Also by Donald Yacovone

*Samuel Joseph May and the Dilemmas of
the Liberal Persuasion, 1797–1871*

*A Voice of Thunder: The Civil War
Letters of George E. Stephens*

*A Shared Experience: Men, Women, and
the History of Gender* (coeditor)

*Hope & Glory: Essays on the Legacy of the
54th Massachusetts Regiment* (coeditor)

*Freedom's Journey: African American
Voices of the Civil War* (editor)

*Wendell Phillips, Social Justice, and
the Power of the Past* (coeditor)

With Henry Louis Gates, Jr.

Lincoln on Race and Slavery

The African Americans: Many Rivers to Cross

Teaching White Supremacy

"Westward the Course of Destiny, Westward ho!" Chromolithograph, 1873, by George A. Crofutt. (See copyright page for full caption.)

Teaching White Supremacy

America's Democratic Ordeal and the

Forging of Our National Identity

Donald Yacovone

Pantheon Books

New York

A cataloguing-in-publication record has been established for this book by the Library of Congress. LCCN 2021058205 | ISBN (hardcover) 9780593316634 | ISBN (ebook) 9780593316641

www.pantheonbooks.com

Frontispiece caption: Illustrator and publisher George Crofutt worked with Prussian-born painter John Gast to create an enduring symbol of the nation's "manifest destiny." The *"beautiful and charming female"* figure of Columbia, as Crofutt wrote, bore the *Star of Empire* on her forehead and in her arm carried *"the emblem of education"*—The School Book—as it proclaimed on its cover. The white figure, with transcendent powers, swept away all nonwhite peoples to carry progress and American supremacy across the continent. George A. Crofutt, "Westward the Course of Destiny, Westward ho!," chromolithograph, 1873.

Jacket image: Detail from "Westward the Course of Destiny, Westward ho!," 1873, chromolithograph after a painting by John Gast, 1872. Everett Collection/Bridgeman Images
Jacket design by Kelly Blair

Printed in the United States of America
First Edition
2 4 6 8 9 7 5 3 1

For our teachers,
but especially for
Thomas J. Farnham,
Edward W. Sloan III,
and
Leonard W. Levy

You've got to be taught to hate and fear,
You've got to be taught from year to year,
It's got to be drummed in your dear little ear
You've got to be carefully taught.
You've got to be taught to be afraid

Of people whose eyes are oddly made,
And people whose skin is a diff'rent shade,
You've got to be carefully taught.
You've got to be taught before it's too late,

Before you are six or seven or eight,
To hate all the people your relatives hate,
You've got to be carefully taught!

—"You've Got to Be Carefully Taught,"
from the 1949 musical *South Pacific* by
Richard Rodgers and Oscar Hammerstein II

Contents

Introduction

When the teacher fails to meet the intellectual wants of
a child, it is the case of asking for bread and receiving
a stone; but when he fails to meet its moral wants, it is
giving a serpent.

—Horace Mann, *Thoughts,* 1872

I learned firsthand the reality of Horace Mann's warning when I enrolled in a teacher-training program in the 1970s. My college sent me to a high school in central Connecticut for my first classroom experience on the other side of the teacher's desk. Student teaching was to be the capstone experience of my undergraduate education—as it turned out, far more than I ever imagined. I will never forget the first time I entered the schoolteachers' lounge, a disheartening space with an awkward array of tired, empty seats placed against the four walls. The worn linoleum floor remained empty except for a few teachers and an old wooden armchair strategically placed in the center of the room. In it sat an orating grandee, likely a department head, whose painfully white skin and frizzy bald skull were accentuated by his thick black-rimmed glasses. As I passed into the small chamber, I could not avoid him, nor could I ignore his gesturing arms or his sermon about the white man's burden. Then and there, I decided that high school teaching would not be in my future.

But scholarship would, and I have spent most of my career studying abolitionism and nineteenth-century African American history.

Several years ago I began a study of the antislavery movement's legacy. I focused on the century *after* 1865 to understand how the "collective" or "popular" memory of the original freedom struggle helped create the modern civil rights movement. As part of this project, I wanted to measure how abolitionism had been presented in our nation's K–12 school textbooks. I naïvely imagined a quick look at a few volumes and then a speedy return to my primary research. Instead, I found myself overwhelmed by the collection of *nearly three thousand* U.S. history textbooks, dating from about 1800 to the 1980s, at the Monroe C. Gutman Library at Harvard University's Graduate School of Education. I stared at the shelves in shock. But it also proved inspiring. I immediately plunged in and resurfaced with a solid sense of what schoolbooks were like *before* 1865—so I could fully grasp the later history of the history I wished to understand. But in a clear inversion of Robert Frost's "The Gift Outright," I was the collection's before the collection was mine. Within a short time, I found myself immersed in a study of how slavery, race, abolitionism, and the Civil War and Reconstruction have been taught in our nation's K–12 schoolbooks from about 1832 to the present. Hence, this book.

One morning as I examined a library cart bursting with about fifty elementary, grammar, and high school history textbooks, a bright red spine reached out to me through time and space. *Why is this familiar?* I wondered. As I opened the book's still-crisp white pages, my gasp must have jolted those wonderful librarians working near me. It all came rushing back. Somehow I had never forgotten the book's image of Eli Whitney, included not for his notorious cotton gin but instead for "inventing" the concept of interchangeable parts—thus laying the groundwork for industrialization. *Exploring the New World,* by O. Stuart Hamer, Dwight W. Follett, Benjamin F. Ahlschwede, and Herbert H. Gross—published and reprinted between 1953 and 1965—had been assigned in my fifth-grade social studies class in Saratoga, California.

Just like a legion of the early textbooks I had been reading, *Exploring the New World* never mentioned the antislavery movement. Slaves, on the other hand, proved necessary to pick cotton—"Who else would do the work?" the authors asked. This textbook, and nearly all the texts I reviewed, was not published by a Southern segregationist press, and certainly not by the Klan or other far-right publishers—although such presses emerged with a vengeance in the 1920s and still operate, especially online. No, the thousands of textbooks that have stained the minds of generations of students, from the elementary grades to college, were produced almost entirely by Northern publishing houses, situated mostly in New York, Boston, and Chicago, and by Northern-trained scholars and education specialists. Indeed, several of the most famous and influential American historians of the first half of the twentieth century, nearly all trained at Northern colleges and universities, produced some of the most racist texts I had the displeasure to read.

At the same time, however, my fifth-grade textbook also stated that the people of the North did not believe that men and women "should be bought and sold." *Exploring the New World,* published during the Cold War, followed the same pattern set at the close of the nineteenth century, seeking sectional reconciliation regarding issues related to slavery and the Civil War. Its authors also wished to avoid cultural strife (and the reality of slavery and racism) and promoted national unity in the early 1960s by asserting that during the Civil War everyone (white) was brave, everyone (white) fought for principle, and Gen. Robert E. Lee represented all that was noble, gallant, and heroic in American society. "His name is now loved and respected in both North and South," they explained. "We know that he was not only a gallant Southern hero but a great American." What we have been teaching our children for nearly all American history suddenly became real, and personal.

.   .   .

The depth, breadth, and durability of American white supremacy and racial prejudice is certainly no revelation to modern historians and social analysts, Black and white. To understand why it has proved so dominant, so irresistibly appealing, even essential, we must survey its development and range. No better place exists to trace that development and cultural importance than in the long history of the nation's textbooks. Embodying the values to be treasured by rising generations of Americans, textbook authors passed on ideas of white American identity from generation to generation. Writers crafted whiteness as a national inheritance, a way to preserve the social construction of American life and, ironically, its democratic institutions and values. Given the extent of the nation's belief in white supremacy, one would be astonished if it had not been a guiding principle of our textbooks.

But this is not a book about a collection of bad books; nor is it an exposé of damaging educational theory. Instead, it is an exploration of the origins and development of the idea of white supremacy, how it has shaped our understanding of democratic society, and how generation after generation of Americans have learned to incorporate that vision into their very identity. Belief in white supremacy and Black inferiority existed long before the creation of the American republic and, along with a sincere—but *not* contradictory—belief in democratic republicanism, always has occupied the center of the American soul. James Baldwin, the celebrated African American writer and critic, recalled in 1965 that "I was taught in American history books that Africa had no history and that neither had I. I was a savage about whom the least said the better, who had been saved by Europe and who had been brought to America." After school, he returned home and thought, "Of course, that this was an act of God. You belonged where white people put you." And it always had been so. In the 1920s, for instance, if an African American student had asked a teacher why no Black people appeared in their history textbook, the answer would be that African Americans "had done nothing to merit inclusion." As the Black scholar Charles H. Wesley reported in 1925, through textbooks and classroom instruction, the Black student quickly realized that "his badge of color in America is a sign of subjugation, inferiority and contempt." In 1939, the NAACP surveyed popular American history textbooks, and as one Black student concluded from the association's findings, since textbooks "drilled" white supremacy "into the minds of growing children, I see how hate and disgust is motivated against the American Negro."

Surveying American history school textbooks from the early

nineteenth century to the present day will provide a more profound insight into the full depth of the national commitment to white supremacy. It also allows us to trace exactly *how* white supremacy and Black inferiority have been, as that student from the 1930s learned, drilled into student minds generation after generation. In the process, we will gain an understanding of just how much such ideas have permeated American culture and continue to exert their toxic influence.

If nothing else, this exploration focuses on the responsibility of *Northern* leaders and educators for the creation and dissemination of white supremacy and construction of the "color line." For most of modern American history, scholarship and popular thought have blamed the legacy of Southern slavery for the distressing persistence of racial inequality. And of course, slave owners and their descendants do possess a unique and lethal responsibility for racial suppression. But it is also the case that if no slaves ever existed in the South, Northern white theorists, religious leaders, intellectuals, writers, educators, politicians, and lawyers would have invented a lesser race (which is what happened) to build white democratic solidarity, and in that way make democratic culture and political institutions possible. As one of our greatest authors, Toni Morrison, once explained, in the United States the rights of man were "inevitably yoked to Africanism." In other words, American democracy depended on Black inequality to sustain white equality.

History textbooks proved a perfect vehicle for the transmission of such ideas, those deemed central to the survival of the nation's democratic experiment. But their influence would, at first, be slow to develop. While U.S. history textbooks began appearing after 1800, the number began to significantly increase only after the 1820s as New England, New York, and parts of Virginia established publicly supported high schools that mandated the teaching of history. While private elementary and grammar schools and academies existed throughout the country, along with private tutors, publicly supported ones existed mostly in the North, with few in the South, outside portions of Virginia and North Carolina, until after the Civil War. Most Americans, for much of the nation's history, simply did not attend any high school or its equivalent. As late as 1930, only about 30 percent of teenagers graduated from a high school, and in sixteen Southern and Western states, only 14.2 percent of whites and 4.5 percent of Blacks of high school age attended public schools. The disadvantages heaped on African Americans, in a segregated world, are evident from the fact that in 1900 only ninety-two Black high schools existed in the country, and sixteen years later a total of only sixty-four had been established for Washington, D.C., and the entire South.

Those numbers would only grow, however, and by 1962 about 70 percent of American teens graduated from high school. But attendance in the lower grades and literacy in general would always be high, catapulting sales of U.S. history textbooks to astounding levels. In 1912 the U.S. Commissioner of Education estimated that annual sales of all textbooks had soared to at least $12 million, about $300 million in modern currency! Just six years later the value had almost doubled. By 1960, fifty U.S. textbook publishers hauled in about $230 million in sales, which leaped to over half a billion dollars by 1967, and by 1975, yearly sales of textbooks surpassed $600 million. This nearly insatiable demand for textbooks blossomed in the 1890s, when several American publishers formed a trust, the American Book Company, that muscled its way into the market using every tactic "short of manslaughter," as one publisher complained, to dominate sales. Book agents employed bribery, influence peddling, and even free vacations to win adoptions from school superintendents. According to one investigation in the *Atlantic Monthly*, the entire "school-book business" had become a "portentous evil." While repulsive and disgraceful, such behavior clearly pointed to the enormous national demand for history textbooks.

Until recent days, Americans have always emphasized the importance of learning, especially through history. In 1857 Amos Dean, the Vermont-born president of the University of Iowa, explained that history was not philosophy teaching by example but *"God teaching by examples."* In history, he maintained, we could see the *"record of human progress."* About thirty years later Francis Newton Thorpe, a political scientist from the University of Pennsylvania, advised American schools and colleges that history and economics were the two most important areas of study for American youth, one pertaining to the past, the other to the future. "Together," he wrote, "they mirror the life of the nation." Before the end of the century, the influential Johns Hopkins University historian Herbert Baxter Adams exclaimed that "history is the grandest study in the world" and that it should be taught to all American youth. Rather than an aggregation of "dead facts," history embodied "the self-conscious development of the human race," a "living fact," and "self-knowledge." Clio, he explained, was "a living muse, not a dead cold form." While history writing was preoccupied with the activities of "great men," Adams reminded his readers that "good men" and "devoted women" made the past, and, thus, our future.

Far from mere aggregations of dead facts, history texts served as reservoirs of values, patriotism, and a national ethos. As other studies have shown, from the start history textbooks sought to create unity through storytelling, creating a national identity that could serve as a road map to the future. As the early-twentieth-century education reformer and peace advocate Fannie Fern Andrews remarked, history existed as "training for citizenship in its broadest sense." Our "boys and girls must be made to feel . . . that they themselves are in its very current," a 1902 textbook explained, and history should foster integrity in the private and public lives of "each individual citizen of the republic." History explained how democracy came about and offered indispensable assurances during times of national crisis. Even in the late twentieth century, history remained honored as a "way of learning," providing the perspective necessary to act justly in the world. Michael Kammen, the Pulitzer Prize–winning Cornell University historian, reaching back into the eighteenth century, described history as "a moral science" necessary to understand ourselves and test our ideals by our actions.

In part, we are right to see history textbooks as "prayer-books" of our national civil religion, as "engines of democracy and equality." But we have been selective in what we cherish in them and blind to what, in time, has proved disconcerting, if not shameful and humiliating. Thomas A. Bailey's *The American Pageant* became one of the most popular textbooks of the mid-twentieth century, with at least thirteen editions in his lifetime and many more after his death. As he wrote in his autobiography, Bailey had sought to craft a general survey of the nation's history that would "reveal it as a beacon-light success in democracy." And his work is largely recalled as a lively paean to America as a model democracy. But behind the animated pages and colorful images lay equally important subtexts that determined what became enshrined as "history" and "democracy." Bailey explained that when he wrote his textbook, he focused on "the movers and shakers, not about the stagehands who shifted the scenery or the housewives who cooked the meals of the men who controlled events." Only because of "public pressure," he complained, did some textbook authors include "more pictures of prominent black leaders for Negro rights—Frederick Douglass, Booker T. Washington, Martin Luther King, Jr., and others—and to say something favorable about them." But no such images ever appeared in his book, and he never even mentioned King. "Descendants of slaves," he said, did not want to be reminded of slavery's legacy. Astonishingly, such exclusion proved an advancement over what his contemporaries were still writing and what had come before.

Thomas Maitland Marshall's *American History*, published in 1930, embodied the assumptions and biases that characterized nearly all American history textbooks published before the 1960s. The very first page of his book shrieks: "THE STORY OF THE WHITE MAN." Marshall said very little about the establishment and growth of the institution of slavery but dwelled considerably on what he viewed as "slave character." Regardless of his situation or condition, he wrote,

> the negro of plantation days was usually happy. He was fond of the company of others and liked to sing, dance, crack jokes, and laugh; he admired bright colors and was proud to wear a red or orange bandana. . . . He was never in a hurry, and was always ready to let things go until the morrow. Most of the planters learned not the whip, but loyalty, based upon pride, kindness, and rewards, brought the best returns.

A group of influential textbook authors and writers repudiated such fantasies of racism and white supremacy immediately after the Civil War, hoping to fulfill an Emancipationist view of the conflict and especially of Reconstruction. Authors like Thomas Wentworth Higginson, a supporter of John Brown and commander of the 1st South Carolina Volunteers during the war, and Charles Carleton Coffin, an abolitionist and the North's best-known war correspondent, had crafted immensely popular histories of the nation designed for school-age children. But their works always struggled against simultaneously published Northern and Southern history textbooks that repudiated such egalitarian aims, and they largely—though not entirely—waned by century's end.

At the advent of the twentieth century, the overwhelming majority of American textbooks began with Marshall's assumption that the history of the United States was the history of the white man, his struggles against Native Americans (usually rendered as "red savages"), and his need to control the lives of African Americans. The history of the country was, in part, depicted as their intolerable efforts to challenge, even destroy, "the superior race." As a 1918 text explained to students, whatever non-English people had done to help create the United States, *"the forces that have shaped that life have been English."* The nation had a fixed identity, books asserted, one inherited exclusively from Great Britain. Growing up in 1890s Ohio, the influential historian Arthur M. Schlesinger, Sr., had been accustomed to seeing Black and German and Irish immigrant neighbors. Nonetheless, his schoolbooks taught that England was "the one and only mother country." Additionally, historians who helped shape national character and interpret the past for thousands of students, like the industrialist James Ford Rhodes, who was president of the American Historical Association, relied on the earlier "science" produced by men such as Harvard University's famed ethnologist Louis Agassiz. For generations, Rhodes and scores of subsequent authors parroted the foul gurgling of Agassiz and others and informed their readers that Blacks were either a separate species or vastly inferior humans, "indolent, playful, sensual, imitative, subservient, good natured, versatile, unsteady in purpose, devoted, and affectionate." Most textbooks, and certainly those appearing since the beginning of the twentieth century, presented Blacks as a foreign, repellent element, an unwanted presence, a necessary evil, or a threat, and *always,* as one 1914 textbook asserted, "a problem that it took many years to solve."

The real problem to solve, however, has been the persistence of white supremacy and its enduring and destructive cultural assumptions. Freedom and slavery, democratic ideas and white supremacy, existed long before the nation's founding. The tensions produced by these competing forces were embedded in the essence of the American republic and, as the prolific and influential historian Ira Berlin wrote, in "the meaning of the American experience." As early as 1765, the Revolutionary leader James Otis understood that *all* colonists "are by the law of nature freeborn, as indeed all men are, white or black." But as modern commentators have observed, despite a ghastly war fought over slavery and more than 150 years of concerted efforts by African American and white activists, "the notion of America as white and Christian has stubbornly refused to dissipate." The soul of the nation remains white. How that happened is the story this book seeks to explain.

.   .   .

Without teachers, we are lost. As Henry Adams reminded us a century ago, a "teacher affects eternity; he can never tell where his influence stops." An earlier New Englander, Amos Bronson Alcott, had placed equal importance on the role of teachers, insisting that they must possess "Wisdom, Truth, Holiness," or such virtues "will not appear in his pupils." The nineteenth century clearly understood how vital teachers are to the moral and intellectual health of the nation. I have tried to make this book have special meaning for them so that they can avoid the catastrophic consequences of Horace Mann's 1872 warning. The serpent of white supremacy has spewed its venom for far too long—ironically, even from the lips of that icon of teacher education. And so I dedicate this book to them, but especially to the teachers who made the most dramatic impact on my life as a historian. I have no idea what I would have become without the patient guidance of my undergraduate adviser at Southern Connecticut State University, Thomas J. Farnham. What he saw in that immature malcontent so long ago, I'll never understand, but I was blessed that he did and that we remain close friends. Two other teachers, now sadly gone, proved especially significant to me. Edward W. Sloan III at Trinity College helped me mature as a scholar and with amazing foresight sent me to the Claremont Graduate University. There Leonard W. Levy gave me the opportunity of a lifetime. He made clear his preference for grit, hard work, and determination and offered his wisdom, patience, and support. Because of him—and my fellow graduate students at the Claremont Graduate School (as it was then known)—I had some of the most exciting, challenging, and fulfilling years of my life. Meeting Dr. Levy that first time at his majestic home in the dreamy foothills of Claremont, California, was like ascending to Clio's divine temple. I always followed his orders, especially to "learn to compose on the typewriter!" (a what?) and to sink my teeth into projects and not let go until I found the answers. His example, and his commands, have been inspirational. For individuals as for nations, I heard him declare, the past matters. The only question is whether *we* will learn from it.

Virtue may be its own reward, but it sure helps to have the support and insights of colleagues, friends, and family. I have been so very fortunate to benefit from the incisive analysis, profound learning, generosity, and comradeship of James Brewer Stewart. His influence touched every aspect of this work, and I shudder to think what the result would have been without him. When I imagine the ideal scholar-teacher, he is the model. I owe an enormous and unrepayable debt of thanks to Diane McWhorter for introducing me to her agent Charlotte Sheedy. I am forever indebted to Charlotte for offering her unmatched wisdom and to her "anonymous reader" who reviewed a large portion of the manuscript and provided invaluable suggestions. Most important, she introduced me to the book's skilled editor, Vicky Wilson, and her talented staff. I cannot be more grateful. All of them embody the good this country possesses.

Colleagues mean everything in the world of scholarship and writing, and I have been blessed to draw on the talent, wisdom, and advice of Michael Birkner, as well as that of Thomas Balcerski, Alan Berolzheimer, Frank Bremer, Dennis Downey, Eric Foner, Judith Ann Giesberg, Dean Grodzins, Caroline Janney, N. Gregory Mankiw, Mark Schneider, and especially Michael Woods for his generous assistance with that evil genius John H. Van Evrie. I also wish to thank Peter Wirzbicki for alerting me to the work of Caroline Putnam and Sallie Holley and their Virginia school for African Americans. I am extremely grateful for the challenging exchanges with Clifton Berry and Mathew Foggy of the Unpaid Labor Movement. They have helped more than they will ever know. Since 2006 everything I have written has been because of Henry Louis Gates, Jr., and Abby Wolf, executive director of the Hutchins Institute. Thomas Wolejko, the Hutchins media and technology coordinator, always offered dependable advice. C. Douglas and C. Mary Alves, Peter C. Kiefer, and David Gordon embody the phrase "old friends," and my project has benefited, as always, from their thoughtfulness and love. I can't thank Peter enough for sending me the five-volume *Bryant's Popular History of the United States,* David for his advice and legal skills, and Doug and Mary for everything else. Dian Kahn provided me with essential illumination on contemporary education issues. The New England Regional Fellowship Program, administered by the Massachusetts Historical Society, sent me down this path, although it is entirely blameless for the results. Robert J. Benz of the Frederick Douglass Family Initiatives, David Harris of Harvard Law School's Charles Hamilton Houston Institute for Race and Justice, June Erlick's *ReVista,* Liz G. Mineo of the *Harvard Gazette,* the *Chronicle of Higher Education,* Alex Gagné and the staff of *Left History,* and the Organization of American Historians blogsite *Process* all published my first forays into the arena of education and white supremacy. I so appreciate their confidence. And what writer doesn't owe an unrepayable debt to librarians? Those at Harvard, especially at the Monroe C. Gutman Library—Rebecca Martin, Carla Lillvik, Karen Carlson Young, and Ning Zou—made my work a joy and a revelation. Equally important, Widener's interlibrary loan office heroically endured my relentless requests, and Amy Newark at Lexington's Cary Memorial Library helped with Muzzey family history. But the most important librarian to me is my wife, Mary E. Yacovone. Her help through the years I spent on this project has been a blessing, and I know just how lucky I am to have found her, even if it was on the MBTA's Greenline.

Teaching White Supremacy

1

The Contours of
White Supremacy

> To the Caucasian race by reason of its physical and mental
> superiority, has been assigned the task of civilizing and
> enlightening the world.
>
> —Samuel Train Dutton, *The Morse Speller,* 1896

S amuel Train Dutton was superintendent of schools in Brookline, Massachusetts, when he wrote the ever-popular *Morse
Speller,* which enjoyed its thirteenth edition in 1903. For about
half a century, however, he reigned as the nation's leading authority
on school administration and public education. He also had led New
Haven, Connecticut's schools, served as superintendent of New York
City's famed Horace Mann School, and had been named professor
of school administration at Columbia University. At the time of his
death in 1919, he was general secretary of the League of Nations'
World's Court League, the founder and first secretary of New York's
Peace Society, and had been a member of the International Commis-
sion on the Balkan Wars. He also helped organize colleges in Turkey
and China and chaired the Armenian and Syrian relief efforts. As the
country's leading educator at the beginning of the twentieth century,
he also earned worldwide renown as a diplomat and philanthropist.
For all his philanthropy and insistence that American schools teach
about slavery and the Civil War, Dutton also asserted that schools
must explain "how the ancient Egyptians differed from the Negro,
and why." Moreover, as he advised teachers, the failures of American
missionaries had proved that Native Americans and Africans were fit

only for manual labor training, the kind of education appropriate for the "heathen and the savage" as well as the "vicious and defective." The white race must take up these responsibilities as its prime mission, Dutton declared in 1896. Such Northern-born leaders who dominated American educational thinking reflected the countless ways, both subtle and blatant, that white supremacy permeated the culture.

Many historians and commentators today understandably see slavery as the nation's "original sin." But slavery alone cannot account for the enduring nature of prejudice against African Americans and others who lacked the "whiteness" so highly valued by educators like Dutton. Groups from Native Americans to the Irish, and some English immigrants, had endured slavery or slavery-like conditions during the era of national development. English indentured servants, especially in colonial Virginia, at times could hardly be distinguished from slaves, as their masters did everything in their power to extend their terms of service and exploit their labor. In the ancient world, people we would now recognize as "white" endured slavery, even in England. And prior to the early nineteenth century, thousands of Europeans had become slaves of North Africans. The difference in North America is the unique combination of African American slavery and the simultaneous gradual development of democratic/republican principles. Determining who should participate in this dramatic and revolutionary process, repudiating the strictly class-based organization of European society, mandated an ideology of white supremacy and acceptance of it as normal and natural. The impact of that ideology is undeniable and defining. As the popular historian and commentator Arthur M. Schlesinger, Jr., wrote over twenty years ago: "White Americans began as a people so arrogant in convictions of racial superiority that they felt licensed to kill red people, to enslave black people, and to import yellow and brown people for peon labor. We white Americans have been racist in our customs, in our conditioned reflexes, in our souls." Borrowing from Herman Melville, Schlesinger confessed that in American history, "the world's fairest hope" had been linked "with man's foulest crime."

Slavery, however, did not require racism to thrive. As a power relationship, it was an ancient institution whose benefits readily justified its means. Even John Locke, the seventeenth-century English theorist who so profoundly influenced the development of American liberty, agreed that slavery was fit punishment for captured enemies. One colonial Massachusetts judge even asserted that lawfully captured members of "Heathen Nations" could be justly enslaved. But in American colonial settlements with embryonic republican (and religious) ideas concerning rights and representation, unassailable qualifications for citizenship appeared necessary to guarantee success and justify those excluded. As Massachusetts judge John Saffin argued in 1701, God had set "different Orders and Degrees of Men in the World," and any idea of universal equality would "invert the order that God had set." Some were born to rule, and others were "born to be slaves, and so to remain during their lives." Thus it proved more than an astonishing coincidence that both slavery and representative government were introduced in Virginia in the very same year. Ideas of ethnic or racial inferiority defined who could be trusted with citizenship—who would be the controlled race and who would be the controlling one, two ends of the same developing social and political contract. Each must be added to the political and social calculus to explain the unique development of American culture. But the ideology of white supremacy, not slavery, proved the more ubiquitous and more enduring institution. It became the standard by which citizenship was defined, and it determined who would prove worthy of power. White supremacy linked the Northern and Southern parts of the nation and distributed equal responsibility for slavery's prolonged existence and the even longer life of racial repression. And it failed (temporarily) to uphold democratic society only when the nation could no longer agree on its parameters.

Rather than Southern slavery, however, it was *Northern* white supremacy that proved the more enduring cultural binding force, planted along with slavery in the colonial era, intensely cultivated in the years before the Civil War, and fully blossoming after Reconstruction. Inculcated relentlessly throughout the culture and in school textbooks, it suffused Northern religion, high culture, literature, education, politics, music, law, and science. It powerfully resurfaced after the Civil War and Reconstruction to reassert control over the emancipated slaves to become the basis for national reconciliation, exploded in intensity with renewed immigration in the 1920s and '30s, and endured with diminishing force to the present day. It succeeded as the superstructure of democratic society by allowing normal political conflict to proceed with the assurance that the assumed dangerous mudsill class (once controlled by enslavement) could pose no threat to the social order. Hence democratic equality rested on racial inequality and malleable definitions of whiteness. Moreover, it offered something more alluring than wealth, more effective than politics, and *far* more appealing than education. For even the poorest of its adherents, indeed especially for them, white supremacy imparts a sense of uncontested identity and, as the American philosopher and social critic Susan Neiman wrote, an otherwise unattainable level of "dignity, simply for belonging to a higher race."

The Rev. Henry M. Field, brother of the Supreme Court justice Stephen J. Field, who helped decide the landmark 1896 *Plessy v. Ferguson* case, had been born in Stockbridge, Massachusetts. The so-called "color line," he explained in 1890, "is not peculiar to one section of the country; that it exists at the North as well as at the South." It would be a mistake, he warned, to "ascribe what we call race-prejudice to the peculiar perversity of our Southern brethren." Although Reverend Field and his own children had been raised by the former Massachusetts slave Elizabeth Freeman, also known as Mumbet, he felt powerless to reject racism. Such sentiments, he contended, were "a matter of instinct, which is often wiser than reason. We cannot fight against instinct, nor legislate against it, if we do, we shall find it stronger than our resolutions and our laws."

North and South cherished white supremacy with equal fervor, but how each section expressed it differed over time and place. It had a patchwork quality, at times allowing African Americans more freedom in some areas of the slave South than in cities or towns of the nominally free North. Complicating the picture is the fact that there had never been any enduring definition of a race, even the white race. Criteria continually shifted, including and excluding nationalities depending on conditions, levels of immigration, and political need. Whiteness, and the idea of race, should be seen more as a "fluid, variable, and open-ended process." While it always subjected people of color—and some European nationalities—to inferior positions, the extent, intensity, and ideological motivation or justification varied considerably over time. As described by whites, races were defined by perceptions and appearances. Although assumed to be biological reality, races are in fact socially constructed categories intended to highlight the superiority and permanence of Caucasians, even as those considered to be Caucasian changed. Indeed, the more immigration made the North heterogenous, the more intense became its ideas of white supremacy. Thus in the 1850s New York's John H. Van Evrie, the father of white supremacy, might define Jews as white, but as immigration exploded in the 1890s, most white Americans excluded them from membership in the Caucasian race.

African American blood, Howard University professor Kelly Miller wrote in 1918, "flows like a stream through our national history." But precisely where that blood flowed preoccupied Americans from the outset of their history. Samuel Sewall, remembered primarily for his role in the Salem witchcraft trials, also authored the first antislavery tract in American history. His 1700 *The Selling of Joseph,* largely neglected during his lifetime, denounced slavery and the slave trade as barbarous and unchristian. In his day, about one-fifth of New England families owned slaves, and by 1750 the region's slave population had reached about ten thousand, located mostly along the coast and in the region's lush river valleys. But as Sewall discovered, his antislavery views proved immensely unpopular. Few whites, he learned, "can endure to hear of a Negro's being made free." Moreover, Sewall and his fellow white settlers believed that even if freed, they "seldom use their freedom well." He believed that such a profound difference existed between Europeans and people of African descent, "in their conditions, colour & hair," that "they can never embody with us, and grow up into orderly Families." They would always, Sewall concluded, "remain in our Body Politick as a kind of extravasate Blood." Their blood might flow throughout American history, as Kelly Miller wrote, but whites would always see that blood as flowing outside the regular veins and capillaries of the nation's body politic. They would always be alien, threatening, disdained. No matter how Blacks might use their freedom, the African presence raised such fearsome concerns for Sewall that it made him wonder if he would retain his cherished whiteness "after the Resurrection."

Prior to North American colonization, Europeans had no settled opinion on the nature of African peoples. Many lived freely in England and across Europe. Even in slave-trading Spain, the Black explorer Juan Garrido and the Black poet and university professor Juan Latino lived there or in the country's colonies in full freedom. Moreover, the European Catholic Church's commissioning of appealing depictions of the African saint Maurice and his martyrdom amounted to a near obsession. Even the 1600 English translation of Leo Africanus's *Geographical History* described the African Kingdom of Timbuktu as a "well-ordered, prosperous, civilized society in which learning flourished as well as trade."

But the hundred years of the African slave trade prior to English colonization created, in the minds of the white settlers, an association of Africans with slavery. Englishmen, whether peripatetic Capt. John Smith or Massachusetts Bay's John Winthrop, were familiar with African slavery in the Caribbean and accepted it as a necessary and proper legal institution. Indeed, the slave trade from Africa and the Cape Verde Islands proved so profitable for New Englanders that it moved Winthrop to thank "the Lord to open to us a trade with Barbados and other Islands in the West Indies." Even before the first African slaves appeared in Massachusetts Bay, the Puritan settlers had enslaved their Native American enemies, and many contended that the Bible's "curse of Ham" explained the African's signifying black skin. Smith thought Africans especially appropriate for enslavement as they originated in the "fryed Regions of blacke brutish Negers." He also set the pattern that would ripple down throughout American history by warning that Africans were "as idle and as devilish as any in the world." They might be natural slaves, he thought, but they represented a dangerous element to insert in the new English settlements. Despite Smith's reservations, white settlers displayed no moral qualms about owning slaves, only about their availability and affordability.

When we hear the phrase "Jim Crow society," we think of the South's infamous culture of segregation and compulsory inferiority of African Americans. But Jim Crow was a Northern creation as much as a Southern one, and it long outlived the institution of slavery. Massachusetts Bay was the first colony to formally legalize slavery in 1641; in 1656 it barred African Americans from serving in the militia; and in 1705 it outlawed interracial marriage, just as the Southern colonies had done in the 1660s. Northern colonists carefully crafted laws to eliminate the possibility of social equality between whites, Native Americans, and people of African descent. Repudiating intermarriage carried powerful legal and symbolic weight, relegating African Americans to the status of "otherness" and alienation, helping to guarantee that Black blood would not flow in white veins. Any Black convicted of raping a white woman would at the very least suffer castration, but a white who raped a Black woman would suffer no penalties whatsoever. Rhode Island even outlawed the right of a Black woman, regardless of legal status, to sue a white man for paternity.

As would become a mainstay of history textbooks, Americans commonly understood that Northern slavery developed only as a mild "domestic" version of what took place in the South. Such was not the case, however, and while it was never as extensive as Southern slavery, it could be every bit as cruel. Northern owners, in what may seem counterintuitive, did not value slave children, as they brought additional costs, remained unproductive for many years, and became an unwanted distraction in the masters' homes. When enslaved women gave birth, owners often considered the newborns to be burdens and gave them away "as soon as possible . . . like puppies." The practice was so common and devastating to Black families that as late as 1774, Black Bostonians petitioned the colonial legislature to defend their marriages and families. "Our children are also taken from us by force," and some were sold soon after birth.

"Thus," they decried, "our lives are imbittered to us." But such justified protests and assertions of rights only increased the intensity of white supremacy. The more people of color accepted white practices, methods, and opinions, the more they adopted white institutions such as Christianity, and the more they lived like those about them, as the University of North Carolina history professor John Wood Sweet wrote, "the more adamant [white] settlers grew about drawing new lines of exclusion."

The European "Enlightenment" of the eighteenth century served only to codify and fortify Northern white supremacist assumptions. The famed Scottish philosopher David Hume, for instance, in 1748 expressed all too clearly what white Europeans and Americans would believe for the next two hundred years. African people, he wrote, were "naturally inferior to the whites. There never was a civilized nation of any other complexion than white." No one "eminent either in action or speculation [existed], no ingenious manufacturers amongst them [Africans], no arts, no sciences." And any such person who did display a high degree of learning would be "like a parrot, who speaks a few words plainly." In 1795 the German physiologist, physician, and anthropologist Johann Friedrich Blumenbach popularized the term *Caucasian.* While he believed that all humans belonged to the same species—an idea that would later be challenged—he asserted that the original humans were white and later diverged into different races. But such diversions, to Blumenbach, constituted regressions from the original form as he believed they appeared in Genesis. As the English author Oliver Goldsmith wrote in 1774, such variations from white "are actual marks of the degeneracy of the human form."

As we are well aware, many of the nation's Founding Fathers North and South owned slaves, and perhaps a few pursued independence to help guarantee preservation of their property. But those who opposed slavery, like Pennsylvania's famed Benjamin Franklin, also despised African Americans and aimed to reinforce white supremacy. As early as 1751, Franklin condemned slavery because he feared the "darkening" of the American colonies. Why should we, "in the sight of Superior Beings, darken its People? Why increase the Sons of Africa, by planting them in America, where we have so Fair an opportunity, by excluding all Blacks and Tawneys, of increasing the lovely white and red?" As he wrote four years later, "almost every Slave *by Nature* [is] a thief." If African Americans obtained protection for "their insolence," one resident of Albany, New York, wrote in 1762, "twill be time for us to leave this Country." Whiteness must reign. Franklin opposed slavery not because of any sense of inherent injustice but because the act of slave owning made whites too haughty, cultivated too strong a sense of superiority, and made them feel too good for common labor. "White children," he worried, would become too proud, disgusted "with Labor, and being educated in Idleness are rendered unfit to get a living by Industry." Franklin saw the world in colors—red, white, and black—and worried over the fate of "purely white People in the world," who, he explained, were "proportionally very small" in number.

The Revolution's success and the decline of Northern slavery did not increase the kind of humanitarianism we associate with nineteenth-century abolitionists—they only hardened ideas of white supremacy. The new "freedom" enjoyed by African Americans in the North amounted to a kind of totalitarianism that threatened the status, security, and identity of whites. John Adams, a lawyer who in his prepresidential days represented both slaves and slave owners in court, held that humanitarianism played no role in the decline of slavery in his region. Instead, he asserted, slaves had become "lazy, idle, proud, vicious, and at length wholly useless to their masters, to such a degree that the abolition of slavery became a measure of œconomy." But Northern slavery's decline (for whatever reason) only increased intolerance for its victims, and freedpeople's new autonomy—the lack of total control inherent in the institution of slavery—became increasingly threatening and demeaning to whites. Thus the word *white* began appearing in the nation's founding documents, in laws governing who could marry, vote, and hold office, and in the Articles of Confederation's rules over taxation for the raising of militia forces based on "the number of white inhabitants" in each state. Although the Constitution did not employ the term *white,* it did not need to as whiteness had become intertwined in all aspects of governance, implicitly and explicitly, as in the nation's 1790 Naturalization Law, which restricted citizenship to immigrants who were "free white person[s]."

The North's Christian churches, where one would expect to find sympathy for the oppressed, only reinforced prevailing social attitudes. By the advent of the nineteenth century, what little racial tolerance that previously existed had evaporated. All churches relegated African American members to separate pews and rear lofts, as far from white congregants and the pulpit as possible. During the 1770s, in the wealthy Rhode Island seaport of Newport, the Rev. Samuel Hopkins preached against slavery. Living in a slave-trading center, Hopkins and his congregation displayed admirable courage in opposing the business that had enriched the town and colony. In 1784 the church even refused brotherhood with anyone who participated in the trade. Hopkins, who considered abolitionism essential to a true Christian identity, regretted that his fellow citizens viewed African Americans in "a mean, contemptable light." Education, he lamented, "has filled us with strong prejudices against them, and led us to consider them, not as our brethren, or in any degree on a level with us, but as quite another species of animals, made only to serve us." But Reverend Hopkins could not fully accept African Americans as his brethren and backed colonization to remove them to the British colony of Sierra Leone. Whites, he asserted in 1793, were "so habituated, by education and custom, to look upon and treat the black as an inferior class of beings" that they would never achieve equality in America. Nor would Hopkins even try. Thus African colonization became a necessity. When he learned that a Black congregant had married a white woman, his church excommunicated both, exclaiming that interracial marriage was "Contrary to the Distinctions that God made." In 1818 Newport's Episcopal Church explained that "white respectability" mandated that "no colored people be allowed to sit down stairs" with whites. That same year a Congregational church in Rutland, Vermont, a state that never legalized slavery but permitted it to endure nonetheless, dismissed its Black clergyman, Lemuel Haynes, whom it had employed since

1788. His race and the fact that he had married a white woman now proved intolerable.

The nineteenth-century North would see only further hardening of white supremacist attitudes among its clergy, and some like the Congregationalist Rev. Nehemiah Adams (1806–78) even thundered against all critics of slavery. Adams, a graduate of Harvard and the Andover Theological Seminary, received his doctorate from Amherst College in 1847 and served congregations in Boston and Cambridge. He had visited the South in 1854, which gave him all the evidence he needed to denounce abolitionists and defend the institution of slavery. He published furiously, attempting to convince fellow Northerners that slaveholders *loved* their property and were filled with "pity," "yearnings of compassion," and "loving-kindness" for them. His views won him enduring affection in the South, and long after the Civil War, South Carolina clergymen published a collection of his sermons on race as *At Eventide*.

But Adams is best remembered for his 1854 volume, *A South-Side View of Slavery*, which saw its fourth edition in 1860 and made him the punching bag of every abolitionist in the North. Prior to his trip south, Adams had described himself as a "lover and friend of the colored race," and he had even helped a freed slave redeem his family and reach Liberia, the crown jewel of the American Colonization Society. Expecting to see the very worst as he traveled to Virginia, South Carolina, and Georgia, instead he found the slaves to be a "better-looking, happier, more courteous set of people [than] I had ever seen." He was mesmerized by the "magnetism of their smiles," which convinced him that slaves were far more content than the average Northern white laborer. He found them so full of joy and true religious sentiment that he gleefully asserted that slaves did not require literacy to know God. They "had sources of enjoyment and ways of manifesting it which suggested to a spectator no thought of involuntary servitude." He assured his readers that to think otherwise was simply a distorted Northern fantasy. Moreover, the slaves he saw lived in the lap of luxury with "broadcloth suits," ironed shirts, polished boots, gloves, umbrellas, and the finest of hats. Others possessed costly blue coats with bright buttons, "white Marseilles vests, white pantaloons, broaches in their shirt bosoms, gold chains, [and] elegant" canes. How could owners treat so pampered a people as "cattle"? he asked.

Adams, quite likely, had read the early work of George Fitzhugh and Edmund Ruffin, some of slavery's more enthusiastic defenders, and came away with a benevolent and paternalistic view of the "peculiar institution." Just as Southerners commonly argued, Adams asserted that slaves lived far better than Northern workers. Additionally, he assured his readers that slavery prevented pauperism. Every slave, he exclaimed, "has an inalienable claim in law upon his owner for support for the whole of his life." While Northern workers could be left to die on the streets, the slave was well cared for, and all society thus benefited from the institution that could be seen in its true light only as a positive good. Unlike the poor of Boston, slaves enjoyed cradle-to-grave protection and welfare. Accusations that slavery was inimical to the Black family simply were not true, he contended, and slave families suffered no more breakups than Northern families did due to death, divorce, or runaways. The infamous whip almost never touched the back of a slave, he assured his readers, and instead was used only for the slave driver's protection. As Blacks could not be emancipated "and remain here," no alternative to enslavement existed. Emancipation, he warned, would be the "most disastrous event to the colored people." Just as other leading Northern white supremacists asserted, Adams held that white and Black could not live together "except by the entire subordination of one to the other." There was simply no coexistence "outside of white domination."

One might dismiss Adams as a perversely unique manifestation of Protestant orthodoxy, but his views, and far worse, could be found among more liberal Protestants. Hartford, Connecticut's Yale-educated minister Horace Bushnell (1802–76) was a prodigious author, with his collected works stretching to eleven volumes. But he is best known for his 1847 text *Christian Nurture,* where he argued against the idea of humanity's innate depravity. "All souls of all ages and capacities," he maintained, "have a moral presence of Divine Love in them." By "all souls," however, he meant only white ones. On the eve of the Civil War, he fantasized that impartial government census data proved that, like the inferior American Indian, African Americans would gradually disappear. The Black could not compete with the white, he advised his faithful. "I know of no example in human history where an inferior and far less cultivated stock has been able . . . to hold its ground" against a superior one. In Bushnell's estimation, Blacks were an inferior race destined for extinction. "Many are too indolent to work, too improvident to prepare comfort for their families. Many fall into ways of crime. Others are a prey to the vices of civilization, under which they die prematurely." Moreover, in a vein that would later become the mainstay of social Darwinists, he declared that one need not mourn the death of such inferiors, "a stock thousands of years behind, in the scale of culture." Such an end, he thought, was not only inevitable but desirable.

·   ·   ·

By the time Bushnell wrote *Christian Nurture,* ideas of white supremacy had cauterized the consciousness of most Americans North and South. As the historian Forrest Wood wrote over fifty years ago, to "suggest that anyone else had a stake in the country's future," other than whites, "was unthinkable." If God had not fixed this idea in the United States, Northern politicians asserted, then nature implanted such thinking directly into an American's very being. Hardly wicked, such principles struck the average American as "just and reasonable . . . wholesome, natural, and right." As the keen observer of antebellum American society Alexis de Tocqueville remarked, "The law can abolish servitude, but only God can obliterate its traces." For white Americans, he concluded, the African American would always be "a stranger." A Concord, New Hampshire, newspaper disposed of the idea of racial equality as "so absurd and preposterous, that we cannot conceive how it can be entertained by any intelligent and rational white man."

Nineteenth-century writers and analysts who helped craft American identity thought only of the nation's English heritage, its presumed "Anglo-Saxonness." And no region of the nation identified more with Anglo-Saxons than New England. Even the radical Massachusetts abolitionist Theodore Parker regarded New Englanders as "the best of the Caucasians." And no one spoke with more authority or more intensity about America's white identity than the philosopher-king of Concord, Ralph Waldo Emerson. He embodied the ideal true American as a descendant *only* of the Anglo-Saxon. He, like Parker and most other New Englanders, believed in a hierarchy of race that placed himself at the very top. The "Saxon seed," he asserted, has an "instinct for liberty," and only the "English race can be trusted with freedom." The African, he explained, would never "occupy a very high place in the human family. Their present condition is the strongest proof that they cannot." Not the Irish, nor the Native American, and certainly not the Chinese could ever attain such an illustrious level. All fell, Emerson wrote, before the "energy of the Caucasian race."

Emerson hoped to recast America into his idealized image of old England. It was "a garden," he wrote in his 1856 work *English Traits,* and under an "ash-colored sky, the fields have been combed and rolled till they appear to have been finished with a pencil instead of a plough. . . . The long habitation of a powerful and ingenious race has turned every rod of land to its best use." For Emerson, England represented a man-made Garden of Eden embodying "national genius" and clearly was the most "successful country in the universe for the last millennium." America, in Emerson's eyes, "is only the continuation of the English genius into new conditions. . . . See what books fill our libraries. Every book we read, every biography, play, romance, in whatever form, is still English history and manners." Merging physiognomy, morals, and ethics as only Emerson could, the English face "combined decision and nerve with the fair complexion, blue eyes and open florid aspect. Hence the love of truth, hence the sensibility, the fine perception and poetic construction." For Emerson, race was the "controlling influence," and "in the Negro," he declared, it "is of appalling importance." On a less abstract plane, Emerson bemoaned the common moral failings of a white person more than anything else, certainly far more than the "captivity of a thousand negroes [which] is nothing to me."

Apparently, the brilliant Black abolitionist Frederick Douglass also was nothing to Emerson, as he went out of his way to prevent him from becoming a member of the same private Boston club that he belonged to. Emerson eventually became a sturdy abolitionist, even sanctified John Brown after his execution in 1859, but he hated the slave as much as slavery.

White supremacy not only marked Concord's titan of nineteenth-century philosophy and literature, but flashed like lightning through many of the nation's most treasured and revered authors, especially some who are still avidly read today. Walt Whitman evokes the poetic incarnation of the American democratic spirit. His clarity and boundlessness make words sing with visions of the cosmos. More than Emerson, he embodied the Transcendentalist merging of idea and thing. Yet with equal passion Whitman merged white supremacy with democratic values. As a New York Democratic editor before the Civil War, Whitman espoused Free Soil politics and the nation's manifest destiny in the West. He opposed slavery's expansion because he saw it as a conflict between "white freemen" and a Southern "aristocracy . . . men who work only with other men's hands." He possessed no sympathy for the victims of that aristocracy, but instead feared the reduction of "brave, industrious and energetic freemen" to "the equals only of negro slaves." Slavery mattered to Whitman only so far as it affected white labor. As he wrote in 1847, the slave played no role in the equation of national freedom. Rather, slavery mattered as a vital issue because it constituted a battle "between the grand body of white working men . . . and the interests of the few thousand rich, 'polished,' and aristocratic owners of slaves." The Civil War failed to change Whitman's views of African Americans, and on city streets they still appeared to him "like so many wild brutes let loose." He disdained the very idea of Black men holding public office in the South during Reconstruction. He accepted it only as a "temporary, deserv'd punishment" for the South's responsibility in causing the devastating Civil War. "Blacks can never be to me what the whites are. . . . The whites are my brothers & I love them," he crowed. Indeed, Whitman's attachment to his white brothers included enduring personal bonds with the former

Confederate soldier Peter Doyle, who had been in Ford's Theatre the night John Wilkes Booth murdered President Lincoln. Whitman went to his grave immersed in ideas of white supremacy and Black inferiority, fused to the notion that African Americans would not and likely could not "do anything for himself. . . . No! No! I should not like to see the nigger in the saddle—it seems unnatural." Like the Rev. Horace Bushnell and other Northerners, Whitman read ethnological studies and believed that "the nigger, like the Injun, will be eliminated. It is the law of races, history, what not."

Mark Twain, who made his home in Bushnell's Hartford, rejected white supremacy, but his Connecticut literary partner, the Massachusetts-born Charles Dudley Warner, embraced it. In 1880 Warner wrote an essay for the influential *Atlantic Monthly* offering a long historical explanation as to why the word *equality* did not mean what it said, especially when applied to African Americans. The "dogma of equality" vexed Warner. "Our objection is deeper. Race distinctions ought to be maintained for the sake of the best development of the race . . . and we doubt that either benevolence or self-interest requires this age to attempt to restore an assumed lost uniformity, and fuse the race traits in a tiresome homogeneity." For Warner, equality raised the deep-seated white fear of race-mixing and genetic decline. Miscegenation, he asserted, would never be "attractive to the American people." After proclaiming that he had read all the world's experts, all its past "sages," on the history of equality, Warner avowed that "inequality appears to be the divine order; it always has existed; undoubtedly it will continue." The only equality he envisioned for the nation was one that preserved "property," recognized the differences in the sexes, and would not "obliterate race traits."

Such a definition of equality fit well into the elite world of the Massachusetts-born Henry Adams (1838–1918). An accomplished historian, public intellectual, and author, he was, in the language of his own day, one of our greatest men of letters. The novelist Henry James pronounced him the "philosophic father to us." His famed *The Education of Henry Adams,* which saw its centennial in the fall of 2018, remains an essential American text, one that blends autobiography, history, and the novel form to achieve unequaled durability and popularity. Because of its place in American and world literature, *The Education of Henry Adams* has been a mainstay of a collegiate education. But we have not fully understood the full scope of its impact or its subversive contexts, much less Adams's role in sustaining white supremacy. Indeed, although the important core of the text traverses the era of the American Civil War and especially Reconstruction, Adams never employed that term. Because of the intensity of his racism and anti-Semitism, he dismissed the era that would decide the nation's future and the African American role in it simply as one that was overwhelmed with sordid political corruption, which had its origins in alleged Jewish intrigue both in the United States and in Europe. Neither an autobiography nor a history, Adams's "trickster" novel would devalue African Americans and attack Jewish life, becoming perhaps the most ingenious and dangerous book of the fin de siècle.

Famously, Adams's account detailed how the nation had arrived at its "tragic" turning point, from the early days when true leaders like Washington, Jefferson, and Madison (and the Adams family) determined the course of human events, to the cultural descent of the late nineteenth century. At the outset of the twentieth century, with immigration reaching unprecedented levels, Adams believed that the nation had turned away from men like himself, jettisoning a more human-centered and unified civilization for an ugly industrial capitalist one. In repudiating modernism, he looked back longingly to an imagined and presumably more humane—and white—eighteenth-century temperament, but more specifically to the European Middle Ages. In a critical but especially foul turn, the book's religious-inspired repudiation of modernism entailed a rejection of the twentieth century as an economic suzerainty dominated by what he labeled the "Jew banker." Despising changes in American life, he blamed the transformation on the "society of Jews and brokers, a world made up of maniacs wild for gold," in which, he lamented, "I have no place."

And in his searing repudiation of the direction of American society, African Americans also had no place. Indeed, his famed text

Henry Adams (1838–1918) wrote sophisticated volumes of academic history on the early American republic. They largely ignored African Americans but judged the Haitian Revolution fairly and dispassionately. In his enormously influential *The Education of Henry Adams,* however, he belittled African Americans, ignored their quest for freedom, judged the post–Civil War years as a Jewish-inspired era of corruption, and refused to employ the term *Reconstruction.* Marian Hooper Adams, photograph, 1883.

considered the crisis over slavery only to the degree that it affected white Americans. If nothing else, he wrote, the advocates of slavery proved only an "object-lesson of the way in which excess of power worked when held by inadequate hands." Of slavery's victims and their integration into American life, he remained silent, and his silence taught generations of students that this central issue, one that drove to the heart of American civilization, did not matter.

Preoccupied with class decline—although ultimately his class only benefited financially from capitalist growth—Adams ignored the most important change of his times, or of any age. Despite the horrific human cost and the historic national transformation that had resulted from the Civil War, African Americans and African American freedom remained invisible to him. In the 1890s, when he crafted his history of the Jefferson and Madison administrations, he could write dispassionately about the Haitian revolutionary Toussaint L'Ouverture. But the *Education* ignored all Black leaders, authors, artists, and intellectuals, male or female—including Frederick Douglass, W.E.B. Du Bois, and even Booker T. Washington. It contained only a few trivializing mentions of Blacks, such as a reference to a "negro cabin" in Washington, D.C.'s Rock Creek Park and to the district's "Negro babies, and their mothers with bandanas." Among the few white leaders he cited who in life had gained renown for advancing the cause of racial justice, the great abolitionist, orator, and labor reformer Wendell Phillips was dismissed as "a model dangerous for youth." Adams then jettisoned the country's leading legal reformer, anti-imperialist, and NAACP head Moorfield Storey as "a dangerous model of frivolity." Adams's *Education* ignored the racial domination of the white South, the rampant violence and lynching inflicted on African Americans that had begun as soon as the war ended, the battle for civil rights legislation, and the struggles for the Fourteenth and Fifteenth amendments to the Constitution, which he lamented.

For Adams, African Americans played no significant part in the nation's history or in the society in which he lived. As he wrote at the close of Reconstruction in 1877, "the Turk of Europe is the counterpart of the American nigger; the Lord only knows how he came there or how he is to be got away." African Americans, to Adams, were just one more annoying part of the landscape. When he traveled to South Carolina in January 1894, he complained that he would have to spend a fortnight there "among the niggers and the mosquitoes." Adams's most famous work, one that has helped influence the way we understand the modern age, left a deeply divided legacy. It brilliantly imagined the most fundamental of changes occurring in Western society, and at the same time perpetuated its worst and most lethal manifestations.

While Henry Adams represented one way Northern elite culture could warp education to serve the needs of white supremacy, the master of the nihilistic cosmic horror fantasy genre, Howard Phillips Lovecraft (1890–1937), similarly shaped a decidedly lowbrow but far more widespread genre. Among his more popular tales are "The Outsider," "The Other Gods," "The Lurking Fear," "The Shadow on the Chimney," "What the Red Glare Meant," "The Horror in the Eyes," "The Rats in the Walls," and "The Horror at Red Hook."

Lovecraft spent most of his life in Rhode Island, after briefly residing in New York City with a Ukrainian-Jewish wife whom he soon left. His work has captured a level of popularity today that Lovecraft never enjoyed during his lifetime, especially among those on the political far right. A literary prize for the fantasy genre is awarded annually in his honor, and there are at least five online journals devoted to his work, along with seven bibliographies of writings by and about him and six video documentaries. Modern filmmakers and authors from Ridley Scott to Stephen King have been influenced by him. However much he might appeal to simple devotees of fantasy—but especially because of that appeal—he remains a wellspring of white supremacy. He combines elements from racial theorists like Louis Agassiz and John H. Van Evrie and his circle with anti-immigrationist ravings and a virulent anti-Semitism that even Henry Adams could respect. While he did not live to see the full development of Nazi Germany, he had freely expressed his admiration for Adolf Hitler. Like so many American racial theorists, the misnamed Lovecraft denounced miscegenation, believing that only "pain and disaster" would result from "the mingling of black and white." What lay behind his many stories is a thoroughgoing commitment to white supremacy and Black inferiority. In his papers at Brown University, this poetic gem resides:

"On the Creation of Niggers."

When, long ago, the Gods created Earth,
In Jove's fair image Man was shap'd at birth.
The beasts for lesser parts were next design'd;
Yet were they too remote from humankind.
To fill this gap, and join the rest to man,
Th' Olympian host conceive'd a clever plan.
A beast they wrought, in semi-human figure,
Fill'd it with vice, and call'd the thing a NIGGER.

While his manuscripts might contain the most toxic examples of his views, Lovecraft's published fantasies expressed parallel opinions, accounting for his popularity on the far right. "The Horror at Red Hook," for instance, is a screed against immigrants, whom he often reviled as either "monsters" or "contagions," terms that proved all too commonplace in the eugenics-dominated 1920s. The population of the Red Hook section of Brooklyn, according to Lovecraft, "is a hopeless tangle and enigma; Syrian, Spanish, Italian, and negro elements impinging upon one another, and fragments of Scandinavian and American belts lying not far distant. It is a babel of sound and filth, and sends out strange cries to answer the lapping of oily waves at its grimy piers and the monstrous organ litanies of the harbour whistles." They could, as one commentator remarked, bring only chaos to the "master race." His continued popularity remains problematic, and whether directly or subconsciously, he appeals to readers as both the "modern pope of horror" and its "grand wizard."

. . .

Horace Mann (1796–1859), another famed New Englander, remains an American icon. More than anyone else, he is responsible for creation of teacher-training institutions (normal schools) and the nation's free public educational system, conceiving of it as a bulwark of democratic republicanism. He also became a leading Massachusetts Whig and Free Soil politician, serving as a state representative and then in Congress from 1847 to 1853. If that was not enough, in his final years he also had become president of Ohio's Antioch College. As the nation's leading educator, Mann bears special responsibility for the direction that American education took. His commitment to free public education remains an enduring legacy, but less appreciated is his equally significant commitment to white supremacy.

When the Massachusetts Unitarian minister and abolitionist Samuel Joseph May took over leadership of the Lexington Normal School in 1842, he proved unrelenting in his determination to admit any qualified young woman regardless of color. The school's board protested, but when May admitted a young woman named Mary Miles, wife of the ex-slave Henry Bibb, it relented. Mann remained largely silent, not wishing to alienate his very useful and influential administrator, but the board made it clear that it would refuse to allow him to admit another. Mann, surprisingly, had rented a room in his own house to a female Black student, Chloe Lee, who had been admitted to another of his normal schools, but could find no one else to rent her living space. Even with Mann's cooperation, young Lee found her experience in his system marred by hostility and "insidious discriminations." And no wonder. Despite his regard for Chloe Lee, African Americans repulsed Horace Mann. Although he considered himself an antislavery advocate, he let Massachusetts know that he would have nothing to do with the radical abolitionism of William Lloyd Garrison. Moreover, his version of abolitionism amounted to little more than colonization, proposing to end slavery by returning all African Americans to Africa and creating what he called an "all-white America."

This icon of American education considered Africans, along

Horace Mann (1796–1859) was the nation's greatest advocate of public schools and teacher education. Yet he scorned African Americans, wished them all removed from the country, and resisted their entrance into the normal schools he helped found. His bronze statue still presides over Boston's State House grounds. Emma Stebbins, sculpture, 1906.

with Asian peoples, to be like trees of a noble forest that "grow in the rocky depths of a cavern, without strength, or beauty, or healing balm—in impurity and darkness." They were little more than unfortunate people "fed by poisonous exhalations from stagnant pools." Africans, who he assumed lived under abject despotism, "intellectually, dwell in a pit denser than subterranean darkness." As for the institution of slavery, Mann cared nothing for its victims but instead fretted—as had Benjamin Franklin—over slavery's impact on whites. Work under the regime of slavery was dishonorable, he argued, something only a slave did. It even affected the country's cherished white women, he warned on the floor of Congress. With shocking language, Mann informed his fellow congressmen that because slavery tainted the very idea of work, Southern white women refused "to join the[ir] black sluts in any sort of household labor." The South and this "lovely land," he mourned, was "blackened with a negro population." That such a person led the national effort to create a public education system reflected commonplace Northern opinion but was a catastrophe of staggering proportions.

Massachusetts, usually thought of as the cradle of abolitionism and liberalism, was the birthplace of Jim Crow and white supremacy. William Lloyd Garrison and similar egalitarian abolitionists, we must remember, were a despised minority. Even on the eve of the Civil War, Wendell Phillips needed bodyguards to protect him at his Boston home and at public events, and he carried a Colt revolver. Horace Mann's support for the Colonization Society and a white America reflected popular opinion better than Garrison or Phillips ever did. Indeed, during the Civil War, the state legislature passed an act of incorporation to reestablish the Massachusetts Colonization Society. Robert C. Winthrop, scion of the famed colonial family, speaker of the U.S. House of Representatives, and longest-serving president of the Massachusetts Historical Society, feared that the Civil War would catapult thousands of unwanted former slaves northward, "an emergency to which no one can be altogether insensible."

The Colonization Society, born in the halls of the U.S. Congress in 1816, found its greatest advocates in the North and especially in

Boston. Never a popular idea in the slave South, colonization struck Northern politicians as the only practical answer to the "problem of the negro." Abraham Lincoln was a lifelong supporter, and most major Massachusetts politicians, from Edward Everett to Daniel Webster, advanced the colonization agenda, considering it essential to the survival of the republic. Edward Everett (1794–1865), orator, governor, congressman, senator, secretary of state, and Harvard University president, was also a lifelong colonizationist. In the House of Representatives, he exclaimed that Blacks were criminals, "ignorant and needy," a threat to the "peace and welfare of the Union," and he urged the entire congressional delegation of Massachusetts to support removal and the American Colonization Society. If a midwestern politician wished to attract national attention, he came to Boston to proclaim his support for colonization.

Caleb Cushing (1800–79), Harvard graduate, lawyer, judge, U.S. attorney general, Democratic congressman, diplomat, and brigadier general during the Mexican War, was one of the state's most experienced and successful political leaders. On July 4, 1833, celebrating American independence, he praised the nation for its "liberty of thought, liberty of speech, liberty of action—liberty in government, liberty in person . . . the cherished desire of the human heart." How lucky he was, Cushing proclaimed, to live in the land of the Pilgrims, where everyone, even the slave, was "born to equal participation in the blessings of life," where liberty had "forever struck" the chains of slavery from "the Negro." Liberty, knowledge, and even Christianity had become the equal "birthright of the European and the African, throughout the New World!" How he could celebrate liberty while also declaring his regret that slavery still existed in the South remains a mystery. But Cushing, like Benjamin Franklin a hundred years earlier, cared little for slavery's victims. Instead, like Horace Mann, he worried that slavery was corrupting the white South, creating disloyalty and turning it into a "plague-spot." Colonization was the only answer because, he declared, even "free blacks in the United States labor under disadvantages arising from color, which no system of laws, however just and equal,—no plans of benevolence, however comprehensive,—can remove." "Full equality" was an impossibility, he concluded, and only colonization to Liberia could give African Americans full freedom. Twenty years later Cushing remained unchanged in his commitment to a white America. "I do not admit as my equals," he proclaimed, "either the red man of America, or the yellow man of Asia, or the black man of Africa."

No one better embodied American nationalism and Northern political leadership than Massachusetts senator Daniel Webster (1782–1852)—and no one more fully embraced the white supremacist principles of the American Colonization Society. Remembered for his oratorical defense of the Union and his pure expression of American nationalism, memory of his support for colonization has fallen completely by the wayside. For the great Webster, slavery, which he said had always existed, caused no sense of urgency. It had underpinned the unrivaled glory of ancient Greece. Justifying slavery in the same way as his contemporaries, in his famous March 7, 1850, speech he urged national compromise on the issue and acceptance of the new Fugitive Slave Law. There existed, he explained, a natural and original distinction "between the races of mankind—the inferiority of the colored or black race to the white race." He backed colonization, but not wishing to antagonize the South, he supported it only to remove the unwanted "free colored people to any colony, or any place in the world."

Like most of his fellow citizens, Webster considered Africans to be heathens, who lived in "petty provinces, ignorant and barbarous, without the knowledge of God, and with no reasonable knowledge of their own character and condition." Whites had done the African a great favor by enslaving them and by acquainting them with civilization and true religion. As the famous inventor and painter Samuel F. B. Morse proclaimed in 1863, religion could do its best work when a barbarous race was enslaved to a Christian one. Slavery then, in words worthy of George Orwell, meant "*Salvation* and *Freedom*." As many African Americans as possible should now be returned to Africa, Webster explained, where they could lift their brethren and stop impeding the progress of "our Anglo-Saxon race, to spread . . . their knowledge and their principles . . . and love of liberty, civil and religious, over the largest possible space on the habitable globe."

Africans could never develop in America, he asserted, where "no man flourishes, no man grows in a state of conscious inferiority, any more than a vegetable grows in the dark. He must come out." While removal of Blacks might aid African development, Webster told the thirty-fifth annual meeting of the American Colonization Society, it would really be for the benefit "especially of the North."

.   .   .

The Philadelphian Septimus Winner (1827–1902), one of the most popular songwriters of the mid-nineteenth century, is best known for "Ten Little Injuns," "Listen to the Mockingbird," and "Oh Where, Oh Where Has My Little Dog Gone." Over the course of his long career, he published two to three hundred such songs, as well as scores of instructional manuals for musical instruments, poems, and many children's books. He also became a teacher of a different sort. Modern memory of him is overwhelmingly sentimentalist, a quaint remnant of times past. But Winner, a conservative pro-slavery Democrat, was jailed for treason in 1862 for composing the anti-Lincoln song "Give Us Back Our Old Commander, Little Mac, the People's Pride," a demand that President Lincoln return George B. McClellan to command of the Army of the Potomac. It sold wildly when first released, but to gain release from prison, Winner had to destroy all unsold copies of the tune. He had sarcastically dedicated the accompanying 1861 "Contraband" song sheet to the Massachusetts politician Maj. Gen. Benjamin F. Butler for his novel use of the laws of war to liberate slaves by declaring them contraband and thus liable to seizure. Winner had more than music in mind and revealed his opposition to African American freedom from the outset of the war. Like so many other Northerners, he did not hesitate to employ demeaning images of African Americans to make a sale. Despite his racism, Winner also was not above "borrowing" tunes that he heard African Americans whistle on the streets of Philadelphia and turning them into his own songs and cash.

No mere sentimentalist or harmless self-styled "crank," Winner was a shrewd businessman who infused American songwriting with noxious stereotypes that diverted attention from the freedom

This song sheet was facetiously dedicated to Maj. Gen. Benjamin F. Butler, who first referred to escaping slaves as wartime contraband. Septimus Winner, "The Contraband," 1861.

struggle, confirmed white notions of Black incapacity, and promoted a national longing for the Old South. His 1865 song "Ellie Rhee" shows that the postwar "Lost Cause" sentimentality that fueled Southern white resistance to Black freedom and full democracy had as strong a hold on Northern imagination as it did on that of the South. Moreover, if Winner's song/poem is any indication, it—like the ideology of white supremacy—started in the North before becoming a mainstay of Southern white resistance.

Ellie Rhee (or Carry Me Back to Tennessee)

Sweet Ellie Rhee, so dear to me,
Is lost forever more;
Our home was down in Tennessee.
Before dis cruel war.
Then carry me back to Tennessee,

Back where I long to be,
Among the fields of yellow corn,
To my darling Ellie Rhee.

CHORUS: Then carry me back to Tennessee,
Back where I long to be,
Among de friends of yellow corn,
To my darling Ellie Rhee.

Oh why did I from day to day,
Keep wishing to be free;
And away from my massa run away
And leave my Ellie Rhee.
Then carry me back to Tennessee,
Back where I long to be,
Among the fields of yellow corn,
To my darling Ellie Rhee.

CHORUS

They said that I would soon be free
And happy all de day.
But if dey take me back again,
I'll never run away.
Then carry me back to Tennessee,
Back where I long to be,
Among the fields of yellow corn,
To my darling Ellie Rhee.

CHORUS

The war is over now at last.
De color'd race am free,
Dat good time comin' on so fast:
I'm waiting for to see.

Winner's "Ellie Rhee," it turned out, was no onetime sprouting of regret for the war and Black freedom. He went to his grave mourning the war, its impact on the *South,* and the "lamentable" loss of its slave wealth. One of his final poems, "Southern Roses," lamented the war's damaging impact on Southern lives and those lost, "life's tearful cost." Expressing the hope that the white South would truly rise again, the Philadelphian counseled his considerable audience that

> Southern Roses still shall bloom
> O'er the dust of fallen brave
> Bloom for sons and daughters fair
> To decorate their early graves
> Over ruins of the past
> Mighty people yet shall rise
> Scorning with a proud contempt
> Unforgiving enemies
> Southern rose long shall bloom
> Glad'ning hearts with hope and trust
> Barren fields grow green again
> when stolen treasure falls to dust.

. . .

Composers, ministers, social leaders, and authors helped shape the contours of white supremacy and ensure its dominance, but it was the law that exercised ultimate power and authority. And far more than any other section of the country, the North, especially Massachusetts, crafted the legal principle that underpinned white supremacy and enforced Black inferiority. The majority decision in the infamous 1896 *Plessy v. Ferguson* case determined the fate of the nation. The notorious doctrine of "separate but equal," which *Plessy* articulated, had its origins in an 1849 case.

In *Roberts v. City of Boston,* Massachusetts chief justice Lemuel Shaw established the damaging principle, which another Massachusetts-trained judge, Henry Billings Brown, later welded

"Our goddess of liberty. What is she to be? To what complexion are we to come at last?" *Frank Leslie's Illustrated Newspaper,* July 16, 1870, p. 288.

into U.S. constitutional law, where it remained for over sixty years and lingered on in practice, if not in law, for generations after. Shaw, father-in-law to Herman Melville, ruled that Boston's racially separate schools were in all respects equal. Moreover, the city could create schools based on "race, religion, economic status, or national origin," even age, gender, and ability. Racial prejudice, according to Shaw, lay outside legal remedy. It was "not created by law, and probably cannot be changed by law," he famously wrote. So no doubt would linger on the issue, Shaw further ruled that "compelling colored and white children to associate together in the same schools" would only *increase* prejudice.

After the Civil War, while Congress began expanding the circumscribed world of African American rights, the Supreme Court moved in the opposite direction. During the 1870s, even before the close of Reconstruction, the Court began emasculating Congress's civil rights laws and especially the Fourteenth and Fifteenth amendments to the Constitution, which ensured Black civil and voting rights. The infamous *Slaughter House* cases of 1873, initiated by New Orleans butchers seeking relief from city regulations, became the opportunity for the Court to distinguish between state and federal citizenship and to determine that the Fourteenth Amendment—despite clear *original* congressional intent—protected only rights that owed their existence to the federal government. All others fell to the states to enforce, with which, the Court ruled, the Fourteenth Amendment had "nothing to do." In his famous dissent, Stephen J. Field declared that his associates on the Court had pulled off a great feat of legal magicianship, turning a constitutional amendment intended to aid newly freed African Americans into "a legal device to protect the wealthiest and most powerful." The civil rights of African Americans thus became the property of the states, guaranteeing their demise. Three years later, in its even more infamous *United States v. Cruikshank* (1876) ruling, the Court overturned convictions arising out of the horrific slaughter of African Americans in the 1873 Colfax, Louisiana, Massacre. In a ruling that would have far-reaching consequences, the Court decided that federal law and the Constitution applied only when states, not individuals, violated a person's civil rights. All other such cases could be handled only by local and state governments, thus ensuring the South's complete domination of African Americans and the constriction of Black rights in the North.

But the Supreme Court did not suddenly imagine that Blacks had no rights that white men were bound to respect. This principle was built into American society, and as the *Roberts* and the infamous 1857 *Dred Scott* cases showed, it dominated legal thinking, despite the later intentions of Radical Republicans in Congress and the new constitutional amendments. And the trail of similar state court decisions was long and unwavering. In 1883, for instance, the New York court ruled in the case of *King v. Gallagher* that "if one race be inferior to the other socially, the Constitution of the United States cannot put them upon the same plane." Indeed, Henry Billings Brown's decision in *Plessy v. Ferguson* was unremarkable at the time—even though it set the blueprint for American Jim Crow segregation—because it reflected commonplace white American and legal views.

The *Plessy* case had resulted from an orchestrated challenge to Louisiana's 1890 law that required "equal but separate" accommodations for whites and Blacks on the state's passenger railroads. The famed Reconstruction judge and novelist Albion W. Tourgée led the legal challenge to the law before the Supreme Court. Tourgée and his associates argued that the Louisiana law violated the Thirteenth Amendment that had ended slavery and immediately elevated all African Americans to full citizenship. But Brown and most of the other justices rejected that line of argument, avowing that at the very least, the Fourteenth Amendment proved that the Thirteenth did nothing beyond ending involuntary servitude. And the Fourteenth Amendment, which Brown admitted was intended to "enforce the absolute equality of the two races before the law . . . could not have been intended to abolish distinctions based on color, or to enforce social, as distinguished from political, equality or a commingling of the two races upon terms unsatisfactory to either." Shaw's decision in the *Roberts* case, Brown declared, confirmed Boston's right to form separate schools based on race, age, sex, poverty, or abandonment. He specifically rejected the idea that "social prejudices may be overcome by legislation" or that the Constitution could compel "an enforced commingling of the two races." Social equality could be achieved only through voluntary efforts by individuals, not through lawmaking. "Legislation," he wrote, "is powerless to eradicate racial instincts or to abolish distinctions based upon physical differences." If one race was inferior to another, "the Constitution of the United States cannot put them on the same plane." And so separate *and equal*—which no state even attempted to create—became the law of the land, permitting the grossest and most *unequal* conditions for African Americans and enshrining white supremacy as the nation's elementary legal principle until 1954.

Born in South Lee, Massachusetts, Henry Billings Brown (1836–1906) had attended Yale and studied law at Harvard. He moved to Detroit, where in 1860 he became deputy U.S. marshal and in 1863 an assistant U.S. attorney. During the war, he did not support emancipation or Abraham Lincoln. In 1875 President Ulysses S. Grant appointed him to the federal bench, where he served until ascending to the Supreme Court in 1891. In his memoir, Brown clearly explained the importance of his lineage and of racial purity: "I was born of a New England Puritan family in which there was no admixture of alien blood for two hundred and fifty years."

Honoring and defending the white race clearly mattered to Brown. Before the Civil War, he had opposed abolitionists. He once heard Wendell Phillips speak and, impressed by his oratory, concluded that Boston's blue-blooded abolitionist was "a dangerous man" and a "demagogue." Not long after the war, Brown briefly lived in Memphis, Tennessee, where he made a point of dining with Jefferson Davis. He never had a "more delightful evening" and found the former Confederate president to be "a most courteous and agreeable gentleman of the best Southern type." He excused Davis's role in the Civil War and found his views "little more than a radical difference of political opinion." He believed that it "would have been a grave mistake to apply the legal canons of interpretation and put him on trial like an ordinary malefactor." His views only solidified further while he was living in Michigan. Surprisingly, in 1872 Brown had addressed a mixed-race audience and urged Black voters to stick with President Grant—who would name him to the federal court—a man who represented the party of "justice, freedom, and equal rights." But that night Brown returned home and recorded his actual sentiments in his daybook. He felt satisfied that he had written his own speech and "fired it off at a big audience of niggers." No doubt the speech helped advance his career. Brown, a scion of New England Puritanism, wished to preserve the white male privilege that had characterized American life. He hated woman suffrage almost as much as he hated Black enfranchisement. As he wrote in his memoir, "no suffrage without nigger—no suffrage, no nigger."

It's richly ironic that the judge who would institutionalize white supremacy and Black inferiority in law came from Massachusetts, while the lone dissenter in the *Plessy* case, Judge John Marshall Harlan, had been a Kentucky slave owner. Separate accommodations would never be "equal," Harlan warned, and the *Plessy* decision would be every bit as "pernicious as the decision . . . in the *Dred Scott* case." And so it would. A careful reading of Harlan's famous dissent reveals his repudiation of legal Jim Crow but not of "social discrimination." Despite his penetrating argument, Harlan held as firmly to white supremacy as did the rest of the justices. The "white race deems itself to be the dominant race in this country," he wrote. "And so it is, in prestige, in achievements, in education and in power. So, I doubt not, it will continue to be for all time if it remains true to its great heritage and holds fast to the principles of constitutional liberty." The Constitution might be color blind, but to Harlan, it could no more create social equality than it could create economic equality. In a very direct way, the *Plessy* case reunited North and South on the principle of white supremacy. As a Springfield, Massachusetts, newspaper predicted in 1892, when the *Plessy* case was winding through the nation's court system, "equal but separate" would "spread like measles in those commonwealths where white supremacy is thought to be in peril." No such danger existed in the North.

.   .   .

William James, the nineteenth century's leading American philosopher, psychologist, and author, boasted that Harvard's Swiss-trained scientist Louis Agassiz (1807–73) represented man on "a heroic scale." Indeed, well before the 1890s, Agassiz had trained nearly all the country's most important naturalists. His influence cannot be overestimated. When Agassiz arrived in the country in 1846, he immediately raised unprecedented interest for his research in biology and ethnology, which gained him election into the American Academy of Arts and Sciences. The very next year Harvard hired him, initiating the modernization and professionalization of science in the United States. To keep him, the university then founded its school of science and the Museum of Comparative Zoology. As Stanford University's founding president David Starr Jordan remarked in 1923, the hiring of Agassiz amounted to nothing less than the "beginning of a new era in American education." His influence grew so rapidly across the nation and became so immense that

Emerson feared he would turn Harvard into a college of natural history. Instead, Agassiz weaponized science to guarantee the subservience of African Americans and enshrine whiteness as the highest scientific category of human development. Next to law and religion, science exerted the most widespread and permanent impact on the institutionalization of white supremacy, and Louis Agassiz was its most potent champion.

Louis Agassiz had formerly been an advocate of monogenesis, the unity of mankind, grounded in firm Christian faith. But once he arrived in the United States, he struggled to retain his original ideas concerning human origins. Although he avoided admitting to a change of heart, he in fact converted to polygenesis almost immediately after arriving in the country, holding that "successive, separate and independent creations" characterized the natural history of plants and animals. In 1850 he published a series of essays in the Unitarian newspaper the *Christian Examiner* to reconcile religious faith with polygenesis. He understood that charges of

Louis Agassiz (1807–73), the Swiss-born Harvard University naturalist and ethnographer, was the most influential American scientist of the midnineteenth century, training nearly all of the country's leading naturalists. His revulsion for African Americans and his insistence on their inherent inferiority knew no limits. The influence of his damaging ideas cannot be overestimated. James W. Black, photographer, carte de visite, 1861.

heresy would damage his career and reputation, so in the Northern press he avoided directly challenging the story of human origins in Genesis and argued that scientific observation only increased human understanding of God's true powers. While his essay professed belief in the "true unity of mankind," he obfuscated his real conclusions by asserting that "the unity of the species does not involve a unity of origin, and that diversity of origin does not involve a plurality of species." All this affirmed the "inequality of races," whatever their origins. For Agassiz, Africans were "today what they were in the time of the Pharaohs. . . . And does not this indicate in this race a peculiar apathy, a peculiar indifference to the advantages afforded by civilized society?" Even the American Indian, "the indomitable, courageous, proud Indian," blazed brightly compared to the "submissive, obsequious, imitative negro."

What changed Agassiz wasn't science or literature. Upon arriving in the United States, he visited Philadelphia and had his first sustained encounter with people of African descent. It horrified him, forcing a complete rethinking of his understanding of human development. He immediately wrote home to his mother, asserting that his prolonged contact with a "degraded and degenerate race" in Philadelphia made him reconsider everything, "all our ideas about the confraternity of the human type and the unique origin of our species." He struggled with his reaction but admitted that "it is impossible for me to repress the feeling that they are not the same blood as us. In seeing their black faces with their thick lips and grimacing teeth, the wool on their head, their bent knees, their elongated hands, their curled nails, and especially the livid color of the palm of their hands, I could not take my eyes off their face in order to tell them to stay far away. . . . What unhappiness for the white race—to have tied their existence so closely with that of Negroes. . . . God preserve us from such a contact." He lectured in the South during that first trip to the United States, asserting in December 1847 in Charleston what he would not say so directly later in Boston. Black and white, he proclaimed, "were physiologically and anatomically distinct species."

In 1850 Agassiz returned to South Carolina and closely examined and, now famously and controversially, had slaves in Columbia photographed for further study, then archived the images in Harvard's Peabody Museum of Archeology and Ethnology. He discovered that great diversity existed within species, such that the "differences between distinct races are often greater than those distinguishing species of animals from one another." For example, the "chimpanzee and gorilla do not differ more from one another than the Mandingo and the Guinea Negro." According to Agassiz, it didn't much matter whether we called these differences, "races, varieties, or species"; all that mattered was whether "these differences are primitive, or whether they have been introduced subsequently to the creation of one common primitive stock." To him, God had created the differences and so had determined "the relative rank among these races." Agassiz, like most Americans, believed that God had determined racial rank and had placed the white at the very top and the "negro" on the bottom. In August 1863, during the Civil War, Agassiz advised the Massachusetts abolitionist Samuel Gridley Howe that in a postwar world, African Americans should enjoy "legal equality," but he rejected any hint of what he called "social equality." That was simply impossible "from the very character of the Negro race," which to Agassiz's mind was inherently "indolent, playful, sensuous, imitative, subservient, good natured, versatile, unsteady in their purpose, devoted, affectionate, in every thing [*sic*] unlike other races." African Americans were children masquerading as adults, he confidently assured Howe, insisting that "no man has a right to what he is unfit to use. . . . Let us beware of granting too much to the negro race in the beginning, lest it become necessary to recall violently some of the privileges which they may use to our detriment, and their own injury." Agassiz would not live to see the full impact of all that he had written, but he undoubtedly went to his grave confident of what it would be. And at least one individual who avidly read his works helped ensure what impact would result.

2

"The White Republic Against the World"

The Toxic Legacy of John H. Van Evrie

He is not a black white man, or a man merely with a black skin, but a different and inferior species of man.

—John H. Van Evrie, *Negroes and Negro "Slavery,"* 1853

John H. Van Evrie (1814?–96), the nation's first professional racist, laid the white supremacist foundations of American democracy. As the ideological spindle on which the pre– and post–Civil War eras swirled, he worked tirelessly to permanently bind white supremacy to the nation's democratic ethos. The North's most belligerent enemy of Reconstruction, Van Evrie employed his unprecedented genius for marketing to inject white supremacist ideals into American political discourse North and South. Immediately after the war, he and his business partner Rushmore G. Horton published a raucous history textbook, *A Youth's History of the Great Civil War in the United States,* to repudiate the policies of the Lincoln administration, reject all political or social equality for African Americans, and guarantee that future generations would cherish white supremacy as the nation's governing principle.

Smart, ambitious, and blessed with boundless energy, Van Evrie fused an unprecedented marketing campaign to an exhaustive command of the works of Louis Agassiz and other ethnologists to bolster the white supremacist foundations of the Democratic Party and the white working class. Best known for his repellent books *Negroes and Negro "Slavery"* (1853), *Free Negroism* (1862), *Subgenation* (1864), and *White Supremacy and Negro Subordination* (1867), Van Evrie also ran a small publishing empire, Van Evrie, Horton & Co., in the heart of Manhattan, the seat of American economic and political power. In addition to publishing Horton's textbook, Van Evrie's firm circulated a flood of similarly-themed pamphlets, texts, and even a novel. He published two combative newspapers, the New York *Day-Book,* which became the *Weekly Caucasian* in 1861 after the Lincoln administration tried to shut down papers that promoted disloyalty and treason, and *The Old Guard: A Monthly Journal Devoted to the Principles of 1776 and 1787.*

Van Evrie, who popularized the terms *white supremacy* and *master race,* has been either overlooked or grossly underestimated by most modern historians and remains unknown to the wider public. A toxic combination of Joseph Goebbels, Steve Bannon, and Rupert Murdoch, Van Evrie too often has been dismissed as a fake Democrat, as an oddity, or as not especially influential, even if perhaps reflective of Northern racists. Nothing could be further from the truth. Nearly all Democrats of the mid-nineteenth century knew of him, and even Abraham Lincoln had read some of his writings. Moreover, his ideas resounded in the U.S. Congress. New York representative James Brooks—a Queens Democrat born in Maine—recited Van Evrie's toxic ideas in December 1867, quoting at length from his defense of "white man's government" and the supposedly gross incapacities of African Americans. Even a Wisconsin state representative read Van Evrie's words to his fellow legislators, asserting that they were the "embodiment of my views." There remains, Rep. Mitchell Steever declared in 1858, a "perfect harmony" with the facts that the "Caucasian race is peculiarly progressive" while the "negro is this moment what he was four thousand years ago."

We have undervalued Van Evrie's impact, ignored his poisonous writings, and failed to understand how much he helped shape modern white supremacist ideology, even in the South. His toxic views may have emerged from his era's textbook teaching of U.S. history and certainly played an enormous role in assaulting the struggle for liberty and civil rights after the Civil War. In so doing, we have completely underestimated the intensity of Northern white supremacy, both before and after the Civil War.

A somewhat elusive character who changed the spelling of his name several times, Van Evrie was born in Canada and moved to Rochester, New York, in the 1830s after obtaining medical training at Geneva Medical College (now Hobart and William Smith College), where his future father-in-law taught. An aggressive social climber, in 1842 he married Sophia Elizabeth Colman, a descendant of the city's founder, the niece and ward of Thomas Hunt Rochester, the sixth son of Col. Nathaniel Rochester. Van Evrie then established a medical practice in the city's Smith's Arcade. He lived briefly in Lucas County, Ohio, but declared bankruptcy in 1843 and returned to Rochester. After his wife's untimely death in 1845, he served in the Mexican War as an assistant surgeon in the 15th U.S. Infantry. The war may have heightened Van Evrie's racist fervor, but it did not create it. In early 1846 he had sought John C. Calhoun's assistance in preventing New York Whigs from enfranchising African Americans, in what he labeled "the most dangerous movement that has ever occurred in this County." He was infuriated by a "*sickly sentimentality* that would sacrifice the whole race of whites in visionery [*sic*] projects to benefit a few blacks." All Democrats, he insisted to Calhoun, must stand up for the preservation "of the purity of the Anglo Saxon race." After the Mexican War, he abandoned his medical career and, with evangelical fervor, took up the cause of white supremacy full-time.

Moving to New York City to build a publishing empire could not have been smarter. Had he remained in Rochester, Van Evrie might have been overlooked or perhaps diminished by the dramatic appearance in the late 1840s of Frederick Douglass. If he had remained in Rochester, a conflict with Douglass would have been all but inevitable and likely would only have increased public sympathy for the Black abolitionist editor and enhanced the influence of his newspaper, the *North Star*. In fact, Douglass later launched blistering attacks on Van Evrie and the New York *Day-Book*, mixing contempt with amusing sarcasm. Did they cross paths in Rochester in 1847 or 1848? It's difficult to believe that anyone in the small city could have remained unaware of Douglass's arrival and his plans to establish an antislavery newspaper. No record has been uncovered of any

John H. Van Evrie (1814?–96), the nation's first professional racist, had a relentless drive to convince the North that the African represented a separate, lower species of human. He refused to employ the term *slave* and asserted that Africans, like mules and oxen, had been created by God to work for the white man. W. G. Jackman, "The White Republic Against the World," lithographed engraving, New York, ca. 1868.

interaction between the two, however. Perhaps after the death of his wife and the increasing antislavery activism in Rochester, Van Evrie quickly sought new, more hospitable surroundings. All we know for sure is that sometime after returning from the Mexican War, he abandoned his Rochester medical career and his only child, whom he placed with his wife's relatives. Ablaze with racial rage, he moved to Washington, D.C., where he obtained a taste for journalism at the Washington *Daily Union,* which published an excerpt from his first tome, *Negroes and Negro "Slavery."* He then moved to the commercial and publishing nexus of the Atlantic world.

New York City in the 1850s had about 800,000 inhabitants, more than one million if we include those living in Brooklyn, then a separate city. The next largest U.S. city was Philadelphia, which sported a population of 600,000. All the Southern cotton spun in New England mills passed through New York, the center of the nation's banking, finance, commerce, and manufacturing. Because of King Cotton, the South poured some $200 million a year into the city. As the nation's leading commercial center and port, New

York operated about sixty piers along eastern Manhattan alone, and as many as nine hundred vessels plied the harbor on any given day. The city handled more shipping every year than all other American ports *combined*. Even in the 1820s, the revenue from tariffs collected just in New York paid nearly all the national government's annual expenses. Not surprisingly, New York City brimmed with publishers, newspapers, journals, and magazines as no other city ever had or ever would. By one estimate, at least 345 different publishers—not including printers, bookbinders, or retailers—operated there as early as 1852. Just a fraction of the newspapers and journals published in New York boasted a circulation of about eighty million subscribers. As the Library of Congress's newspaper database shows, between 1850 and 1860, 773 different newspapers published for varying lengths of time in New York. If we include Brooklyn, the figure leaps to a dizzying 821. In 1859 alone, the New York City directory listed 167 newspapers and journals publishing full-time. If Van Evrie longed for his lethal opinions to have the greatest social and political impact on the largest number of people, New York City was the place to be.

Van Evrie set up shop in the heart of Manhattan, at 162 Nassau Street, steps from the Tweed Courthouse, which went up beginning in 1861, just as he was accumulating unprecedented influence and notoriety. His Nassau Street business operated within a hub of publishing enterprises, all within easy walking distance of one another. Either on his street or on nearby blocks one could find the *American Journal of Photography,* the *American Publisher's Circular,* the *Bank-Note Commercial Reporter, Harper's Weekly,* James Gordon Bennett's *Herald,* the *Christian Ambassador,* the *Christian Intelligencer,* the *Christian Inquirer,* Theodore Tilton's *Independent,* and the *Home Missionary,* as well as the American Baptist home Mission Society, the American Missionary Society, the American Tract Society, and a plethora of other business and commercial publications. But there was no greater irony than that within a block of Van Evrie's Nassau Street publishing hothouse sat the Beekman Street offices of the *National Anti-Slavery Standard.*

In a pattern that should be familiar to modern eyes, Van Evrie

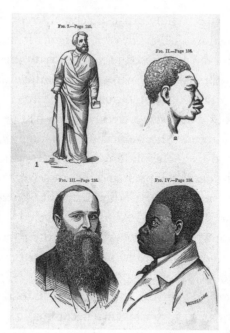

Frontispiece to Van Evrie's best-known work, *White Supremacy and Negro Subordination* (2nd ed., 1870).

simultaneously denigrated African Americans and crafted an image of himself as a superpatriotic defender of (white) democratic society. Indeed, for Van Evrie, degrading African Americans as a subspecies was *essential* for creating nineteenth-century American democracy and an enduring white identity. His inventive and revolting racial theories, ensconced in a multitude of publications, translated the new ethnological "science" of Josiah Clark Nott, George R. Gliddon, and Louis Agassiz, among others, for an eager public. He aimed his diatribes especially at the white working class, those most threatened by the very notion of freedom for African Americans and by immigrants. Yet he simultaneously appealed to New York's Irish and German populations, who also felt directly threatened by the idea of free Black labor. Even in the 1840s, the poorest Irish immigrants proved the greatest enemies of African Americans. They flocked to the Democratic Party, seeing it as a bulwark against Black labor and abolitionists, who they asserted promoted "niggerology." Attacking African Americans became, for the Irish, a direct avenue to gaining whiteness, while urban Blacks suffered so many attacks that they called the brickbats thrown at them "Irish confetti." Like Walt Whitman, Van Evrie used racial bigotry to present himself as the defender of these workingmen and as an influential and successful businessman with their best interests at heart.

The New York *Day-Book,* a weekly paper, had been founded by Nathaniel B. Stimson, who ironically as a young man had worked in a store owned by the abolitionist Arthur Tappan. But Stimson quickly came to despise Tappan and his antislavery principles. The paper originally supported the Whig Party but turned pro-Southern and Democratic. Then in 1855 Stimson discovered Van Evrie. Sometime the next year he began working with the paper's owner, and when Stimson unexpectedly died in 1857, Van Evrie, Horton & Co. assumed control of the newspaper.

Van Evrie quickly turned the *Day-Book* into the *Liberator* of the white supremacist movement, becoming the North's most vocal and persistent advocate of white supremacy and defender of the Southern labor system. The paper, he declared, stood on the Declaration of Independence's presumed "equality of all white men." He boasted that his paper's circulation in the South was greater than that of all Northern papers *combined,* and in 1868 he claimed more subscribers "than any other Democratic journal ever published on this continent." The Charleston, South Carolina, *Courier* reported that the *Day-Book* had over 35,000 readers in the South and an equal number in the North. New York's popular *Frank Leslie's Illustrated Newspaper* pegged the *Day-Book*'s total circulation at 40,000, and if the Charleston paper's estimate was correct, it may have reached 50,000 or 60,000, giving it a far larger readership than Boston's radical antislavery newspaper ever enjoyed.

While some modern historians have downplayed the importance of Van Evrie's career, Walt Whitman's publisher considered the *Day-Book* to be among New York's most influential newspapers, in the same category as the *Herald,* the *Tribune,* and the *Illustrated News,* reaching the very same audience that Whitman sought. Mimicking Van Evrie, Whitman advised readers of the Brooklyn *Eagle* that democracy and white privilege were threatened by immigrants and especially by African Americans, who possessed "about as much intellect and caliber (in the mass) as so many baboons." Papers like the Columbus, Ohio, *Crisis* and the Camden, New Jersey, *Democrat* pronounced the *Day-Book* a prime organ of the Democratic Party, one that "ought to be in every Democratic family." In Boston, the seat of antislavery fever, the *Evening Transcript* had nothing but gushing praise for the New York publisher. As a physician, the paper explained, Van Evrie was in an excellent position to detail how "negroes" were a distinct species, fit only for slavery. The paper found his writings "entirely new, and distinct from that advanced by any other writer." He "at last" had provided Bostonians with "the true philosophy of this distracting question."

The same praise came from newspapers across the South, where Van Evrie was guaranteed to find a welcoming audience. The influential *De Bow's Review,* published in Louisiana and South Carolina, had praised his 1861 *Negroes and Negro "Slavery"* as "the most original, profound, and valuable book that has issued from the press of Europe or America, for many years past." The journal declared him to be "a learned anatomist and physiologist." It gloried in Van Evrie's determination that Africans embodied a completely "different species, physically, from the white man." It proclaimed Van Evrie a "great physical philosopher" who had proved with finality that no connection existed "between the man and the brute." After the Civil War, the *Review*'s support for the New Yorker only grew, and the journal exclaimed that he wrote about white supremacy "con amore." At the same time, the Maryland *Union* expressed its admiration for the *Day-Book* because it gave a voice to former Confederates like the popular author E. A. Pollard and offered blistering attacks on the reputations of abolitionists, calling them out as the real traitors to the United States.

But Van Evrie's reach proved far broader. Without exaggeration, virtually *any* American who read a newspaper from 1858 to 1879 likely had seen one of his publications, a review of his work, or an advertisement. Countless American papers, and even some across the Atlantic, reviewed his publications (sometimes scornfully). Indeed, one English journal branded Van Evrie as America's chief authority on "the negro." While his papers and publications were lethal and offensive, they operated in an environment of toxicity, which only added gravity to his outrageous assertions. The preeminent Civil War–era Black paper, the New York *Weekly Anglo-African,* rightly denounced Van Evrie's work as "coarse and stupid," revealing his "rude and bestial nature." But such opinions, as the *Anglo-African* sadly knew, were commonplace. Even the Transcendentalist-turned-Catholic Orestes Brownson, who decried Van Evrie as one of the "half learned who babble nonsense" and who considered African Americans to be fully human, defended the South's right to hold slaves and denounced democracy as "one of the best hits the devil ever made." New York's better-known editor James Gordon Bennett offered similar opinions in the New York *Herald* and openly defended slavery as "neither evil nor a crime." The idea of unleashing four million Southern Blacks on the nation was his worst nightmare, so for the benefit "of civilization at large," he exclaimed, slavery had to be protected.

The *Day-Book* and Van Evrie, Horton & Co. intertwined a message of white supremacy with Democratic politics to gain the trust and support of the white working class. They wished to be understood as the nation's most important defenders of "the equality, fraternity and prosperity of the democratic masses." A tireless advocate of the Democratic Party, Van Evrie even referred to his Manhattan firm as the "Democratic Publishing House." He pushed the party's agenda of states' rights, limited government, and lower taxes with unrestrained fervor. His defense of the Southern labor system was the core of his ideological campaign to the Northern worker. As the New Haven, Connecticut, *Columbian Register* explained in 1862, Van Evrie appealed to them by "proving" that emancipation would cost the North "*Forty Millions of dollars* more" just for groceries. The paper urged "all white laboring men" to read Van Evrie's work to help avoid the "enormous" loss awaiting the North if slavery ended. Most important, as the New York *Observer* declared in 1859, Van Evrie's *Day-Book* represented a bulwark against "the modern heresies of Abolitionists" and exposed the idea of Black equality as a direct threat to *"equality among white men."* Other city papers offered similar support for his racial theories: one journal maintained that Van Evrie's "arguments are all based on the undeniable fact of the mental and physical inferiority of the negro race." The *Metropolitan Record and New York Vindicator* assured its readers that Van Evrie had proved that "the Creator intended the negro to remain in a state of tutelage or dependence on the superior Race." Because of its campaign for white supremacy, the city's other Democratic newspapers considered the *Day-Book* to be essential to the republic's survival.

Van Evrie dreamed of becoming New York's mouthpiece for state and national Democratic politics. He cultivated influential politicians like Illinois's Stephen A. Douglas, who distributed his pamphlets to his own constituents and described the Democratic Party as dedicated to making "the hemisphere safe for white men's self-government." Even before establishing his New York publishing empire, he had contacted South Carolina's John C. Calhoun to strengthen North-South bonds. But he wished to exert influence and increase sales, not to gain political office or position. "I am," he explained to Calhoun, "no trading Politician, only a citizen." He positioned himself as a defender of the nation as Washington and Jefferson had imagined it. He, like Jefferson, believed that the country depended on the alliance of "the Northern Democracy" and its "natural allies of the South," by which he meant slaveholders. Without this alliance, he feared that the Whig Party—which to him embodied aristocracy and Black freedom—would dominate and control "the Presidency for half a century."

At midcentury, when Van Evrie began attracting national attention, the Democratic Party in fact had become a "solemn pact," however fragile, between its Northern and Southern wings, indispensable to national unity. He sought to strengthen the party's working-class base in the North *and* the South—and enhance his own credibility—by savagely attacking European aristocrats, especially the English. They represented the wellspring of vile abolitionist principles of race-mixing, he maintained, and were kin to the Northern capitalists who exploited both Northern workers and Southern farmers. He would, as a kind of "Marx of the master class," attract working-class support by linking Northern elites and capitalists to European aristocrats. "Those who produce everything enjoy nothing," he explained, "while those who produce nothing enjoy everything." The rich and idle condemned the many to "lives of ignorance, toil and brutality, differing little from the animals that they labor with." He described Europe's monarchies as inherently antidemocratic, basing their survival on the idea that one group of whites could and should subordinate others. The English ruled by illegitimate usurpation, "those who are not naturally superior, while American democracy assures self-government of, by, and for naturally equal whites." He co-opted the language of abolitionism and reform by proclaiming the "doctrine of human brotherhood," which to him meant the "equality of all whom God has created equal, and the inequality of all whom He has made unequal." Antislavery agitation, however, only diverted attention from elite mistreatment "of the white working class." He delighted in comparing "mulattoes" to European royalty, a group renowned for mulish sterility and possessing the "same feebleness, tendency to imbecility, to idiocy and impotency. Nature abhors them both for both are the results of the violated laws." Thus Van Evrie built a national Democratic appeal that grounded the workingman's economic welfare and the nation's political future squarely on anti-abolitionism, class conflict, race hatred, and white supremacy.

He also sought to exploit American xenophobia, arguing that a painful and revolting future awaited the United States and its workers if it followed the example of British emancipation from the 1830s. The English working class, he warned, suffered greatly because of it, enduring exploitation and death because funds that should have gone to their elevation were, instead, lavished on Blacks "basking in tropical suns or reveling on pumpkin in Jamaica." The "despotic and irresponsible oligarchy" of England squandered money on "the negro," he cried, taking food from the workers, the truly oppressed, and instead wasting it "on the Negro."

The Democratic Party offered a natural and inviting home for Van Evrie and his ideas. Its leadership, North and South, embraced him, and he fully exploited all the support he could gather. John A. Quit-man, Mississippi's fire-eating governor, congressman, and slaveocrat, distributed copies of his publications. He paid special attention to the Democratic South and secured similar endorsements from Jef-ferson Davis and the region's preeminent publisher, J.D.B. De Bow. In 1855 a Raleigh, North Carolina, paper endorsed one of his pam-phlets and urged its subscribers to read his work because it "upsets every abolition argument, and shows the whole foundation work" of the movement's "superstructures false and wicked." The next year the New Orleans *Daily Picayune* opined that Van Evrie would have gained wide acceptance in the North if not for the region's "bigoted and intolerant" opinions. To expand his appeal and confirm his own legitimacy, he obtained glowing endorsements for his publications from party leaders like New York's former U.S. senator Daniel S. Dickinson. He sent signed copies of his pamphlets and books to prominent political figures, even those unlikely to accept his ideas, like Ohio's Salmon P. Chase and Massachusetts's Charles Sumner, hoping that such political enemies would publicly attack him and thus generate free advertising.

The 1854 case of Capt. James Smith and his slave-trading brig *Julia Moulton* offered Van Evrie his first major opportunity to combat abolitionist fervor, disseminate his poisonous ethnological views, and gain him the publicity he so craved. Smith, a naturalized German citizen, had been arraigned before the U.S. Circuit Court in New York City for employing his Maine-built vessel in the illegal slave trade. The ship had been crammed with 664 Africans when captured, creating an incident that roiled Congress and caused an international incident as Smith claimed that the secretary of the Portuguese consul owned the vessel. Although convicted at trial and subject to the death penalty, upon appeal Smith pleaded to a lesser charge that carried a penalty of no more than two years imprisonment.

Van Evrie expressed his outrage over the trial, asserting that the illicit international slave trade, in fact, differed not in the least from the American interstate slave trade and was indeed legitimate commerce, "practiced by good Christians and pious men." Rather than facing the death penalty, Smith deserved national praise for "rescuing" Africans, who would be "immeasurably and inexpressibly happier and better off" than any "negroes" who "ever existed in Africa." Men like Smith brought workers to the United States, Van Evrie argued, who could do the work that "Caucasian laboring" populations could not because the "negro's . . . millions of sabacious [*sic*] glands" acted as "safety valves under a vertical sun." God, he declared, had created Blacks "for this labor." Rather than being a criminal, Van Evrie exclaimed, Captain Smith was a philanthropist.

White supremacy bound together the Democratic Party's various factions. Equal political rights "for *all white men* by virtue of their whiteness and manhood" was the party's central governing principle North and South—in law, politics, and foreign policy, at home and in the home. As the St. Paul, Minnesota, *Daily Pioneer* declared in 1857, Democrats campaigned proudly for "White Supremacy against Negro Equality." Stephen A. Douglas's famous 1858 campaign against Abraham Lincoln for a U.S. Senate seat rested on such uncompromising white supremacy. The nation's government, he assured Illinois voters, "is founded on the white basis. It was made by the white man, for the benefit of the white man, to be administered by white men. . . . I am in favor of preserving not only the purity of the blood, but the purity of the government from any mixture or amalgamation with inferior races. . . . I am opposed to taking any step that recognizes the negro man or the Indian as the equal of the white man." Douglas assured his constituents that his unwavering commitment to the "great principle of self-government" was far more important than "all the negroes in Christendom." Democrats found eager audiences for that message throughout the North. That same year Jefferson Davis toured New York and New England to praise the links between the slave-owning South and its allies in the North. Together, he asserted, they had built a republic on the "rock of white supremacy." To thank Davis for bringing his message of Democratic white unity to the North, Maine's Bowdoin College awarded the future president of the Confederacy an honorary degree. He then spoke at the birthplace of American liberty, Boston's Faneuil Hall, on October 11, introduced by a scion of the nation's Revolutionary tradition, Charles Francis Adams, Jr., whose only regret was that he did not spend more time with Davis.

By the time Van Evrie's career began to accelerate in the 1850s, Democrats had become the party of unswerving white supremacy. But as the historian Michael Woods so effectively reminds us, they never quite agreed on "how white men should govern." The party remained a volatile coalition, with many internal splits that would eventually shatter in 1860. None of the factions ever disagreed on white supremacy, only on how the African American should be suppressed and what role slavery would have in that process. They all accepted Van Evrie's notions of polygenesis. As the influential *Democratic Review* explained, "Few or none now seriously adhere to the theory of the unity of races." Science had proved that there "are several distinct races of men . . . with entirely different capacities, physical and mental."

Thus as we have seen, many Northern white supremacists eagerly supported the American Colonization Society (ACS), while Southern Democrats, because of their commitment to the "peculiar institution," expressed only tepid interest in the society's work. The ACS maintained that African Americans were too ignorant, too lazy, or too criminally inclined to live peaceably with whites. Removing them to Liberia would relieve the nation of an unwanted class and bring a people (however inferior) who had been exposed to Christianity and American values to the "dark continent." The "negro," as Rep. Frederick P. Stanton explained in 1852, can rise only in Africa, while in America he was doomed "to inevitable decline." Daniel Webster had proclaimed in 1852 that where the negro went didn't matter, only that he left: "He must come out." From Horace Mann to Horace Bushnell to Daniel Webster, Northern leaders of all political persuasions found in the ACS an answer to the "problem of the negro."

Van Evrie, however, saw no "negro problem." The colonizationist desire to expel African Americans, according to him, flew in the face of God's plans *and* the needs of American democracy. For Van Evrie and Democratic supporters of slavery, God had placed the African in the South for good reason, "as cooperating partners of the whites. . . . We are as essential to each other as boys on the opposite ends of . . . a seesaw." The nation required Blacks, and if by some "ill fate" they left, he insisted, white Americans would "instantly set to work, fit out ships and replace them by fresh accessions from Africa." Without "the negro," he asserted, the "centre of the Continent must remain a desert waste." In Africa, the negro was "useless, [a] non-producing savage." But his "wonderful capacity of imitation," Van Evrie explained, showed clearly that he had been designed by God to "exist in juxtaposition with the superior race, whom he serves and serves well." Freedom, as whites imagined it, was a mistake for the African and denied his natural God-given role in the world. He had, the New Yorker explained, a "natural right" to live out his existence in service to whites: *When they live the life that they are intended for, they are free; when they do not, they are slaves.*

As he explained in his *Six Species of Men,* God created the white race as the superior race—Genesis proved that. But God also created many lower orders of mankind. As his 1867 *White Supremacy* detailed, the Swedish botanist Carl Linnaeus (1707–78) mistakenly believed that God had created mankind as "an order, a genus and species by himself. This is false as a matter of fact, for in the entire world of animal existence there is no such fact as a single species. All the forms of life are made up of groups or families. . . . Each of these is composed of a certain number of species." African Americans are not "colored white men" but rather an altogether different species of human, just as there were different species of birds. The "Creator had so plainly marked" the inferiority of the African in at least six different ways, in color, figure, hair, features, languages, and brain. Blacks were inferior, he argued, just as the owl was inferior to the eagle, yet both were still birds. But such beings were inferiors designed by God to do the white man's work. The "negro" represented the lowest order of humanity, without a history, "no learning, no literature, no laws. For six thousand years he has been a *savage.*"

But the African was not a "slave." That term implied an unjust suppression or captivity of white humans. Van Evrie avoided the term because he maintained that the condition of African Americans in the South was their *natural* order. Granting them full white freedom would have been the real injustice. The term *slave,* he wrote, was a *"misnomer, a word borrowed from Europe, expressing a certain relation of white men to each other a thousand years ago, and senseless when applied to the South."* Accordingly, Americans should no more see the property of Southern white planters as slaves than oxen or horses. They did the work that God and nature intended for them.

But most important, he believed that African Americans should not be removed from the nation because they provided an unambiguous and essential contrast that displayed the naturalness of democracy for whites. Their presence rendered differences among whites insignificant. Far from wanting to remove Blacks from the United States, Van Evrie saw them as *indispensable,* "the happiest conjunction that ever occurred in human affairs." Their presence allowed for the construction of white equality, and no white equality could exist without them. As he would reiterate over the years of his career, without the African presence, the class distinctions and aristocracy of Europe would have continued in the United States. Without "negroes," he wrote in 1867, "without the presence of natural distinctions, without those lines of demarcation fixed forever by the hand of God," the country "would have remained the most aristocratic community. . . . Without the juxtaposition with a different race, without the active presence of the negro, without the constant daily perception of those natural distinctions that separate races . . . neither Jefferson nor anyone else could have risen to the level of the grand [white] truth embodied in the Declaration of Independence." Without Africans' presence, the Federalist-Whig-Republican cabal to strengthen the central government would have succeeded in enforcing the Northern aristocratic domination of the worker. Thus in Van Evrie the "ultra-democrat" merged with the ultimate white supremacist, a combination essential for his appeal in the North.

The rise of abolitionism had convinced Van Evrie that the North did not sufficiently understand the "real nature of the negro" and mistakenly offered pity for "imaginary sufferings of the slave." His fellow citizens thus required his help to better understand the African's true "physiology and psychological" facts. He presented himself as one who had spent years studying "the negro," and his research would strip off "the skin of the negro" and demonstrate that he is "not a black white man, or a man merely with a black skin, but a different and inferior species of man." He had read his Louis Agassiz and all the other American and European ethnologists and claimed that he could reveal the full truth to the public about the "diversity of origin" in the natural world and the "diversity of species" in the human world.

Van Evrie, like most other Americans, accepted the biblical account of Adam and Eve. If God had created all human species as one, he argued, then all would have had the same faculties. Since they did not, he asserted, and since God created all things, he clearly had created "the negro" differently, at a different time, and for a different purpose. Borrowing from Agassiz, Van Evrie emphasized that the African remained unchanged over thousands of years, thereby affirming an original divine purpose, one far different than that intended for whites. Left to themselves, they would be heathens, subsisting on snails and bugs, but as servants "within the precincts of civilized life," their "natural subordination to superior races" manifested as "assigned by the hand of nature." Under those conditions, "the negro" would achieve his true role and full "freedom." To those who believed that Africans could rise to the same level as whites, he declared that even if they were raised by royalty in Oxford, England, and "supplied with all the wealth of the Rothschilds," nothing would change. Africans would have the "same color, the same hair, the same formed limbs, the same animalized pelvis, the same small and receding brain—in a word, with the same physical inferiority, [they] will be the same mental [inferior] that the Creator has stamped upon the race."

· · ·

The Civil War posed an existential crisis for Van Evrie. From the war's outset, he considered it an inherent threat to American social relations, endangering every cherished belief and underlying principle of white supremacy, from his conception of the Founding Fathers' purpose in creating the United States to the divine order of nature.

But the war, especially emancipation and the era of Reconstruction that followed, also provided him with extraordinary opportunities, a national platform of unprecedented scale, and the prospect of obscenely reshaping the nation's understanding of human nature and race. As few others had ever attempted, Van Evrie took full advantage of the crisis to weld Democratic unity and attempt to reforge the nation's white supremacist foundation. He labored relentlessly during Reconstruction to guarantee that whites would enjoy all the advantages of the prewar world, without the formal existence of the "peculiar institution." White supremacy, Van Evrie asserted, would prove essential to maintaining the social structure, guaranteeing white democracy, and subordinating the African as designed by God and intended by nature.

January 1861 saw the publication of Van Evrie's *Negroes and Negro "Slavery."* As the nation moved inexorably toward war, his volume attempted to head off possible strife by tutoring Northerners about the "true nature" of African peoples. New York's *American Publishers' Circular and Literary Gazette* welcomed the effort, explaining that the North's "gigantic falsehoods concerning the negro character, and the social institutions of the South, must be exploded." Van Evrie's book, the journal declared, revealed the fiction of an "irrepressible conflict" between the North and the South. The social systems of the two sections were, the journal quoted Van Evrie, "entirely harmonious in theory, and would be so in practice, if the truth were only revealed concerning the negro." Another newspaper in Iowa similarly endorsed the book and longed for the day that Northerners would travel to the South and see reality for themselves. Then, the paper asserted, their delusions about slavery "would be exploded in sixty days." With war on the horizon, the paper urged Americans to read Van Evrie's book before it was too late.

The New Yorker joined with prominent city Democrats to oppose the war and even reprinted Benjamin Wood's May 16, 1862, congressional speech pleading for an end to the fighting and for an immediate start of negotiations with the South to restore the Union. Wood and his brother, New York mayor Fernando Wood, proved adamant opponents of the fighting and joined with Van Evrie in blaming the relentless antislavery agitation for stirring "the embers of the strife." Van Evrie followed up by accusing Republicans and President Lincoln of nothing less than conspiring to restore the hated old Federalist Party and its antidemocratic aristocratic goals, a view widely shared by fellow Democrats.

At first, his efforts backfired. The English, so frequent a target of his ideological assaults, struck back with ferocity. The *Saturday Review of Politics, Literature, Science and Art,* which over its long history would publish the writings of Oscar Wilde, Walter Bagehot, H. G. Wells, and George Bernard Shaw, condemned Van Evrie as possessing a "malignant ferocity of temper and an indecent vehemence of language" aimed at "the unhappy race whom he longs to rob even of their humanity." The journal concluded that if the audience for whom he wrote possessed a spirit anything like his own, "the prospects of his country would seem to be gloomy indeed." Although Van Evrie did not support secession and longed for a restoration of the prewar world, his views earned him the reputation of a dangerous Copperhead and threats that he and his colleagues at his publishing firm would be arrested for treason. Just a few days after the attack on Fort Sumter, about three thousand men and boys assembled in front of the *Day-Book*'s office and demanded that Van Evrie, Horton & Co. display the American flag. The mob had roamed city streets visiting the offices of newspapers and hotels known to have Southern sympathies and demanded that they all fly the flag. Van Evrie emerged from his building and promised to fulfill the protesters' request, but after their departure, he instead displayed a Tammany Hall banner. The diarist, lawyer, and founder of the city's Union League Club, George Templeton Strong, thought the protest would temper Van Evrie's "treasonable talk" and compel the *Day-Book* to be "more cautious in its utterances." He could not have been more wrong.

When the Lincoln administration temporarily shut down the *Day-Book* for its treasonous rhetoric in the fall of 1861, Van Evrie immediately rechristened it the *Weekly Caucasian* and renewed the fight. Joining Benjamin Wood and other Democrats, he saw reconciliation as still possible if the Southern labor system was re-established as the governing national principle. That effort was "vital to the South, to the North, to the future civilization of America—to the freedom, progress and prosperity of every white man on the American continent." The nation must, he demanded, restore "a government of white men, made by white men for themselves and their posterity forever." He remained adamant in avoiding the term *slavery* and instead proclaimed that the white supremacy of Washington and Jefferson could heal all wounds. Secession, which he considered a dangerous and murderous folly, reflected the South's attempt to "preserve the status quo—to prevent the destruction of the existing order, and the supremacy of the white man over the negro—in short, to preserve the principles on which this government was founded in 1788."

Rather than blaming the South for causing the war, Van Evrie sought to refocus Northern attention on abolitionists. Stamping out them and their Republican Party tools would restore the Constitution and peace. Reinstate white supremacy, he declared, and the "South will themselves 'restore the Union.'" He accused the Republicans, on the other hand, of seeking to destroy white supremacy and use national banks and tariffs to enslave the "working classes of the North." Slavery embodied a "divine mission" in America, he asserted, and the abolitionists were guilty of "impiety to God" for their attacks on it. Lincoln was but their tool and reflective of a Northern mind immersed in "British writers, British books, British policy, and British teachings" that had so perverted the North's understanding. Together with British connivance, the president and his party, Van Evrie exclaimed, were conducting a war on the very idea of democracy. Lincoln embodied a "monstrous undertaking—to abolish the supremacy of the white men [and] the subordination of the negro, and give them the same freedom."

When the Lincoln administration first threatened emancipation late in 1862, Van Evrie erupted in rage and horror. "Lincoln issued his Miscegenation Proclamation," Van Evrie proclaimed, because Britain had "forced him to . . . under the threat to recognize the Confederate States." It resulted from at least thirty years of effort by British agents "and their tools among us" to spread antislavery fictions. Van Evrie's colleague at his publishing house, Chauncey Burr—who edited *The Old Guard,* which Van Evrie dominated and then took over in December 1869—proved as incendiary as his partner. In 1863 Burr accused Lincoln, Vice President Hannibal Hamlin, and Senator Charles Sumner of being mulattoes. The Detroit *Free Press,* an enormous fan of Van Evrie, then advised the president to move to Haiti or Liberia. What could Americans expect from Lincoln's intention to end slavery? Van Evrie asked. Look to Haiti, he answered with stern authority. The principles of Charles Sumner would only get American white women "violated . . . on the dead bodies of their husbands," he screamed. "To overthrow the present relation of the races is to injure both the white man and the negro, and to inflict a deadly blow upon the course of humanity, civilization, and Christianity." History had shown, Van Evrie raged, that Black freedom led only to "crime, pauperism, and vice" in the North, the destruction of commerce in the West Indies, and economic decline among the "white laboring and producing classes." He presented himself not only as the defender of white supremacy but as the savior of African Americans, asserting that he sought to rescue them from a freedom that would prove fatal. By strengthening white supremacy, however, all would flourish.

In addition to agitating the racial waters, Van Evrie's remarks produced real, if regrettable, results. It fortified Democratic power not only in New York but also in Ohio. The Columbus *Crisis* reproduced a portion of his 1862 book and pamphlet *Free Negroism,* which emphasized the threat to white labor posed by emancipation. It helped Democrats push the Ohio legislature to amend the state constitution to ban the resettlement of African Americans anywhere within its boundaries. Shelby County even petitioned the legislature for a special exclusion law proclaiming that white citizens could never live in proximity to such a "degraded race." Newspapers from Connecticut to Wisconsin reprinted portions of Van Evrie's publications as proof of the threat posed by free Blacks. Bridgeport, Connecticut's *Republican Farmer* warned that "Abolitionists and miscegenations" were committing the country to emancipation. Inflamed by Van Evrie's warnings, the Wisconsin *Daily Patriot* denounced the government for turning a "fierce and bloody war solely" into an effort "to emancipate this degraded race from slavery."

Equally important, Van Evrie's views energized powerful enemies of emancipation. During the Civil War, the influential New York inventor and artist Samuel F. B. Morse had become president of New York's Society for the Diffusion of Political Knowledge (SDPK), an organization formed in 1863 and dedicated to opposing the Lincoln administration and Black freedom. Morse, who agreed with Van Evrie's view that Great Britain lay behind the antislavery movement, had joined with twenty-four powerful New York businessmen, including Gov. Horatio Seymour and the corporate lawyer Samuel Tilden, to create the SDPK. Morse agreed entirely with Confederate vice president Alexander Stephens's declaration that slavery had been the cornerstone of Southern society. That statement, Morse explained, reflected the "physical, philosophical and moral truth, that *the two races are not equal.*" Like Van Evrie, he damned abolitionism as a violation of God's laws, declaring in 1863 that the Bible fortified the relationship of "master and slave, clearly ordained by God." Morse and his fellow society members could not imagine a "South without negro slaves." Indeed, Morse had become so dedicated to Van Evrie's ideas of white supremacy that he freely incorporated them into his speeches, including pages of his 1862 pamphlet *Free Negroism,* claiming them as his own.

At the close of 1863, the publishing firm Dexter, Hamilton & Co. brought out a scandalous hoax, a seventy-two-page pamphlet entitled *What Miscegenation Is!,* amusingly authored by a "L. Seaman." The crude pamphlet, pretending to endorse interracial marriage, was the work of two Democratic journalists of the New York *World,* David Goodman Crosby and George Wakeman. It masqueraded as the opinion of an abolitionist who supported "race mixing," a charge relentlessly thrown at antislavery supporters. The audacious effort, meant to have an impact in the 1864 elections, intended to flush out Republicans who, presumably, would endorse the pamphlet, thereby exposing them to relentless Democratic attacks. Many across the North fell for the trick, assuming it was genuine. It sent Ohio congressman Samuel Sullivan "Sunset" Cox into apoplexy, charging

WHAT MISCEGENATION IS!

—AND—

WHAT WE ARE TO EXPECT

Now that Mr. Lincoln is Re-elected.

By L. SEAMAN, LL. D.

WALLER & WILLETTS, Publishers,
NEW YORK.

This pamphlet sought to instill fear that the white man would soon be replaced by the Black man. "Sambo's good time is come—that his millennium is at hand—that his star is in the ascendent. White men, just stand back and let the conquering heroes pass." *What Miscegenation Is!* (1863), p. 5.

that Republicans and abolitionists were nothing but "two links of the same sausage made of the same dog." Clearly, Cox warned, the Republicans were moving relentlessly toward racial equality, lusting for "miscegenation!" The Philadelphia *Age* and the New York *Daily News* considered the pamphlet real and exclaimed that it reflected the deep desires of "Wendell Phillips & Co." Of course, it read like nothing an abolitionist ever wrote, and it is entirely possible that Van Evrie also fell for the hoax, although he probably knew the publishers as they both operated on the same New York street.

Whether duped or not, Van Evrie took advantage of the notoriety generated by the "Seaman" pamphlet and emerged with his own inflammatory eruption that went far beyond anything imagined by the *World*'s reporters. His 1864 book, *Subgenation: The Theory of the Normal Relation of the Races; An Answer to "Miscegenation,"* bore as its title a word that combined *sub* with *genus* to express his unrelenting opinion of Black inferiority. It became another platform for him to discourse on the "natural or normal relation of an inferior to a superior race." The idea of race mixing so disgusted him that he declared that whites should "cut the throats of their children at once" rather than let them live in a world of "degradation and amalgamation." The book repeated the theories he had been disseminating since the mid-1850s, beginning with his principal position that *"there is no slavery in this country; There are no slaves in the Southern States."* "We are," he cried, "fighting about a myth."

He repeated his view that humans, like other creatures, are

composed of different species. In the case of humans, he identified six species, or races of men, in descending order: Caucasian,
Mongolian, Malay (or Oceanic), Indian, Esquimaux, and Negro.
The Caucasian, according to Van Evrie's definition, included Assyr-
ians, Persians, Egyptians, Russians, and Jews. He believed that all
these groups possessed the same characteristics that defined the
"master race wherever found." His willingness to include Jews might
be surprising, but their prevalence in the Old Testament and their
highly literate culture probably influenced Van Evrie's decision. He
may also have been moved by the racist ravings of the New York
businessman, diplomat, and publisher Manuel Mordecai Noah
(1785–1851), one of the most prominent Jewish Americans of the
early nineteenth century. Born in Philadelphia, he grew up in South
Carolina and moved to New York after 1815. There he published

"Negro." From John H. Van Evrie, *White Supremacy and Negro
Subordination; or, Negroes A Subordinate Race, and (so called)
Slavery Its Normal Condition* (1867), p. 308.

the influential *National Advocate,* an organ of the Tammany Hall Democratic political machine. A great promoter of Jewish rights in New York, he appeared to establish his "white" credentials by relentlessly attacking African Americans. He made a career out of demeaning the city's Blacks as the lowest form of life and insisting on their removal from the country, seeing them as a threat to white democracy.

As he wrote elsewhere, Van Evrie insisted that Americans did not understand the "negro," much less scientific theories of ethnology, and it was his mission to educate them. Color, he warned, was the least important of the differences between the Caucasian and the African. "In figure, hair, features, language, senses, brain, mental faculties, moral powers, down even to the very elementary particles of his blood, he is as distinct from the white man as the horse from the ass, or the camel from the dromedary. In color he is black. His figure is stooping and his gait shuffling." In other publications, Van Evrie went a step further and decried the African's inability to grow a beard. "Equal beards," he wrote, would have been an "outward symbol of equal manhood." Because the African could only manage a "little tuft on the chin," he could not possibly be the equal of the Caucasian. Any Black who could grow a full beard clearly must have a "large infusion of white blood." He persisted in these ridiculous assertions although even a cursory glance at his own image revealed that, as opposed to the flowing beards that appeared in his books to show white superiority, he could only manage a few chin whiskers.

In a dangerous move, Van Evrie elevated ethnologists like Louis Agassiz over the nation's religious and biblical authorities. He often employed this tactic to incite reactions and increase publicity about his views, although it likely lost him more readers than he gained. The Boston *Congregationalist,* for instance, objected to his ideas concerning separate species and human origins as a "fruitless effort." Evangelicals, devoted to missionary work among African people, also opposed him. The Yale graduate and Congregational minister Leonard Bacon, for instance, explained that all "men are alike in their capacity for religion." But Van Evrie fought back, explaining that only the Caucasian had such ability, while "the savages of

Africa have no such religious instinct." The idea that all of humanity originated from "a single pair, Adam and Eve," he had asserted, quoting Agassiz, "is neither a Biblical view nor a correct view, nor one agreeing with the results of science." Theologians "who would strive to use the Bible to prop up their narrow and bigoted assumptions as to the proper relation of the different races of men, will be regarded in the future as belonging to the same class as those who assailed geography, astronomy and geology with their ecclesiastical anathemas." The misreading of scripture and the "falsification of science," he maintained, resembled the misguided effort by the church to stifle Galileo. One could be a devout Christian, he insisted, and still not accept the idea that the earth had been created in six days. What science proved, he wrote, was the "absolute natural equality of those whom God had created equal." This supported true democratic society, in which equal men were entitled to equal "rights, like laws," and "like duties." This embodied the democracy that God intended, "born in a society founded on subgenation" and "made the corner-stone of a new government."

. . .

Congressional Reconstruction generally aimed to incorporate freed people and Northern Blacks into American society with equal constitutional protections and responsibilities. As Eric Foner, the country's leading authority on Reconstruction, has written, in the South it was "a massive experiment in interracial democracy without precedent in the history of this or any other country that abolished slavery in the nineteenth century." The era represented a colossal effort to transform and refound the nation and its governing principles: in short, to eliminate the world as Van Evrie understood it. Northern victory in the war, and subsequent attempts by Republicans to reform and reunite the nation, produced all the furor and rage that Van Evrie could muster. What he and his colleagues had labeled "Lincoln's reign of terror" was the fruit of antislavery lies adopted by the Republican Party to seize control of the federal government, "drive the South to resistance," and under the banner of "preserving the Union" implement the abolitionist agenda of

"Negro equality." From the very beginning, Van Evrie declared, this had been the party's "revolutionary and treasonable design," which it sought to complete in the postwar era. While the South's defeat proved painful for the New Yorker, it also became an opportunity like no other he had ever experienced. The unprecedented and sophisticated campaign of resistance he mounted would carry his name and his inflammatory words to every part of the nation, fortify Democratic resistance to racial equality, and give a new birth, not to freedom, but to white supremacy.

The momentous, unprecedented, and sometimes contradictory Republican effort to transform the nation should not blind us to the widespread resistance to those plans in the North, aimed at preserving white supremacy. "Slavery is dead," the Cincinnati *Enquirer* moaned, but "the negro is not. There is the misfortune. For the sake of all parties, would that he were." Congressman "Sunset" Cox, a favorite of Van Evrie's, proclaimed at the war's end that in "the school house, the church, or the hospital, the black man must not seat himself beside the white; even in death and at the cemetery the line of distinction is drawn." This, the New York *Daily News* proclaimed, represented the essential defense of the "social rights of the white race." Without laws to enforce such "respect," the long-serving New York congressman James Brooks warned, there would be "mongrel schools and school houses . . . mongrel [street] cars . . . mongrel taverns . . . [and] complete mongrel social existence from the cradle to the grave." The New York *World,* a leading Democratic newspaper, denounced Mississippi's Black senator Hiram R. Revels as "a lineal descendant of an orangutan." Even those who were sympathetic to abolitionism and supported Black enfranchisement, like the future president James A. Garfield, possessed "a strong feeling of repugnance when I think of the negro being made our political equal and I would be glad if they could be colonized, sent to heaven, or got rid of in any decent way." Even some Garrisonian abolitionists like Lydia Maria Child exalted white New England culture and believed that only through intermarriage could African Americans gain equality and "whiteness." For one of the abolitionist move-

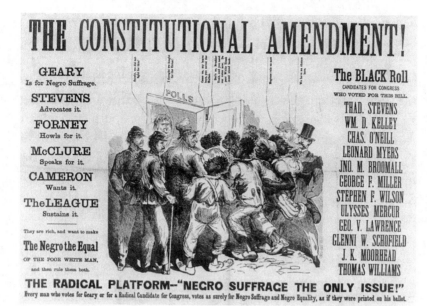

THE CONSTITUTIONAL AMENDMENT!

GEARY
Is for Negro Suffrage.

STEVENS
Advocates it.

FORNEY
Howls for it.

McCLURE
Speaks for it.

CAMERON
Wants it.

The LEAGUE
Sustains it.

They are rich, and want to make

The Negro the Equal
OF THE POOR WHITE MAN,
and then rule them both.

The BLACK Roll
CANDIDATES FOR CONGRESS
WHO VOTED FOR THIS BILL.

THAD. STEVENS
WM. D. KELLEY
CHAS. O'NEILL
LEONARD MYERS
JNO. M. BROOMALL
GEORGE F. MILLER
STEPHEN F. WILSON
ULYSSES MERCUR
GEO. V. LAWRENCE
GLENNI W. SCHOFIELD
J. K. MOORHEAD
THOMAS WILLIAMS

THE RADICAL PLATFORM—"NEGRO SUFFRAGE THE ONLY ISSUE!"
Every man who votes for Geary or for a Radical Candidate for Congress, votes as surely for Negro Suffrage and Negro Equality, as if they were printed on his ballot.

A poster attacking postwar Republican efforts to enact a constitutional amendment for Black suffrage. A group of African Americans are shown crowding ahead of white war veterans and other whites toward a door marked "Polls." One veteran complains, "Surely, we did not fight for this." Another declares, "I thought we fought for the Union." A disheveled bearded man encourages the Blacks, saying, "Come on, my brave boys, you saved the Nation." One responds, "Dat's so Brudder Yank, and you need our votes now. De poor White Trash must stand back." At right, two white men complain, "Negroes rule us now" and "We have no chance here." "The Constitutional Amendment!," 1866.

ment's most influential reformers, intermarriage was the best tool to extinguish "blackness."

No solid foundation for a transformation of the nation's ideas of race during Reconstruction ever existed. At the close of the Civil War, eighteen of twenty-five Union states denied African Americans the right to vote, and even in 1870 with passage of the Fifteenth Amendment to the Constitution, thirteen of twenty-six Northern states still denied African Americans the suffrage. During the postwar era, as at the time of independence, the more freedom Blacks attained, the more whites insisted on control and domination. The women's equal rights movement, as embodied by Elizabeth Cady Stanton, denounced "Black" Republicans as a party of "negro worshipers." She allied with Democrats to attack Reconstruction and Black enfranchisement. Such equality, she warned—foreshadowing the later approach of the Ku Klux Klan—would subject white women to the loathsome control of "Chinese, Indians, and Africans." Lynching and murder became common occurrences in the South, and at best African Americans enjoyed only dangerously ambivalent support in the North. So it is no surprise that some African Americans gave up all hope of peaceful coexistence and applied to the Colonization Society for help. "We see no prospect of success here. The white people have too much the advantage of us," as Mississippi African Americans lamented in January 1868. "They have all the land, all the money, and all the education." Their former owners made them work and refused to pay wages. Whites systematically denied them teachers for their children, and those who did manage to offer instruction to African Americans in the cities were "scorned and hated."

To Van Evrie, these examples of white supremacy, especially in the North, represented a natural and powerful instinct among whites. In one of his more popular works, the 1867 *White Supremacy and Negro Subordination,* he described such measures as an essential defense mechanism intended to preserve the white race: they sprang "from a fundamental organic necessity, impelling us to preserve our structural integrity." Without that instinct, the white race, the highest of the human species, would disappear. While uncontestably "superior," the white race still appeared to Van Evrie as fragile and under constant assault, especially in America. In ancient times, he argued, "nearly five hundred millions of whites [had lived] in Africa." But they had been swallowed up by interbreeding, or what he called "mongrelism," and disappeared. Very likely, he obtained this notion from the Pennsylvania-born author and diplomat Bayard Taylor, who in 1854 asserted that Ethiopians were a darker version of Egyptians and "an offshoot of the great Caucasian race." Van Evrie became obsessed with the "threat" of interbreeding and throughout his writings issued warnings concerning the deadly fate awaiting those who intermingled with lower species. It would be the surest way for the white race to "most rapidly lose its vitality and perish or disappear as a nationality." The master race, he warned, must maintain its purity or fall into the trap of European monarchies and become sterile like a mule. Beginning in the eighteenth century, he argued, European monarchies—this time Britain *and* France—joined forces to aid American "savages" in order to prevent independence and resist "the onward march of American civilization." The fate of the nation and the white race, he warned, stood at the precipice, and if the nation fell into the mongrel pit, it would "utterly perish from the earth."

At the onset of 1868, Van Evrie still perceived the Democratic Party as the only effective bulwark against Republican attempts to mongrelize the country and to "raise our poor, tax-ridden and disorganized country up out of this horrid slough of negro-stinking equality and despotism." He warned, however, that the same "conspirators" who had controlled President Lincoln and led the nation into a pointless war, now, in 1868, sought to reinforce their success in destroying half of the nation by installing a "military hero" in the White House. They had eagerly suppressed the Democratic "party of the people" to increase taxation and adopt legislation that was "always for the benefit of the rich, and against the interests of the poor." In an overconfident mood, however, he then turned his venom against the Democratic Party's "president-makers." They had betrayed the people in 1860, he howled, by supporting his former ally Stephen A. Douglas when they should have nominated New York's Horatio Seymour, who, he claimed, would have kept the Democratic Party united, defeated Lincoln, and avoided the cataclysmic Civil War. He even claimed that Dean Richmond, chairman of the New York State Democratic Committee—and a wealthy railroad magnate—had confessed to him that the party had made a terrible mistake in 1860 and helped bring on the war. As Richmond had died in 1866, no one could verify Van Evrie's tale. Nonetheless, the Democrats did nominate Seymour as their candidate in 1868, heading a white supremacist ticket that promised to undo Reconstruction.

While he continued to rail against the Republicans as the

A campaign badge supporting Horatio Seymour and Francis P. Blair, Jr., Democratic candidates for president and vice president of the United States, 1868.

"*mulatto* party," Van Evrie also broke with his former Democratic allies, denouncing the party as "a miserable machine to get spoils." The party, as it always had been, was a coalition of forces with conflicting interests. Van Evrie decided, wisely or not, to strike out on his own. He increased his control over Chauncey Burr's journal the *Old Guard* and used it to lash out at both parties, pledging to defend the Democratic masses himself and call out "all such mongrelized dolts as political asses." Without reliable political partners, he would lead the effort to restore the white republic. "We do not mean to reconstruct" the nation, he exclaimed, but to "restore the Union." "Reconstruction," to Van Evrie, meant the "Africanization" of American society. He would have none of it.

While Van Evrie's break with the Democratic Party might have been a failure of judgment, his commitment to white supremacy clearly had outdistanced his former political allies who inevitably became entangled with conflicting interests. For Van Evrie, the ideology of white supremacy trumped political loyalty, and as he always sought influence, not political office, declaring his independence simplified and focused his mission. It also won him admirers across the country, bringing him the publicity he craved and needed to continue his work. Both his newspapers and his books and pamphlets, as he intended, gained him national attention and support. The Trenton, New Jersey, *Daily True American* and the Detroit *Free Press* lavished praise on his 1867 *White Supremacy* text—the New Jersey paper extolled it as the result of years of "patient study and investigation," especially vital at this historical juncture to counter the "mistaken philanthropy" of Northern politics. The Ohio *Demo-*

cratic Enquirer recommended his writings, especially his *Six Species of Men* (1866) to "every voter in the United States." The Maryland *Union* valued his effort to give voice to former Confederates like E. A. Pollard, author of *The Lost Cause* (1866), who also published essays in Van Evrie's monthly journal the *Old Guard.* The *Union* also delighted in his attacks on U. S. Grant, the "military hero" whom he had warned that Republican conspirators were going to place in the White House: a man, the paper remarked, who was "overrated."

A month after President Grant took office in March 1869, Van Evrie went on the attack. Less a warning to Grant than a call to arms, Van Evrie's *Old Guard* letter to the president warned that if reformers and Radical Republicans had their way, the country would quickly sink into "the abyss." Amalgamation and equal rights threatened the republic now more than ever. In his letter to Grant, he reprinted a portion of one he had earlier sent to President Andrew Johnson praising the former president for his keen understanding of the Constitution, which had made him the "foremost man of all this world." Grant should, Van Evrie advised, follow Johnson, allow the Southern states to "govern themselves," and leave the subordinate race to "their care and guidance." Do not "quail before the Abolition madman," he cautioned Grant. Restore the Constitution as it was and the Union as it was, and all would be saved. The war had been an evil revolution, he warned, one designed to destroy a "homogeneous" country and place it under a "mongrel government." Grant and the "flower of American youth" had been used and deceived by Lincoln, who had aimed to destroy the republic. "Never before in the annals of mankind has there been a fraud so shameless, a wrong so gross, or a crime so atrocious committed by any government or ruler" than that carried out by Lincoln and his conspirators to overthrow the government and "strike down the principles on which . . . *the founders of American liberty established self-governing States on a white basis.*" But now, he exclaimed, the *"army has overthrown this grand American system and on its ruins set up a nation based on a Mongrel citizenship."*

After 1868, freed of any need to defer to the Democratic Party, Van Evrie directed his resourcefulness and enormous energy toward directly influencing public opinion. For instance, he worked through Edward A. Pollard, who had achieved fame in 1858 with his first book, *Black Diamonds Gathered in the Darky Homes of the South*. After the war, Pollard became one of the chief inventors of Lost Cause mythology, with his history of the Old South and the war, *The Lost Cause: A New Southern History of the War of the Confederates*, with which he gained an enduring legacy. To Pollard, slavery had been the ideal social and cultural institution that bound master and slave into a system of "mutual attachment," a kind of extended family. But Pollard did not sink into despair over its loss; instead, after reading Van Evrie, he came to realize that white supremacy mattered more than "slavery" and represented a social order that could exist quite well within the postwar Union. Indeed, following Van Evrie's lead, he began putting the word *slavery* in quotation marks. Absorbing the New Yorker's writings, he scorned the idea that African Americans were white men with black skin. What mattered now was not restoring "slavery" but gaining control and opposing "the entire series of measures to endow the negro" with power, what he saw as the Africanization of the South. Such a result would give the white South the choices of "mongrelism or utter ruin." "Slavery," he said, just as Van Evrie had argued, never existed and had no structure to sustain it. Black-white relations in the Old South, Pollard asserted, had existed not by law but "in powerful harmony with the laws of nature." Pollard did not merely adopt Van Evrie's ideas but praised him directly as "a gentleman who has written on Southern subjects with great power and felicity." At present, Pollard explained in 1868, the South was fighting a war it could not lose. She "finds herself this time in distinct and firm alliance with a party in the North, in sympathy with the educated reason of the world, and with all human instincts in her favour, defending the doctrine of the superiority of races, and maintaining the broad and noble interests of the white man's government in America." For Pollard, because of Van Evrie, the Old South's Lost Cause might "be but the introduction to a larger contest."

Van Evrie took his fight for the "larger contest" directly to the nation. In addition to influencing important writers like Pollard, he injected the ideology of white supremacy into high culture through poems and at least two novels, one by Virginia's most successful fiction writer of the nineteenth century, John Esten Cooke. A Confederate veteran who had served on the staff of General J.E.B. Stuart, Cooke hated war but understood the North's obsession with romanticized Civil War stories. Writing in the tradition of Sir Walter Scott and James Fenimore Cooper, he published about thirty-five works of fiction, history, and recollection. His 1870 romance of the Old South, *The Heir of Gaymount,* became one of his most successful novels of the postwar period—a book published by John H. Van Evrie. It extended Van Evrie's war on Reconstruction by other means. Cooke intended to show that Black freedmen, who now labored under the government's rules rather than nature and God's will, were "far less efficient than they were before, under the most indulgent masters." Van Evrie clearly saw the advantage of allying with Cooke and bringing his fiction to a large Northern audience, which would simultaneously increase the visibility of his press and fortify white supremacy.

Even more important, Van Evrie emerged as a marketing genius who understood his audience and knew exactly how to reach them. He made sure that reviews, commentary, and announcements of his publications appeared in newspapers across the nation, from Boston to New Orleans, and from New York to Michigan, Kansas, and on to California. Just in the year 1871, he ran advertisements in more than *fifteen hundred different American newspapers,* and a word search in the Library of Congress's newspaper database revealed many thousands more for the era. Every time he published a new book or recycled an old one with a new title to meet each new abhorrent change—such as the Emancipation Proclamation, the end of the Civil War, civil rights legislation, or an unfavorable election—he sent out advertisements to countless newspapers such as the *Saturday Evening Post* and the Boston *Evening Transcript.* After the Supreme Court's 1857 *Dred Scott* decision, for instance, he threw together a pamphlet that offered the "historical, legal, and physical aspects of the 'Slavery' Question in a concise compass" and offered it cheaply (25 cents) with large discounts for bulk orders. Never missing an opportunity, he used the advertisement to push for subscriptions to the *Day-Book* and the *Old Guard*. He then ran advertisements for everything his firm published in *Harper's Weekly*, one of the North's most popular journals.

Like Walt Whitman, he also attracted publicity by reviewing his own works. In the Kansas *Weekly Herald*, for instance, he offered praise for his own opinions and his weekly newspaper. The *Day-Book*, according to the review, advanced his assertions that whatever color a person of African descent might be, the negro would always possess "the same other marks of distinction and inferiority." The Kansas paper "praised" his efforts, which he performed "in a most masterly manner." In Boston, New York, Philadelphia, Baltimore, and Buffalo, and in New Jersey, Connecticut, Michigan, and Wisconsin, countless newspapers carried lists and glowing endorsements of his firm's publications. He even advertised in religious journals like the *American Quarterly Church Review*, ensuring that his work reached influential pastors who might reconsider their views on his unorthodox positions.

As his advertising made clear, Van Evrie also targeted the South, where he knew he would have wide influence. To readers in Virginia and Georgia, he described his *Day-Book* as a weekly devoted to "white supremacy, State Sovereignty, and federal Union." In rural Mississippi, he advised readers that his monthly paper, the *Old Guard*, was the "*only*" Democratic magazine in the country. He pushed his updated edition of *Negroes and Negro "Slavery"* to readers in New Orleans and Washington, D.C., and he even targeted his *Day-Book* to readers in tiny Winnsboro, South Carolina, ensuring that no one escaped the Van Evrie name.

In a stunning revelation that sounded more like the 1960s than the 1860s, Van Evrie's publishing house ran promotional campaigns that possessed all the advertising feel of the Fuller Brush Company. Van Evrie, Horton & Co. placed an offer in local newspapers, even in Milledgeville, Georgia, declaring that anyone who formed a club of fifty or more *Day-Book* or *Old Guard* subscribers and collected ninety dollars in subscription fees would receive "by express, carefully boxed, a $55 Grover & Baker Sewing Machine." To encourage those who remained uncertain, the company would supply free sample copies of the paper. By appealing in such a manner, the company affirmed its support for, and identification with, working- and middle-class white *families*. Moreover, Van Evrie wisely chose to entice readers with one of the best sewing machines of the era, one that had received endorsements from across the social and political spectrum, from the wife of the abolitionist editor Joshua Leavitt to J. H. Hammond, a U.S. senator from South Carolina. Even the New York *Evangelist* declared that the company's sewing machines would bring on the "needle woman's millennium" and was destined to become a "household god."

Beyond his newspapers, Van Evrie's books received equally lav- ish praise across the North, and not just from prewar defenders of slavery. His work became central to how many white Americans would understand the political, social, and moral issues at stake. Just before the start of the Civil War, for instance, the Hartford, Connecticut, *Courant* directed the public's attention to *Negroes and Negro "Slavery,"* which it celebrated for its "considerable ingenuity and much learning." At the same time, the *Metropolitan Record and New York Vindicator* exclaimed that his book was based "on the undeniable fact of the mental and physical inferiority of the negro race, as proved by physiological and anatomical facts; by the lack of mentality, their lower animal structure and mental organism, their inability to make any progress unaided, and their inaptitude for even the higher mechanical pursuits. . . . The Creator intended the negro to remain in a state of tutelage or dependence on the superior race." White supremacy would trump any disagreement over the future of slavery. During the Civil War, Van Evrie increased his campaign, placing advertisements in nearly every Democratic-leaning paper in the country, denouncing the drive for emancipation.

Such views only intensified after the Civil War, as military combat turned into Reconstruction's political and civil strife. As early as 1866, one Pennsylvania paper and another in Iowa offered gushing praise for Van Evrie's publications, especially the *Old Guard* because it published a "superb steel portrait" of Robert E. Lee, "the only genuine likeness on sale in the North." Pennsylvania and Ohio Democratic-leaning papers overflowed with similar endorsements. In 1868 the Detroit *Free Press* declared that Van Evrie's *White Supremacy and Negro Subordination* (1867) displayed the "fundamental necessities of the American system." We must return to them, the paper warned, "or collapse in the anarchy, disintegration" of "Mexico and all other mongrelized communities." In 1868 the Trenton, New Jersey, *Daily True American* described the same text as the result of years of "patient study and investigation." It was essential, the paper argued. As Reconstruction advanced "mistaken philanthropy" by misguided "political teachers," Americans must recognize that Blacks were not whites with dark skin and fully appreciate "the difference in the capacity of the races."

.   .   .

Through pamphlets, newspapers, books, and marketing, Van Evrie, Horton & Co. took its white supremacist principles into every acre of the political landscape, seeking to influence the partisan struggles roiling the nation—ones that would define the future. And it was that future that Van Evrie and his partner Rushmore G. Horton sought to shape. Little is known about Horton, but the 1856 campaign biography he wrote of James Buchanan is revealing. He saw the future president as someone who "went to the utmost limit of constitutional power in protecting the Southern States" and controlling African Americans. "All regarded the doctrine of equality with negroes with something like indefinable horror," he wrote, and considered anything approaching social and legal equality as outrageous and degrading.

The guns at Appomattox had hardly quieted when the two published their school textbook, *A Youth's History of the Great Civil War in the United States, from 1861 to 1865* (1866). The press not only reprinted the book in 1867—perhaps to honor Horton after his death that year—but, ever mindful of New York City politics, even brought out a translation for the city's German population. While Horton received authorship credit, the book embodied the vile words and white supremacist principles that Van Evrie had been spewing since the 1850s, especially his invented antislavery conspiratorial drama that he argued lay behind the war. By recasting the narrative of the sectional crisis, Van Evrie and Horton aimed to reshape the war's legacy and define American race relations.

"This book has been written in the cause of Truth," the text began. But in fact, *A Youth's History* emerged as part of a long line of political tracts over the course of American history to the present day that feast on a paranoid style merged with conspiratorial fear. Their book made clear that the history of the United States had always been a conflict between those who "did not believe in the people" and wanted a strong central government to control them, and those who would have "the people" control the government. Symbolized by the battling figures of Alexander Hamilton and Thomas Jefferson, the country had been riven by Tory antidemocratic forces that warred against "the democratic principle." Tories then became Whigs and Republicans who employed the British-born "popular delusion about negroes" to gain political power. For Horton and Van Evrie, Abraham Lincoln was the modern incarnation of Toryism, embodying John Quincy Adams and the Alien and Sedition Law. With the likes of William Lloyd Garrison, Wendell Phillips, and John Brown, he conspired to carry out the "British free negro policy . . . a pet measure of all kings and despots of Europe." To do so, they argued, Lincoln assumed dictatorial powers in order to realize the abolitionist delusion.

In their version of history, the North had been the aggressor. The Northern states, under the Federalist-Whig-Republican thumb, remained committed to British-style monarchy, and even before Washington was placed in his grave, the conspiracy sought to destroy the Union because the South had become so "thoroughly democratic!" Since its founding, the nation had endured a struggle between those desiring a strong, centralized monarchical government and the South's democracy. With the coming of the Civil War, the old Federalist Party's opposition to democracy had "ripened, at last, into the late terrible strife." The "old monarchist party of New England" had used the issue of the "negro" to attack

ABOLITION OFFICERS DRIVING NEGROES FROM THE PLANTATIONS.   Page 291,

"Abolition Officers Driving Negroes from the Plantations." Rushmore G. Horton's *A Youth's History of the Great Civil War in the United States, from 1861 to 1865* (1866) claimed that "Negroes" had been happy on their plantations and that Union soldiers had forced them into "freedom."

Southern democracy. With the cooperation of British agents in Canada, Horton and Van Evrie argued, the North had "agitated the negro question" relentlessly and successfully destroyed democracy and the Union, while simultaneously preserving the "aristocracy in England." Inverting history, their text claimed that the revolutionists Abraham Lincoln and William H. Seward had forced secession on the South, which withdrew from the Union to preserve "the sacred principles of liberty and self-government which our forefathers established." Without secession, they argued, the South faced the intolerable consequences of "amalgamation and social death."

In Horton's telling, the North then sent an "abolition army" into the South. Having issued the Emancipation Proclamation "in the style of a dictator," Lincoln then aimed to compel negroes to "be 'free' to do as they pleased, to go where they pleased, and to be as lazy and useless as they pleased." But the "slave" population of the South remained entirely loyal to their masters and refused to leave their plantations. The "invading" army found "the negroes" so devoted to their white masters that Yankee soldiers had to tie them up and threaten to "bayonet them" to force them out of their homes. Horton even included an engraving showing Union troops handcuffing slaves to expel them from their plantations. "So," he wrote, "in hundreds of thousands of broken hearts all over the land, the name of abolitionism will be coupled with thief, robber and murderer as long as time shall last."

The book attracted much attention, some of it appropriately hostile, but it also won approval across the North. While the Chicago *Republican* found the book "so puerile an attempt to poison the rising generation against the cause of the Republic," the Harrisburg, Pennsylvania, *Patriot* maintained that it should be "in the hands of every young man in the country." Reprinting a review from the Boston *Traveler*, the Bennington, Vermont, *Banner* summarized the book's argument that the Civil War had been fought not to preserve the Union and republican institutions but "to destroy both." John Brown had been nothing short of "a fiend," the South had been fully justified in leaving the Union, and Democratic enemies of the Lincoln administration and the war like Clement Vallandigham had been heroic; the paper even declared that the wretched and murderous 1863 New York City Draft Riots had attained heroic status. We can't know how widespread school adoptions of the book were, but in 1879 at least one school in, of all places, Boston used *A Youth's History.*

Van Evrie appeared to abandon his white supremacy campaign by 1879 and likely returned to his medical profession for a living. Perhaps he concluded after the adoption of the Fourteenth and Fifteenth amendments that his campaign, like the South's secession, had been a failure. While he died in obscurity in Brooklyn, New York, in 1896, his campaign for white supremacy would receive dramatic confirmation at that very moment by the U.S. Supreme Court's decision in *Plessy v. Ferguson.* As the father of American white supremacy, he may not have achieved all he desired, but his impact proved considerable nonetheless.

In addition to his firm's history textbook, Van Evrie's other works found eager audiences long after his death. In 1908 the Richmond,

Virginia, *Times Dispatch* recommended his *Negroes and Negro "Slavery"* to its readers, advising them that it was an excellent book "and easy to get." Lost Cause crusader Mildred Lewis Rutherford, who published twenty-nine books and pamphlets and a monthly magazine during the 1920s, and who served as the official historian of the United Daughters of the Confederacy, marshaled the Horton schoolbook to defend the Jim Crow South. She cited *A Youth's History* to charge Lincoln with being a dictator who "overthrew the government . . . by issuing a military edict [the Emancipation Proclamation] . . . which changed the fundamental law of the land." She assured her readers that Reconstruction had "made the Ku Klux Klan a necessity." Her reprint won applause from Lyon Gardiner Tyler, the son of President John Tyler and president of the College of William and Mary, as a needed antidote to Northern propaganda about the Civil War and the deification of Lincoln. The Southern Publishing Company in Dallas, Texas, offered the Horton text in 1925, as well as other school history texts, like the 1932 *The Lone Star State: A School History,* which advanced all the usual condemnations of carpetbag criminals, lazy negroes, and heroic Klan members. The Horton text was an undeniable example of the Northern white supremacist foundations of the Southern descendants of slaveholders.

Van Evrie's *White Supremacy and Negro Subordination* has been kept in print by the Confederate Reprint Company and by its ideological heirs right up to the present day. The online Dixie Project still promotes Van Evrie's publications, claiming that he has been "slandered by mainstream sources today even in spite of the fact that many of his conclusions have been proven by events of history subsequent to the War Between the States." Moreover, infuriated by the presidency of Barack Obama and encouraged by the fulminations of the Trump presidential administration, alt-right and neo-Nazi websites are making freely available Van Evrie's incendiary works that demean, dehumanize, and objectify people of African descent.

Van Evrie found his final resting place in Rochester's Mount Hope Cemetery. Perhaps his abandoned daughter, Catherine Van Evrie— who lived until 1922—brought the body back home from Brooklyn for interment there. In a final irony, however, Mount Hope also holds the remains of Frederick Douglass and Susan B. Anthony. But while Van Evrie's headstone lies broken and abandoned, without even a birth date, every year scores of people visit the cemetery to pay their respects to the two other Americans who labored so much to create an ideal democracy.

3

From "Slavery" to "Servitude"

Initial Patterns, 1832 to 1866

Were a grand family procession to set forth in the order
appointed by Providence, the white men would go first,
the white women with their children second, and next the
colored Servants.

—Emma Willard, *Via Media,* 1862

Joseph Emerson, the head of Wethersfield, Connecticut's Female
Seminary, explained in 1828 that the most important text his
students could read—next to the Bible—was the nation's history. A "profoundly Christian enterprise," Emerson wrote, American history displayed the record of the "first government, that was
ever established upon the genuine basis of freedom." This land of
revivals, he advised his students, had been born "a garden that the
Lord delights to bless." Since at least 1823, however, Emerson had
been regularly vacationing in Charleston, South Carolina. Somehow what he saw there never made it into the history lessons concerning "the genuine basis of freedom" that he offered to his young
scholars. Nor did his approach differ from that of other authors
and educators of the 1820s and '30s. Elizabeth Palmer Peabody, a
renowned educator, a friend of Emerson's, and a charter member of
Boston's Transcendentalist Club, published instructions to teachers
in 1832, providing over eighty pages of questions that should form
the basis of a history curriculum. She covered Columbus, the exploration of the Americas, Mexico, the Aztecs, and even Native Americans. She advised teachers that young students should develop an

understanding of other religions and different forms of government, which would "lay the corner-stone of a true liberality of heart." But she offered not a word about African Americans or the institution of slavery. While slavery as a political problem would emerge in American textbooks in the 1840s and '50s, none ever discussed the antislavery movement prior to 1860—when John Brown could not be avoided. African Americans received no attention, except when later discussion moved toward how the South raised and harvested cotton. As individuals, they never appeared in a text. Only after the Civil War would textbooks discuss African Americans and even then, with the exception of the Reconstruction era, only to describe them as "ignorant, far inferior, and well suited to [a] hot climate" and a "problem" that defied solution.

Most early textbooks avoided any detailed discussion of the institution of slavery and its conditions, out of either ignorance or, lack of concern, or for fear of damaging sales. As the years passed, however, they could not dodge conversation about the *political* controversy over slavery, not only because the issue roiled the nation but because Americans understood history as primarily a political narrative. And as the nation entered the 1850s, that narrative became increasingly contentious and frayed to the point of disintegration. Beginning with the controversy over the 1820 Missouri Compromise—which temporarily decided the fate of slavery in the lands acquired in the 1803 Louisiana Purchase, allowing it in Missouri and adding the free state of Maine—and especially after the Mexican War, the political impact of slavery became enormous and unavoidable. While textbooks completely ignored the rising and fractious antislavery movement, their tentative and inconsistent coverage of the mounting political tensions clearly displayed most authors' confusion, if not outright fear.

Such fears, however, became a driving force for one of the country's most successful textbook authors. Emma Willard, the icon of the women's education movement, used her commanding national platform and her impressive mastery of American history not only to instruct her generation of students but to rescue the nation from the approaching abyss. During the 1850s, she crafted best-selling textbooks with passion, skill, and determination to head off the smoldering sectional crisis, but she did so by advancing the kind of white supremacy that John H. Van Evrie would later imagine and disseminate with unprecedented skill. While it remains impossible to link Willard's textbooks, or any others before the Civil War, to Van Evrie, what they recorded—and what they avoided—certainly shaped his everyday environment. It is no coincidence that as soon as the war ended, Van Evrie and his partner Rushmore G. Horton published their own children's textbook about the war, seeking to forestall acceptance of any Emancipationist understanding of the war's meaning, replacing it with a vile and unrepentant assertion of white supremacy. In that way, Van Evrie bridges the pre- and postwar eras, linking the textbooks that likely nourished him to those that later absorbed his own poisonous views.

·   ·   ·

In 1827 only Massachusetts and Vermont required public schools to teach history, with New Hampshire following in 1846 and Virginia in 1849. In 1851 California mandated instruction in grammar schools regarding the federal and state constitutions. What little public education existed remained mostly above the Mason-Dixon Line, and the majority of the nation's teachers were either born or trained in the North. Especially in the South, formal education, public or private, remained largely an elite enterprise, especially after grammar school, for much of the nineteenth century. But as public education began to spread and states North and South established private academies, the demand for textbooks increased dramatically. Between 1820 and 1849, sixty-nine different history textbooks appeared, and by 1859, 439 existed for all branches of history. By 1855, spending on all textbooks had increased to over $5 million, outselling all other categories of books. Surprisingly, by midcentury the United States produced more textbooks than all European nations combined. National interest in history blossomed during the early nineteenth century, from popular narratives to accounts in journals and newspapers. As one journal observed in the 1830s, "No department of literature amongst us is cultivated with more assiduity than history." The ever-popular Samuel G. Goodrich, who also wrote under the pen name "Peter Parley," once observed that "history is the most important of all studies. . . . It acquaints us with the true character of our race, and enables us to know ourselves better."

Especially for the first two generations of textbook authors, however, "our race" and "ourselves" meant only the Europeans who encountered the New World. Their work took on a rather inflexible model in which "history" occurred only in European exploration, colonization, Revolution, Constitution-forming, party politics, and successive presidential administrations—and nowhere else. The format and racial assumptions about what constituted history largely precluded authors from dealing with other subjects, although they occasionally included sympathetic accounts of Native Americans, and female authors might include a famous woman in their books. For most, however, the layout, appearance, and order of events appeared largely the same, with each paragraph numbered. Often a list of questions would appear at the end of a chapter to draw students' attention to issues and events that had priority. With some variation, this model persisted and dominated textbooks into the early twentieth century. From a young reader's perspective, the format could prove onerous and at times oppressive. William Swinton's 1872 *First Lessons in Our Country's History . . . Aiming to Combine Simplicity with Sense* clearly proved intolerable to one student, who stabbed Harvard University's copy with a sharp implement right through the back cover and halfway into the text. A few could be innovative, such as Thomas Howland Mumford's 1856 *The Child's First History,* a breezy colloquy between a little girl named Madge, her sister Anne, and their aunt. Their discussions focused on Native Americans but failed to include any actual history and, of course, never mentioned a word about slavery or African Americans.

Noah Webster's 1832 *History of the United States* proved typical of many textbooks published before the Civil War. The Connecticut-born Webster, of dictionary fame, insisted that history must be "the principal school book in the United States." It should impress "truths upon our mind and imbue students with correct principles of morality and life." Every child, he thought, "should lisp" the lessons of the past. His book detailed Spanish colonization and discussed Native societies but clearly focused on New England as the archetype of New World settlement. The nation as Americans had come to know it in the 1830s, he wrote, owed everything to the Puritans, especially those of Connecticut, who represented the greatest influence on the Revolution and the creation of the Constitution. "For the progress and enjoyment of civil and religious liberty, in modern times, the world is more indebted to the Puritans . . . than to any other body of men, or to any other cause." He cared nothing for African Americans or the history of slavery, giving it only passing mention in the North, and managed to discuss the development of cotton cultivation in the South without revealing who grew and harvested the crops. In his textbook, Webster did manage to describe "Negroes" as one of the world's principal peoples, but he was utterly ignorant of African civilizations and did not believe that any worth mentioning ever existed. He described Africans—as if all were identical—as "black" with smooth skin, short, woolly hair, and "the nose flat and short; the lips thick and tumid; the teeth of an ivory whiteness. The body of the negroes is generally well formed and of full size, but the legs are often bent outwards, and the heel projects farther than that of Europeans." (During the Civil War, whites often referred to African American troops as "long heels.") Elsewhere, Webster wrote "that of the wooly haired Africans, who constitute the principal part of the inhabitants of Africa, there is no history, & there can be none. That race has remained in barbarism from the first ages of the world; their country has never been explored very fully by civilized man." For Webster, American history was the record of his Puritan forebears and no others. Thus was the standard of whiteness-in-history set for the next two centuries.

The sense of white American identity that infused Webster's conceptions of history and society permeated nineteenth-century education at all levels and in all subjects. From the start of their education, children absorbed a hierarchical understanding of race and civilizations. Students memorized assumed characteristics of differing civilizations and peoples and where they—as white

Americans—stood in the racial hierarchy. As one 1793 teacher's guide instructed, "nature has formed the different degrees of genius, and the characters of nations which are seldom known to change." Thus, as an even earlier geography manual instructed, anyone of African descent belonged to a "brutish people, having little more of humanity but the form." An 1815 text, meant to encourage reading, instructed students that the "mental powers" of the "negro," "in general, participate in the imbecility of their bodies." By the 1850s, geography manuals simply dismissed African peoples as "destitute of intelligence." And while the descriptions might alter over time, the hierarchy did not, with the white or Caucasian at the top and the Ethiopian or Black always at the bottom. As John H. Van Evrie had argued, only the white race had been created in the Garden of Eden, with other races and peoples developing at other times through the influence of climate, chance, geography, or God's will. As one 1826 geography textbook instructed, students of all ages would never doubt that the white race always furnished "the greatest number of beautiful figures."

Many textbooks simply used older ones as models, but as the century wore on, authors increasingly relied on the works of professional and popular historians, such as the massive ten-volume history of the United States by George Bancroft (1800–1891), whose work dominated the nineteenth century. One of the nation's most influential historians, Bancroft was also a teacher, a Democratic Party activist, a diplomat, and, in 1844, secretary of the navy during the Polk administration, when he established the Naval Academy at Annapolis, Maryland. In 1845 he served as acting secretary of war and signed the order sending Gen. Zachary Taylor across the Rio Grande, which started the Mexican War. Bancroft became one of the first American scholars to earn his doctorate in Germany, where his Harvard advocates had sent him. His immense talent had been seen from the start of his career, and in 1822 Emerson dubbed him "an infant Hercules." As the most commanding historian of the nineteenth century, Bancroft claimed he took nothing on faith, considered "tradition" to be "a careless story teller," and often went directly to original sources. His *History of the United States,* begun in 1834, had become by 1860 eight massive volumes that celebrated the American quest for political, social, and religious freedom; and in 1874 he concluded his story, to the end of the American Revolution, with yet two more volumes. For the rest of his career, Bancroft revised his volumes, which eventually saw well over twenty editions. Only the twentieth century's history titan—and admiral—Samuel Eliot Morison ever rivaled the sheer dominance of George Bancroft.

With astonishing detail and sparkling generalizations, Bancroft detailed the English settlement of North America. When he came to the settlement of Virginia, he marveled at it as an "asylum of liberty" that, "by one of the strange contradictions in human affairs," also became the "abode of hereditary bondsmen. The unjust, wasteful, and unhappy system was fastened upon the rising institutions of America by the mercantile avarice of a foreign nation." Many textbooks later copied this Bancroft phrase, "the mercantile avarice of a foreign nation," sometimes without attribution, seeking to divert attention from American responsibility for the development of slavery. Attempting to preserve the innocence and purity of the American founding, Bancroft blamed England for the evil practice and at the same time diminished the responsibility of his ideal democratic republic by correctly describing slavery as an institution as old as human civilization. He also compared the contradiction of American slavery and American freedom to that of the ancient Hebrews who burst their own chains but bound others to their will. Greeks enslaved Greeks, he advised his readers, and Anglo-Saxons "trafficked in Anglo Saxons and Africans sold Africans." Even the European traffic in slaves had been established before "the colonization of the United States and had existed before the discovery of America." While all true and with a level of detail that existed nowhere else, his narrative shifted the responsibility for the imposition of slavery on the American colonies to Europe, completely ignoring the legal record of all the original colonies that offered complete security to the institution that he so clearly hated.

In the era before the Civil War, by one historian's account, "less than one-half of 1 percent of all text space in history books" discussed the institution of slavery. Some books in the 1830s did contain criticism of the "peculiar institution"—such as those of the Connecticut-born Samuel Griswold Goodrich (1793–1860)—but during the 1840s and '50s, such authors dropped those statements in subsequent editions of their books in response to market demand, especially in the South. Historians of education and history textbooks often heap praise on Goodrich for criticizing the institution of slavery, especially because he became the nineteenth century's most popular schoolbook author and the "preeminent authority on childhood historical literacy in America." His popularity, particularly his remarkable "Peter Parley" series of books, did achieve a level of success not seen again until the age of the Internet. Some students confessed that they read their copy of his books "until it was torn to pieces." Goodrich became so influential and respected a figure that President Millard Fillmore appointed him U.S. consul to France

"Negro Slaves at Work in the Field." While Charles Goodrich hoped that slavery would end, he instructed young students that "slaves are generally well treated, that is they have enough to eat, drink, and wear, and are not often required to labor beyond their strength." He stressed that slaves were "the property of their masters who have a right to punish them for bad conduct, and to sell them." Illustration from Goodrich's *The First Book of History for Children and Youth,* 3rd ed. (1848), p. 81.

in the early 1850s. "I think you have done more to diffuse useful knowledge among the rising generation," Fillmore declared, "than any other modern writer either English or American." Goodrich/Parley claimed to have published 170 books, selling seven to twelve million copies. Quite possibly he sold 50,000 copies of all his Peter Parley texts and about 300,000 copies of all his other books every year, some of which still sold in 1912. His success at writing became so immense that his brother Charles could not stand idly by: he quit the Protestant ministry to follow his brother into a career of writing history textbooks. Imagine that! For thirty years, "Peter Parley" imitators made a living off that name, with seven imposters just in England. His success proved so staggering that in a fit of jealous rage, Nathaniel Hawthorne compared Goodrich to a host of maggots that "feed on cheese."

Goodrich's biographer asserted that the New England author deliberately scattered antislavery messages throughout his texts. During the 1830s, various editions of his *First Book of History for Children and Youth* did discuss the beginning of slavery in 1619, calling it the unhappy foundation "for that system of slavery, which now pervades the Southern States." Although Goodrich claimed that most slaves were "well treated," he still wrote that they could obtain no education, retain no property, and enjoy "no liberty, no right to consult their own wishes, or, like the rest of mankind, pursue happiness in their own way." Moreover, the death of an owner might well mean the destruction of a slave family, with members "very often . . . never see[ing] each other again." He especially expressed his disdain for the slave auction, which could lead to the purchase of a mother by one person and her children by another. The agony of the mother, he wrote, was "past description." As for the Middle Passage, he explained, it was a "barbarous" enterprise with "poor creatures" stuffed belowdecks, many of whom suffocated and died. Others could not endure the horror and threw themselves into the sea. He advised his readers that slavery represented a "bad system altogether, and all good people believe that it is wrong." He hoped the time would not be far distant when "there will be no slaves in our country." One need not wonder, then, that some in the South damned Goodrich's works, especially the "Peter Parley" texts, as "full of insidious poison, even in the pictorial illustrations." Even after most of his books underwent a pro-slavery purging, some Southerners still rejected them, and *De Bow's Review* damned Northern-produced textbooks as "abolition works." The journal cried out for textbooks "written, prepared and published by Southern men." New England–authored books, the *Review* asserted, taught children about "their fathers' cruelty and oppression" toward "the unfortunate victim of bondage." They would have none of it.

"I have taken advantage of every convenient occasion to excite hatred of injustice, violence, and falsehood, and to promote a love of truth, equity, and benevolence": many commentators point to such Goodrich statements, and early editions of his histories, as a clear indication of how Northern schoolbooks damned slavery. A closer examination, however, reveals a far more ambiguous story. Although he lived until the eve of the Civil War, Goodrich never publicly commented on the growing sectional strife during the 1850s, and of course, he never discussed the abolitionist movement in any of his books. In his posthumously published memoir, he admitted to seeing "threatening clouds in the sky" and "ominous thunders in the distance." But he had seen conflict before, having served in the War of 1812, and believed that danger always "passed away" and that the nation would only grow and prosper—"and so I trust will be, the future."

More important, Goodrich was no abolitionist. A Daniel Webster Whig who joined the Republican Party in 1856, he directly witnessed growing sectional strife, but made clear that "we are not abolitionists. . . . We make no war on slavery where it is established. We accept it as sheltered by the compromise of the Constitution. Within this boundary it is sacred." In the very book that included Goodrich's most damning statements about slavery, he also offered the usual Northern solution to the slavery "problem" by advocating the American Colonization Society's plan to remove African Americans to Liberia. African people should be free, he wrote, but in Africa, not in the United States. There "they may enjoy happiness and freedom in the native land of the Negro race." Moreover, in his

"Peter Parley" books, he repeated Benjamin Franklin's fears about the impact of slavery on *whites*. By 1848, almost all his criticisms of slavery had been eliminated from his books.

Goodrich's work, in the end, had no discernible impact on the rise of the abolitionist movement. Indeed, when Goodrich traveled to the South in 1846—to see the region for himself and to acknowledge his large readership there—he found no hostility whatsoever. *De Bow's Review* may have carped about his baneful influence on the South, but in fact, Goodrich reported, "I was kindly received, and had the honors of a public welcome." This should not be surprising. His 1847 text on North America, meant for elementary school students, contained absolutely no commentary on slavery. It began with Adam and Eve, moved on to the Tower of Babel and Spanish exploration, and did not get to English colonization until one hundred pages into a two-hundred-page text. While it mentioned the founding of Jamestown, Virginia, it said nothing about the introduction of slavery. The book ended with the War of 1812, managing to dodge every controversial subject. The same was true of his extremely popular *A Pictorial History of the United States*. Originally published in 1843, by 1866 it had sold over half a million copies. After 1843, editions were purged of any hostility to slavery and adopted a strict Republican Party line on politics and sectional tensions, without a mention of abolitionists, colonization, or even Liberia.

Perhaps Goodrich's popularity in the South and elsewhere in the United States can be explained by his 1844 *Peter Parley's Geography for Beginners*. Making sure that students began their education with "correct" racial views, the ubiquitous "Peter Parley" explained to youngsters that the world was composed of different peoples, "some are white, some brown, some black. Some are wild and savage, and some are kind, gentle." One could find the sweet-looking Turk or the warlike savages from "Caffraria" (Kaffraria), South Africa. Students learned that "white people" came from Europe, and that "Negroes" or "black people" are just slaves "or their descendants." In describing various people of Africa, he employed the words *ignorant, barbarous, uncivilized, indolent, weak,* and *degraded.* Regardless of the country they currently live in, he wrote, negroes were "fond of dancing. . . . When the sun goes down, dancing begins from one end of Africa to the other." His text illustrates every part of the United States with informative captioned notes and questions to review. But when offering an illustration of Africa, the book simply said: "The teacher will here put such questions as he deems necessary." For the most part, "Peter Parley" confessed that the African continent "is unknown to us, and many portions of it are inhabited by ignorant and weak nations and tribes." But in North America, he advised his readers, forty million white people lived "on the continent." And since "the first settlement of America by white people, many interesting events have occurred. Several great states have risen." What might appear to modern readers as antislavery sentiment in Goodrich's popular books, in fact, sought only to show the "alien" and inferior character of Blacks and emphasize the supremacy of American whiteness. If he sought an end to slavery, it was only because he wished to end the African presence in America. His readers in the pre–Civil War South would find little to fear and much to admire in this famous New Englander.

Another New Englander, Salma Hale—a New Hampshire lawyer, state representative, and congressman—had been publishing history textbooks since the 1820s. In the last edition of his work, published in 1848, he declared that the introduction of slavery into the American colonies had been a "traffic abhorrent to humanity, disgraceful to civilization, and fixing the foulest stain upon the character of the age and people." But like so many authors who followed him, he could not get the exact year of the introduction of slavery into Virginia correct, and cited 1620 rather than 1619 as the critical date. Also, as in so many other texts of the era, he spent far more time discussing the importation of prospective English wives into the Virginia colony than the importation of slaves, which he reduced to a single sentence. He wondered if South Carolina's climate was sufficiently harsh to "justify holding their fellow-men in bondage," but he said nothing more about the "peculiar institution" for the first three hundred pages of his two-volume textbook. Hale seemed at war with himself, clearly disapproving of slavery but also not wanting to focus on the issue, since his book sought to establish the legitimacy of the new republic and its accomplishments. So he largely silenced his sentiments, ended his story in 1817, and instead of voicing an opinion about the problem of slavery, he placed an appendix at the end of volume two that listed the distribution of slaves by state between 1790 and 1830—entirely without commentary.

For most authors, avoidance was the preferred approach to dealing with the intractable problem of slavery. Marcius Willson's 1845 text similarly dodged the problem and preferred discussing Spanish exploration of the New World to the introduction of slavery, which he did not mention until covering the settlement of colonial Georgia and opposition to James Oglethorpe's slavery ban. When he came to 1820, however, Willson found that he could not avoid the issue. But instead of detailing the controversy over the extension of slavery into Missouri and the West, he simply stated that the debates "arrayed the South against the North, the slaveholding states against the non-slaveholding states, and the whole subject became the exciting topic of debate throughout the Union." The narrative in a later edition abruptly ended in 1848 and left the reader with an unsettling warning that the world's monarchies had predicted "our ruin":

> Let our prayer then be that the same God who brought Our fathers out of bondage, into a strange land, to found an Empire in the wilderness, may continue his protection to Their children; nor visit upon them the national and domestic sins of which they are guilty. Let us indulge the hope, that in the Western World freedom has found a congenial clime. . . . Let us endeavor to cultivate a spirit of mutual concession and harmony in our national councils.

Willson chose an unsettling and confused method of alerting students that something dangerous and volatile had been brewing in their country, issues that many authors of the 1850s also desperately tried to elude.

As the nation approached the 1850s, however, a number of textbooks like Willson's revealed increasing levels of anxiety and uncertainty. Even nineteenth-century New York's celebrated pantologist Egbert Guernsey (1823–1903) found his encounter with American history a disturbing reminder that his own generation seemed increasingly incapable of living up to the achievements of their fathers and preserving the republic. He had begun life in Litchfield, Connecticut, of firm Puritan stock. He attended Yale, earned a medical degree from the Medical College of New York University, and after receiving a law degree from the College of St. Francis Xavier, became the city's best-known homeopathic doctor. In his spare time, he trained in pharmacy, managed a drug company, won appointment as the Williamsburg city physician, and in 1860 helped found New York Medical College. He also helped edit the New York *Evening Mirror* and founded and edited the Brooklyn *Daily Times* in 1855 and the *Medical Union* in 1873. In 1853 he published his first medical text, *Homeopathic Domestic Practice.* He then became a life member of the New-York Historical Society and the American Geographical Society, and during the Civil War helped found the city's Union League Club. As a league member, Guernsey helped organize the 20th United States Colored Troops and in 1864 marched down Broadway with them as they set off for the South, eventually serving in Louisiana and the Department of the Gulf. Before his medical career rocketed to local renown, he also published the first edition of his U.S. history text in 1847—with a simplified version for the elementary level—a volume that saw its ninth edition in 1851 and its fifteenth in 1869.

His *History of the United States of America, Designed for Schools* began with an unwavering belief that the nation's "fathers" had "worked out the great design of God, and were aided by him in their glorious consummation" in founding the republic. Guernsey's book followed a traditional narrative pattern through the colonial era and the Revolution and ended with biographical sketches of the presidents and their "noble" achievements. Unlike most other volumes of the era, however, Guernsey provided a genuinely sympathetic account of Native Americans and, astoundingly, referred to the Cherokees as a "beloved people." He even noted resemblances among the Mongolian, Alaskan, and Native American peoples, implying a common origin and hereditary lineages, entirely without the obnoxious racial speculations that usually followed such assessments. Most other textbooks, like the 1855 two-volume *A Child's History of the United States* by John Bonner, celebrated the extinction of Native Americans. Bonner sought to imprint on the American mind that U.S. history was the record of the "White Man's" progress over the godless red savage. Indeed, Bonner turned the continent's Native male inhabitants into evil oppressors, making "their women . . . do all the hard work." Noble savages, perhaps, but Bonner also referred to them as "heathens," "half naked," and "ignorant." Guernsey proved a rare exception, offering a remorseful account of Indian removal and clearly blaming "white men" for their demise.

Although Guernsey failed to provide any sustained account of slavery in the United States, no reader could come away from his text without perceiving the author's disapproval of it. When discussing Spain's colonization in the New World, he referred to two slaving vessels of Lucas Vasquez de Ayllón that stopped along the South Carolina coast and tricked Indians into an onboard visit. He then suddenly pulled anchor and headed for Santo Domingo to sell them: "Husbands torn from their wives, and children from their parents." While he also misstated the year of the first arrival of slaves into Virginia, he provided—as few other texts had done—a summary of the alleged 1741 slave plot to burn New York City. Although the existence of such a plot hinged on sparse and coerced evidence—it likely never happened—it did lead to the trial and the ritual burning of fourteen Blacks, the hanging of eighteen more, and the transportation to the Caribbean of about seventy-one other assumed conspirators. In retrospect, Guernsey wrote, the New York authorities created the alleged plot in their imaginations and "executed innocent men." He compared the disgusting affair to the Salem witchcraft trials to "show into what extravagances men may be led, when their actions are uncontrolled by calm dictates of reason." Clearly, he implied a warning about the nation's increasing political strife, especially after 1850. But he only hinted at such dangers (which young students would easily miss) and refused to specify precisely what threat the nation faced.

Moreover, he worked hard to absolve the colonists of any responsibility for the existence of slavery. As Jefferson had done in the first draft of the Declaration of Independence, Guernsey blamed England, and the "mercantile avarice of a foreign nation" (words he lifted directly from the historian George Bancroft), for imposing slavery on the American colonies. If there was a moral failing at work, it was clearly not the fault of our "fathers." He glossed over the contentious 1820 Missouri debates and failed to detail the ever-increasing political controversy over slavery, even after the Mexican War and California's request for statehood. Then suddenly the Union appeared to be in peril: "Disunion was not only heard at the north and the south, the east and the west, but boldly and threateningly in the Hall of our National Legislature." He warned students, as other popular textbooks did, that "elements of strife were thus convulsing the country, and threatening civil war." Then he immediately backed off and assured readers that peace would continue because the U.S. Senate possessed "the most powerful minds that have ever existed in our government or the world."

But by the time he revised his text in the 1850s, Guernsey's former confidence had withered. The deaths of President John Tyler and Senators John C. Calhoun, Henry Clay, and Daniel Webster shook his confidence. The very best men he had relied on in 1847 were now gone. But he could not quite lay blame for his trepidation where it squarely belonged. He advised students that by 1852, the nation had achieved unprecedented growth and social development. New cities, canals, railroads, and manufacturers were the accomplishments of "sovereign" people. But the future, he warned, depended on the intelligence and virtue of those people. Should they falter, Guernsey cautioned, "the cause will be found in the grasping avarice, the vice and ignorance of the people." But, clearly, not in the institution of slavery.

Samuel Griswold Goodrich's brother Charles (1790–1862), enticed into textbook writing by "Peter Parley's" remarkable success, published several editions of his U.S. history textbook throughout the 1850s; it was revised and expanded in 1867, long after his death. For Charles Augustus Goodrich, even as late as 1858, American

PERIOD I.

DISTINGUISHED FOR DISCOVERIES.

EXTENDING FROM THE DISCOVERY OF SAN SALVADOR BY COLUMBUS, 1492,
TO THE FIRST PERMANENT ENGLISH SETTLEMENT, AT
JAMESTOWN, VIRGINIA, 1607.

CHAPTER I.

SPANISH EXPEDITIONS.

I. COLUMBUS.[1]—1. The honor of the discovery of America[2] belongs to Christopher Columbus, as an individual, and to Spain, as a nation.

Columbus was born about the year 1435, in Genoa, a city of Italy. At the age of fourteen, after having acquired some knowledge of geometry,

Landing of Columbus.

geography, astronomy, and navigation, he entered upon a seafaring life. About twenty years later we find him in Lisbon, attracted by the spirit of maritime enterprise, of which that city was then the centre.

[1] In Italian, *Colombo* ; Latinized, it becomes *Columbus*, by which name he is best known. In Spanish, his name is written *Christoval Colon*. See p. 10, note 1.
[2] There is reason for believing that the Northmen, in the 10th century, found their way to

QUESTIONS.—1. To whom belongs the honor of discovering America? To what nation? —When and where was Columbus born? What is said of Columbus at the age of fourteen? Twenty years later? Why did he go to Lisbon?

(7)

While many midcentury textbooks contained no illustrations, most that did presented the founding of America as an enterprise fusing whiteness with Christian destiny. Charles A. Goodrich and William H. Seavey, *History of the United States of America, for the Use of Schools* (1867), p. 7.

history displayed nothing but the nation's "virtue, enterprise, courage, generosity, [and] patriotism," and his book provided sound examples of how to avoid "vice," which should incite students "to copy such noble examples." One might have expected him, as a former minister, to craft a narrative that emphasized the religious influences necessary for the success of a "free" government. He offered little substance about the establishment and development of slavery, although he clearly did not approve of it. He dismissed the nullification crisis during the Andrew Jackson administration, when South Carolina denounced the federal tariffs of 1828 and 1832 as utterly unconstitutional and thus null and void within the state, as a political crisis caused by mere "discontents" in South Carolina. Instead of revealing the tenuous nature of the American union, according to Goodrich, the incident displayed President Jackson's superior leadership and skill. He breezed past the 1850 Compromise, sparked by California's request for statehood, the status of slavery in lands acquired in the Mexican War, and the demand for a new Fugitive Slave Law, with an unexamined reference to a "spirit of anarchy and discord" that infected the nation like a virus, then conveniently ended his narrative. The remainder of his book catalogued American achievements in invention, agriculture, trade, and commerce. Not even Peter Parley had performed so massive an act of evasion.

But in the mid-1850s, some authors revealed a growing uneasiness. Bonner's juvenile two-volume text could not dismiss the consequences of the Mexican War. The female narrator whom he employed to relate some of his history declared outright that the Mexican War had been unjust. "War is only justifiable when it is in defense of national honor or national rights; and we, not Mexico, were the aggressors." Authors such as Benson J. Lossing (1813–91), a New York journalist with over forty books to his credit, struggled to maintain an aura of self-confidence. Most textbook authors continued to evade any serious exploration of the issues that not only divided North and South but also set Northerners at each other's throats. Lossing, a self-trained writer, editor, and amateur historian, possessed a talent for reaching a general readership. A solid Democrat, he wrote to support his politics, but his primary dedication was to sales, and at least two of his works sold 50,000 to 60,000 copies. His 1854 *Pictorial History of the United States,* with the standard textbook format, was reprinted at least three times in the 1860s, with the last revised edition printed in 1876. Curiously, after surveying the periods of discovery, colonization, and Revolution, he referred to the nation's subsequent history as the "Confederation," which would have fit comfortably with the Democratic Party's preference for a weak central government. Lossing failed to mention slavery's founding in Virginia, and the word *slavery* did not appear in the text for fifty-five pages, until he declared that Henry VIII's revolt against the pope led to his making the people of England "his slaves." He evaded further mention of slavery until his discussion of the Monroe administration, when he abruptly alerted the student to the eruption of a "violent and protracted debate" in 1820 in Congress. The final compromise resolutions, to Lossing's mind, settled the matter and secured the "Confederation." The return of controversy in 1850 threw the nation back into violent debates, embittering North and South and shaking the "Confederation" to "its centre." But he depicted Henry Clay as the nation's savior, standing between the "Hotspurs of the North and South." Lossing remained loyal to the Democratic Party until 1859, when he joined the Republicans.

Benson Lossing's *A Primary History of the United States for Schools and Families* (1863) offered history as a dramatic tale for students and families, who could be imagined only as white. Frontispiece.

In much later writing, he held the South and the "wicked sophistries of the Calhoun school" responsible for causing the Civil War. Unfortunately, he came to that conclusion rather belatedly.

. . .

As Northern publishers and authors, especially New Englanders, dominated the textbook industry (and publishing in general), Southern commentators became increasingly frustrated with the "Yankee-centric" quality of the historical narratives. By the 1850s, calls for texts specifically designed for Southern students and readers became increasingly common—and more desperate. Calvin Wiley, the superintendent of North Carolina public education, expressed typical frustration with "Yankee" textbooks "with all the bias which is given to them . . . which they pass to our children." They breathe "hostility to Southern institutions," he protested. But the region's exceedingly low literacy rates, with as many as one in seven white North Carolina adults illiterate, and the paucity of Southern publishing houses strangled demand for and efforts to produce any textbooks at all. In 1857 Hinton R. Helper, the famed North Carolina racist *and* critic of slavery, examined the 1850 U.S. Census and with vexation concluded that the "people of the South are not a reading people. Many of the adult population never learned to read; still more do not care to read." Even when Southern presses did publish textbooks, they sometimes only added to the frustration of critics. Astonishingly, one press in Louisville, Kentucky, brought out the first edition of Noah Webster's *History of the United States,* a book that largely ignored the South and, as *De Bow's Review* groaned, spread the "praise and glorification of the first citizens of the New England and Northern States . . . as a set of incomparable patriots, irreproachable moralists, and the most exemplary models for future imitation."

What Southern critics sought, and had great difficulty finding, were texts that favorably examined the "subject of the weightiest import to us of the South. . . . I mean the institution of Negro Slavery." Although slavery once had been seen as a misfortune, such was no longer the case, J. W. Morgan—a Virginian—explained in *De Bow's Review*. Books that did not praise the "doctrines" that "we now believe" should be banned and never come "within the range of juvenile reading." Morgan damned current textbooks as flying the "black piratical ensign of Abolitionism." Continued use of such works would only corrupt the minds of youth and "spread dangerous heresies among us." Even spelling books could not be trusted, as they contained covert condemnations of "our peculiar institutions." The North had declared a moral war on the South, Morgan exclaimed, so for "common sense" and "self-preservation," would not "some one speedily undertake the good work?"

But no general history of the United States that met the guidelines espoused by such critics in *De Bow's Review* ever materialized from a Southern press. Moreover, as "Peter Parley" discovered, his works still found eager readers south of the Mason-Dixon Line. Additionally, while Southern publishers could not compete with those in the North, they did offer a few alternatives. Between 1850 and 1857 a Baltimore publisher brought out Martin Kerney's *Catechism of the History of the United States,* and despite the fact that it alleged that the young George Washington chopped down an apple tree, it still sold thirty thousand copies. Between 1858 and 1865, Bartholomew R. Carroll published a similar catechism in Charleston, South Carolina, which went through twenty editions. Carroll, who had published a documentary history of South Carolina in 1836, offered his chronological list of questions and answers as a work without "sectional favor." While hampered by an irritating format, Carroll nonetheless managed to provide a reasonably accurate history of the development of American slavery within a transatlantic colonial context—one that explained the South's overwhelming reliance on agriculture. Like his Northern competitors, he could not avoid commenting on the American character. The "typical" Southerner, he explained, possessed "frankness, hospitality, taste, and refinement," while those colonists who settled in New England proved "amusing and intolerant." Perhaps thinking of the Webster volume, Carroll went on to describe those who settled Connecticut as especially intolerant and progenitors of a place where "public services" were constantly interrupted by insolent boys who would be "publicly whipped" for their outrageous conduct. Carroll's work laid foundation stones for the myths of Cavalier and Yankee. But regarding slavery, he said little. His questions and answers did include the 1820 Missouri Compromise and the volatile disputes of the 1850s, confessing that "the subject [slavery] was introduced into every debate." He admitted that Stephen A. Douglas's 1854 Kansas-Nebraska Act, which in effect terminated the Missouri Compromise of 1820, "disturbed the harmony and quietude of the people," and he even acknowledged the bitter civil war that had erupted in Kansas. But just as his narrative approached the precipice, Carroll turned to geography and statistical descriptions of the country, as his Northern brethren did, avoiding commentary on what clearly was tearing the country apart.

The one book that might have met most requirements that Southern critics demanded turned out to be William Gilmore Simms's history of South Carolina, not a general U.S. history, which antebellum Southern authors never showed interest in writing. Originally published in Charleston in 1840 and quite successful, the book's subsequent revised versions remained in print through 1937, but most editions after 1842 ironically came out under a New York City imprint. And why not, since the few Southern presses that existed lacked the resources and distribution networks of the dominant Northern publishing houses. Moreover, they proved a welcoming home to texts that bore prime responsibility for sustaining white supremacy, even if some expressed disapproval of slavery. Simms, who became one of the Old South's most successful literary figures, typified American fiction's obsession with violence and murder. "Perhaps," he wrote in 1835, "one of the most natural and necessary agents of man in his progress through life, is the desire to destroy." He is best known for his countless novels about colonial South Carolina and the South, especially *The Partisan: A Romance of the Revolution* (1835). Besides the history of his home state, he also crafted popular biographies of the Revolutionary War heroes Francis Marion and Nathanael Greene and of the colonial adventurer and explorer Capt. John Smith.

Simms also crafted a brief "memoir" of South Carolina's Revolutionary War hero John Laurens as an introduction to Laurens's published war correspondence. His careful account, stressing character and the glory of winning American independence, proved unusually "selective." For Simms, the young Laurens exemplified "frank earnestness, resolute zeal and American directness of purpose." There are hints of mild criticism in the work: impulsiveness, perhaps overzealous youthful misjudgment, ultimately led to Laurens's death in a British ambush on August 27, 1782. But nothing in the "memoir" would arouse suspicion in the average reader who knew little or nothing about Laurens's service, and opinions, during the war. Although Simms made absolutely no mention of it in his account, during the war John, and his more famous father, Continental Congress president Henry Laurens, had supported the raising of Black troops to fight the British. John Laurens, in fact, had been delegated by Alexander Hamilton to convince South Carolina to support the effort. John wrote to his father, "My plan is at once to give freedom to the negroes, and gain soldiers to the states. . . . A well chosen body of 5,000 black men, properly officer'd, to act as light troops . . . might give us decisive success in the next campaign." Ironically, that letter was included in the very collection that contained Simms's "memoir." He simply would not acknowledge this effort or any other that brought the institution of slavery and white supremacy into question.

Simms intended his history of South Carolina both for the general public and "for the use of schools." Unlike standard textbooks, his narrative tale was unencumbered by annoying numbered paragraphs and queries. His handling of the region's early period proved surprisingly sympathetic to the Native Americans, although in the end he could not avoid calling them "savages." Nonetheless, struggles against Native peoples dominated the beginning of his history, and he did not bother to mention slavery until ninety-five pages into the text, and then only as another of the colony's commodities. A few pages further on, however, he detailed the importance of slavery, clearly viewing it as a blessing. The "vast increase of negro slaves," he proudly explained, "opened boundless plains of virgin fertility and freshness to the sun." Rice production exploded, he wrote, and if not for slaves, the colony could not have flourished.

With verve and style, he wrote about South Carolina's conflict with Spanish Florida in the late 1730s and about the September 1739 Stono Rebellion, when twenty slaves attempted to throw off their enslavement and reach Fort Mose in Spanish Florida. As many as a hundred enslaved Africans participated in the rebellion, with fifty caught and executed. But for Simms, rather than a slave rebellion, the Stono uprising was an episode when "raw" African savages, prompted by the base "appetites and passions" of the Spanish, were lured away and led astray from their rightful place in slavery. "The negro cannot long resist temptations which appeal to his appetite; his passions are too strong; his intellect too mean and feeble . . . and the cunning enemy soon used the semi-barbarians at his pleasure." The captive Africans, according to Simms, did not seek freedom and liberty—things only whites could covet—but acted only out of base passions. But more important lessons came out of the slave experience for Simms. Black slavery had the ironic effect of making whites more jealous of their own liberty and less willing to endure any subservient role in the British Empire. In a pairing that proved reminiscent of John H. Van Evrie's later formulation of the nature of white democracy, Simms asserted that the American Revolution and independence depended on slavery. "Negro slavery had the farther effect," he wrote, "of making them [whites] jealous of their own liberties, while elevating them to a high sense of their own dignity and character." To defenders of the Old South or of the newer North, American independence and democracy appeared to rest firmly on white supremacy and Black slavery.

.   .   .

Although we often think of female textbook authors as common in the twentieth century, they certainly existed in the years before the Civil War, and in the case of Emma Willard proved absolutely pivotal. Some early female authors went unrecognized because they understood popular prejudice against them and displayed their authorship only with their first initials and a last name. Thus the

1855 text by A. B. Berard, *School History of the United States,* actually was written by Augusta Blanche Berard (1824–1901). She had served as the U.S. "postmistress" at West Point for about twenty-five years—with members of her family occupying the same position for over sixty years—continued in the position until 1897, and was buried in the academy's military cemetery. Additionally, she taught at the Pelham Priory School in Westchester County, New York, and published a number of other books, including *Reminiscences of West Point in the Olden Times* (1886), *A School History of England* (1873), and *A Manual of Spanish Art and Literature* (1866).

Berard's history, like so many other early textbooks, displayed a bias toward New England, and to give women a place in her narrative, she asserted that Mary Chilton, who was thirteen in 1620, was the first Pilgrim to land on Plymouth's "Forefathers' Rock." When discussing the founding of Pennsylvania, she also slipped in a comment that a "mother's love" had saved William Penn. But unlike Noah Webster, Berard did not ignore the South, although she sought to convince the reader that the Southern colonies shared little in common with the Northern ones because of slavery. She identified Spain as the chief progenitor of the institution of slavery in the Western Hemisphere and, like other textbook authors, took her cue from Jefferson in blaming England and the Royal African Company for forcing slavery on the colonies. Once slaves had been introduced, however, removing them proved nearly impossible because, she explained, they "thrived" in the warm climate of the South, although their removal was "much to be desired." Unlike other early authors, she explored the ramifications of Texas annexation, which incited opposition in the North by inclusion of so large a slave state in the Union. She too recognized the 1850s as an era of political strife and consternation. "On the subject of slavery, taxation, important duties, and internal improvements," she warned, "much bitter party feeling has risen." Politics had become so contentious, she cautioned, that "God has raised up for us wise and peace-loving statesmen" to avert a crisis. But as in so many other texts of the 1850s, confidence did not spill from her narrative, and she ended her study with prayers for an anxious future.

Few textbook authors, male or female, could equal the success or impact of Emma Willard (1787–1870). The legendary founder of the Troy, New York, Female Seminary (1821)—now known as the Emma Willard School—has become an icon of women's education. At the beginning of the twentieth century, the president of Middlebury College exclaimed that Willard had begun a "movement which has revolutionized the ideas of the civilized world on the subject of women's education." For some, she also became a feminist heroine. The historian Anne Firor Scott saw Willard as a model of feminist advocacy. "Justice will yet be done. Woman will have rights," she proudly quoted Willard. For Scott and many others, Willard embodied the "claims and rights of women" everywhere. But as the historian of women and literature Nina Baym reminds us, Willard definitely was no "proto-liberal" or a feminist in any modern sense. Instead, she worked tirelessly to better situate women in the context of her own times, improving their status through educational opportunities and posing no challenge to male supremacy. In fact, she often remarked that the "husband and father" represented "the only natural sovereign." Thus she adamantly rejected the women's rights movement and any reform beyond the field of education, and she especially repudiated abolitionism. No African American student ever attended the Troy seminary during her lifetime, and the first did not become enrolled until 1948.

Willard, who had been publishing since 1828, saw her various history textbooks go through repeated reprintings, revisions, and expansions. Her first book was reprinted fifty-three times, the last edition appearing in 1873, three years after her death. It was translated into German and Spanish, for use on the West Coast, Cuba, and South America. Her popularity cannot be overstated, and she sold over one million copies of all her textbooks collectively. Daniel Webster even kept a copy of her *Republic of America,* which saw many editions between 1830 and 1843, on his desk. Equally important, next to "Peter Parley," she became one of the most popular textbook authors in the South and even retired early from the Troy seminary so that she could devote herself to encouraging female education there.

Emma Willard (1787–1870) was the nation's greatest advocate for female education. She founded Troy, New York's Female Seminary—now the Emma Willard School—and published some of the most popular U.S. history textbooks of the antebellum era. Like John H. Van Evrie, she considered people of African descent to be an inferior species of human, destined by God to do the white man's labor. Her seminary did not admit a Black student until 1948, the year after Jackie Robinson broke the color barrier in professional baseball. Illustration from Ezra Brainard, *Mrs. Emma Willard's Life and Work in Middlebury* (1918).

Willard was not only the nation's leading advocate for women's education but also an ardent nationalist. In the 1846 abridged *History of the United States,* she clearly revealed her aims in writing her books. History, to her, was the best means to "sow the seeds of virtue," so that the "youthful heart shall kindle into desires of imitation." The decline of public virtue, to her mind, called out for the "need to infuse patriotism into the breasts of the coming generation." The closer the country came to a cataclysmic rupture, the more earnest became her pleas for patriotism. On the eve of war, on March 1, 1861, she sent Congress a petition she had drawn up with fourteen thousand signatures of women from fourteen states to plead with political leaders to repudiate the sectional prejudice that threatened to destroy the nation's peace and unity. The next year she offered a plan for national reunification. In her *Via Media,* Willard made clear that she disapproved of slavery and, thinking it would display her generosity, asserted that she could never accept a

statement by Henry Ward Beecher—whom she accurately quoted—
that "if I had been God, I would not have made them [slaves] at
all." Like John H. Van Evrie, she believed that God had created
Africans to serve whites and that the role of "the negro race" in the
nation did not include "political equality." Nor should they enjoy
"all the political privileges of the whites." Repudiating women's and
Black rights, she went on to declare that only white men should
concern themselves "with making constitutional laws or legislative
enactments." Failing to understand that the South insisted not only
on keeping but expanding the institution of slavery, she thought
national unity could be maintained by North and South training
"the negro[es]" and then sending them to Liberia.

Willard's 1846 textbook, following lines set out by William
Gilmore Simms's South Carolina history, emphasized conflict with
Native Americans, alternately referring to them as Indians and "savages." Significantly, she singled out Pocahontas as a unique example
of Native American womanhood and female moral authority. She
accurately dated the start of colonial American slavery at 1619 but
avoided discussion of its importance. The book did include lists of
student questions for review, among them the beginning of slavery.
But it placed no emphasis on the "peculiar institution" and instead
understandably focused on the rise of the new nation and its quest
for independence, aimed at producing the civic virtue that she
deemed necessary for national survival. Her narrative, emphasizing
war, independence, political development, and nation building,
became jarred by the debates over Missouri slavery beginning in
1819. She had told her readers almost nothing about the development of slavery in American history, but the unsuspecting student
now suddenly read that a "question was now debated in Congress
which agitated the whole country. It had reference to a subject,
which, at this time, more threatens the stability of the Union, and
consequently the existence of this nation, than any other. This is
slavery." She quickly dropped the subject, however, and went on
to discuss foreign policy issues and cotton production, without
reference to where cotton was grown or who produced it. She then
abruptly terminated her book with the death of President William

Henry Harrison in 1841. Clearly, like Goodrich, Berard, Lossing, and nearly all other textbook authors of the antebellum era, she was unprepared to explain where the national debates over slavery came from but greatly feared where they were headed.

Her expanded text of the early 1850s revealed that she had undergone a remarkable transformation in her thinking about American history and the place of slavery and race in it. She now saw the study of American history as essential for youth and critical for the nation's survival. It would not only discourage vice but would suppress "bold and criminal ambition." It would encourage a desire for "greatness," offering examples "which our children can draw from." Compared to ancient and corrupt Europe, she declared, "the character of America is that of youthful simplicity, of maiden purity," and the country had proved itself "the most virtuous among nations." The settlement of the American continent, to her mind, had been a long process of redeeming a wilderness from godless savages and transforming it into a home for the American "new race." This transformative power could be seen in the story of Pocahontas, who, she now wrote, in marrying John Rolfe became a hero and white.

Willard spent little time recounting the history of colonial slavery, and as so many others had done, she now used the incorrect 1620 date for its introduction to the English colonies. Unwilling to examine slavery's history, she simply asserted her disdain for its introduction. Clearly seeking to retain the idea of national "maiden purity," she shifted blame for slavery's introduction to England. Just as John H. Van Evrie focused on the alleged English threat to American liberty, Willard turned her sights on Great Britain for forcing slavery on an unwilling nation. Moreover, she asserted, "the Queen herself became afterwards a party to this atrocious merchandize." Having now developed a conspiratorial view of slavery and American history, she was willing to detail aspects of the slave trade that she and others previously had largely ignored. With remarkable accuracy for her time, she emphasized that before the American Revolution about "nine millions" of Africans had been brought to the Western Hemisphere, with "hundreds of thousands" imported into the United States. As no other textbook author had done, not even Charles A. Goodrich, Willard condemned the horrors of the Middle Passage and the entire trade, in particular focusing the youthful reader's attention on the seizure of African children: "They shriek,—they seek to burst their chains, that they may plunge into the deep." Those who survived were "sold like cattle—and bought to labor beneath burning suns, till they die!" The introduction of slavery, Willard now asserted, had been "an evil so vast in its consequences, and so difficult now to eradicate."

Asserting that England had forced an impossible choice on unsuspecting Americans, and disdaining the African presence, her textbook argued for the kind of compromises that had created the republic in 1787. The three-fifths clause of the Constitution, defining representation in Congress, and the end of the slave trade, for instance, had proved to be workable agreements that rescued the new nation from the abyss: "an example to future times." Now, however, the South could never abandon slavery "without ruin," and the national government could never compel its termination, because "the American republic is powerless" due to the constitutional guarantee that each state was "a sovereign." Any movement to end slavery, she warned, would bring about the "downfall of the American republic." Only "gradual emancipation" offered the prospect of ending an evil and retaining national unity. But exactly what she meant by "gradual emancipation" remained unclear.

Much as her contemporary John H. Van Evrie would argue a short time later, Willard decried abolitionism as a dangerous evil fomented by English monarchists to destroy the American nation, which stood alone against corrupt Europe as an "anti-monarchical state." American abolitionists, a group she never described, fomented anarchy and played directly into English hands by claiming "negro slavery to be that one sin, by which alone humanity is debased." Their opposition to the 1850 Fugitive Slave Law, she argued, had been cooked up by the British, who had sent their agent, the abolitionist George Thompson, to the United States to stir up a crisis. This subterfuge, she argued, followed the script of the nation's foreign enemies. Abolitionism, she warned, was a plot fomented by "our enemies" who "SEEK TO DIVIDE US." Sane minds instead would look to gradual emancipation, which would preserve the South's interests and over time could remove the unwanted element. She argued that the South had modified and "softened" slavery to the point that it eliminated its worst aspects and thus made compromises possible. The North should recognize the South's efforts at improving "the colored race," and that Southerners were turning their "servants" into "intellectual, moral, and religious beings." She now maintained, as Van Evrie would shortly afterward, that no "slaves" existed in the South, only servants. Southerners did not own Black humans, just their "time." In "a great part of the South" now, most "blacks are allowed . . . the holding of property, and the disposing a portion of their own time. . . . They are, as they should be, called servants, rather than slaves." The American Colonization Society's Liberian project was a safety valve, where the "surplus colored population" could go, offering relief to the nation and at the same time transforming Africa "into [a] Christian civilization." Such "emigrants," she imagined, while enjoying a far better life as American "servants" than they would have led in their homeland, could now return there and become a "gleam of moral light" that would illuminate "the darkness of their [brethren's] minds." Following this invented path could ensure American "maiden purity," "abolish" slavery, and attain national compromise.

In the momentous dawning of 1860, the nation's textbook authors struggled to sustain patriotism, face the increasing political and social strife, and somehow set it within a national narrative. Willard saw in history a model for compromise, but like John H. Van Evrie, she sought to alter the nation's understanding of slavery rather than change its actual circumstances. The English Quaker poet, novelist, and antislavery advocate Mary Howitt (1799–1888) tried a more direct approach. Howitt had written, translated, or edited about 110 works, and in 1860 she brought out an American edition of *A Popular History of the United States,* which had been published in England the year before. With an outsider's perspective, vast experience in literature (along with her equally accomplished husband, William), an international reputation, and a firm antislavery commitment, she was positioned to overturn the popular understanding of American history. She had met and become friends with the radical abolitionist William Lloyd Garrison in 1840, when he attended the World Anti-Slavery Convention in London. As she recorded in her autobiography, the 1840s were a critical time for her, as abolitionism "wholly absorbed my thoughts." In August 1845 she again met with Garrison and confessed:

> I am just now deeply interested in the Anti-Slavery question, the real, thorough Abolitionist view, which would cut up this original sin root and branch, and spare none of its participators. Our friend, William Lloyd Garrison is now in London, with one of the most interesting men I ever saw, a runaway slave, Frederick Douglass. The narrative of his life, written by himself, is most beautiful and affecting.

About five years later Howitt published *Our Cousins in Ohio,* what she described as a true story of distant relatives who lived near the banks of the Ohio River at the "Cedars." At the home of

Mary Botham Howitt (1799–1888) was a popular English author. Her remarkable *A Popular History of the United States* reflected her Quaker horror at the institution of slavery. It had only one American edition and, predictably, was quickly forgotten. Steel engraving after a painting by Margaret Gillies, undated.

"Herbert and Meggy," a former slave named Adele tells "the children and their mother a great deal about her sufferings." She was brought to Indiana by her owners, who managed to keep her in servitude by threatening to send her son back to Georgia if she did not continue to serve the family and so fully pay for his freedom. Howitt's anti-slavery sympathies could not have been clearer, as was her joy when local abolitionists rescued Adele and her son.

Howitt's two-volume history, in which she confidently revealed her gender, relied heavily on some of the best American histories available at the time, works by George Bancroft and especially by the abolitionist Richard Hildreth. In every way, Howitt's work sur-passed all previous histories in its fluid literary style. A true narrative without the vexing paragraph numbers and questions, she began with Viking explorations of North America and moved quickly to Columbus and the early explorers of the Western Hemisphere. She described the region's native inhabitants as willing trading partners and offered sympathetic accounts of the Aztecs, crushed by Cortes and Spain. Her first mention of slavery came without special treat-ment, referring to it as a practice that resulted from the need for labor, with the Dutch as North America's principal traders.

Her book was one of the few to pay special attention to slavery in the North, especially in New York, and to New England's par-ticipation in the slave trade. She noted with subtle disapproval the fact that Virginia hardened its slave laws during the early 1660s and reminded readers, which would have infuriated *De Bow's Review*, that the new slave codes eliminated any reference to the adoption of Christianity as an exemption from enslavement. In an unmistakable rebuke, she wrote that the new codes refused to consider the killing of a slave as a criminal act. As virtually no one else had, Howitt discussed South Carolina's 1712 slave code, detailing the enumerated crimes and punishments, which she reprinted from Hildreth's mas-sive six-volume U.S. history, allowing the code to speak the horror for itself. She then decried such laws still enforced in the South, which, "not contented with outraging humanity in the person of the slaves, proceeds to insult and blaspheme Christianity." Likely borrowing from Egbert Guernsey, she detailed the so-called 1741

New York slave revolt, also comparing it to the Salem witchcraft trials. She denounced as bogus the subsequent New York conspiracy trial that led to the execution of so many African Americans, and she condemned New York's white officials as committing judicial murder and bearing shameful "blood-guiltiness."

With her unprecedented criticisms of American slavery, Howitt went further and disparaged the North's favorite racial reform, the activities of the American Colonization Society. The society claimed to be benevolent and Christian, she wrote, but "the true benevolence" would be to "gradually, wisely and justly abolish slavery—[and] to prepare the black man to be a good and useful citizen of a great and free country." Moreover, as no one had ever even considered including in a textbook, Howitt cast doubt on the genuineness of the American liberty won in the Revolution. Discussing the growing breach between the American colonies and her own country over parliamentary and colonial powers, she could not help but observe the "inconsistency of contending for their own liberty and depriving other people of theirs." Although she completed the book in 1859, Howitt tellingly ended her arresting account of American history in 1850, with the compromise over slavery. Perhaps in fear of endangering the book's sales, she avoided any further discussion and instead indulged in a catalogue of American achievements and grand economic developments, ending her assessment with the astonishing declaration that "politically and morally, the Republic of the United States has been a grand, successful experiment." Within two years, however, that "experiment" would come to a disastrous end, entirely because of the institution that she had so honestly and directly attacked with her well-crafted work.

Through the years of the Civil War and shortly after, publishing houses scrambled to reprint past moneymakers. The Philadelphia firm E. H. Butler & Co. reprinted Samuel G. Goodrich's richly successful *Pictorial History of the United States,* and two presses combined to bring out brother Charles's updated *History,* with additional chapters tacked on to cover the Civil War. But neither mentioned the abolitionists, who after the war enjoyed a sense of celebratory appreciation that they had never seen prior to 1865. Brother Charles may have been the first textbook author to mention John Brown by name, although as would be standard fare after Reconstruction, he characterized him as "mad." While the new edition, which came out in 1867, strongly condemned slavery, it lacked any coherent discussion of the beginning of Reconstruction. Hence the message to white students: Black lives did not matter.

Most of brother Samuel's *Pictorial History* had remained essentially unchanged since the 1850s, with the exception of its final pages. Now the revised and expanded version asserted that Southern leaders had misled the people of the South, teaching them to "despise and hate the people of the North." With wonderful cunning, they had led their fellow citizens to believe that slavery, "in every way injurious to them—was absolutely necessary to their prosperity." They even invented the right to secession to protect their interests and prove that the United States was nothing but a compact that could be dissolved "at will." The book presented the standard Republican position that the North had recognized the South's right to slavery where it existed, thus freeing the North from the taint of abolitionism and exculpating it from any responsibility in causing so disastrous a conflict. With the war over, both brothers' revised books expressed decidedly more hostility toward the institution of slavery, but somehow Samuel Goodrich's *Pictorial History* forgot to mention the Emancipation Proclamation.

4

The Emancipationist
Challenge, 1867 to 1883

Our country may still be teacher and leader of the nations toward a higher and nobler civilization—toward justice, right, and liberty.

—Charles Carleton Coffin, *Building the Nation,* 1883

Textbooks quickly incorporated the Civil War into the narrative of the nation's history. But it would take several years before they began to fully explain the meaning of the transformation overtaking the United States as a result of the war. John Bonner's two-volume 1855 *A Child's History of the United States,* for instance, had celebrated the extinction of Native Americans and perceived U.S. history as the record of the "White Man's" progress over the godless red savage. It largely ignored slavery and Blacks. The 1866 edition, however, displayed a dramatic conversion, not only focusing on African Americans but emphasizing their heroism during the war and their assistance to the Union cause. Although he did not name South Carolina's Robert Smalls, he did inform readers that a Black man had seized a Confederate vessel and that a Black woman had saved the life of a Union soldier. Such heroism, Bonner wrote, implicitly repudiated the prejudice against the freedpeople and demonstrated that "there was something manly in the negroes after all." The book celebrated emancipation and credited Northerners with pushing Lincoln to "strike a blow at slavery." He even predicted that "you will live to see the day on which" Lincoln issued the Emancipation Proclamation "kept as a national anniversary."

Other texts from the 1850s similarly saw revisions that took up the themes of emancipation and even predictions that the freedpeople would receive the "rights of citizens." Blacks would see, Bonner wrote, "equal civil and political rights and privileges with other citizens, such as the elective franchise."

In the first years after the war, although textbooks began to include African Americans and slavery in the national narrative, stereotypes and derogatory characterizations persisted and actually became more intense against Native Americans. Charles A. Goodrich's 1867 edition of his popular textbook carefully located many tribes on a detailed map but resorted to simpleminded and pejorative assertions about Native American life, claiming "them" to be "taciturn and unsocial, except when roused by some strong excitement." When angered, Indians became determined enemies that no danger could deter, "neither absence nor time could cool them." The book dismissed Native women as "squaws" and drudges. William Swinton's 1872 *First Lessons in Our Country's History* seemed better calculated to inflame, if not incite prejudice, then educate. His book at first appeared to be sympathetic, beginning with the assertion that "from the first day that white colonists set their feet on the soil of North America, the natives of that soil were doomed." But the fault lay with the Natives, not with the invaders. The guns that Indians obtained from whites "made them reckless in their destruction of game, and rendered their petty wars more frequent and more bloody." The rum whites sold Native inhabitants turned them into "brutes." Even the clothing they obtained from whites caused them to abandon furs and hides, leading to "sickness and consumption." In response to white greediness and seizures of land, "the red man became crafty, revengeful, and murderous. And this state of feeling lasts even down to the present day."

The revised 1867 textbook of "Peter Parley's" brother Charles A. Goodrich also retained discouraging elements of the 1858 edition, including the annoying numbered paragraphs. It spent more time discussing the colonial era's importation of prospective English wives than slaves, and it continued to date the introduction of slavery at 1620. It failed to discuss the antislavery movement and still labeled

John Brown "mad." But William Seavey's revisions of the text clearly displayed the dramatic impact of the antislavery movement and the Civil War. In an unprecedented addition inserted after discussion of the nation's founding, Goodrich and Seavey now included a strong antislavery statement. Despite the American Revolution's proclamation of the rights of man, the new edition declared, "and in violation of the principles enumerated in the Declaration of Independence, by which the revolt had been justified to the world, [slavery] remained undisturbed in all the states." Moreover, despite some Northern moves against slavery and the judgment of the "wisest and best men of the time," an institution so "repugnant to the principles of Christianity and so fraught with danger to society, religion, and the state" remained "riveted" to the South.

Students now obtained a glorious view of the American Revolution but one tempered by the nation's failure to end slavery, as Seavey wrote, despite the Founding Fathers' justifications of independence grounded in the "rights of man." Moreover, because of the Civil War, slavery moved to the center of the national narrative. Slavery and the justifying ideology of states' rights, the book explained, lay at the heart of the conflict. The revised text damned the Civil War as *"wicked,"* the result of "restless ambition of designing men" begun by some of the slave states "jealous of the growing political power of the free states." Secession, intended to perpetuate "the system of human bondage," instead "has struck the chains from every American slave." Additionally, slavery had caused the South to fall economically behind the North and produce "a large class, known as *poor whites,*" a people "sunk in a condition of misery, ignorance, and depravity, but little removed from that of the slave." Similarly, while Swinton's *First Lessons* portrayed the Emancipation Proclamation as a central result of the war, the revised text, like so many others, ignored the role of Black troops. Even when discussing battles that included regiments of Black soldiers, Goodrich and Seavey failed to mention their participation. They discussed the July 18, 1863, Union assault on Battery Wagner, outside Charleston, South Carolina, but failed to mention the 54th Massachusetts Regiment's role in the attack or the death of its legendary commander, Robert

Gould Shaw. Astonishingly, it included an account of the April 12, 1864, Confederate attack on Fort Pillow, but only to point out the viciousness of the engagement, not the fact that Nathan Bedford Forrest's soldiers massacred the surrendering Black troops—which went unmentioned. Such works, published shortly after the war, dramatically highlighted the national struggle over slavery but did not fully challenge the nation's racial hierarchy—yet.

Even into the 1870s, textbooks continued to follow the standard formats, often made the same errors, and continued to emphasize a political narrative, to the exclusion of the antislavery movement and most everything else outside politics. But significant changes had begun. David B. Scott's *A School History of the United States* was one of the first to emphasize the impact of Eli Whitney's cotton gin on the growth of slavery, and it more thoroughly incorporated the issue of slavery into the politics of the mid-nineteenth century, without the genuflections to Henry Clay, Daniel Webster, and John C. Calhoun that had been so much a part of the prewar narrative. Moreover, Scott's textbook examined the war that exploded in Kansas after Stephen A. Douglas's 1854 Kansas-Nebraska Act as indicative of the bitterness over slavery that erupted "throughout the country," a process that the student now learned had been building for thirty years. In an unusual innovation, his textbook halted its narrative to specify the distinct political causes of the Civil War, which it identified as the transformation of the South since 1793 and the development of slavery. Each section of the country, Scott explained, "was grievously mistaken about the feelings of the other, and a single spark was all that was needed to fire the magazine." But unwilling to risk sales in the South or to be forced to question American racial views, the author abruptly dropped all discussion of slavery and the results of the war, then breezed through 1865 so he could discuss the settlement of the Pacific coast.

John J. Anderson, a New York City grammar school principal, published a catechism-style elementary school text in 1867 and a popular grammar school history the following year, which saw reprintings until at least 1882. Each volume retained all the vexing qualities of traditional textbooks but shifted emphasis to explain the coming of the Civil War. They both expressed hostility to secession, and the catechism, though it contained no sense of narrative, did instruct young students in the "memorable proclamation" of Abraham Lincoln. Anderson closed the book with the adoption of the Thirteenth Amendment to the Constitution, which ended slavery, punctuating the new theme emerging in schoolbooks. His traditional school history text, which was used in New Haven, Connecticut, in the 1880s and in Southern Black schools, made a point of describing John Brown's raid at Harpers Ferry not as the act of a madman but as a central event in the chronology leading up to the Civil War. Regarding national strife over slavery, he rehearsed the traditional political narrative from 1820 through the contentious 1850s but left out anything not directly related to political history, such as the abolitionist movement. Unlike most other texts published right after the Civil War, Anderson's book did discuss the beginning of Reconstruction and Congress's battle with President Andrew Johnson, even his impeachment. In a dramatic move, he characterized Congress's war with President Johnson as a heroic determination to prevent restoration of the Union "until certain guarantees of protection should be extended to the colored population."

But textbook authors could not explain the full significance of the war to their readers until that meaning played out in the pivotal battles over Reconstruction. The new civil rights laws, the passage of the Thirteenth, Fourteenth, and Fifteenth amendments to the Constitution, and debates over the role of African Americans in the political and social structure had to take place before textbooks could express precisely what all the debates, combat, and sacrifices signified. The dramatic consequences of emancipation clearly began to engulf the nation as soon as the fighting ended. As Confederate forces slowly demobilized in the East and the final clashes in the West played out in the spring of 1865, African Americans and their white political allies started planning for what they hoped would be a new era of freedom. Hardened by experience but nurtured by the democratic promise embedded in the country's highest ideals, antislavery forces leaped at the chance to remake the nation

Frederick Douglass (1818–95) embodied the African American quest for freedom, liberty, and equality. No understanding of the impact of white supremacy, before and after the Civil War, is possible without his perspective. Charles Milton Bell, photographer, 1881.

and redirect its history. Reconstruction, the immensely promising *and* frustrating era resulting from the war, required leaders of the caliber of Frederick Douglass and Senator Charles Sumner. They, along with the rest of the North, confronted the most fundamental of questions concerning the meaning of the Civil War, the nature of the economic order, the limits of social control, the definition of freedom—and exactly who should benefit from it.

Understandably, many in the North, having grown weary of death and destruction, craved peace and tranquility. Hardly a family existed that had not suffered some grievous loss or profound trauma, and Lincoln's assassination only accentuated the North's grief. As a result, some—especially the new president, Andrew Johnson— looked for ways to quickly heal the country, forget the past, and reunite all white citizens for a more benign future. But after so much sacrifice and suffering, and two hundred years of brutal enslavement and racial repression, antislavery forces across the North refused to let this moment slip. "Don't tell me," Frederick Douglass thundered, that the people down there have become so just and honest all at once that they will not pass laws denying to black men the right to testify against white men in the courts of law. Why, our Northern States have done it. Illinois, Indiana and Ohio have done it . . . and if the Legislatures of every Southern State to-morrow pass a law declaring that no negro shall testify in any court of law, they will not violate that provision of the Constitution. Such laws exist now at the South. The next day, the Legislatures may pass a law that any black man who shall lift his arm in self-defense, even, against a white man, shall have that arm severed from his body, and may be hanged and quartered. . . . Slavery is not abolished until the black man has the ballot.

Just so there would be no misunderstanding, Maj. Martin R. Delany, editor, writer, abolitionist, and the highest-ranking African American in the U.S. Army, advised President Johnson that to "secure and perpetuate the Union," the national government needed to enfranchise Black men. Moreover, it must recognize the "political equality of the power that saved the nation from destruction— a recognition of the political equality of the blacks with the whites in all their relations as American citizens." Delany symbolized the African American role in the war, an indispensable force that had served as soldiers, sailors, scouts, and stevedores, without whom no victory would have been possible. At the close of 1865, Massachusetts's legendary abolitionist senator Charles Sumner reiterated Delany's stand and counseled his colleagues that "the power that gave freedom must see that freedom is maintained." He warned the president and his reluctant colleagues that the newly freed people of the South must not be "handed over to the tender mercies of [their] former owners." Slavery, Sumner advised, "must be abolished not in form only, but in substance, so that there shall be no Black Code, but all shall be Equal before the Law." Reports he received of atrocities inflicted on former slaves outraged and disgusted him. How could the U.S. Senate tolerate the incineration of little Black girls?

he cried out. Such frightful barbarism must not be tolerated, he exclaimed, and the North must recognize that one war had been replaced by another: *"The South is determined to have Slavery,—the thing, if not the name."* Without federal protections and guarantees, he warned, the South would immediately return to the "old system, with all its mitigations rescinded and all its horrors intensified." That same December Sumner introduced a bill to outlaw any discrimination or denial of rights "on account of race or color." All persons, his civil rights bill made clear, were "recognized as equal before the law." It passed the Senate on January 11, 1866.

Charles Sumner (1811–74), statesman, Massachusetts senator, and pivotal Radical Republican, was the North's most important advocate for African American civil rights. Frederick Douglass praised him as the "Wilberforce of America." This 1854 lithograph by Leopold Grozelier (1830–65), after a portrait by William Wetmore Story, hung in Douglass's Washington, D.C., home.

Sumner was well informed about white Southern resistance to the end of slavery. No shortage of information existed about the South's unwavering resistance to *any* change in the status of freedpeople. In fact, given the extraordinarily permissive surrender terms that General Grant offered to General Lee and the Confederate army, many rebel soldiers came away from the battlefield entirely without a sense of defeat. And the unremitting violence they inflicted on African American Union soldiers—when they could get away with it—fully revealed the South's unrelenting determination to reject defeat and Black freedom. Occupying Union troops, Freedmen's Bureau agents, and a host of journalists, abolitionists, teachers, and missionaries—Black and white—who either labored in or canvassed the South, informed Northern leaders of the brutal Southern opposition to Black freedom and Northern rule. As the Pulitzer Prize–winning historian Leon F. Litwack wrote over forty years ago, "The planter class made every effort to retain the essential features of the old work discipline." *Any* departure from the old racial order on the part of the freedpeople unhinged the "entire network of controls and restraints" and undermined the "very basis of the social order" as well as the labor system. White Southerners could not tolerate the fact that their former property had won freedom, much less that they would dare to act like free people. They must, Southern whites insisted, show utter and "complete deference."

African Americans who went south to assess the situation for themselves understood that the future of Black freedom hung precariously between Northern hatred of the defeated rebels and the relentless fanaticism of Northern white supremacists. Jermain Wesley Loguen, an African Methodist Episcopal Zion clergyman and Syracuse, New York's legendary underground railroad activist, returned to Tennessee in July 1865 to visit the plantation he had escaped from thirty-two years earlier and to preach to the emancipated. Hoping he might discover someone he previously had known, Loguen instead found his own mother, who, old and "feeble," nonetheless traveled ten miles to "hear her long-lost son." He also discovered much change. In the "place of slave-pens," he reported to New York's influential *Weekly Anglo-African,* "you will see churches and schoolrooms filled with happy souls." Local Blacks, he reported, stood ready to assist those who came "to help in the great work of elevation." But the *Northern* whites he found roaming the Nashville-Knoxville region turned out to be "meaner than the Southerners; yes, meaner than the rebels themselves." The African American, he warned, desperately needed the presence of the Union army to achieve "his God-given rights granted and guaranteed to him." Without such protection, Loguen explained, Black rights were doomed.

A concerned Northern public could rely on skilled reporters to go south to assess the depth of white resistance. John Richard Dennett (1838–74), an 1862 Harvard graduate who had worked with freedmen at Port Royal, South Carolina, became the university's professor of rhetoric in 1870, then resigned his post after only two years to take over as literary editor of the *Nation*. Tall, robust, and looking like he just stepped out of a Thackeray novel, Dennett had been hired by the *Nation* in 1865 to report on his travels throughout the South. This New York–based journal, meant to be the successor to William Lloyd Garrison's *Liberator*, had been established with the backing of John Brown supporter George Luther Stearns, Pennsylvania abolitionist James Miller McKim, and other prominent reformers. Its owners hired the British-born E. L. Godkin and Wendell Phillips Garrison—the Liberator's son—to manage and edit the journal. Over the course of its long history, stretching to this very day, the *Nation* was home to many of the country's leading intellectuals. It began life as an aggressive critic of the South and an advocate for Radical Reconstruction. It hired Dennett to reveal the full extent of white Southern resistance to the North and the fate of African Americans. By interviewing whites, Dennett confirmed the startling reality that Douglass and Sumner had declared to all who would listen. The white South regarded the enfranchisement of African Americans as utterly unthinkable and would not tolerate it. Putting Black and white on the same political footing "would make the South fight," Dennett reported and, as Reverend Loguen had warned, would require a permanent standing army to enforce. Near Kingstree, South Carolina, Dennett encountered an anonymous white landowner who denounced all Blacks as thieves and candidly confessed, "I look forward to the extermination of the freedmen."

In the year following the end of the war, Dennett and the *Nation*'s other reporters revealed the lethal challenge faced by those just liberated. As the journal warned in August 1865, the "slavocracy exists to-day in almost as much force as it existed before a shot had been exchanged." In some ways, it was even stronger, the *Nation* insisted: "Its spirit is fiercer and more bitter than it was before the war. . . . Our Southern slaveholders . . . still retain the slaveholding spirit without keeping the slave" and had become more of an "oligarchy—as ever existed." Southern whites felt as though they had been beaten by their inferiors, "flogged by the peasant" as they quaintly expressed it, and fully meant to rise again. The South would not accept either defeat or Black freedom. To underscore its point, the *Nation* revealed the horrifying fate of a freedman in Jonesboro, Tennessee, who had escaped from his plantation and sought protection in a Union camp. His former master caught up with him and savagely severed the man's feet.

Frederick Douglass recognized that the North remained riven by racists like John H. Van Evrie and a Democratic Party that sought Reconstruction's complete defeat. Even without such entrenched political opposition, the North struggled with conflicting political interests and unstable racial views to find the most reliable and just path to re-create the United States without slavery. Although many white Northern leaders lacked confidence in Black enfranchisement, it nonetheless represented the strongest path to maintaining control over the former rebels, reinforcing Republican political control, and offering some guarantee for the protection of the freedpeople. But under Godkin's leadership, the *Nation*—like the rest of the North— soon wavered in its support for Black rights, believing that enough "has been done for the negro, and that he may now be left to take care of himself." Since Northern whites had almost no contact with Blacks and understood little or nothing about the realities of Black life even in the North, some wondered if the "Negro" would die out *"just as the Indians have."*

Yet even as the reform spirit began to wilt in 1869, the *Nation* acknowledged that the "last thing we can do for him [the former slave] is to pass the Fifteenth Amendment." Until that point, however, equal suffrage had been the very *minimum* change that reformers, abolitionists, and Northern Republicans had insisted on for the freedpeople and the South. The Federal government, the journal had asserted in 1866, "is bound by every consideration of justice, honor, and decency either to see that the freedmen enjoy complete security or to furnish them with the means of protecting themselves." They had earned at least that. Moreover, such action would ensure that the war would be seen as one not of conquest but rather "of liberation." Dedicated political leaders like Sumner looked to Haiti and Russia for lessons on how to confront the problem of the newly emancipated. While most white Americans viewed the freedpeople as only a labor problem, the eloquent Boston abolitionist Wendell Phillips reminded them that they were "not simply freedmen. They are a part of the American commonwealth; and we seek their education, elevation, and happiness." The United States, he insisted, "owes him land; it owes him education. . . . It is a debt that will disgrace us before the people if we do not pay it." Anything less, he avowed, would be a moral outrage.

.   .   .

While the antislavery vanguard of Phillips, Douglass, Sumner, and their colleagues—along with the Republican Party—struggled after 1865 to create the future, the American past and the textbooks that recounted it increasingly took on an entirely new sense of urgency and mission. Because the struggle for justice and full democracy lay at the heart of Reconstruction, authors began diminishing—and for a time eliminating—the demands of white supremacy that had previously dominated American history textbooks. Their work reflected the beginnings of a changing national identity and so helped reshape national memory and redefine what in the past now mattered to Americans.

At the most general level, school textbooks always have played a central role in the creation of historical memory. The values and critical events that a country incorporates into its memory build the broadest possible political consensus, along with personal and national identity. Historical memory, as Yale University's David Blight explains, functions as a kind of "master narrative" that citizens carry with them to guide their thinking and shape social and political life. As one author of the 1890s advised, schoolbooks aimed to "awaken the spirit of patriotism" with "the heroes of the home, the hospital, the flood, and the field, men and women alike . . . bright examples for the young to follow." Before 1861, most history textbooks had stressed white domination over Native Americans and political narratives that glorified the American Revolution and the presidency—resisting any systematic discussion of the issue of slavery and completely ignoring the Black contributions that made America possible. But between the Civil War and the turn of the twentieth century, a new, more inclusive master narrative emerged. The facts about the eras of exploration, colonization, revolution, and the political growth of the American republic, of course, remained. George Bancroft and Francis Parkman would always beguile the reader with the romance of conquest and emergence of the new democratic republic. That history rightly endures, as part of the story of how the United States came about. But after 1865, the Civil War and the national struggle over slavery—even novels like Harriet Beecher Stowe's *Uncle Tom's Cabin*—moved to the center of the country's new master narrative, becoming a primary focus of the American teaching curriculum. Moreover, in a stunning move, textbooks began incorporating the history of slavery and Blacks into the mainstream of American history in a way that would not be seen again for nearly seventy years.

Elisha Mulford's *The Nation: The Foundations of Civil Order and Political Life in the United States* (1870) reflected the new master narrative that emerged after the war to reshape the nation's textbooks and its political and social goals. Mulford (1833–85), now largely forgotten, was born in Montrose, Pennsylvania, and attended Yale, where he ignored the growing antislavery movement and focused on obtaining legal training. After graduation, he dropped the law and attended Union Theological Seminary and the Andover Theological Seminary, an orthodox Protestant bastion founded by refugees from Harvard who could not tolerate the university's turn toward Unitarianism. He entered the Episcopalian Church, traveled to Germany, and studied with the influential philosopher Georg Wilhelm Friedrich Hegel. While he never achieved stability, a permanent pulpit, or a teaching position, his major works had enduring impact. Mulford's *The Nation* played a critical role in forging Reconstruction's antiracist, egalitarian foundations, and his 1881 treatise, *The Republic of God,* helped shape the social gospel movement of the late nineteenth and early twentieth century.

In many ways, Mulford's 1870 work is an astonishing production, fully deserving Charles Sumner's praise of it as "a very thoughtful masterful book, showing scholarship, taste & good principles." In unprecedented ways for a work outside the canon of antislavery rhetoric, Mulford's study repudiated white supremacy, the "Aryan spirit and Aryan life." His exploration into political philosophy rejected any identification of the nation "with a race," which he saw as antithetical to "moral unity and moral order." Indeed, his work proclaimed that a country that rested on the "rights of a race, and not the rights of man" was a country that would die. The Civil War had transformed him. Even before imagining such a work, while ministering to a congregation in New Jersey, he had concluded that Christianity must be the foundation of a true community, uniting "rich and the poor, in one common service," to realize the "common Fatherhood of God, and the Brotherhood of Christ." He soon came to view the Civil War not only as a struggle between freedom and slavery but as a contest for the very life of the nation. The South's assault on the Union, he later wrote, was a sin "in league with hell." But his New Jersey congregants failed to appreciate his new ideas, ostracized him, and eventually forced his "retirement" to Friendsville, Pennsylvania, where he wrote *The Nation.*

For Mulford, the country owed its existence to God and must embrace all who lived in it. No "sect and no faction" could claim any "exclusive possession" of it. The very idea of nationhood was "*a continuity . . .*, reaching back to the fathers and forward to the children." It was a "predetermined" whole, not simply the sum of its parts. It existed as a "moral organism," and its citizens were "moral parts" who found fulfillment in freedom. As personhood derived from God, "the life of each must be held sacred, his worth must be allowed, his dignity must be regarded, his freedom must have in the nation its maintenance and its sphere." Citing James Kent's *Commentaries on the Law,* a four-volume analysis of law and legal theory that helped shape American jurisprudence, Mulford grounded the quest for equal rights in Kent's idea that all people "born in the nation" are its citizens—without exception—"irrespective of ancestry, and consists with a national not a racial principle" (2:39). For

Mulford—as for Sumner and those who led Reconstruction's effort at national transformation—a nation could reach full realization only with full freedom. Slavery had been the country's "necessary antagonist," and in order for the "nation" to reach fruition and fulfill God's intent, it "must overcome and destroy slavery, or at last be destroyed by it."

Elisha Mulford (1833–85) was the author of *The Nation: The Foundations of Civil Order and Political Life in the United States* (1870). An enemy of white supremacy, Mulford embodied the egalitarian Emancipationist ideals of the North after the Civil War. James Harvey Young, oil on canvas, 1890, now in the Yale University Art Gallery.

Mulford believed that a true nation fulfilled a divine mission, but a "confederacy" lacked divine foundations and was "the exclusive possession of those who have constructed it; its government is their agent, its justice the scheme of their legislators." For a "confederacy," the "end of society is the securance and furtherance of private interests, its order is the balance of those interests, its government is the representation of those interests; its primary and exclusive function is their protection." The Civil War had been a struggle not between freedom and slavery, but between a legitimate, rights-driven, divinely inspired "nation," and a class-riven confederacy and dictatorship. Mulford imagined this confrontation as ultimate moral combat, in which the Confederacy was "in league with hell." In conception, the Confederacy denied the divinely inspired origin of the nation and humanity "and the sacred rights it bears in its divine image." The government of a "nation," on the other hand, was grounded in the "determination of its manhood and in the spirit of the people. And not in the accidents of life, as property or occupation, or rank, or color, or race." Citizenship in "the nation," Mulford avowed, inherently repudiated class domination and white supremacy. Published in the midst of Reconstruction, Mulford's book was a rich and explosive declaration of universal American freedom.

After the postwar civil rights legislation and the February 1870 adoption of the Fifteenth Amendment to the Constitution guaranteeing African American suffrage (or so some Americans assumed), the nation's textbooks took on a far more vigorous Emancipationist perspective. Samuel Eliot's 1874 textbook unmistakably instructed students that tensions had *always* existed between North and South, and that the "great line of distinction was run by slavery." Moreover, sectional conflict over "this thorny subject, so far from being smoothed by the compromises of the Constitution, stood up as bristling as ever." Eliot (1821–98), a Harvard graduate, Trinity College president, member of the Massachusetts Historical Society, and grandfather to historian Samuel Eliot Morison, pinpointed 1831 as the critical turning point in the nation's history. The Nat Turner slave rebellion and the near-simultaneous appearance of William Lloyd Garrison's *Liberator* had changed the character of the country. Southern moderates disappeared, replaced by pro-slavery hotheads, while in the North attempts to repress Garrison and his antislavery colleagues transformed the nation's political life into a profound contest between slavery and freedom. Northern abolitionism had been bound to grow, "notwithstanding all the weakness of its friends and all the strength of its foes." This, Eliot proclaimed in unprecedented language for a textbook, led to the Civil War, a tragic event that endowed the nation with "the sense of suffering in a great cause, and of contributing to great ends—the emancipation of four million slaves [and] the union of forty million freemen."

Other texts censured the Supreme Court for its abominable

1857 *Dred Scott* decision, which one 1879 book explained not only displayed the "failure of the Supreme Court as an arbiter" but also drew the North's attention to the "impracticable demands of the slave-owners." Others included activities outside the standard political narrative, such as the antislavery petition campaign of the 1830s, the creation of the American Anti-Slavery Society, and the growth of the abolitionist movement. Beginning to display liberation from traditional formats, Alexander Johnston's 1882 *History of American Politics* relied on many Emancipationist sources, including histories by George Bancroft, the early volumes of Herman Von Holst's *Constitutional and Political History of the United States* (1876–81), Horace Greeley's 1866 *American Conflict,* and U.S. senator and vice president Henry Wilson's *Rise and Fall of the Slave Power* (1872–77). One Catholic U.S. history text even emphasized the role of Massachusetts in establishing slavery in the American colonies, noting that it was the first colony to legalize it and then threw itself into the slave trade just "as soon as they had any commerce at all." In its discussion of the 1820 Missouri Compromise, it laid out the pattern that would inevitably lead to war, holding the South responsible for its dedication to a vast army of slaves that would "produce great wealth to the planters." The 1820 crisis had clearly revealed the full depth of the sectional strife that would lead to war: a South dedicated to the expansion of slavery and the North insisting on its "confinement." As abolitionists cried out for slavery's elimination, William H. Seward in an 1858 address declared an "'irrepressible conflict' between free and slave labor." Moreover, the Catholic text treated John Brown respectfully, avoiding the common accusation that he was a madman. While it gave only passing mention to the Emancipation Proclamation and failed to discuss the antislavery movement or the use of African American troops during the war, it did provide a paragraph on the first American cardinal in 1875.

. . .

While we know that predominantly white schools across the country employed such textbooks, we know much less about those used in the South's new, post–Civil War schools for the emancipated.

A few examples may suggest how the transformation in historical memory could help advance democratic values. In the mid-1870s, approximately 177,000 African American children lived in Virginia, but only about 52,000 attended school. Average attendance hovered around a frustrating 29,000. Because of prejudice, poverty, geography, or school location, for every eighteen Black students, only three managed regular attendance, even in a school system that operated only half the year. But attendance represented only part of the challenge. John Wesley Cromwell (1846–1927), an African American educator, editor of the *People's Advocate,* and Republican Party activist, reported on Virginia Black education in 1875. Born in the state but raised in Philadelphia, Cromwell had graduated from the Institute for Colored Youth in 1863 and in 1874 earned a law degree from Howard University. He taught in American Missionary Association and AME Church schools and served as a postal clerk in Washington, D.C. He earned the reputation as a leading civil rights advocate, worked closely with the Black intellectual Rev. Alexander Crummell, and became one of the country's earliest chroniclers of African American history.

Attendance proved a daunting challenge, Cromwell pointed out in 1875, but the educational materials available to teachers and students could be far more damaging. No amount of honesty and dedication on the part of teachers, he warned, could overcome the devastating impact of ethnologists like Josiah Clark Nott and George R. Gliddon, whose white supremacist ideas suffused textbooks of all kinds, especially those originally published before the Civil War. Whatever the subject—geography, spelling, reading, even civics and history—Cromwell found their influence pervasive, systematically assaulting the idea of African American worth. A "firm, unshaken faith in the ability of the race" would be impossible to build, Cromwell cautioned in 1875, while such pernicious "education" justified oppression and checked Black "aspiration."

That same year, however, saw publication of a book that Cromwell would have approved: *Young Folks' History of the United States* by Thomas Wentworth Higginson (1823–1911). A Unitarian minister, thoroughgoing abolitionist, and John Brown "secret six" member,

Higginson had commanded the 1st South Carolina Volunteers during the Civil War. In print until at least 1909, his textbook remained enormously popular throughout the 1870s and '80s, in both public schools and private academies, from Massachusetts to Wisconsin and south to Virginia and South Carolina. It broke the textbook mold with fluent prose, illustrations, subject bibliographies, and even suggestions for readings in literature and poetry. With Higginson's antislavery credentials and his integration of slavery and abolitionism into the mainstream of American history, the book would have had a dramatic impact on its readers. It became a mainstay among the African American students at the Black school in Lottsburg, Virginia, founded in 1868 by the Garrisonian abolitionists Sallie Holley (1818–93) and Caroline F. Putnam (1826–1917).

Having met at Ohio's Oberlin College, the two women founded the Holley School during Reconstruction, operating it without tuition fees or salaries for themselves. Instead, they relied on their antislavery and women's networks for support, especially the wealthy New Yorker Gerrit Smith, and the Massachusetts reformers Louisa May Alcott and Sarah Blake Shaw, along with Sen. George Frisbie Hoar. Holley and Putnam possessed the deepest commitment to their students, both remaining at the school's helm until they died. In an 1885 letter to her former abolitionist colleague in Massachusetts, Samuel May, Jr., Putnam revealed that the two women used Higginson's book and that theirs was "the only school in Virginia that teaches his [Higginson's] history—praising John Brown!"

Higginson's exceptional text and its New England antislavery focus was certainly one that the two women working in Virginia would be gleeful to have. Virginia might be the oldest colony, he confessed, but he would start his history in "geographic order," beginning with the "new England states, because this arrangement will be easier to remember, and less confusing, than to regard only the order of time." Nor did his regional prejudice prevent him from detailing slavery there, as well as in New York, Pennsylvania, and Virginia. His antislavery background could be plainly seen, and he was one of the first authors to discuss Judge Samuel Sewall's 1700 antislavery pamphlet, *The Selling of Joseph.* He described the careers of the Quaker abolitionist Benjamin Lundy and William Lloyd Garrison. At the same time, he set the antislavery movement in the mainstream of American history, detailing the founding of the New England Anti-Slavery Society in 1832 and quoting at length from Garrison's explosive 1831 opening editorial statement in the *Liberator*. Garrison opposed all war and all bloodshed, he explained, thus dispatching to the trash heap of history the charge that he incited the Nat Turner rebellion. Higginson brought the debate over slavery out of Congress and into the streets, chronicling the intense opposition to Garrison and his colleagues throughout the North, the Bostonians of "property and standing" who threatened to lynch him, and those in Alton, Illinois, who did murder the antislavery editor Elijah P. Lovejoy.

Thomas Wentworth Higginson (1823–1911), a Unitarian minister and radical abolitionist, was one of John Brown's secret supporters. During the Civil War he commanded the African American 1st South Carolina Volunteers. Later a prominent editor, he published a highly successful history textbook, *Young Folks' History of the United States,* in 1875.

In detailing the political history of the country, he abandoned the prewar deification of Daniel Webster, Henry Clay, and John C. Calhoun. He instead called Calhoun "the great leader of the pro-slavery party," which sought to "uphold the interests of slavery, extend its influence, and secure its permanent duration." Texas annexation in 1845 represented no glorious example of the nation's "manifest destiny" to expand across the continent, but rather exemplified *slavery's* aggressive expansionism. To the more economically minded student, Higginson stressed that when the Union incorporated Texas, it absorbed its $7.5 million public debt. " 'Texas,' " he cheekily wrote, became " 'Taxes' with the letters differently arranged."

In Higginson's book, the 1850 Fugitive Slave Law became the key event leading directly to the Civil War; this law he damned as unconstitutional "as well as inhuman." Rather than dwelling on the standard political leaders of 1850 like Henry Clay, as most textbooks did, his work emphasized the antislavery orators Charles Sumner, Horace Mann, Wendell Phillips, and Theodore Parker. He offered no space to African American activists like Frederick Douglass, William C. Nell, Lewis and Harriet Hayden, James McCune Smith, or Henry Highland Garnet. He did, however, detail the tragic impact of the Fugitive Slave Law, discussing the Shadrack and Anthony Burns cases in Boston, the Jerry McHenry rescue in Syracuse, New York, and the truly heartbreaking tale of Margaret Garner in Cincin-

Frederick Juengling, "The Last Moments of John Brown," engraving after an 1884 painting by Thomas Hovenden, now in the Metropolitan Museum of Art.

nati, Ohio, who preferred to kill her children rather than allow them to be reenslaved.

Thereafter, Higginson's narrative became an antislavery political history, culminating in the failed uprising of John Brown, whom Higginson had supported and consistently characterized as an earnest liberator of the oppressed. He quoted the words of Virginia governor Henry Wise, who signed Brown's death warrant, and rejected any accusation that Brown was insane and instead described him as "a man of clear head, of courage, fortitude, and simple ingenuousness . . . a man of truth." He even began the legend that on the way to the gallows Brown kissed the forehead of a slave child. For Higginson, the history of the United States was a history of the struggle over slavery and, ultimately, its death in the Civil War. While he never mentioned his own combat service, he did detail the service of African American troops, specifically mentioning those who were first in the field, the 1st Kansas Volunteers and the 1st South Carolina Volunteers—the regiment he commanded. An African American student could find much to admire and affirm in Higginson's portrayal of Black military service and sacrifice, including the battles at Battery Wagner and Fort Pillow, and especially the Black troops that became the first Union forces to enter Richmond, Virginia, the Confederate capital. His book sped with antislavery fervor to the end of the Civil War and almost lyrically to the closing words from Lincoln's Gettysburg Address, that "government of the people, by the people, and for the people, shall not perish from the earth."

In Selma, Alabama, for its part, the Burrell School used postwar editions of John J. Anderson's *A Grammar School History of the United States*. Founded in 1866, Alabama's first school for African American children had been a joint venture of the American Missionary Association and the Freedmen's Bureau, and it operated in conjunction with city officials. It started out in a carpenter's shop but two years later received its own building, purchased by the AMA, and funded by an extraordinary grant of $10,000 from Jabez Burrell of Oberlin, Ohio. The principal was John Silsby, a stern temperance advocate, but a man dedicated to Black freedom who understood all too well the local hostility to the city's African American population. A "great moral warfare yet remains to be endured," he informed the AMA, "as slavery is not yet fully dead much less is the Negro enfranchised." Indeed, Selma's former slave owners continued to oppress their former workers, still lashing children who didn't work fast enough for their taste. But the Burrell School and Silsby remained dedicated to the freedpeople. Not only did he win election to the Alabama Constitutional Convention, but he did his best to ensure that whites respected Black voting rights by also becoming the register of voters. In 1880 the Burrell School offered instruction to 421 students, making it one of the largest of the eleven AMA schools still operating. When local officials later proved less than dedicated to teaching Black students, the AMA took full control of the school and in 1903 moved it to Florence, Alabama, where in 1937 it became an African American high school.

John J. Anderson's text, like many other prewar textbooks, underwent dramatic changes, especially in its 1882 edition. Some traces of the book's antebellum origins remained: it still gave more space to the need for English wives than to the introduction of slaves. But as the chronology progressed, Anderson spent an increasing amount of time discussing issues related to slavery, such as the alleged 1741 New York conspiracy. Now the book focused on events leading up to the war and the responsibility of slavery in causing the bloody conflict. Texas annexation, for Anderson, became a contest between those who rejected the increasing threat of the slave power over the government and those who supported it. When it came to California's request for admission into the Union and the resulting 1850 Compromise, he gave no praise to Webster and Clay but instead made clear that the "slave power" had caused the national crisis. His narrative, similar to that of Higginson's book, described a nation absorbed by the struggle over slavery and similarly lauded John Brown as a liberator, not a madman, clearly responsible for terrifying Southern leaders. Moreover, responsibility for the conflict rested squarely on the shoulders of Southern politicians who could not accept and did not believe Lincoln's and the Republican Party's stand against the extension of slavery, rather than its abolition.

Categorically, they had left the Union to preserve slavery, not to uphold some abstract argument about states' rights. Moreover, Reconstruction proved a battle between a Republican Congress and a recalcitrant President Johnson, in which Congress passed legislation that offered "certain guarantees of protection" for the "colored population" in the form of the Fourteenth and Fifteenth amendments. This could represent an inspiring message for African American grammar schoolchildren.

But the textbook employed at the Southland College and Normal Institute, near Helena, Arkansas, may have possessed greater power than all others. Founded by the Quakers Calvin and Alida Clawson Clark in 1864 as an African American orphan asylum, Southland won support from the Friends Home Mission Board, and in 1866 men of the 56th U.S. Colored Troops Regiment erected its first building. Despite continuous local opposition, the school grew, becoming a teacher-training facility in 1869 and a college in 1872. White opposition finally brought down the facility in 1925, but before its demise, the school educated generations of teachers using a history textbook thoroughly imbued with a powerful Emancipationist theme.

Josiah W. Leeds's *A History of the United States . . . Designed for General Readers and for Academies* must have been written with Southland in mind. Leeds, a Pennsylvania Quaker who had married a Virginian, recounted the antislavery background of the Civil War in an appealing narrative style. At the book's outset, he advised readers that he had little interest in military history, something that "accomplishes little or no good for humanity." Rather, he would focus on whether "we, as a people, by any low estimate of honor, truth, or equality of rights, are in danger of becoming utterly corrupt." His text established slavery's presence beginning with Columbus, who bore responsibility for introducing "a wretched, life-long servitude-victims of a system." As no one had ever done previously, he traced the first slaves *"introduced upon our soil"* to St. Augustine, Florida, in 1565.

Leeds carefully wove slavery into his narrative, beginning with attempts to enslave Native inhabitants and moving on to more general enslavement of African peoples. He accurately cited 1619 as the correct date for slavery's introduction into Virginia and compared it to the practice of the ancient Israelites who enslaved strangers and those considered heathens. As Yale historian Edmund Morgan would do almost one hundred years later, Leeds explained how indentured servants became an important precedent for the practice of permanent slavery, as masters did everything in their power to extend the length of an individual's indenture. He also explored the lives of slaves by detailing the 1712 South Carolina slave code (as Mary Howitt had done in 1860), allowing its harsh provisions to speak for themselves. He provided truly astonishing detail about the history of the slave trade, describing the *asiento* of the 1713 Treaty of Utrecht that gave England a monopoly over slave importation in the Spanish Caribbean. The *asiento,* orchestrating multinational slave trading rights with Spain, withstood financial crashes, Leeds wrote, and "fulfilled its unholy office." Between 1676 and 1776, he declared dramatically, Great Britain bore prime responsibility for sending three million "negroes, most of them between the ages of 15 and 30 years," into slavery. Sparing no one, Leeds denounced the trade that led to the deaths of about a quarter million more who were bought directly on the African coast, then "succumbed to the horrors of the 'Middle Passage' and were buried beneath the waters of the Atlantic." He had no way of knowing that likely over two million of the approximately twelve million Africans transported by all countries to the Western Hemisphere as slaves died before their arrival. While he charged that England as a matter of policy deliberately introduced slavery into its North American colonies to suppress colonial economic development, protect English manufacturing, and prevent any move toward colonial independence, he did not attempt to exculpate Americans from responsibility for its persistence. Indeed, he made clear that slavery existed in all the colonies and emphasized New England's dominance of the slave trade.

Leeds's textbook then recorded how the country had rid itself of slavery and the important role that Quakers played in its demise. In unprecedented fashion, he described the country's early antislavery history, starting with the 1688 Germantown, Pennsylvania, petition, then the protests by Benjamin Lay, John Woolman, and Anthony Benezet. He reprinted a long account of Society of Friends antislavery activities in Pennsylvania and New England written by the Quaker abolitionist and poet John Greenleaf Whittier. His was the first textbook to try to detail international abolitionism, discussing the careers of Granville Sharp, Thomas Clarkson, William Wilberforce, William Pitt, and the 1807 suppression of the English slave trade. Even as he retained the standard political narrative, he infused it with the rise of the antislavery movement, especially the work of Benjamin Lundy and William Lloyd Garrison. He made abundantly clear to the reader that abolitionism grew outside the standard political narrative and outside the halls of Congress, but nonetheless played a central role in American history. His account, however, proved no apologia of sectional supremacy, as "the moral responsibility for the existence of slavery in the United States, rested upon the North as well as the South. Northern ship-owners and merchants participated in the gains of the slave traffic, while cotton, tobacco and rice, the products of slave labor, largely passed through the hands of northern factors, yielding them lucrative profits." As a pacifist, he rejected the Civil War, believing it "folly" and would have been entirely avoidable if the nation had listened to Connecticut's peace advocate and diplomat Elihu Burritt. The cost of the war, instead, easily could have paid compensation for emancipation, the education of all the former bondsmen and illiterate Southern whites, and built half a dozen railroads to the Pacific and a system of canals connecting the Mississippi River to the Atlantic coast and the Great Lakes. As if that were not enough, two million men might still be alive to enjoy the fruits of real emancipation. Nothing remotely like Leeds's history had ever appeared in a classroom.

In 1891 Southern Black schools no longer had to rely on white-authored textbooks, with all their uncertainties, but instead had access to books that offered the kind of social and moral affirmation that John Wesley Cromwell sought. Schools in Virginia, and especially in North Carolina, could use *A School History of the Negro Race in America from 1619 to 1890* by Edward Austin Johnson (1860–1944).

Educator, lawyer, and Republican Party activist, Johnson had been born into North Carolina slavery but in 1883 graduated from Atlanta University. He taught in Black public schools in Atlanta and then in Raleigh, North Carolina, where in 1891 he earned a law degree from Shaw University, the South's oldest historically Black university. While attending Shaw, he served as principal of the Washington School, which he had attended as a boy. Two years later he became the law school's dean and successfully argued cases before the North Carolina Supreme Court. He went on to become an important state Republican Party activist and by 1900 had attended three national Republican Party conventions as an official delegate. But increasing racial prejudice, especially ending Black voting rights, and declining opportunities eventually forced Johnson to leave the state, and in 1907 he settled in New York City. He then became the first African American to serve in the state legislature, where one of his initial acts was to craft new civil rights legislation. With immense energy, he wrote his history of African Americans—while completing his law degree—out of concern that the children he taught would never

Edward Austin Johnson (1860–1944), a light-skinned former North Carolina slave, rose to become a lawyer, teacher, author, and prominent Republican Party activist. He moved to New York in 1907 and was the first African American elected to the New York state legislature. In 1891, justifiably fearful that African American children would never be taught their own history, he published *A School History of the Negro Race in America from 1619 to 1890.* This image of him appeared in *How to Solve the Race Problem: The Proceedings of the Washington Conference on the Race Problem in the United States* (Washington, D.C.: National Sociological Society, 1904), p. 188.

gain awareness of the significant African American contribution to the nation's history and development. His text accomplished its goal and became the first by an African American author to win approval by the North Carolina State Board of Education.

Black children should have the opportunity, Johnson wrote in the text's introduction, to study the "many brave deeds and noble characters of their own race," a chance they would rarely be given in books by white authors. Books written "exclusively for white children," he bemoaned, emphasized the "inferiority of the negro." Most textbooks depicted the negro as "only a slave," and Blacks' work on behalf of American freedom remained unknown. But he assured his young readers that bravery, patriotism, and hard work knew no race. Rather than emerging from primitive societies, he explained, their African heritage was grand, and African learning in the ancient world was no different from that of fabled Greece and Rome. He urged his fellow Black teachers to carry the message of Black accomplishments to their students. *Negro,* he proclaimed, should always be written with "a capital *N.*"

As tangible evidence of Black ability and accomplishment, Johnson focused on the Boston poet Phillis Wheatley (c. 1753–84). Captured as a child in West Africa, in 1761 she was transported to Boston, where the Wheatley family purchased her. Unprecedented for a textbook author, Johnson paid close attention to her life and career, portraying Wheatley as a woman of immense talent and learning, in an obvious repudiation of white supremacist arrogance and disparagement of African American ability and culture. He even included an engraving of her, based on the one that had appeared as the frontispiece of her book of poems. He went on to include biographical accounts of Benjamin Banneker, "a mathematical and astronomical genius," as well as the nineteenth-century author, poet, and antislavery orator Frances Ellen Watkins Harper, to show Black contributions in every field of study and endeavor, accomplished despite overwhelming obstacles.

Beyond individual achievements, Johnson focused on the African American contribution to "the American cause," from the Revolution through the Civil War and, in an additional book, the Spanish-American War. Basing much of his work on the writings of the antebellum Boston abolitionist and Black chronicler William C. Nell, Johnson discussed the Black role in the Revolution, especially the contributions of Crispus Attucks and Primus Hall. Uniquely, he devoted an entire chapter to Frederick Douglass and went on to detail the Black role in the Civil War and Reconstruction's effort to advance Black rights and education, which so many textbooks ignored. As no other schoolbook had ever attempted, he emphasized the great success of Black churches, especially the African Methodist Episcopal, African Methodist Episcopal Zion, Methodists, and Presbyterians, the colleges those denominations established, and the surprising amount of wealth that African Americans accumulated, all in spite of unrelenting white repression.

. . .

A core set of textbooks published after the Civil War showed clear evidence of a transformed national mentality, especially regarding slavery, the place of African Americans in the historical narrative, and as suggested by Elisha Mulford's 1870 *The Nation,* the very purpose of the United States. A few even attained the kind of sympathetic inclusiveness that would have satisfied a John Wesley Cromwell or an Edward Austin Johnson. Moreover, as time passed, textbook authors could ground their work in an increasingly progressive body of more comprehensive histories, such as William Cullen Bryant and Sydney Howard Gay's massive and enormously successful five-volume *A Popular History of the United States,* published between 1876 and 1899. Indeed, the Bryant and Gay history proved so influential that its prime author, Gay, at his death was remembered not for editing the *National Anti-Slavery Standard* or for his abolitionist career in New York, but as the author of the multivolume history. While Gay disdained William Lloyd Garrison and Frederick Douglass, his text glorified the antislavery cause, offered stunning stories of the Underground Railroad, interpreted the war as a slaveholders' rebellion, emphasized the centrality of the Emancipation Proclamation, and gave special attention to the formation of the 54th and 55th Massachusetts Regiments. Significantly, volume four dealt harshly with white racial attitudes and the suppression of Black communities. "The great mass of the Northern people," Gay's history declared, "were absolutely destitute of any humanity for the blacks, or any principle in regard to slavery . . . and they cared nothing for the condition of those . . . held as property and treated as beasts." The series' fifth volume, written by the journalist and Lincoln biographer Noah Brooks, offered nothing but praise for Radical Reconstruction and its intention to guarantee to freedpeople "the exercise of their civil rights."

Such popular texts and schoolbooks became a liberating force, originating in the radical antislavery movement and finding renewal in the postwar work of Frederick Douglass and countless other Black leaders, Charles Sumner and the Radical Republicans, and "liberty's hero," Wendell Phillips. Their impassioned words and the heroic efforts of thousands of African American and white educators, missionaries, and Freedmen's Bureau agents created an unprecedented and hopeful atmosphere. Even former Black soldiers, such as the 54th Massachusetts's Sgt. George E. Stephens, who taught freedpeople in Virginia, and Sgt. Stephen A. Swails, who became a lawyer, trustee of the University of South Carolina, and president pro tempore of the South Carolina senate, found both symbolic and representative expression in the new textbooks. For a brief time, the eloquence proved simply extraordinary.

> That to man may be given his birthright,
>   To knowledge, the future waits;
> Equality, freedom to labor,
>   And labor, the wealth it creates. . . .
> Fraternity, rise to thy mission,
>   The noblest since order began,
> Till the nations are brothers united
>   In one federation of man!

Hezekiah Butterworth (1839–1905), in his poem "The Banner That Welcomes the World," expressed not only his opposition to war but an egalitarian vision, as he also did in his popular history text for elementary school students, *Young Folks' History of America.* American educators at the close of the nineteenth century anointed Butterworth as "one of the most widely-read American authors," best known for his enormously popular travel and history series for young readers, "ZigZag Journeys." The first volume in the series— which eventually grew to eighteen—sold forty thousand copies, and his 1882 *ZigZag Journeys in Classic Lands* sold ten thousand copies *before* publication. His history textbook went through ten editions between 1882 and 1900, and by one estimate, over one million copies of his books sold across the United States, enthralling the nation's young readers. It didn't hurt that his Boston publisher produced lavishly illustrated and beautifully bound works of leather, cloth, and gold. The *Journal of Education* declared Butterworth a "master workman" and predicted that his 1896 biography of Lafayette, *The Knight of Liberty,* would seize the attention of American youth. He also published countless poems and essays in Theodore Tilton's *Independent,* in the *Atlantic Monthly, Harper's,* and *Century,* and in newspapers and journals across the country. A poet, author, educator, peace and temperance advocate, and sober enemy of cigarettes, Butterworth published about one hundred different books. At the time of his death in 1905, Americans from coast to coast lamented the passing of the "Pathfinder for American Youth."

Little has been written about Butterworth, and his first thirty years are largely a mystery. Born in Warren, Rhode Island, he likely suffered from diabetes and related afflictions for most of his life, preventing him from completing a degree at Brown University, marrying, or serving during the Civil War. Instead, he had spent much of his youth teaching himself, participating in church activities, and working on his family's modest farm. He began editing a local newspaper and publishing essays in the Boston *Congregationalist* and *Appleton's* journal. But he remained largely unknown until the popular Boston children's magazine *The Youth's Companion* hired him in 1870. He remained there for the next twenty-five years. Most of what he wrote for an eager public, especially his "ZigZag" volumes, fortified traditional values and appealed directly to a white, youthful, and sentimentalist readership. His writings about America

manifested an unswerving devotion to romanticized history, especially the European conquest of Native Americans and repellant
stereotypical life in the Old South. They paid handsomely, however,
allowing him to purchase a winter cottage just north of Orlando in
Belleview, Florida. But when it came to formal education, Butterworth wrote with style, dedication, and passion, and his *Young Folks'
History* placed the problem of slavery at the center of the American
experience.

At first, his text said little about slavery, relating the standard
Virginia tales of Capt. John Smith, then moving swiftly to New
England and the romance of struggle with and conquest of Native
Americans. Like nearly all other textbooks, his blamed England for
introducing slavery into the colonies, selling "good people to be
slaves in Virginia." His narrative went on to describe an America
that sought to end slavery but could not because England "forced
the slave-trade upon the reluctant colonists." Having established
English responsibility for slavery and labeling the trade "heinous,"
he confessed that colonists North and South "owned Africans without remorse." He then blamed the Revolution's failure to end slavery
on South Carolina and Georgia, which possessed an unquenchable
desire for slaves, and sought to establish the long-term cause of the
Civil War.

Rare for a children's text, however, Butterworth's devoted an entire
chapter to slavery as a prelude to the Civil War. With the Louisiana
Purchase and the cotton boom, he explained, "slave-holding became
lucrative," and the South became immersed in it. But he assigned
primary responsibility for the South's devotion to slavery to the
man whom prewar textbooks had always praised, John C. Calhoun.
He, more than anyone, Butterworth wrote, bore responsibility for
the pro-slavery ideology that the South came to adopt after 1831.
Because of Calhoun, the South perceived that the "peculiar institution" was ordained by God and that there could be no opposition
to "this heaven-ordained institution. . . . So Calhoun taught. So
the South learned to believe." Butterworth also found the Southern
church morally culpable, preaching not only the divine origins of
slavery but considering it as the "proper condition of the negro." As

profits rolled in for slaveholders, with the backing of both church and state, Butterworth explained, "it was little wonder that a fanatical love for slavery possessed their hearts." Anyone who disagreed was tarred and feathered, and "many were shot; many were hanged; some were burned. The Southern mobs were singularly brutal, and the slave-owners found willing hands to do their work."

Having established the South's irreversible dedication to slavery, Butterworth went on to describe the condition of the enslaved. His young readers might have been horrified by his description of someone "regarded not as a person, but as a thing. He had no civil rights; nay, it was defended by the highest legal authority that a slave had no rights at all which the white man was bound to respect." No sweet days of the Old South lingered in Butterworth's account. He informed students that a slave had no right to marriage, no control over his family, and was subjected to flogging and even murder if his owner so desired. Any kind of resistance on the part of the enslaved justified beating, whipping, or even execution. Owners could and did sell off children, they separated husbands and wives, and if slaves ran away, vicious dogs chased them down. "Public whipping-houses became an institution," while churches proclaimed that slavery "enjoyed the sanction of God."

After 1820 the entire nation fell into the grasp of slave owners, Butterworth continued, who constituted "a great political power. . . . Their policy never wavered to gain predominance for slavery, with room for its indefinite expansion." The slave power grew so forceful and its influence so pervasive that the North became its willing abettor. Indeed, Northern capitalism came to depend on slavery: "The cotton planter borrowed money at high interest from the Northern capitalist. He bought his goods in Northern markets. He sent his cotton to the North for sale. The Northern merchants made money at his hands, and were in no haste to overthrow the peculiar institution out of which results so pleasant flowed." Moreover, slave owners convinced themselves that "the condition of the slave was preferable to that of the free European laborer."

After describing the hopeless condition of slaves and the North's callous disregard for their welfare—and more precisely, its greedy profiteering off their backs—Butterworth set the stage for a dramatic departure. "All looked very hopeless for the poor negro," he wrote. "The South claimed to hold him by divine right." It looked to a future of infinite expansion, and a "powerful sentiment in the North supported her claims." Everything seemed arrayed to "assert for ever the right of the white man to hold the black man as an article of merchandise." Just as desperation reigned, William Lloyd Garrison and his newspaper, *The Liberator,* detonated like a starburst in Boston to challenge the slave power. Butterworth reveled in presenting the New Englander as a heroic figure who battled slavery virtually alone and in dire poverty, subsisting on "bread and water" until his paper sold, allowing him then to indulge in a "bowl of milk." While ignoring Garrison's Black Boston allies and his other initial support, Butterworth justifiably emphasized the courage of the few New Englanders who eventually rallied to his standard, and the enormous opposition that swelled up against them. But within seven years, the initial apostolic dozen would expand to several thousand, and the "war against slavery was now begun in earnest." Garrison led a devoted band that possessed "a zeal which knew no bounds and permitted no rest."

As Higginson had done, Butterworth depicted John Brown not as a fanatic but as a man with "the blood of the Pilgrim Fathers" flowing in his veins. He sought no fame, only justice. "He saw a huge wrong, and he could not help setting himself to resist it." From the wars in Kansas to the war in Virginia that he hoped to provoke, Brown acted as "God's servant, and not man's." As no one else revealed at the time, Butterworth explained that his actions at Harpers Ferry included Black and white insurrectionists. And while Brown may have been a "detestable rebel" to slave owners, he was a martyr to antislavery activists. Brown may have exercised poor judgment, the historian concluded, and his actions proved "unwise and unwarrantable; but his aims were noble, his self-devotion was heroic."

Butterworth possessed a marvelous ability to dramatize and simplify the national crisis, bringing it down to a struggle between the forces of slavery and those who sought its demise, with the Lincoln

"Slaves Escaping to Union Troops." Hezekiah Butterworth sought to humanize the enslaved and their quest for freedom. Illustration from Butterworth's *Young Folks' History of America* (1882), p. 433.

administration and the Republican Party caught in the middle, simultaneously seeking to hold the Union together and limit slavery's growth. He saw the strife as a "death-grapple" in which each party asserted its power to "conquer or be crushed." With rich, agile prose, Butterworth made the true nature of the conflict vividly clear. In the contest over freedom and the nation's future, the North chose freedom and the South took the path to slavery and inequality. Butterworth quoted the Confederacy's vice president, Alexander Stephens, expressing the South's commitment to the great "truth" that "the negro is not equal to the white man" and that "slavery is his natural and normal condition."

Lincoln's Emancipation Proclamation was a necessary and practical war policy, Butterworth explained, but "in war opinion ripens fast," and the decision to issue it quickly turned revolutionary. Thus the "slaves of men who were in arms against the government were declared free," and then they turned against their former owners. What began as a practical political measure quickly became a "moral war measure," and the North understood it that way. On January 1, 1863, "bells pealed joyfully in the great cities and quiet villages of the East" and rang throughout the West. No one had ever imagined this happening, not the "hunted fugitive, not the wretched slave in his cabin. . . . No political prophet ever saw the opening of those doors of events that made his [the slave's] freedom a necessity to the life of the nation. The Red Sea opened as by the dividing hand of God." For Butterworth, as for Elisha Mulford, the war had committed the country to freedom, and Reconstruction would fulfill its central mission: "Citizenship was no longer to be dependent upon color. . . . Henceforth, American law would present no contradiction to the doctrine that 'all men are born equal.' . . . No State might henceforth pass any law . . . to abridge the privilege of any class of American citizens." The war destroyed slavery, and Reconstruction established equal justice, committing the nation to fully implementing the principle of equal rights. In Butterworth's *Young Folks' History of America,* the Emancipationist repudiation of the white world of John H. Van Evrie could not have been more explicit.

One year after publication of Butterworth's book, the pinnacle of the Emancipationist interpretation of the war emerged from the pen of the North's most illustrious and respected Civil War reporter. With unequaled authority and with skills honed on battlefields from Virginia to the Carolinas, Charles Carleton Coffin (1823–96) crafted his *Building the Nation* textbook to impress on the minds of America's "Boys and Girls" that the injustices of slavery and white supremacy lay at the center of the American experience. So that there would be no misunderstanding, Coffin began by declaring that "slavery was a degradation of labor" and that the nation's Founding Fathers had not advanced beyond the "feudal age to recognize all men, irrespective of race and color, as entitled to the privileges of the Constitution." For Coffin, slavery was more than an exploitive labor system. It was a totalitarian social system that ruled as "a great political power . . . making itself felt in all affairs of State." *Building the Nation,* he informed his young readers, would not only explain how that happened but would lead all Americans "toward a higher and nobler civilization—toward justice, right, and liberty."

Coffin was born in rural Boscawen, New Hampshire, the youngest of nine children, three of whom died as infants. He attended two local academies but never continued on to college. Instead, like Butterworth, he educated himself, becoming an omnivorous reader and, as one chronicler remarked, treating every book that came within reach as a fish in his mental dragnet. He also grew up listening to his grandfather and local residents regale him with the drama and romance of their experiences in the American Revolution. He came by his antislavery principles honestly, as a youngster reading his father's antislavery newspapers, especially the New Hampshire *Herald of Freedom* and Garrison's *Liberator.* In his bedroom hung a copy of the famed Josiah Wedgwood medallion of a kneeling slave with the motto, "Am I not a Man and a Brother?" It was, he recalled, the last thing he saw in the evening and the first thing in the morning. He also witnessed firsthand the ugly reaction of his neighbors when a Black family moved into town, and his father's principled response when he employed one of the family members out of sympathy for them and disgust with his neighbors. As an adolescent, Coffin attended antislavery lectures in Concord whenever Garrison, the English abolitionist George Thompson, Abby Kelley Foster, or Theodore Dwight Weld came to town, and he loved the poetry of the abolitionist John Greenleaf Whittier. By the age of seventeen, he joined the antislavery wing of the Whig Party and

Charles Carleton Coffin (1823–96), the Civil War's best-known reporter, dedicated his postwar career to writing the history of the war. He repudiated the institution of slavery and instilled in the rising generation a dedication to liberty for all regardless of color.

became acquainted with the future U.S. senators Henry Wilson and Charles Sumner, as well as several other influential Massachusetts politicians. He followed them into the Republican Party; in 1856 he came out for John C. Frémont, and in 1860 he was a member of the delegation that informed Abraham Lincoln that he had won the party's nomination for president. Years later, in one of the nearly two thousand popular lectures he gave, Coffin declared that Lincoln had been "selected by divine providence to perform a great part in the [nation's] historic drama."

During the 1850s, Coffin had worked as a self-trained surveyor, served briefly as a civil engineer with two New Hampshire railroads, and erected telegraphic lines in the Boston area. But his passion for journalism soon won out, and he began writing for several Boston-area newspapers and for Horace Greeley's New York *Tribune*. Beginning in 1854, because of his talent and Republican Party connections, he joined the staff of one of Massachusetts's most influential newspapers, the Boston *Journal*. When war broke out in 1861, he quit the editorial desk and took to the field, quickly becoming the Union's leading war correspondent, with his dispatches appearing under the nom de guerre "Carleton" read across the North. From First Bull Run to Appomattox, from Virginia west to St. Louis and south to Charleston, "Carleton" roamed the battlefields, not just the command tents, exposing himself to fire on the front lines to get the story right. A fellow reporter witnessed him racing across battlefields "over breastworks, para pits, rifle-pits, rocks, fallen trees . . . with his head down like an animal which trails by scent." He won the appreciation of the troops and the riveted attention of readers back home. Newspapers from around the country and in Europe, for example, reprinted his eyewitness account of the historic battle at Gettysburg in July 1863. In 1866 most of his dispatches were republished in a five-hundred-page collection, *Four Years of Fighting*, which nearly every boy in Boston had read; it proved so popular that it was translated into French and German for European readers. On his death in 1896, the Boston *Journal*, the paper where he had worked for so long and that had sponsored his "Carleton" dispatches, declared Coffin the war's most influential reporter.

Coffin well earned his fame. He had reported on nearly every major battle of the war: Bull Run, Antietam, Fredericksburg, Gettysburg, the Wilderness, Petersburg, Cold Harbor, and about eleven others. He had walked the streets of Savannah, Charleston, and even Richmond the day it fell to Union troops. His reporting covered the war from start to finish, and exceedingly rare for a white journalist, he recorded the reactions of those freed from bondage by the Union army. He considered their perspective to be central to understanding the meaning of the war, if not the defining meaning itself. Late in the war, he interviewed an African American woman in Savannah who just had been liberated by Union troops. She told Coffin that she had heard General Sherman announce that all in the region were now free. "I didn't believe it," she sadly responded. "Yes, you are free," Coffin repeated. Her heartbreaking response spoke volumes and helped shape Coffin's. "But that don't give me back my children . . . that have been torn from my breast, and sold from me, and when I cried for them was tied up and had my back cut to pieces! . . . O Lord Jesus, have mercy! How long, O Lord? . . . O Blessed Jesus, they say that I am free, but where are my children!—my children! Her hands fell,—tears rolled down her cheeks. She bowed her head,

"Fit Only to be a Slave." Illustration from Coffin, *Building the Nation* (1883), p. 307.

and sat moaning, wailing, and sobbing." In Virginia, he witnessed escaped slaves emerge from hiding as Union forces approached. The immense smiles on their faces impressed him deeply, but joy evaporated when he saw those limping behind the initial group—old men broken by relentless work, with long beards and crippled hands, and toothless women, almost blind, trudging from the woods held erect by sticks serving as canes, with "little negro boys, driving a team of skeleton steers." For Coffin, the Union troops were liberators, re-creating hope, translating it "from eternity into time."

As he drank in the scene, Coffin spied a light-complexioned woman with long hair and hazel eyes who sat on the broad steps of her former owner's piazza contemplating an unknowable future. The jubilation of the others who gloried in their liberation had no noticeable impact on her; she had, Coffin wrote, "no heart to join in the general jubilee." While her former owner had never physically abused her, he had sold off her husband and her children. "Life was a blank," with no beatings necessary, Coffin lamented, to comprehend the full tragedy of slavery. She spoke with refinement and directly, unlike anyone else, and Coffin had to stare to determine if she had any discernable African blood in her veins. She confessed to being the daughter of her former owner and said her newfound freedom amounted to only "gall and wormwood." Coffin remarked that he had "read of such things. But one needs to come in contact with slavery, to feel how utterly loathsome and hateful it is." She sat on the piazza for hours, staring simultaneously into the desolate past and "a dreamless, hopeless future." When he wrote about his nation's history for the children of the future, he thought of the real impact of the curse of slavery.

No wonder education mattered so much to Coffin. As early as 1857, he had served on local Massachusetts school committees. He supported Horace Mann's teacher-training institutions and aided one for women in Salem, Massachusetts, that in 1856 had graduated the Philadelphia-born African American author and abolitionist Charlotte Forten. After the war, he attended many teacher institutes to obtain a better grasp of educational needs. Whenever he gave one of his countless history lectures for Boston's Lowell Institute or for the legendary Old South Meeting House, he insisted on lecturing in the late afternoon so that students could attend. And it was for children, especially boys, that he wrote approximately twenty-five books on history, biography, war, and liberty. Astonishingly, the Boston Public Library owned *fifty* copies of his history of the Revolution, *The Boys of '76,* all of which were continually out on loan. Educators gloried in his publications, since children seized them like ripe apples, finding them both instructive and as "charming as novels." For at least thirty years, the *Journal of Education* reported in 1895, children, especially boys, read him with an "insatiable appetite." That year the *Journal* declared that "no other author has written so much about history for so many young readers, and written it so well as Mr. Coffin."

Coffin designed *Building the Nation* (1883) as the culminating text of a huge four-volume series, "The Rise of the People: Stories from American History, for Young Readers." It began with the rise of liberty in Europe, traversed the colonial era and the American Revolution, and ended with the rise of abolitionism and the election of Abraham Lincoln, the prelude to the Civil War, and liberty's rebirth. As he wrote in the series' first volume, *The Story of Liberty,* he understood the history of Western civilization as a "march of the human race from Slavery to Freedom." Before writing *Building the Nation,* Coffin returned to the South to see for himself the reality of that freedom for African Americans. Statesmen and political economists had assured the nation countless times, he explained in the spring of 1878 in *The Congregationalist,* that "the negro could not take care of himself." But his tour of the South proved otherwise, confirming what he already knew. African Americans still did most of the work, he declared, and if not for them, "the white population of the South would be in the depths of poverty." Indeed, the whole industrial world of the North Atlantic turned on the spindle of Southern cotton, all made possible by the same freedpeople who whites insisted could not take care of themselves. In Alabama, a well-dressed Black baggage handler told him that his wife owned twenty acres of land "and was putting in her cotton." Well, these "poor creatures," Coffin wrote with the bitterest sarcasm, "if left to themselves, would lapse into barbarism." He knew better, and now so did his readers.

Fortified by unrivaled experience both on and off the battlefield, Coffin crafted his textbook to assess what the colonists had done with the liberty they had won in the Revolution. When America achieved independence, he advised his students, kings no longer ruled the land, but the world "was wondering what they would do with it." Unlike any other textbook author, Coffin planted the problem of slavery right at the Constitutional Convention. How would slaves be counted when the convention determined representation in Congress? Would slavery survive at all? Could the United States even come into being when Northern leaders like New York's Gouverneur Morris denounced slavery as a curse? Americans had led the world, he reminded his readers, in advancing "the rights of men, but the idea had not dawned upon them that negroes had any civil rights, or that slavery was wrong." Moreover, when Thomas Jefferson crafted the immortal words of the Declaration of Independence proclaiming the equality of all men "he was not thinking of negroes."

THE RISING POWER.

Coffin graphically drove home the power of slavery over the entire nation, illustrating the bond between Northern industry and Southern agriculture. "The Rising Power," from Coffin, *Building the Nation* (1883), p. 284.

Coffin used the example of the Connecticut Yankee Eli Whitney and his cotton gin to explain how slave labor became integrated into the economy and how Northern industrialization became dependent on Southern agriculture and Southern slavery. Moreover, every time a national crisis occurred, such as renewed war with Britain in 1812, he reminded his students that America could never triumph because of the destructive impact of the institution of slavery. His text also gave unprecedented attention to the activities of women, including illustrations of their activities and accounting for their contributions to the history of religion and the temperance movement. In a singular move, he devoted an entire chapter to American racism. To white Americans, he wrote, a "colored person was called a 'nigger.' He had no rights." Even though Black men fought alongside George Washington to win American independence and stood with Andrew Jackson in New Orleans against invading British troops in 1814, "the nation accorded [them] no rights under the Constitution." No matter how gifted or well educated Blacks were, their country condemned them to "menial service" in the kitchen or the stable.

Rather than offering obscene characterizations of slaves as living easy, luxurious lives, Coffin emphasized the harsh conditions they endured. "The Comfortless Cabin," from Coffin, *Building the Nation* (1883), p. 389.

In travel, schools, and churches, segregation and inferiority reigned, and African Americans in the South made agriculture flourish but received only the whip in gratitude. "It is natural," Coffin instructed students, "for men to hate those whom they have wronged." Because New England and New York had figured so prominently in the slave trade, the North developed "an intense prejudice against free negroes, and a desire to get them out of the country." To fulfill their disgust and ease their conscience, Yankees helped organize and actively supported the American Colonization Society. To these activists, Coffin warned, every colored person was a "nigger" who "had no rights."

Having devoted a chapter to American race hatred, Coffin offered students one on the antislavery movement, chronicling its relationship with English abolitionists. He gave a central place to the work of antislavery women, a near revolutionary move compared to other textbooks, focusing on the life of the Pennsylvania abolitionist leader Lucretia Mott, even offering a nearly full-page engraving of her. In his discussion of Mott, Prudence Crandall, Benjamin Lundy, Wil-

To drive home the true horrors of slavery, Coffin recounted the tragic ordeal of Margaret Garner, who preferred to slay her children rather than permit them to be reenslaved. "Death Rather Than Slavery," wood engraving after a painting by Thomas Noble, *Harper's Weekly,* May 18, 1867; reprinted in Coffin, *Building the Nation* (1883), p. 403.

liam Lloyd Garrison, Wendell Phillips, and others, Coffin made sure students understood that abolitionism had been inextricably linked to the defense of free speech and all other constitutional freedoms. These individuals, he impressed on his readers, were heroic defenders of justice, the very essence of what the nation should be about.

But as *Building the Nation* emphasized, the country's history had been misdirected, deflected from fulfilling the liberty first enunciated in the Magna Carta, in favor of achieving the slaveholders' dream. People of African descent became things—not people, husbands, wives, children—all dragged to the slave marts of the South to be sold as cattle, "to work in the cotton-fields, beneath the broiling sun, driven by a brutal overseer sitting on a horse, with a whip in hand, which he delighted to crack over them." This, Coffin exclaimed, was the institution that the white Southerner proclaimed was a "divine institution, ordained of God for the well-being of the human race." He detailed the tragic case of Margaret Garner, reproducing the devastating engraving of her capture in Cincinnati by slave catchers, to graphically illustrate the tragedy of slavery and the subordination of Northern freedom to the demands of the South. For the South, as slavery apologist George Fitzhugh put it, servitude was a necessary "educational institution" and "was worth ten times all the common schools of the North." All the controversial events of the mid-nineteenth century, Coffin explained, from the annexation of Texas and the Mexican War to the Fugitive Slave Law, indeed the entire movement of history of the era, aimed at securing and then expanding the institution of slavery.

Given the irrepressible Southern desire to preserve, protect, and expand the institution of slavery, Coffin could only view John Brown in a heroic light. Unable to avoid him and unwilling to dodge the impact of his actions, Coffin drove student attention right to him and the "important part" he played in the "great drama of history." From the age of twelve, John Brown's soul had burned for "justice and right." He followed his own star, directed by no one. Concluding that the South would never be talked out of slavery, he resolved to be "an instrument in the hands of the Almighty to give freedom to the slaves." Coffin correctly reported that five African Americans participated in the raid at Harpers Ferry, and like Higginson, he included a romanticized account and image of Brown kissing a slave child on his way to the gallows. For Coffin, Brown was the embodiment of the courageous hero: "They who make great sacrifices for truth, justice, and liberty can never die."

But even as the Emancipationist vision of the meaning of the Civil War came to its zenith in Coffin's work, it was already under attack. The influence of progressive authors like Elisha Mulford, Thomas Wentworth Higginson, Hezekiah Butterworth, and Charles Carleton Coffin would linger until the beginning of the next century. But the white South's unwavering resistance to Reconstruction and its utter repudiation of racial equality, combined with the Democratic Party's poisonous attacks, eviscerated the North's fragile embrace of Emancipationist ideals. Increasingly, history textbooks retreated from articulating the principles of liberty and full equality that had underpinned the era of Reconstruction. The process would be halting and contradictory but proved relentless and certain. "Lost Cause ideology," the new "master narrative," erupted across the country during the 1880s and '90s, even as Northern students still read Butterworth and Coffin. But by 1906, this ideology had purged the notion of universal liberty from textbooks, in favor of the vision of permanent national reunification constructed out of John H. Van Evrie's idea of white supremacy.

5

Causes Lost and Found, 1883 to 1919

Rebel rule is nearly complete in many states . . . and is gradually capturing the nation's Congress. The cause lost in the war, is the cause regained in peace, and the cause gained in war, is the cause lost in peace.

—Frederick Douglass, *Lessons of the Hour,* January 9, 1894

By the time Douglass mourned the loss of gains achieved by the Civil War, Reconstruction had reached an ignominious end, and the fate of African Americans lay entirely in the hands of white supremacists. The white press derided and damned his 1894 speech condemning racism and lynching as "incendiary," "dangerous," and even "nihilistic." When Sen. Charles Sumner died in March 1874, he seemed to have taken the nation's crumbling "idealistic fervor" with him. Even ratification of the Fifteenth Amendment four years earlier had only heightened, rather than diminished, Northern white supremacy. "The white man—the man of the superior race," the New York *Herald* cried in February 1870, "will always have ascendancy." The North remained committed to what the Rev. Samuel T. Spear called in the New York *Independent* "Negrophobia," whether expressed confidently and categorically by a John H. Van Evrie or paternalistically by a former abolitionist. Negrophobia, Spear observed, was the characteristic construction "of the white American mind." Most of the North—and soon most of the South—ultimately would agree with Lincoln's former secretary of the navy, the Connecticut Yankee Gideon Welles, that slavery's death was a national blessing. They would also eagerly approve of Welles's estimation that "the Negro is not, and never can be the equal of the white. He is of an inferior race and must always remain so." The Emancipationist vision of the future that Elisha Mulford, Hezekiah Butterworth, and Charles Carleton Coffin had infused into their writings in the 1870s and '80s had been fading even before they put pen to paper.

Although the North always had disdained African Americans, at the war's end it willingly experimented with political equality in the South to restore the Union, assist the former slaves in their transition to freedom, and prevent any future attempt at secession. But when the Reconstruction experiment appeared to prove a dismal and disastrous failure, they abandoned any attempt to force political equality on the South and allowed whites to return to complete power. The calamitous end to Reconstruction, however, had no impact on the North's understanding of its role in the Civil War. Its "master narrative," or what Robert Penn Warren memorably described at the war's centennial in 1961 as a sacred "treasury of virtue," was grounded exclusively on a heroic restoration of the Union *and* on the end of slavery, not on equality. Recognizing the "error" of Reconstruction thus became part of the national reunification effort and ironically buttressed the North's "treasury of virtue."

One book published in 1874 helped convince the North that Reconstruction based on Black civil rights had been an unfortunate and ill-advised diversion. Equally important, that book proved essential to the interpretation of Reconstruction that Americans would obtain from textbooks for the next eighty years. And true to form, this white supremacist evaluation of Reconstruction was written not by a former Confederate but by a lifelong enemy of slavery from Maine.

James Shepherd Pike's *The Prostrate State: South Carolina Under Negro Government* was the single most influential assault on the Emancipationist goals of the Civil War and Reconstruction eras. The white supremacist counterpart to Elijah Mulford's *The Nation,* Pike's work convinced the North of the inherent incapacity of African Americans for *any* role in government. The most comprehensive assault on the North's "mistaken" goals of Reconstruction, it detailed how the experiment with Black power in South Carolina had created "the most ignorant democracy that mankind ever saw." Pike (1811–82), born in Calais, Maine, had emerged as a prominent antislavery Whig, then became an influential Republican journalist for the Boston *Courier* and chief Washington correspondent for Greeley's New York *Tribune.* In the Civil War, he served as Lincoln's minister to the Netherlands. In the 1850s, he had won widespread Republican support for his vicious attacks on the Democratic Party and especially on Illinois senator Stephen A. Douglas, denouncing both as dangerous guardians of slavery and "enemies to their country and enemies to their [own] race." Despite his abolitionism, prior to the 1860 election he issued vile assertions that African Americans were an "ignorant and servile race" that ought to be exported to the West Indies. His later denunciations of Black ability and unyielding condemnations of Reconstruction found enthusiastic support from Charleston to Boston. In Boston, the prominent former abolitionist James Freeman Clarke hailed Pike's book as authoritative and decisive. Clarke even visited South Carolina to verify the accuracy of Pike's assertions and returned declaring that everything his fellow New Englander had written was "confirmed by every man whom I saw." Even the future novelist William Dean Howells explained in the February 1874 *Atlantic Monthly* that, as Pike claimed, South Carolina had completely fallen "prey to the black and white thieves who 'govern it.'" Howells, who had been a John Brown supporter, declared that Pike spoke the truth—South Carolina had become a "dismal and devoured State."

Frederick Douglass led a small contingent of abolitionists and reformers who repudiated Pike's allegations. Through Washington, D.C.'s *National New Era* newspaper, Douglass denounced Pike's campaign against Reconstruction as calculated to "fire the negro-hating heart to deeds of violence against the black race." Others defended the state's government, pointing out the significant construction of new roads and schools, the establishment of social services, and the advancement of African Americans out of enslavement. Even in Pike's home state of Maine, the Portland *Daily*

Press scorned his pathetic tears for a "prostrated" South Carolina. "Very little was said about a prostrate state," the paper sarcastically observed, "when a large majority of the inhabitants . . . were held as property." Whatever corruption afflicted the state, the *Daily Press* maintained, was a deserved punishment. Whites reaped "the whirlwind," the paper advised, having sown the seeds of their own misery. They defended slavery, they seceded, "they lost, and now they suffer the consequences both of their oppression of a majority, and the results of their system of outrage." In Congress, Samuel Cox, the former Ohio Democrat who began representing New York in 1869, waved Pike's book before his colleagues in 1876, declaring that it proved that South Carolina's Reconstruction government was "rotten to the core." If federal troops remained there, he exclaimed, they should do so only to "lop off the rottenness." He confidently asserted that Pike's book had categorically demonstrated that "Negro government" was "the blackness of darkness in robbery and rascality." In response, South Carolina congressman Robert Smalls, a former slave, asked Cox if he "had got a book on the history of the City of New York," a remark that set his Republican colleagues rolling in the aisles with laughter. But in the end, the attacks on Pike were few and far between. Even New York's famed journal the *Nation* denounced Reconstruction governments as "socialism," and the intelligence of the state's Black population as only "slightly above the levels of animals." From South Carolina to Delaware, to New York, and on to Minnesota, newspapers around the country accepted Pike's assertions as final proof of the utter and complete failure of Reconstruction. "Negro supremacy," a Minnesota paper exclaimed, made a "mockery of government." Even the *Spirit of the Age* in little Woodstock, Vermont, concluded from Pike's book that Reconstruction amounted to nothing more than a "huge system of brigandage."

Pike had actually begun his assault on Reconstruction a year *before* his visit to South Carolina at the outset of 1873. In March 1872, writing for the *Tribune,* he began a series of essays on the state with "A State in Ruins," in which he contrasted the prewar days of white supremacy to the current Black rule of "ignorance and barbarism." He could not accept the idea that "300,000 white people are put under the heel of 400,000 pauper blacks, fresh from the state of slavery and ignorance the most dense." His "knowledge" of conditions in the state came from Sen. William Sprague of Rhode Island, whose business interests in South Carolina led him to decry "corruption," and from Gen. Wade Hampton, head of the state's "Redeemer" white supremacists in 1876–77, who never wavered in his effort to restore white rule. Pike's *Tribune* essays, reprinted across South Carolina and the nation, demanded expansion into a book.

The Prostrate State, presumably based on his personal tour of South Carolina, in fact did not differ from what he had previously written in his newspaper accounts. But the combined anger, outrage, and rebuke that laced his book screamed like a siren that shattered the uncertain repose of Northerners. His account proved convincing, not just because he played on popular prejudice, but because he bonded his previous denunciation of slavery to what he presented as immoral corruption in Reconstruction South Carolina, thereby appearing as a consistent conservative critic. It fell to the true conservative, he wrote, to "expose the evils of slavery and aim to prevent its spread." He must then "expose the frightful results of the rule of ignorance, barbarism, and vice, and visit with unsparing condemnation of affairs as perilous and as threatening to the future peace and prosperity of the country as any that ever preceded it in our history." Thus Pike presented himself as consistent, moral, and principled, yet his governing principle was white supremacy.

Instead of being victimized by the state's "old aristocratic society," Pike asserted that South Carolina now suffered under the "dregs of the population habilitated in the robes of their intelligent predecessors, and asserting over them the rule of ignorance and corruption." No government existed in the state, Pike shouted: "It is barbarism overwhelming civilization by physical force. It is the slave rioting in the halls of his master, and putting that master under his feet." A thieving anarchy had befallen the state, he argued, led by "Sambo," who "takes naturally to stealing, for he is used to it." After years of Black rule, Pike avowed, "the Treasury of South Carolina has been so thoroughly gutted by the thieves who . . . had possession of the

State government" that there was "nothing left to steal." "The Negro" and his carpetbagger allies operated a "system of brigandage" that stripped whites of their wealth, robbing "the poor and rich alike, by law." They confiscated estates "by law" and did so "simply to enrich themselves personally."

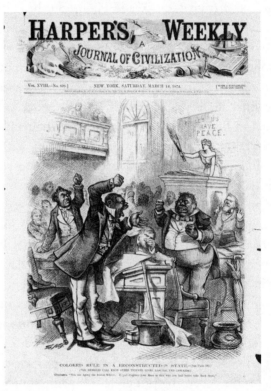

Harper's Weekly was once a steady enemy of slavery and an advocate of Black freedom, but like the rest of the North, it succumbed to the propaganda of white supremacists. It offered the nation graphic illustrations of the presumed inherent inferiority of African Americans and the profound "errors" of Reconstruction that James Shepherd Pike's *The Prostrate State* would inject into popular culture. "Colored Rule in a Reconstructed State," wood engraving by Thomas Nast, *Harper's Weekly,* March 14, 1874.

The world had turned upside down, Pike insisted, and Reconstruction South Carolina possessed about as much sense as a crazed world of talking squirrels. Indeed, Pike's blistering and horrified account reduced Reconstruction and all African Americans to the level of abject stupidity. The typical Black legislator, Pike spewed, "did not know what he was going to say when he got up; he did not know what he was saying while he was speaking, and he did not know what he had said when he sat down." Pike spared no words to have white Americans understand the complete lunacy of African Americans exercising political power. "The speaker is black, the Clerk is black, his door-keepers are black, the little pages are black, the chairman of the Ways and Means is black, and the chaplain is coal-black. At some of the desks sit colored men whose types it would be hard to find outside of Congo." Such language helped define the way schoolbooks would later present their destructive histories of Reconstruction. In fact, a 1930 textbook by Helen Giles, a teacher at Columbia University's Horace Mann Elementary School, quoted Pike's racist rant (unattributed) as irrefutable evidence of the horrors of Reconstruction.

.   .   .

While the white North gloried in its Civil War "treasury of virtue," African Americans bore the burden of white complacency. In 1883 Frederick Douglass had explained that the end of slavery failed to alter the terms of American liberty—for African Americans, liberty remained only a word, and "our citizenship is but a sham," the right to vote "only a cruel mockery." Douglass knew all too well the task that the North faced and what it would take to extinguish slavery *and* white supremacy. The "miserable dream" of the prewar republic must be debunked if African Americans were to gain full freedom and equality. Douglass, more than anyone, could testify to the "invisible chains of slavery" that endured despite the South's defeat. As Wendell Phillips remarked shortly after the end of the war, "We have abolished the slave, but the master remains."

The 1898 report of the New England Teachers' Association (NETA) on American history textbooks admitted that the issue of slavery remained a "thorn in the flesh to text-book makers." But the association determined that the problem would eventually fade because of a generational shift. Immediately after the Civil War, Northern opinion dominated, and teachers could not avoid "dwelling on the evils of slavery, and picturing the South as marching perversely, through long years, to its final ruin." At that time slavery had to be seen as a moral evil, "wholly without excuse." But now, the association reported, a New South had arisen on the ashes of the old, and a younger generation unbiased by any experience with the Civil War had come to consider "that there might, after all, be something to say on the other side." Textbooks were becoming legitimate apologists for the South, the report stated, explaining Southern "adherence to slavery on scientific rather than moral grounds." The report then concluded that as a result, we will have greater "objectivity" on the issue of slavery.

The "science" that the NETA believed had reshaped American history in the 1880s and '90s emerged from the pen of, among others, the Connecticut-born and Harvard-educated John Fiske (1842–1901). A giant of a historian at three hundred pounds, Fiske authored a dozen works of history and ten other books on religion and philosophy, although he is usually remembered for his studies of New England and early American history. He was the nation's leading promoter of the English social Darwinist Herbert Spencer, believing that Spencer had revolutionized thinking on human development as a process that went from the primitive to the complex, and from savagery to civilization. History was the record of the working out of this cosmic order. For Fiske, this "science" was divine truth, and political ideas had to follow from its "law of evolution." Even as a young man, he had proclaimed that "there is nothing in this world like *SCIENCE.*" And as Fiske once advised an associate, he had studied evolution "in order that he might understand history."

In 1884 Fiske published *Destiny of Man, Viewed in the Light of His Origin,* his rumination on the relationship between Darwinism and Christianity. For Fiske, Darwinism—the idea of natural selection—displayed the process of human perfectibility, but that process was episodic. While humans had separated themselves from other animals, "the interval between the highest and lowest men far surpasses quantitatively the interval between the lowest men and the highest apes." Thus "the brain of a Shakespeare and that of an Australian savage would doubtless be fifty times greater than the difference between the Australian's brain and that of an orangoutang." Moreover, the most developed humans came out of the Mediterranean world, then "widened until [in] our day it covers both sides of the Atlantic." Such Darwinian progress, he argued, had spread most effectively to Europe and "into the hands of men of [the] English race" like Emerson. Not surprisingly, Fiske, one of the most popular historians of the late-nineteenth-century United States, was president of the Immigration Restriction League.

"Savage Indians." Author John Fiske explained, "Some of these Indians were more savage than others" (p. 3). The source he cited for the image was Henry Wadsworth Longfellow's *Hiawatha,* illustrated by Frederick Remington. John Fiske, *A History of the United States for Schools* (1895).

Fiske's 1895 textbook *A History of the United States for Schools* began by inculcating assumptions of white supremacy into readers. This book, especially regarding the origins of slavery and the presumed inherent nature of Blacks, reflected the same assertions, and employed some of the same language, as histories used in the South. By the 1890s, Northern and Southern views on slavery and white supremacy had converged. Even while he admitted that for "nine or ten generations" America had drawn on a multicultural world for its development, he nonetheless asserted that the nation still found its origin and meaning "in the history of Europe, and chiefly in that of England." Those settlers colonized a North America that Fiske maintained had been occupied only by two types of natives: the "savage" and the "barbarous." He briefly discussed the development of slavery, emphasizing its appeal because of the need for "cheap" labor for work that "did not require much intelligence." He dismissed its role in the North as inconsequential, as "negroes" could do no labor "that could not better be done by white men." In the South, however, "everybody took it for granted that negroes would not work except as slaves," so history followed a different course. Fiske set the development of American slavery within the context of colonial unfree labor and even described indentured servants as "white slaves." Unlike his predecessors, he accurately dated the introduction of slavery to 1619 but never noted the irony of the dual establishment of slavery and representative government in the same year, although he paired the two events together in his discussion of Virginia. As the book progressed, he instructed his readers that the Constitution protected slavery and that Eli Whitney's cotton gin helped transform Southern agriculture, vastly increasing the demand for slave labor. The rising demand for slaves then made the South "anxious to defend the institution of slavery against possible attacks from the North."

Fiske offered no judgment on the rise of abolitionism in the early nineteenth century and presented a thorough and dispassionate account of the growing national political strife over slavery through the election of Lincoln. While he excluded African Americans from the antislavery movement, and from history in general except as "slaves" or participants in "mobs," he did highlight abolitionism as an aspect of the antebellum reform movement. He characterized William Lloyd Garrison as the movement's leader, Wendell Phillips as its orator, and Theodore Parker as its minister, even providing appealing illustrations of them. He also discussed the antislavery stand of John Quincy Adams when he served in Congress. He saw the 1850 Fugitive Slave Law as a mistake that could violate the constitutional rights of free African Americans as well as of the slave, but thought Harriet Beecher Stowe's *Uncle Tom's Cabin* did more to change Northern attitudes about slavery than any fugitive slave rescue. As a New Englander, Fiske would not condemn the antislavery movement, but he did describe John Brown as a merciless "religious fanatic" and Adams as someone who would not allow the subject of slavery to "rest in quiet" and remarked that the more Southern opposition he encountered, the "more ruthlessly he carried on" his attacks.

Avoiding censure and blame, Fiske carefully detailed the nation's political struggle over slavery and the coming of the Civil War. When discussing the murderous 1863 New York City Draft Riots, he referred to African Americans as the "innocent cause of the war," a phrase commonly employed in the North during the 1860s. But Fiske rendered African Americans only as bystanders, denying them any agency and casting them as beneficiaries of white initiatives and sacrifices, utterly uninvolved with gaining their own freedom— except as occasional fugitive slaves. He and many other authors provided a glorified, but dangerously attenuated account of the Emancipation Proclamation, failing to mention that it called for the recruitment of African American soldiers. As other texts had done before his, Fiske's completely ignored the 179,000 African Americans who served in the army—and the thousands more in the navy—and never mentioned any battles involving Black troops or the merciless Confederate policy against them, much less the fact that even President Lincoln confessed that the war could not have been won without them.

All this set the stage for his brief rendering of Reconstruction, a misstep he believed had been caused by the tragic assassination of Lincoln, which "deprived the Southerners of their kindest and most powerful friend," a view that became standard in at least twenty different textbooks for both Northern and Southern students. Even Hilary A. Herbert and Woodrow Wilson considered Lincoln's assassination a "calamity" for the South. Fiske discussed Congress's battles with Andrew Johnson and the legislation and constitutional amendments that aimed at securing freedom and political equality for African Americans and "poor whites." But to Fiske, the "iron clad" oath of allegiance to the United States that prevented former Confederate political and military leaders from voting or serving in restored state governments proved fatal to the South. The oath, he avowed, barred "good people" from serving and allowed "a swarm of greedy Northern adventurers, known as carpet-baggers," to seize control of the South with the assistance of "negro votes" and an occupying army. In a version of history that parroted James Shepherd Pike's, corrupt Northerners used their "negro" allies to tax whites for their own profit. Justified white resistance then arose against "corruption" as the Klan heroically fought fraudulent Black and Yankee rule, stolen elections, and stolen money. In Fiske's telling, as more and more whites regained their civil rights, "the better class of Southern citizens came back into power," and life "improved."

Fiske's and Pike's rendering of the war and especially Reconstruction increasingly dominated history education and public perception. They reflected a swelling interpretive trend during the 1880s and '90s that celebrated the end of slavery but also offered withering views of African Americans—and a repudiation of equal rights—that would endure for generations. This unmistakable trend in history, political science, and even geography moved relentlessly toward a white racial consensus, matching Northern popular prejudice that perceived African Americans as incapable of operating within a free labor system. By 1890, as the *New York Times* reported, white Americans earnestly believed that "imprudence and improvidence are among the most characteristic traits of the negro."

Moreover, Fiske's and Pike's views received a dramatic boost during the 1890s when the new generation of highly trained scholars, particularly at Columbia University, expanded on their understanding of the war and particularly of Reconstruction. Columbia's John W. Burgess and especially William A. Dunning—both specialists in history and political science—dominated scholarly and popular understanding of the era, shaping "generations of students at all levels of education." They would use their influential academic positions to solidify the nation's understanding of race and history. By 1897, Dunning had convinced most Americans that the very term *Reconstruction* was a literal "synonym for bad government." As far as Black political equality was concerned, Dunning taught that the "enfranchisement of the freedmen and their enthronement in political power was as reckless a species of statecraft" as ever existed. Moreover, he emphasized that the change had emerged not from Charles Sumner's "trite generalities of the Rights of Man," but from a naked Republican grab for political domination. White resistance to it, with what Dunning evasively called "extra-legal devices," proved absolutely essential for the reestablishment of order and white supremacy.

.   .   .

Despite the influence of Fiske, Pike, Burgess, Dunning, and their Southern counterparts at the turn of the century, textbooks surprisingly remained contested ground. Even the hearty Fiske discovered that one needed thick skin to "write a history of this country, without giving offense to anyone." If one wanted to avoid controversy, he groaned, "one should stop at 1492." From the 1870s until about 1912, contrary to what most modern American historians have thought, an Emancipationist vision endured in many histories and at all grade levels. These texts not only approvingly mentioned antislavery sentiment in the North but understood that the postwar Republican Congress sought national reunification *and* a just path to full freedom for the former slaves. Books that embraced such views exerted a vital, if short-lived, impact, challenging the nation's basic historical narrative and particularly its meaning. At the same time, Lost Cause dogma, with its unwavering assertions of white supremacy, began to overwhelm the nation's history education as Jim Crow segregation saturated all of American culture. Nevertheless, those textbooks that retained an Emancipationist interpretation of the Civil War and Reconstruction eras, even for a few decades, sowed seeds for the growth of the new century's civil rights movement.

For the very youngest students in elementary and grammar schools at the end of the nineteenth century, schoolbooks provided few details or even a coherent narrative of the nation's history. Like textbooks for Southern schools, those used across the North in primary education rarely discussed the development of slavery and often relegated important issues and events, such as the Emancipation Proclamation, to footnotes. But it would be a mistake to assume that that strategy always diminished the historical importance of slavery and emancipation for the student. Indeed, when discussing the introduction of slavery into Virginia in 1619, an early 1870s text offered one of the most dramatic footnotes a young child might ever encounter: "From this circumstance, small as it seemed at the time, the most momentous consequences ensued,—consequences that, long after, rent the republic with strife, and moistened it with blood." It made clear to students that the controversy over slavery fractured the new republic, that the issue of slavery lay at the heart of every election during the 1850s, and that the Supreme Court's infamous 1857 *Dred Scott* decision—usually ignored by textbooks for young students—transformed slavery from a local to a "national institution." Even elementary school teacher manuals of the era, which listed supplemental source materials, sustained an Emancipationist viewpoint by urging students and teachers to read works by Abraham Lincoln, Ulysses S. Grant, William Cullen Bryant, and John Greenleaf Whittier on John Brown, Harriet Beecher Stowe's *Uncle Tom's Cabin,* and the Philadelphia poet and diplomat George H. Boker's lyrical tribute to Black military service, "The Black Regiment." Another teacher's manual, crafted by Stanford University professor Mary Sheldon Barnes in 1893, made sure that instructors integrated slavery into all of American history, from the colonial era through to the Civil War. While her racial views remained ambiguous, Barnes advised teachers to use the 1850 Fugitive Slave Law as an opportunity to explore the antislavery movement with the theme that "slaves were men, and not property." John Brown, she instructed, could be used to reveal the ambiguities of abolitionism, explore reactions to his career, and assess his historical importance. Barnes avoided all harsh assessments of the antislavery movement and advised teachers to read biographies of the egalitarian abolitionists William Lloyd Garrison and Wendell Phillips and especially the 1869 history of the antislavery struggle, *Some Recollections of Our Anti-slavery Conflict,* by the Garrisonian abolitionist Samuel Joseph May.

At the close of the nineteenth century, women emerged as a major force in the world of education, thanks in part to the work of Horace

Mann and the tireless advocacy of Emma Willard. Helen W. Pierson (1835–1906), a Nova Scotia–born New York author, earned a national reputation in the 1850s as a writer, editor, correspondent, and author of countless sentimental stories—even about escaping slaves—that appeared in *Frank Leslie's Magazine, Harper's Monthly,* and *Godey's Lady's Book.* She gained fame after the war for her immensely popular series of children's primers and juvenile fiction, especially for her histories "in words of one syllable." Her children's histories of France, Germany, Great Britain, and the United States reached a large national audience, even in the South, where they were used long after her death. According to one New York newspaper, her "one syllable" texts routinely served as popular Christmas gifts. It would be difficult to overemphasize her influence.

The 1889 edition of Helen W. Pierson's elementary school textbook *History of the United States in Words of One Syllable* repudiated the Emancipationist vision of the Civil War. The 1883 edition had damned slavery for destroying Black families and leaving the slave with "no hope and no joy in his life." But six years later, on the very same page with the same illustration, she praised the easy lives slaves enjoyed. The Civil War became a romanticized patriotic battle of "brave boys in blue and grey." Her 1889 edition ignored the end of slavery, and her earlier favorable discussion of Reconstruction entirely disappeared. "Slaves in Field of Sugar Cane" appears on p. 101.

Writing a book employing only one-syllable words proved an impossibility, but the meme served to advertise her approach and spawned similarly simplified textbooks for the young. While Pierson wrote disparagingly of Native Americans, she presented slavery as a divisive force in American history, with the North—and astonishingly, Thomas Jefferson—seeing the slave trade as an evil that "tore the black man from his home and sold him to those who would pay the most." Slavery proved so important to her narrative that she devoted an entire chapter to it, depicting the North as believing it "wrong to buy and sell men, and to break up homes," and the South as committed to having Black men perform the labor that white men "could not do." While she never employed the multisyllabic term *abolitionist,* she did introduce Garrison—without his first name—as a man who believed that all slaves should be "free at once." She also linked him indirectly to the Virginia insurrectionist Nat Turner: Garrison "taught the slave he had a right to be free, and so this black man rose and took his rights." Ironically, borrowing from Lost Cause dogma, Pierson also instructed her young readers that the South had seceded in defense of "states' rights," but only for the "right" to own slaves. In a crucial move, she discussed not only the 1863 New York City Draft Riots but Black military service, particularly the fact that Black troops were the first Union forces to enter Richmond, effectively ending the war and "the curse" of slavery. In her attenuated discussion of the postwar period—the term *Reconstruction* had too many syllables—she singled out one essential fact for her readers: "A law [was] made which said that men of all races and hues should have a right to vote."

More advanced textbooks used in the 1880s and '90s set their narratives in the clear light of the sacrifices of the war, and Reconstruction imparted the idea that the United States had been given a "special mission" grounded in a "divine order" and was "trusted with liberty" and the responsibility to enlarge it. They made clear that slavery lay at the heart of the sectional strife, that abolitionists rightly opposed it, and that the assaults on free speech and a free press by anti-abolitionists aimed to destroy any commitment to Black liberty. They also weaved the history of slavery throughout their narratives, including in the Northern colonies. One text designed for use in public and private schools by Horace Scudder, the Boston editor of the influential *Atlantic Monthly,* blended socialist concerns of the 1880s with the history of slavery and referred to the South's slave population as a "working class" exploited by a white leisured master class. Another text squarely placed blame for the introduction of slavery into the American colonies on English "lords and capitalists." Reminiscent of the argument advanced by Benjamin Franklin in the previous century, Scudder asserted that a class of poor Southern whites emerged who lived "from hand to mouth" and in "ignorance" because they had learned that work was only for slaves. While Scudder advanced a disparaging characterization of Southern slaves, he blamed the slave system, not inherent attributes, for the low status of Black Southerners. Southern Blacks lived in squalor and degradation, he asserted, because slavery denied them education, banned them from establishing their own businesses, and prevented them from ever becoming full citizens. He depicted slavery as a damaging institution that made a few men rich and impoverished everyone else, and he balanced his critical characterizations of Southern slaves with their justifiable right to resist, even rebel against, their oppressors.

Mary Elsie Thalheimer's 1881 text, *The Eclectic History of the United States,* incited renewed sectional strife when the Southern Historical Society declared it "unfit . . . owing to unfairness in treating sectional questions in connection with the late war." Her book, which remained in print through 1900 because her brother was CEO of the monopolistic American Book Company, raised the ire of Southerners not just because it "hides its poison" so ingeniously, but because it proved so popular that former soldiers and their sons acted "as agents for its dissemination" throughout the South. The "poison" that so disturbed the Southern Historical Society lay clearly on the opening page. Employing Confederate vice president Alexander Stephens's famous phrase, Thalheimer explained that slavery, not states' rights, had been the "cornerstone" of the Confederacy. She lambasted the secessionists for bitterly protesting the alleged centralization of the Union's federal government, then producing a government more centralized than the one they opposed. Moreover, she instructed her readers that no government on earth could accept a legitimate "Constitutional right" to secession. As slavery underpinned the South, Lincoln had had no choice but to attack it to restore the Union; hence the Emancipation Proclamation. Thalheimer detailed the Proclamation's provision for arming Black soldiers, even discussing the first Black Union troops armed in Kansas and in South Carolina, just as the Bostonian Scudder had emphasized the heroism of Robert Gould Shaw and the 54th Massachusetts Regiment at Battery Wagner, South Carolina. In both texts, Black heroism had thoroughly dispelled the notion that African Americans could not be effective soldiers. She proudly declared that within one year fifty thousand Black troops marched against slavery and "contributed much to the final victories of the Union on the Mississippi." In a final blow, her text held the Confederacy responsible for deluding its people and opined that it should have abandoned the fight just as soon as it began calling for the arming of slaves.

As the publications of Columbia University's John W. Burgess and William A. Dunning and the Harvard-trained John Fiske illustrate, most American colleges and universities had become fertile breeding grounds for white supremacy. Whether considering the liberal arts, education, geography, science, medicine, or the law, most schools of higher education promoted, justified, and detailed the legitimacy—if not inevitability—of white supremacy. In many ways, Harvard University led in this effort, especially through its schools of medicine—which rejected all Black applicants—and the sciences, as Louis Agassiz's career made clear. As the Harvard Law School professor Randall Kennedy once wrote, the university "has been indelibly scarred by slavery, exclusion, segregation, and other forms of racist oppression." But Harvard also admitted some African American students over the course of its history and at the turn of the twentieth century produced some of the nation's most gifted and influential Black scholars, including W.E.B. Du Bois, Alain Locke, and Carter G. Woodson. Equally important, two Harvard University historians and textbook authors combined at the turn of the century to become a stunning force in the perpetuation of the Emancipationist interpretation of American history. Edward Channing (1856–1931) and Albert Bushnell Hart (1854–1943), despite their personal beliefs in white supremacy, nonetheless helped train Black scholars and fought the advance of Lost Cause dogma in scholarship and the teaching of U.S. history.

Channing published a monumental six-volume history of the United States between 1905 and 1925, for which he received the Pulitzer Prize, and in 1898 he came out with a history for high schools and colleges that remained in print for twenty-five years. He had earned one of the first history Ph.D.s granted by an American university and enjoyed a close bond with his Harvard colleague Hart. As one would expect with a name like Channing, he had deep New England roots. His mother was the sister of the famed author and Transcendentalist Margaret Fuller, and his great-uncle was the legendary Boston Unitarian minister William Ellery Channing. History draped his upbringing and shaped his character. Although a firm Lincoln-style nationalist and personally unsympathetic to the radical abolitionists, he read their writings and the best available studies of their careers and recommended these sources to the students who used his textbook. Such thoroughness mattered. With lively prose and a diligence that only a scholar could bring to the task, Channing's account moved slavery to the center of American history and made clear that responsibility for the controversy that rent the republic fell squarely on the South. He believed that the North in general and the Republican Party in particular "stood firmly and squarely on the ground occupied by the fathers of the Constitution . . . that the national government should [not] be used as a machine to extend slavery."

His text reflected the then-common perception that most slaves did not suffer extraordinary abuse, but at the same time he acknowledged violent slave resistance in the North and South. He emphasized the ruthlessness of slavery in South Carolina, with its devastating rice plantations, and the "unusually brutal harshness of the masters and overseers." As no one else had done with such thoroughness, he charted the rise of antislavery sentiment from Samuel

Sewall's 1700 *Selling of Joseph,* to the Pennsylvania Quaker opposition to slavery, and to the state's antislavery congressional petition campaign in the 1790s. Channing, foreshadowing the later response to Garrison and his colleagues, presented early Southern legislators' reactions to this first petition campaign as volcanic, assailing the "memorialists with tremendous fervor." Clearly, Channing wrote, "they scented danger from afar." He also detailed the importance of the Ordinance of 1787, Vermont's move to outlaw slavery in its state constitution, John Adams's authorship of Massachusetts's 1780 constitution, which declared that "all men are born free and equal," and the liberalization of Protestantism, all of which to him were clear signs of society's cultural progress.

With enormous care and detail, Channing charted the rise of radical abolitionism, beginning with the emergence of William Lloyd Garrison in 1831, and the South's determination to silence him to the point of offering a $5,000 bounty to anyone who would kidnap and drag the outrageous offender to Georgia for justice. He also detailed the North's opposition to him, even his near lynching in 1835, the repression of his colleagues, and the destruction of New England schools that taught African American children. While other texts would have employed this history to discredit the antislavery movement, Channing instead instructed students to understand them as harbingers of "more fruitful results" to come. That fruit, for Channing, was the growing political resistance to slavery, such as the antislavery petition campaign to Congress in the 1830s. He singled out John Quincy Adams for defending the abolitionists' right to petition Congress, which he linked to basic American civil rights. He highlighted the 1837 murder of the antislavery journalist Elijah P. Lovejoy, which, he rightly observed, led to the emergence of the movement's most eloquent advocate, Wendell Phillips, and the beginning of the transformation of Northern public opinion. Even John Brown, condemned by most authors as ruinously insane, appeared not as a legitimate cause of Southern anger and mistrust of the North but rather as a critical actor in a process that ultimately led to the demise of slavery and, astonishingly, to the liberation of Southern *whites*. In a stunning move, Channing quoted the 1881 remark of the Boston journalist, entrepreneur, and activist Edward Atkinson that one day he expected to see former Confederate soldiers joining with their children to raise a monument to Brown "in token of the liberty which he brought to the white men of the South."

On the issue of slavery, Channing wrote firmly and eloquently, but he failed to include African Americans in his narrative, ignoring their role in the antislavery movement and in the Civil War. They appeared as a cause but not as historical actors, more a problem than a people. But he also hailed defeat of the Confederacy as the death not just of slavery but also of its principle that "the negro is not equal to the white man; that slavery, subordination to the natural race, is his natural and normal condition." While offering only a cursory assessment of Reconstruction, Channing laid blame for its failure on Andrew Johnson and the South's unswerving resistance to civil rights for the former slaves, not on carpetbaggers and scalawags. "The Southern whites," he wrote, "were determined to deprive the freedmen of their rights guaranteed to them by the [new constitutional] amendments, and thus to defeat the object of reconstruction." They beat, shot, and intimidated the former slaves to deny Black voting rights and "regain control of the Southern state governments, and ultimately succeeded."

Channing's assessments, despite their shortcomings, furthered an Emancipationist view of the nation's central crisis at a time when that view had come under withering assault across the country. They were surpassed in eloquence, determination, and commitment only by those of his Harvard colleague Albert Bushnell Hart. Harvard's professor of history and government for over forty years, Hart always referred to himself as a "descendant of Abolitionists." Born in Clarksville, Pennsylvania, he graduated from Harvard in 1880 and received a fellowship to study history and government in Germany with one of Europe's leading scholars of the United States, Hermann von Holst. Hart then returned to Harvard and became one of the most influential, and certainly the most productive, American historians of the early twentieth century. His almost countless publications and writings—books, pamphlets, essays, and speeches—fill about 250 archival volumes.

Albert Bushnell Hart (1854–1943), Harvard University's prolific American historian, set aside his own racial prejudice to become dissertation adviser to some of the country's most influential Black scholars, including W.E.B. Du Bois. He continued to assist his former students long after their graduation and became an adviser to African American educators in the District of Columbia.

One cannot overemphasize Hart's importance to the nation's teaching, its understanding of American history, the development of African American history, or the continuation of the Emancipationist historical viewpoint. Not only did he become one of the nation's most prolific historians, writing influential biographies, histories, and reference works, but he also edited "The American Nation," a dominating twenty-seven-volume series, published between 1904 and 1918, covering the full range of American history—which included his own *Slavery and Abolition, 1831–1841.* His six-hundred-page high school textbook, *Essentials in American History,* came out in 1905, the year before *Slavery and Abolition,* setting a striking pace of labor, and it remained in print for at least fifteen years. Perhaps his most enduring contribution, however, was his teaching career. While most of his fellow department members would have nothing to do with African Americans, he and his colleague Edward Channing took on Black graduate students, among whom were those who would shape Black history in the twentieth century: Carter G. Woodson, founder of the Association for the Study of African American Life and History; Charles H. Wesley, who published over fifteen works on African American history, taught for decades at Howard University, and became president of Wilberforce University; and W.E.B. Du Bois, an NAACP founder, editor, and the nation's leading African American scholar and social critic of his or any other generation. Hart considered Du Bois to be his most gifted student of any race and lobbied tirelessly to find him employment after his graduation. Because of Du Bois's immense talent, Hart saw in him the nation's most effective argument against racism, even his own. Indeed, largely because of Hart, Harvard's history department granted fourteen doctorates to African Americans, about 25 percent of all such degrees awarded prior to 1940. He also served as mentor to Oswald Garrison Villard, William Lloyd Garrison's grandson, a pivotal social activist, and a founding member of the NAACP. Clearly, Hart left an enormous imprint, helping to make the modern civil rights movement a possibility.

Hart understood, as so many of his contemporaries did not, that a profound contradiction lay at the heart of American society. The nation professed principles of equal opportunity and civil rights, but violated those norms in its abhorrent treatment of those Hart labeled "the unorganized race." As a scholar, he sought balance and detachment, but when it came to the history of slavery, he concluded that it could have existed only "with blood, iron, and tears." He understood abolitionism as a humanitarian effort, part of a wider moral transatlantic movement that embodied the progressive force of "modern civilization." Defenders of slavery, on the other hand, represented the "obsolete, the abnormal, and the impossible." Moreover, his scholarship embraced the egalitarianism he found among the Garrisonians and acknowledged the thriving, respectable, and intellectually accomplished African American communities of the North. White abolitionists, he wrote, traveled with their Black colleagues, "sat upon the same platforms with them, ate with them, and one enthusiastic abolitionist white couple [even] adopted a negro child." As few other scholars had done, Hart included Black abolitionists in his history of the movement and described Frederick Douglass as a "man of extraordinary power and magnetism, a remarkable speaker." Even more unusual, Hart praised Black female abolitionists such as Sojourner Truth and Harriet Tubman as "striking" and "heroic." His account carried considerable weight, as he revealed that he once had heard Tubman speak.

His 1905 *Essentials in American History* reflected much of the positive characterization of abolitionism that marked his scholarship. By covering antislavery activism outside New England, especially in New York, Pennsylvania, and Ohio, he gave students a deeper appreciation of the movement and its diversity, and he maintained the link between the movement and a vigorous defense of civil liberties. But his work turned ambivalent when it came to Garrison and his colleagues. Interracial activism disappeared from his account, and Garrison became unsympathetic and uncompromising, although determined to "lift up the standard of emancipation in the eyes of the nation." John Brown also came off ambivalently in Hart's textbook, depicted as a heroic man without remorse or guilt who had also convinced the South that "slavery was no longer safe within the federal Union."

As for slavery, Hart contextualized it throughout the New World and portrayed it as cruel from the start. Because the profits derived from slave labor became enormous, he taught that it had thoroughly situated itself in the culture, giving the master uncontested control over his property. Hart assured his readers that the "right to own a slave included the absolute right to sell him, and there was no legal obligation to sell families as a whole." Citing John C. Calhoun, Hart explained that democracy and slavery coexisted in the Southern mind, promoting social stability. "Slavery," Calhoun once remarked, "forms the most solid and durable foundation on which to erect free institutions." As for the Civil War, no ambivalence existed in Hart's account—it was all about slavery. The South would remain in the Union only, as Georgia's Robert Toombs had declared, when "the North shall call slavery right." As only a few other high school texts had done, Hart's book acknowledged the African American military role in the war, including Thomas Wentworth Higginson's 1st South Carolina Volunteers, Robert Gould Shaw's 54th Massachusetts Regiment, and the 179,000 Black troops who eventually served.

But Hart's work collided with his own larger Emancipationist mission when he wrote about the slave. In his rendering, slaves remained an abstraction and a stereotype. One day a slave might be devastated by the sale of a family member or even himself, but the very next he would be "cheerfully fiddling on his way to the dreaded far South." He never completed his study of the United States through Reconstruction, so his textbook relied on current scholarship, which included the work of the archenemy of the Emancipationist framework, William A. Dunning, and the equally racist Princeton scholar Woodrow Wilson, who had written his own history of the era in 1893. On the one hand, Hart's history moved African Americans to the center of Reconstruction, detailing how the national government attempted to integrate them into the reunified nation. He even emphasized the career of the Radical Republican Thaddeus Stevens, presenting him as a dedicated abolitionist and unrelenting advocate of Black suffrage, although likely only to preserve Republican "ascendency." But then he related the "tragic" story, as laid out by Dunning, that Reconstruction had collapsed into anarchy, misrule, and theft through carpetbaggers and scalawags who understandably provoked Klan terror. Hart then instructed his readers that the "whole country" became "weary of the squabbles" and allowed the South to reinstate white supremacy.

Dunning's scholarship had rejected Reconstruction as a doomed effort to elevate "ignorant and degraded black men" to power. The Freedmen's Bureau, intended to assist the former slaves in their transition to freedom, had been a ridiculous effort to address African Americans with "pious homilies and moral platitudes obviously above their intelligence." Dunning defended the oppressive Black Codes that all but eliminated African American freedom as a necessary effort to "bring some sort of order out of the social and economic chaos" caused by emancipation. Since Blacks were not on "the same social, moral, and intellectual plane with whites," Dunning believed they needed to be regulated. He even dismissed accusations of Klan terror as "of but slight consequence compared with the end," which he described as the necessary "social and political ascendency of the white race."

Hart, one of the most influential voices of the Emancipationist viewpoint, knew better than to accept such a twisted depiction of Reconstruction. But in a great irony, as the editor of Harper & Bros.' twenty-seven-volume "The American Nation" series, he had to craft an introduction for Dunning's revolting history of Reconstruction, the twenty-second volume in the series. Hart's introduction was painfully evasive and even ventured the alternative theory that the North experienced its own version of Reconstruction, complete with "unfit officials, the plundering of public treasuries, and the degradation of civic standards." His textbook, however, still reflected Dunning's influence because, like his Harvard colleague Edward Channing, he likely bent to his publisher's will for the sake of greater sales. Channing later so regretted his acquiescence to his publisher that he damned his own *Elements of United States History*, for beginning students, as a "Book of Lies." Hart probably slanted his narrative to succumb to the demands of popular prejudice and his own publisher, the American Book Company, which was notorious for its monopolistic business practices and its willingness to do whatever it took to increase sales.

. . .

Despite the shortcomings of textbooks by Channing and Hart, and the avalanche of those that embraced the white supremacy of Dunning and Wilson, the influence of the Emancipationist viewpoint persisted into the early twentieth century. At the turn of the century—an era presumed by modern scholars to offer only clichéd accounts of the "peculiar institution"—about a dozen histories provided informed accounts of slavery's introduction and destructive development. Several in the 1890s helped students understand its original acceptance by placing it in a world of various types of unfree labor, and nearly all quite accurately used environmental factors— the South's oppressive heat—to explain its persistence: white men simply would not work in such conditions when they could force others to do it for them. The influential Massachusetts father-and-son team of William A. and Arthur M. Mowry stressed that slavery shaped the character of the nation and that the cotton gin made it "almost an absolute necessity." Their work, as few others, dwelled on the condition of the enslaved and advised students that the auction block came to symbolize the "evils of the system," one that produced enormous wealth for a few and poverty for everyone else. "Slave labor," they wrote, "was and always must be one of the most wasteful forms of human industry."

At the beginning of the twentieth century, at least seven additional textbooks described a world of unfree labor to explain slavery's introduction, detailing how such an environment could transform a white labor system into one of enslaved Africans. No sentimentalism, no Lost Cause dogma about slaves loving their masters, disfigured these texts. They depicted the new system as one in which slavery enriched a select few in the South and eventually an industrial elite in the North. Most placed responsibility for slavery's expansion squarely on Eli Whitney's cotton gin, which "extinguished" any opposition in the South and marked a spindled line directly to the Civil War. As one 1901 history explained to students, the New Englander's invention "increased the value of slave labor beyond human calculation." No student assigned these texts could come away with anything but scorn for Southern slavery and how much it contradicted the very principles that underpinned the nation.

As William H. Mace explained in his 1904 *A School History of the United States,* if Americans thought it unjust for England to tax Americans, "it could hardly be right for Americans to buy and sell Africans." Moreover, after 1900 a half-dozen textbooks emphasized this contradiction as the birthmark that had disfigured the nation since 1619. Even John Bach McMaster, whose own history denigrated Reconstruction and earned a devoted readership and profits from 1897 to 1930, advised students that "at the very time the men of Virginia thus planted free representative government in America, another institution was planted beside it, which, in the course of 250 years, almost destroyed free government." The year 1619 became pivotal to explaining the development of American history, and textbooks inculcated the unavoidable fact that "Negro slavery and white republicanism began at the same time in Virginia." As William Estabrook Chancellor, the New Jersey superintendent of schools, explained in 1903, "from Virginia both slavery and democracy spread until, two and a half centuries later, they came to that inevitable and fearful collision, our Civil War."

These same histories built on the positive assessments of the antislavery movement that had been characteristic of Emancipationist books in the 1870s and '80s. While most textbooks afterward ignored African American participation in the movement, some went to unusual lengths to highlight the African American role, usually focusing on Frederick Douglass. At the very time that public discourse promoted segregation and was extinguishing African American history from public consciousness, a history by the Minnesota school superintendent Sanford Niles stoutly resisted the trend. Niles not only devoted an entire chapter to the abolitionists but included attractive images of William Lloyd Garrison, Wendell Phillips, John Greenleaf Whittier, *and* Frederick Douglass, along with one-page biographies for each highlighting their heroism. Niles also dwelled on racist Northern opposition to abolitionists and to African Americans. Under the headline "Mob Spirit," he chronicled Northern mob attacks on Black churches and communities and on operations of the Underground Railroad, a venture he characterized as run by whites and Blacks, men *and* women.

For beginning readers, textbooks that sought to inspire children with the story of "American progress" characterized the antislavery movement, led by William Lloyd Garrison, as embodying the idea that "all slaves should be set free." Even the controversial John Brown appeared as a hero who "lost his life in trying to help slaves free themselves." Another text meant for elementary readers, *The Story of the Great Republic* (1899), characterized abolitionists as a Christian moral force who believed it "unjust and even sinful to allow one class of human beings to be bought and sold, and treated like cattle." Texts that still adhered assiduously to the old format of presenting only the nation's political history, nonetheless depicted the North, and especially New England, as home to people who "looked upon slavery as a sin against God and a crime against man, and commenced a fierce and bitter agitation against its extension." Even John Brown, whom one 1896 elementary text characterized as perhaps unwise in his plans, still appeared as honest, determined, and a "stern enthusiast of Puritan descent" who had "resolved to make a practical effort to free the slaves." This same work instructed students that America could not sustain slavery and fulfill its true destiny: "A real republican form of government based on human slavery was simply an impossibility."

From 1896 to 1912, a time dominated by Lost Cause dogma and Jim Crow segregation in the North and the South, at least *fifteen* different textbooks presented William Lloyd Garrison and the radical antislavery movement as a moral force against the nation's deepest crime. They bonded it to the survival of basic American civil liberties and even linked the movement to the rise of the unprecedented literary outburst of the mid-nineteenth century. One 1903 account explained that the abolitionist movement "had the future with it." Because of the abolitionists, especially because of how much hatred they incited, their cause drew the attention of all Americans as an ultimate "struggle between slavery and freedom." Wilbur F. Gordy's seventh-grade text, first published in 1898 and reprinted until 1935, described the "heroic William Lloyd Garrison and his brave followers" as "right in their leading idea that slavery was wrong." The abolitionists' work, another textbook explained in 1902, forced the nation to confront its central contradiction, "the final struggle between freedom and slavery," and to defend "oppressed humanity." Moreover, as a 1903 history made clear, the issue of slavery was a national, not merely a Southern concern, "an intolerable crime against humanity, for which the whole nation was accountable no less than the slaveholding states." So that even the youngest students would comprehend the issues at stake, a 1912 elementary schoolbook explained that both American political principles and Christianity rejected "the practice of holding men in lifelong bondage on account of the color of their skin and the accident of their birth."

John Brown eventually emerged in textbooks as the most vivid example of a crazed New England obsession with opposing slavery, oppressing the South, and causing the Civil War. But at the turn of the century, a dozen schoolbooks presented him as a sincere, sane, and determined descendant of Puritans who gave his life for the slave. One 1895 elementary school history even asserted that he sought to end slavery with as little bloodshed as possible. For some authors, his act may have helped spark the Civil War, but he remained a hero, met his fate courageously, was "an instrument in God's hands," and "died in the unwavering belief that he had contributed to a great cause." William M. Davidson's 1906 textbook described Brown in political terms, as the leader of a "band of insurgents" who attacked Harpers Ferry hoping to "bring about a revolution which would ultimately lead to the abolition of slavery." Even those authors who disapproved of the raid and quite accurately thought it played a major role in provoking the South to secede from the Union, nonetheless saw Brown as moral, honest, and determined, reflective not of Northern aggression but of the crisis that slavery posed to the nation.

These same textbooks agreed on the causes of the Civil War, rejecting out of hand Lost Cause assertions that the South had merely been defending constitutionally guaranteed "state rights." As one 1903 high school history concluded, states' rights assertions were entirely a function of slave owners' interests. Wilbur F. Gordy's 1898 text stated categorically: "Slavery the Real Cause of the War." So that students would comprehend the full significance of the Kansas-Nebraska Act—it destroyed the Compromise of 1850, gave birth to the Republican Party, and initiated fighting in "bleeding Kansas"—Charles Kendall Adams and William P. Trent's 1903 schoolbook included a dramatic United States map marked "Areas of Freedom and Slavery in 1854." The South, as one 1902 author concluded, was simply "out of tune with an enlightened world" and served only as the "champion of the detested institution of slavery." Even a 1912 elementary school history explained that the Civil War had been caused by "slavery and nothing else."

While most textbooks—even some in the Emancipationist framework—ignored African Americans or relegated them to secondary roles, when it came to the Civil War the narratives decidedly shifted. The Emancipation Proclamation and Black military service refocused attention squarely on the Black contribution during the most critical moment in the nation's history. The impact of Lincoln's Proclamation, which one elementary text advised young readers was "almost as famous as the Declaration of Independence," gave many authors the opportunity to discuss the heroism of 179,000 Black men. In the face of the South's declared intention to treat them as "insurrectionists," textbooks emphasized this essential African American contribution to the survival of the republic. They "fought bravely on many a bloody field" and in the navy, one 1890 text asserted, and another from 1901 proclaimed emancipation and the resulting Black military service as "the greatest event of the century." Wilbur F. Gordy's ever-popular *History of the United States for Schools* even included an attractive full-page illustration of Black Civil War soldiers.

The history of Reconstruction gave these authors additional opportunities to retain the centrality of African Americans to the national narrative and reject the ever-growing dominance of the version of the past created by Pike, Fiske, Burgess, and Dunning. At least seven different texts explicitly repudiated any racist interpretation of Reconstruction. The Quaker Josiah Leeds's 1877 account outlined Federal efforts to support the freedpeople, condemned Klan violence, and emphasized the work of the Freedmen's Bureau and even the educational efforts by the Peabody Education Fund for whites *and* African Americans. The freedpeople needed and deserved such efforts, these authors taught students at the turn of the century, and those who opposed them, including President Andrew Johnson, did so to "reduce the blacks to real slavery under some [other] plausible name, and retain representation for them, while denying them political rights." The North opposed any "restoration of the Union which should leave the blacks in the power of their former masters." The Thirteenth, Fourteenth, and Fifteenth amendments not only sought to "settle the question of slavery forever," but to assist African Americans in their transition to full freedom. No groaning over the enfranchisement of the "most ignorant class of Americans" touched these textbooks, which instead asserted that the new constitutional amendments existed exclusively to give "the former slaves all the legal rights which white citizens had held." They blamed Reconstruction's failure neither on allegedly "ignorant" former slaves nor on corrupt carpetbaggers and scalawags but squarely on the white South, where it belonged. Francis Newton Thorpe's 1901 *History of the American People* noted that white "secret societies, known by various names, as 'The Invisible Empire,' 'the Caucasians,' 'the Ku-Klux-Klan,' [and] 'The Knights of the White Camellia,' . . . attempted to do by violence what they were prevented from doing by law; that is, to control the negroes by a reign of terror." This legacy, Thorpe exclaimed, in "its terrible details surpassed the darkest ages of history."

.   .   .

These textbooks retained a surprising level of Emancipationist fervor at the beginning of the twentieth century, but precious few would endure for the next twenty years. Jim Crow culture spread across the North with a velocity that would have thrilled a John H. Van Evrie, fueling a wave of accounts that ignored or relentlessly denigrated Blacks as unworthy of freedom or incapable of responsible conduct. Even in Boston, the historic seat of egalitarian abolitionism and Radical Republicanism, the new generation of reformers could feel the tidal surge of white supremacy. During the 1905 celebration of the centennial of William Lloyd Garrison's birth, the great lawyer and founding president of the NAACP, Moorfield Storey, could only lament, "We are passing through a reaction against the great principles of freedom and equal rights" to which Garrison had devoted his life.

Just seven years later, one of the most influential publishing houses in the country, New York's Charles Scribner's Sons, released Hilary A. Herbert's popular assault on the antislavery movement, *The Abolition Crusade and Its Consequences*. Herbert, the Alabama lawyer, Confederate veteran, and former secretary of the navy for Grover Cleveland, denounced African Americans as "slothful and incapable of self-government" and held Garrison and his abolitionist allies entirely responsible for bringing on the Civil War. In Herbert's eyes, Garrison was a fevered fanatic who had damned even the kindest slave owner as a "wicked monster" and attacked the South so the North could confiscate its "property." The Civil War was entirely unnecessary, as in time the South would have abandoned slavery on its own. Moreover, the abolitionists owned responsibility for rejecting the moderate Reconstruction policies of Abraham Lincoln in order to transform government in the South "from white to negroid." Hence resistance to Reconstruction was, according to Herbert, essential to protect "white civilization."

Herbert's white supremacist view of the past, especially of Reconstruction (which he had begun attacking over twenty years before his assault on the abolitionists), increasingly became the standard account for history textbooks. Even those that celebrated the antislavery movement and the extinction of slavery as a result of the Civil War poured out their pent-up white supremacist venom when it came to Reconstruction. Perhaps the most important example emerged from the pen of John Bach McMaster (1852–1932). A central figure from the heroic age of nineteenth-century historians, McMaster joined the fraternity of Henry Adams, George Bancroft, Edward Channing, John Fiske, Richard Hildreth, John G. Palfrey, Francis Parkman, and James Ford Rhodes in writing an epic multivolume history of the United States. His eight-volume contribution, published between 1883 and 1913, covered the nation's history from the Revolution to the Civil War. He later produced a two-volume history of American participation in the First World War and a dozen other books. He became so important a scholar that the University of Pennsylvania endowed a professorship in American history just for him, which he occupied from 1883 until his retirement in 1922. The New York–born McMaster, who grew up during the Civil War excited by the soldiers, strife, and drama, always held the South responsible for causing the war and celebrated the end of slavery. But his father, James McMaster, before the Civil War, had founded a financial house in New Orleans and bought a sugarcane plantation next door to one owned by the celebrated future Confederate general P.G.T. Beauregard, who commanded the artillery batteries that fired the first shots at Fort Sumter. That legacy would eventually seep through the veneer of his abolitionist sympathy, like blood through a bandage, when he wrote about Reconstruction for American students.

McMaster's *School History of the United States* remained in print from 1897 until 1930. He covered white participation in the antislavery movement well beyond the traditional focus on Garrison, and he condemned the assaults on free speech and the press that attempted to suppress criticism of the South and slavery. In the end, McMaster wrote, such efforts only increased Northern "antislavery sentiment." Indeed, any fault in his account—beyond ignoring African Americans—lay in his overemphasizing the level of popular support garnered by abolitionists of all stripes. While he characterized John Brown's raid on Harpers Ferry as a "fool's act," no accusations of insanity sullied his narrative. Instead, he called Brown a "man of intense convictions" who possessed "a deep-seated hatred of slavery." As for secession and responsibility for the Civil War, McMaster assured students that he had read all the relevant declarations from Southern leaders and resolutely concluded that "according to its own statements," the South left the Union "because the people believed that the election of Lincoln meant the abolition of slavery." He offered no diverting discussion of states' rights or constitutional guarantees; the war had come about because of slavery, plain and simple.

But when it came to Reconstruction, McMaster duplicated hundreds of similar accounts that characterized it as simple thievery by carpetbaggers and scalawags. In what was fast becoming *the* standard interpretation, McMaster described how a plague of Northern invaders teamed up with "dishonest" white Southerners to take advantage of "ignorant negroes" and seize control of Southern state and local governments to facilitate their lustful plunder. He condemned Northerners who issued warnings to the freedpeople that whites sought to reenslave them, even after describing those very efforts. As Pike and Dunning had done, McMaster explained that white Southerners had formed "defensive" organizations like the Klan to fight the evil carpetbaggers and their Black allies. The violence perpetrated by the Klan and similar groups, McMaster made abundantly clear, represented a necessary response to "corruption." He did rebuke the South for grudgingly approving the Fifteenth Amendment guaranteeing Black voting rights and then passing the Black Codes to suppress those rights. This situation, he explained, only convinced Northerners that the South refused to accept the results of the war and the abolition of slavery. But "to the men of the South, who feared that the ignorant negroes would refuse to work, these laws seemed to be necessary." McMaster's racial bias clearly oozed through his account of one of the pivotal eras in American history. So there could be no misunderstanding, he justified white supremacy in a 1903 speech delivered in Cleveland, Ohio:

> In society, general equality is restrained for the public good. On this principle the blacks are excluded. They are required to bear no burdens, perform no duties. The blacks are a peculiar people, unacquainted with civil liberty and incapable of appreciating its benefits. . . . No white man will stand shoulder to shoulder with a negro in the trainband or the jury room, or invite him to his table or into his pew in church. Why then put him on an equality on election day?

In the 1880s, as Hezekiah Butterworth and Charles Carleton Coffin were publishing their Emancipationist manifestos, other authors took up the more popular cause of national reconciliation. Seeking to diminish the divisions of Civil War and Reconstruction, they emphasized patriotic sacrifices, the development of American liberty, and the debt modern generations owed to "the fathers." Some deemphasized the history of slavery, avoiding the discussion and relegating important facts to footnotes. Textbooks published in the South or for the Southern market said as little as possible about slavery and far more about Confederate heroism. George Frederick Holmes, a Southern philosopher and University of Virginia professor, acknowledged in 1886 that "the true history of the times must wait till a later day" when "renewed harmony reigned." So in his text, he avoided any meaningful discussion of slavery and the Civil War, but made sure to instruct students that the federal government had "no authority to interfere in the emancipation of slaves" or in their treatment. Many textbooks even took up the old prewar version of history, ignoring abolitionism altogether, restricting their narratives to political history, and avoiding any mention of African Americans. A few still refused to provide a serious account of Reconstruction, and one only offered a hint in a footnote that after the war "political strife" continued. The author of a 1901 schoolbook found the subject of Reconstruction so upsetting that he skipped it entirely, jumping directly from the Civil War to the Spanish-American War. A volume by the Elmira, New York, team of Joel and Esther Steele simply declared that after the war "the South was slowly adjusting herself to the novel conditions of free labor" and said former soldiers from both sides "engaged in quiet avocations." This pathological avoidance of the central issues that divided the nation—characteristic of their publisher, the American Book Company—is all the more astonishing since Joel Steele had served in the Civil War.

Educators already had insisted that any overt Emancipationist perspective be purged from textbooks, as the 1898 New England History Teachers' Association's report implied. In her teacher's manual—which had fully integrated slavery into the narrative of American history—Mary Sheldon Barnes also advised teachers to avoid any discussion of the "morality of slavery." Stick to the facts, causes, and consequences, and focus on "the effects upon the slave and the slave-holder." Such an approach, she asserted, was essential for the development of patriotism—what she considered to be the primary goal of history instruction. Midwestern authors adopted the same approach as early as 1878, when Asbury University (later DePauw University) professor John Clark Ridpath—whose parents lived in Virginia—avoided discussing slavery in his desire to make young boys and girls "love the inspiring story" of American history.

The Emancipationist Hezekiah Butterworth succumbed to the desire for national unification—and profit—and turned one of his famed children's books into the epitome of Lost Cause racist sentimentalism. His 1886 *ZigZag Journey in the Sunny South* incomprehensibly began with the "romance" of the European conquest of New England's Native Americans. It then launched into one of the most disturbing renditions of the "Sunny South" written by a Northerner since Septimus Winner. It would have better suited the work of Thomas Dixon, Jr.—inspiration for the 1915 film *Birth of a Nation*—than the author of the pivotal 1882 *Young Folks' History of*

Hezekiah Butterworth's 1886 *A ZigZag Journey in the Sunny South* vacillated between the exotic and the ridiculous when depicting African Americans (p. 239).

America. Butterworth described the Old South's history as "a poem" and repellently opened his *ZigZag* "journey" with the assertion that "the negro is superstitious to such a degree" that he provided a "lively coloring" to the "Sunny South." Butterworth then offered young students a "typical" sunny Southern tune:

> Nigger swine fer to eat good grease,
> Hoo-dah! Hoodah!
> Possom fat, hog liver, chicken-foot grease,
> Hoo-dah! Hoo-dah! Hoo.
> Kink up de wool, nigger, fling out de toe,
> Shuffle up de pigeon-wing—cut, jesso!
> Hoodah! Hoodah! Hoodah! Hoodah!
> Hoodah! Hoo!

In 1903 Butterworth participated in a dedication ceremony in Barrington, Rhode Island, for a new historical memorial composed of a large "white quartz boulder" with a smaller black stone on either side. The attached plaque read: "In memory of the slaves and their descendants who faithfully served Barrington families." His conversion to white supremacy was now complete.

From the late 1880s to 1919, portrayals of Southern slavery increasingly reflected the supremacist fiction profitably affirmed by Butterworth. Few authors in this period detailed the evils of slavery but instead emphasized its many benefits to the South, the North, and most especially the *slave*. Accounts of the introduction of slavery at Jamestown described a world of unfree labor, but now justified it. Textbook after textbook explained that the uncivilized African, legitimately captured in war, was well "suited" to the South's "hot and malarial climate," which would have been fatal to the white man if forced to labor under those conditions. Besides, Africans were a "heathen race" who could only benefit from the experience. One 1913 history assured students that "there can be little doubt that the vast majority of the negroes" were far better off than "they could possibly have been by remaining in their native forests." As Woodrow Wilson explained in his 1893 history, masters "almost uniformly" treated their property "indulgently and even affectionately." They refused to overwork their slaves, who "were comfortably quartered, and were kept from overwork both by their own laziness and by the slack discipline to which they were subjected." As one 1911 textbook elaborated, in theory slavery might be an evil, but in practice it benefited the African who received training "in habits of industry, taught trades, and governed firmly but not unkindly." Some cruel masters may have existed, a few authors confessed, but most slaves lived better than the white working class in "most countries, and the sick, children, and the aged were cared for." Moreover, master and slave formed loving relationships. In one 1909 history, Lawton Evans, a superintendent of schools in Augusta, Georgia, explained that for generations slaves knew no other life, and most "were content to remain as they had been born. A real affection existed between the master and his slave," he wrote. "Never before in history did so tender a feeling exist between an enslaved race and those who held them in bondage." A 1914 two-volume *grammar school* text assured students that "from the little pickaninnies to the oldest old aunties and mammies," all Blacks admiringly fixated on the activities of their masters, and when the workday ended, "they enjoyed getting together for a rollicking time." Another textbook, without referring to Sally Hemings, emphasized the loving relationship between Thomas Jefferson and his slaves, claiming that they "thought that no one could be better than their master. He was kind to them, and they were ready to do anything for him."

" They enjoyed getting together for a rollicking time "

"They enjoyed getting together for a rollicking time." Illustration from Arthur C. Perry and Gertrude A. Price's two-volume *American History* (1914), 2:135.

A few authors acknowledged that slavery could be "hard," even cruel, which in their view fueled dishonesty and violence in the slave. Others dismissed any cruelty associated with bondage as essential to maintaining social control. Andrew C. McLaughlin and Claude H. Van Tyne, university history department heads and constitutional scholars, declared in their 1916 junior high school history that since Africans were primitive barbarians, "there appeared to be no way to control them except to place them under an absolute master." From the early nineteenth century to the twentieth, descriptions of slavery always vacillated between characterizations of it as benign and beneficial and as a possible spur to rebellion. In most cases, however, authors assigned blame for slave violence, such as the 1831 Nat Turner rebellion, to meddlesome abolitionists like William Lloyd Garrison—not to the institution of slavery. Indeed, one 1913 textbook took such pains to explain that slaves had received favorable treatment that it attributed the rise of abolitionism to something other than the slaves' condition. A textbook by Smith College professor John Spencer Bassett explained that slavery grew harsher only *after* the rise of the antislavery movement, which halted the "real advance in rudimentary civilization over African barbarism" and destroyed the "harmony between master and slave." A history by Henry E. Chambers, a Johns Hopkins University Ph.D., and a high school teacher, enjoyed ten editions by 1900. Chambers sidestepped all controversies concerning slavery, explaining that whatever conditions those in bondage endured, the important fact remained that slavery "first placed the United States among the great commercial nations of the world." Not only did slavery catapult the United States to world power, but the "systematic training bestowed upon him during his period of servitude, and his contact with higher intelligence, have given to the negro an impulse to civilization that neither his inherent inclinations nor his native environment would of themselves have bestowed." By 1919, the teaching of slavery had been transformed from Charles Carleton Coffin's Emancipationism into a curriculum indistinguishable from the views of John C. Calhoun.

In this period, when it came to slavery, U.S. histories intended for the general classroom proved no different from those aimed specifically at the Southern market. Both characterized slavery as emerging from a world of unfree labor and emphasized Northern profits in the slave trade. Both emphasized the great value of slaves who performed labor that whites either could not or would not do. One history of South Carolina described slavery's introduction into the New World as "an act of humanity" that relieved South American Natives from "the horrible slavery of the mines." George Frederick Holmes, the British Guyana–born president of the University of Mississippi, asserted that slaves met the colonial era's unfulfilled labor needs, furnishing workers "for clearing the forests, enclosing the lands, cultivating the soil, and for other manual services." Mary Tucker Magill's long-used history of Virginia repeated the assertions that African peoples could withstand Southern sun "better than the whites" and that they made great profits for the North and the South. She too depicted slavery as a benign institution, in which slave owners kept Black families together and maintained affectionate relations with their slaves. Any other description, she asserted, amounted to distortion and propaganda. Slave owners, another well-used 1914 text asserted, sought to preserve the "best interests of both races." Even owners who might desire to free their property could not do so, since emancipation would unleash "a large class of homeless and irresponsible persons" on society and incite "horrible negro uprisings."

Texts for Southern schools, like their Northern counterparts, contended that slavery had provided a refuge for an unfortunate race, who lived better than white workers and were "nursed in sickness and protected in old age. In many cases the negroes were taught to read and write and had the benefit of religious instruction." One beginner's history explained in 1919 that under the direction of a skilled overseer, "negroes made excellent farm hands." They loved their owners and "grew up together" as "playmates and friends." John H. Van Evrie's associate John Esten Cooke crafted a Virginia history text that presented the same image of the slave as a person whom the master treated well and considered a "humble friend and retainer." As proof of slaves' favored status, borrowing from Van Evrie, Cooke maintained that even after the Emancipation Proclamation, they remained "at home, in perfect quiet, cultivating the soil as before . . . best friends of their master's family." Just as

Yankees described slaves as having "a rollicking time," Southern authors taught that the African "savage" benefited from the "great blessing" of slavery.

Textbook assessments of the antislavery movement during this period followed the white supremacist trajectory of Hilary A. Herbert. At least fifteen different ones condemned it as an assortment of malcontents, radicals, fanatics, and mentally unhinged persons dedicated to destroying slavery—and slaveholders—at any cost. Their agitation, petitions, and novels—especially *Uncle Tom's Cabin*—spread false information in the North about slavery and enraged Southerners. Nearly all agreed with future president Woodrow Wilson's 1893 assessment that William Lloyd Garrison and his associates were imprudent and repellent, rejecting any compromises, and amounting to nothing less than "fanatics and stirrers up of sedition." The abolitionists bore responsibility for inciting the South and creating the series of endless crises that led to the Civil War. Nearly all these accounts focused on Garrison—although several offered passing mentions of other prominent white antislavery leaders—inevitably labeling him a "firebrand and fanatic." Even the more temperate rendering in David Montgomery's 1895 *The Leading Facts of American History* maintained that Garrison had "lost his reason" and only "enflamed the South, rather than assured them that the North would share in the burden of ending slavery." *The Essential Facts* of 1909 damned Garrison as "violent in his denunciation of slavery, and . . . resolved to free the negroes if he had to destroy the Union to do it. . . . Many people thought he was crazy on the subject." The North Carolina–born William E. Dodd, who taught at the University of Chicago for twenty-five years, published his own schoolbook in 1915, calling Garrison's newspaper *The Liberator* "yellow journalism" and abolitionists an aggregation of impractical idealists, village merchants, the unsuccessful, and debtors, whose claims that there could be "no property in man" did not differ from socialists' declarations that "there could be no property in land." He dismissed Wendell Phillips as a mere "transcendentalist" and Charles Sumner as "raised" by Garrison and Phillips to become the North's primary "anti-Southern agitator." As one 1918 text concluded, intolerant antislavery propaganda had only threatened and aroused the South, forcing it into "an open defense of slavery." In the end, the nation's schoolbooks advised students, the abolitionists simply failed to comprehend that because of the "inferiority of the negro," Blacks were safer in bondage than free.

The anti-Emancipationist eruption from the 1890s to 1919 that produced identical views of the abolitionists in Northern and Southern textbooks reached a fevered pitch when it came to discussions of John Brown. Again, Woodrow Wilson set the tone, describing Brown as intense, rugged, and unwilling to acknowledge any authority but his own. More important, he was "fanatical almost to the point of madness," terrifying the South, and posing a horrifying existential threat to Southern women. Spewing the classic white supremacist indictment, Wilson cried out that Brown terrified women into fearing "a fate worse than any form of death or desolation." Even the most tolerant authors, who claimed to have read Emerson, Whittier, and Higginson, believed that Brown's "foolhardy" and "unbalanced" plans had only convinced the South that it could never be safe in the Union. Others simply asserted, without any evidence whatsoever, that Brown sought to arm slaves to murder their masters. Indeed, several damned and dismissed him as a fanatical antislavery "murderer" who "was probably insane." A 1911 history and another for "Beginners" published in 1919 even charged that what Brown had really had in mind was a follow-up to Nat Turner, a kind of "bloody Monday" race war that would incite "black men against the white." The danger he posed, as an 1899 textbook asserted, lay in stirring up "negroes," a people "so ignorant" and so easily led that they readily could have been convinced to commit—as Wilson had charged— "the most horrible crimes."

.   .   .

We are accustomed to hearing arguments that the South withdrew from the Union to preserve its "constitutional rights," a phrase that appeared in nearly all schoolbooks published in and for the South. There, statewide education boards controlled the textbook adoption process and favored texts that white-dominated public opinion insisted on. Not until 2018 did the Texas school board finally adapt to modern scholarship and mandate that slavery be taught as the primary cause of the Civil War. But many educators and certainly contemporary advocates of Lost Cause dogma have not understood the more complicated legacy of slavery and secession in Southern schoolbooks.

A few Southern states, under the relentless demands of the United Daughters of the Confederacy, adopted texts that followed John H. Van Evrie and Rushmore G. Horton's insistence that Lincoln "invaded" the South to destroy slavery at the bidding of Great Britain. Most textbooks agreed with Henry Alexander White, a Robert E. Lee biographer and historian of South Carolina, who asserted in 1906 that "President Lincoln commenced the war against the South." Most Southern textbooks adopted the line that "the Southern States did not secede from the Union to preserve or extend slavery. They did so because they had vainly striven to maintain the rights guaranteed to them under the Constitution." Precisely what "rights" did the South seek to protect? As Agnes Scott College professor Lida A. Field explained in her popular 1890s history, the South had *never* abandoned the "right" that "any state might at will withdraw from the Union." Southern authors tirelessly depicted the Republican Party as a sectional force utterly hostile to the South. Susan Pendleton Lee, the wife of Robert E. Lee's cousin, explained, in her "*unprejudiced* and *truthful* history of the United States," that under duress from the hostile North, Southerners "took their affairs into their own hands and left the Union," under the provision "that the Constitution sanctioned the rights they claimed."

But these very same texts went on to detail exactly why secession and those presumed constitutionally sanctioned protections proved so vital to the South. They saw the North as a hypocritical aggressor, determined at the very least to limit the growth of slavery and at the most to compel its end. These textbooks buttressed their affirmations of "constitutional" rights and guarantees with arguments for a Southerner's right to carry his "property" anywhere in the Union, and they defended that species of property as thriving under the "guidance" of benevolent masters. The truth is, White asserted, "the people of the South are doing all that they could to help the negroes to be honest and truthful. They were teaching the Africans how to work and how to live. They fed and clothed them well and treated them kindly. Every day the negroes were becoming a better and a wiser people." Susan Pendleton Lee wrote more honestly about the meaning of "constitutional protections" when she instructed teachers to inform their students that Southern states possessed the right to "deal with slavery in their own borders, and . . . the non-slaveholding States had no right to interfere." Mary Tucker Magill's ever-popular introduction to Virginia history assured young readers that slavery was a blessing to the slave, who enjoyed conditions far better than those in Africa, especially because "they were taught to know about God and about other things which were good for them." John Brown, ignoring the South's "good work" for the benighted African, embodied the North's hatred of the South, and Lincoln then dispatched an army to compel the Southern states to remain in a Union that hated them. The years leading up to the Civil War, Southern schoolbooks taught, were dominated by a clash over slavery and the "struggle for power between North and South." One asserted with clarity that even though the North represented an antislavery cudgel that constantly beat the South, slavery "could not be forcibly abolished without a violation of this compact." Another confessed that slavery had been a "curse" and if not for the cotton gin would have disappeared. Nonetheless, the Union had "no authority over the system of slavery; it was a question for each of the original states to decide." All the texts cited John Brown's raid at Harpers Ferry as undeniable proof of the North's drive to abolish slavery. A 1913 high school account by two professors at West Texas State Normal School went so far as to assert that slavery was a part of the "organic law of the Union." The Texans then quoted an unnamed Virginia congressman to assure students that "slavery is interwoven with our very political existence." So interwoven, the authors maintained, that Lincoln's Emancipation Proclamation was "without warrant in the Constitution."

From a Southern point of view, the Civil War might have been a war of "conquest," but Southern textbooks expressed little ambiguity over its cause. North and South had become "two distinct peoples," as one 1889 text maintained, after forty years of "forensic combat." The "sentiment with which the system of slavery had come to be regarded by the North and South divided" the nation "irreconcilably." Slave property amounted to over "twenty-five hundred million dollars," Henry Chambers asserted. It had been sanctioned by the Constitution, a document that never would have been ratified unless it had protected slavery. After an antislavery party came to dominate the government, the slave states withdrew, and "their interpretation of the constitutional compact justif[ied] them in the act." In fact, Southern motives had never been in doubt until the twentieth century's battles over race. When the former vice president of the Confederacy, Alexander Stephens, published his own classroom history in 1872, he clearly expressed the South's position. When the North placed a minority president in the White House, backed by a party hostile to slavery and favoring increased power for the central government, Southerners considered the "Federal Union perilous to their rights, security, and safety." It always had been about slavery.

Similarly, Reconstruction always had been about Blacks and the degree of white supremacy over them. Painfully obvious in all the textbooks—whether written from the Emancipationist perspective or from that of Dunning, Pike, and their acolytes—is their complete and utter failure to detail the realities of Reconstruction violence inflicted on African Americans. None bothered to recount, for instance, the 1873 Colfax, Louisiana, massacre that claimed the lives of about 150 African Americans, including 48 executed *after* the end of a gun battle between Black and white forces. In fact, after 1865 former Confederates never ceased to commit acts of violence on Blacks, including whippings, murders, lynchings, and rapes. In 1866 bloodlust attacks on African Americans shattered New Orleans and Memphis. In the 1870s, the Northern press warned that a "war of races" plagued the South. Reconstruction came to an end, not because of a lack of Black initiative, as most authors asserted, but because of the explosive and vindictive violence and terrifying assassinations carried out by white Southerners. Reconstruction did not fail—it was overthrown. Those responsible came not just from the

Klan and allied terrorist groups, but also from the Democratic Party, the natural home of Northerners like John H. Van Evrie. As one Ohio newspaper editor declared, these groups advanced the "reign of the bowie knife, of the revolver, and of ruffianism" across the South. They killed with a purpose, choosing ministers and politicians, any Black leader, to cause as much intimidation and disruption as possible. They also assassinated the white Republican allies of African Americans, including one sitting member of Congress from Arkansas. In Louisiana, prior to the election of Ulysses S. Grant, Republicans cried out that two thousand of their supporters had been "killed, wounded, or otherwise injured." In one Louisiana parish a state authority stumbled across a pile of twenty-five dead Black Republicans. In fact, from South Carolina to Texas, white militias roamed the countryside to intimidate or kill Black and white Republican voters. How many thousands died or suffered serious injuries cannot be known. But we do know that after Reconstruction a wave of lynchings spread across the country—by one calculation, 4,084 between 1877 and 1950. None of this proved worthy of mention in the nation's textbooks.

Beginning in the 1890s, as the Emancipationist agenda waned, Northern and Southern authors converged on how to cover Reconstruction. As Frederick Douglass lamented, the cause gained in the war had become lost, and the Lost Cause then gained the peace. Even those texts that once presented Radical Republicans as a positive force to guarantee that "the negro should be intrenched in his rights" and to make "certain the safety of the freedmen," inevitably returned to the central theme of white supremacy. Again and again, authors depicted the failure of Reconstruction, not from violent white resistance but because of a combination of corrupt carpetbaggers and scalawags and "illiterate negro voters," the "most ignorant part of the population." According to Alexander Johnston and Winthrop More Daniels, Northern-born authors who both taught at Princeton University, the freedpeople were "so ignorant and timid that they knew but one way of voting, to vote together and vote against whites." Another dismissed Southern Black voters as "poverty-stricken ignoramuses." One day African Americans might become full citizens, Johnston and Daniels asserted in their popular textbook used between 1882 and 1902, but only when "the negro shows himself worthy of it." Correspondingly, Southern authors emphasized Reconstruction's "gift of freedom" to African Americans, a people clearly unprepared for it, as they remained "demoralized," "idle," and "vicious." Without white direction and control, Northern and Southern authors emphasized, the freedpeople wandered about lost and proved "so ignorant and inexperienced that they hardly knew what to do with their freedom." Another textbook dismissed Black Southern legislators as "so ignorant that they did not even know the letters of the alphabet." The New York City educators Arthur C. Perry and Gertrude A. Price, who believed that Black slaves had always had "a rollicking time," taught students that "ignorant negroes did not even understand what freedom meant." While some proved "industrious and thrifty," the South soon became "overrun with poor deluded negroes who daily became more insolent and more dangerous." They dismissed even free Blacks in the North as lawless, lazy, and "living in idleness."

Northern educators and academics like John Fiske, John Bach McMaster, John W. Burgess, William A. Dunning, Andrew C. McLaughlin, Claude H. Van Tyne, Woodrow Wilson, and Brown University president Elisha Benjamin Andrews threw their professional expertise, prestige, and authority behind condemnations of Reconstruction and support for white power. Andrews, showing that he had read his James Shepherd Pike, in a two-volume history denounced Black Reconstruction political leaders as tools of carpetbaggers who abused their power to fleece "white property-holders." African Americans, he asserted with finality, "were quite too unintelligent to make laws or even to elect those who were to do so." That Southern whites would resist such illegality and chaos should have been expected: "Only doctrinaires or the stupid could have expected that the whites would long submit." So as soon as the federal bayonets departed, by fair means or foul, whites were certain "to remove the scepter from colored hands." He could hardly believe that anyone in the North could have been "so dull" as to expect that Black suffrage would work. Moreover, like Woodrow Wilson, he admonished that emancipation made it "notoriously unsafe for white ladies to venture from home without an escort." He concluded his assessment of Reconstruction with the pronouncement that "the superior race should rule."

As Pike, Dunning, McMaster, and an endless array of textbook authors insisted, the chaotic freedpeople and their Northern white Reconstruction collaborators posed an unprecedented threat to Southern white wealth, property, and lives. Popular literature fortified the universality of such beliefs, especially the novels of Thomas Dixon, Jr., which proved indistinguishable from historical accounts. His 1902 *The Leopard's Spots* cried out that so long as the "Negro is here with a ballot in his hands he is a menace to civilization. The Republican Party placed him here. . . . Their attempt to establish with the bayonet an African barbarism on the ruins of Southern society was a conspiracy against human progress. It was the blackest crime of the nineteenth century. . . . Negro supremacy in politics, and Negro equality in society." To defend the South against this "menace," the United Daughters of the Confederacy and the Sons

A mounted Klansman. In a text that the author sought to place in the hands of every Southern white child, Laura Martin Rose exclaimed that the Ku Klux Klan "has been justly called, 'the salvation of the South,' and its history should be written in letters of light." Rose, *The Ku Klux Klan; or, Invisible Empire* (1914), pp. 77, 82. In some editions, this image served as the book's frontispiece.

of Confederate Veterans united with Laura Martin Rose to place her 1914 text *The Ku Klux Klan; or, Invisible Empire* in every school and library in the South. The influential Vanderbilt scholar Walter L. Flemming even allowed Rose to reproduce portions of his history of the South in her own book. In Rose's hands, the Klan became a noble effort to protect the "homes and women of the South." Carpetbaggers, "men imbued with passions of the lowest order," who excluded "the best class of white people" from the vote, invaded the South, teaming up with "home-made Yankees," better known as scalawags, and "ignorant and brutal negroes" to rape the South. They had placed "black heels on white necks." "The negro," Rose protested, "considered freedom synonymous with equality, and his greatest ambition was to marry a white wife." The brave former Confederate soldiers then rose up with this secret organization to put a stop to "a bondage worse than death." The Klan's prime mission, she proclaimed, was to teach "the inevitability of Anglo-Saxon Supremacy."

In a 1901 history published simultaneously in New York and New Orleans, the former Confederate chaplain John William Jones explained to students that the Klan served as a bulwark against "Negro and carpet-bag supremacy," protecting decent Southerners from "pillage, and other outrages of the negroes." Such assessments of the Klan appeared identically in textbooks by Northern and Southern authors. Two Northern university professors even went so far as to inform students that the Klan, Pale Faces, and the White Brotherhood had been organized by young former Confederate soldiers "seeking merely fun and excitement." Nearly all other texts, however, in the first two decades of the twentieth century, maintained that Southerners sought not to reestablish slavery but to defend whites against the Northern-backed exploitation of the South. Thus Southerners had formed the Klan out of "sheer desperation" in an effort to end corruption. A 1910 schoolbook—which remained in print until 1932—by three Southern scholars explained that the North remained "ignorant of the true condition of affairs and prejudiced in favor of negroes." The Klan proved essential for whites "to regain control." Northern authors followed the same path to white supremacy and parroted the same justifications of Klan activities. As a 1903 history authored by the president of the University of Wisconsin and a professor of English at Columbia University explained, the Klan represented an understandable reaction to Northern efforts to remake the South and establish Black political equality. Peace would return, the two academics asserted, when the warring parties in the South agreed that "the welfare of the negroes would be better served" by industrial education "than by political methods." Even Wilbur F. Gordy's text, used until 1935, which had been so sympathetic to the abolitionists and that even understood that the Radical Republicans meant "to protect the freedmen in their civil rights," saw the Klan as necessary to restore order and white rule. Gordy insisted that in the future, after the "negro becomes intelligent he will doubtless be allowed to cast his vote as he pleases." In 1919 Waddy Thompson (1867–1939), a Louisiana and Georgia businessman and educator, concluded in his Boston-published textbook that by asserting such "self-protection," white power returned to state governments, Reconstruction ended, and an "era of prosperity" began.

In a speech before the Wisconsin Bar Association in June 1918, the great civil rights attorney Moorfield Storey appealed to the legal community to defend the law as their duty and social responsibility. He mourned that the nation had given up on defending law and the rights of African Americans: "Men say that it is for the Southern States to deal with the situation, and that we must not interfere." But he reminded his fellow lawyers that Northerners had said the same thing in 1850, "that slavery was a Southern question and that none but the Southern man could understand or deal with it." Monuments to Civil War soldiers, and "the green graves in Southern and Northern land alike, bear witness to the falsity of the claim." Such memorials "prove that the whole nation pays for the fault of any part." The blood of the white man, he said, borrowing from Abraham Lincoln, had been "drawn by the sword to pay for the blood of black men drawn by the lash." It was not the "negro question," a phrase constantly invoked in the early twentieth century, that disturbed the nation's peace and prosperity. It "is a white man's problem which confronts us. The fault is in us, not in our colored neighbors. It is our senseless and wicked prejudice against our fellow men which is the root of all our troubles." It would have broken his heart to know that the problem he so grieved over was about to grow even worse.

6

Educating for "Eugenocide" in the 1920s

Nothing is more certain than that the Fathers of the Republic intended America to be a "white man's country."

—Lothrop Stoddard, *Re-Forging America: The Story of Our Nationhood,* 1927

The Vermont-born educator Lucy Langdon Williams Wilson (1864–1937) reflected the social and biological imperatives that spurred American schooling in the 1920s. Earning a Ph.D. in science education at the University of Pennsylvania in 1897, she attained sufficient fame as the founder of Philadelphia's first botanical laboratory (1893) and as an educator for girls to have her portrait painted by Thomas Eakins, the city's legendary realist painter, sculptor, and teacher. She associated with Louis Agassiz's former Harvard students and spent twenty years teaching Darwinism to young women. What she lacked in knowledge of American history, she more than compensated for with her drive to demonstrate how whiteness succeeded in early America. Her popular elementary school history text, used between 1898 and 1933, taught beginning students how "white people came to live in America." The nation's first years, in her telling, became the story of how "simple, untaught savages" threatened "Americans" and "how the whites defended themselves." During the same era, a teacher's guide outlining the objectives for history curriculum said little about slavery and nothing about African Americans, but it did insist that junior high school students should understand why there are "so many grain elevators in Buffalo." A similar manual instructed teachers to explain to students why African Americans received no education during the "slave era" and also about those who taught the freedpeople after the Civil War. When it approached the issue of Blacks and whites attending "the same schools in your city," the manual advised that "no additional presentation is needed." White and Black, one 1923 textbook instructed, "must be kept severed socially," while the "dominant race" possessed ultimate responsibility for making "the negro" useful. At the beginning of the twentieth century, white supremacy, always central to the American experience, had become an anxious compulsion.

The new century's mounting white anxiety, especially in the North, emerged from an unexpected source. Despite the failures of Reconstruction and pervasive Jim Crow discrimination, Black social and economic progress proved sufficient to fully justify a New England reformer's 1911 observation that African American "progress during the last half-century will be one of the marvels of history." At the 1900 Paris Exhibition, W.E.B. Du Bois had celebrated the rising Black middle class in a display of more than 360 images. His presentation highlighted several thriving—although segregated—Black communities of the South and became an affirming background to the later success of "Black Wall Street" in Tulsa, Oklahoma. Black culture attained unexpectedly dramatic heights with the founding of the Hampton Institute, Howard University, Fiske University, Spelman College, and scores of other schools and colleges, along with the celebrated career of Booker T. Washington and the establishment of the Tuskegee Institute. The proliferation of Black journals and newspapers, the emergence of accomplished writers, scholars, scientists, and artists, the numerous Black women's organizations, the flourishing churches, the well-publicized Black military service in the Spanish-American War and the First World War, and the rise of the NAACP and the modern civil rights movement all displayed an astonishing and enviable level of social, economic, and cultural progress since 1865.

But once again, the more freedom and success African Americans enjoyed, and the more accomplishments they displayed, the more apprehensive and distressed whites became. As the NAACP president Moorfield Storey explained in 1911, the "more the negro succeeds, the more jealous are his unsuccessful white competitors, and the more they undertake to punish him for their own incompetence." Black achievements, coupled with the tidal wave of Jewish and Catholic immigration beginning in the late nineteenth century, marked an unmistakable social transformation in the United States—a profoundly disturbing experience for white Americans. As one Massachusetts newspaper reported in 1928, between 1890 and 1914, 17.5 million immigrants had arrived in the country; the "alien flood" did not halt until Congress passed the 1924 Immigration Act. Most textbooks of the era approved only of those immigrants who came from Northern Europe and before 1880. Typically, one 1921 account recorded that

> most of the immigrants coming to this country have been from the lower classes of eastern and southeastern Europe, and they give much trouble. They are for the most part very ignorant, and, having been downtrodden in their old homes, they have no respect for law or government. In fact, many of them would like to see the government of the United States destroyed. How to deal with this undesirable class of immigrants is one of the most serious problems that we have to-day.

Immigration rendered "true" American identity uncertain, besieged, and threatened in the eyes of whites, a drifting away from the Anglo-Saxon foundations they had celebrated since the onset of European colonization. Rather than the Flapper Age of Dapper Dan and a shimmering Coco Chanel, the 1920s became the Age of Rage. Americans seethed with a dread fear that the American English garden that Emerson had imagined in his *English Traits* was being uprooted and replaced by nonnative species from alien lands. No longer did Americans see themselves as nourished and watered by a crystalline Lake Placid; now they saw themselves as inundated in the east by an Adriatic assault joined to a dark Guinea Gulf tidal wave and in the west by a Yellow Sea tsunami. Never before had

Americans felt so crushing a need to make America great and white again.

In 1916, as a horrifying war raged in Europe, the Harvard-trained eugenicist Lothrop Stoddard (1883–1950) had warned that the white world faced its greatest threat. The "white race," he cried out, "is in real peril today." Only if the war came to a halt and whites united could they hope to "REPEL ANY SUBSEQUENT COLORED ATTACK." Wake up! he exclaimed, "the yellow, brown and black hordes wait for their opportunity." Fueled by war, immigration, labor strikes, and fears of Bolshevism, traditional white Americans suffered a "psychic crisis" of unprecedented ferocity, sparking a quest for a reaffirmed national identity and desperate demands for social and cultural control. The process can be traced in the way textbook authors aggressively asserted the "alien" and inferior nature of Blacks, in the immense popularity of eugenics, and especially in a wave of lynching and organized violence, such as the 1921 destruction of the Greenwood District of Tulsa, Oklahoma, aimed at expunging "alien" people, and especially at African Americans.

From Coatesville, Pennsylvania, to Ocoee and Rosewood, Florida, from Valdosta, Georgia, to East St. Louis, Illinois, and

Ruins after the race riots, Tulsa, Oklahoma, June 1921.

Tulsa, Oklahoma—containing the West's most successful Black community—whites incinerated, shot, and hung African Americans and demolished Black communities, in an unrelenting orgy of violence. The outrages reached a shocking peak in what historians have referred to as the "Red Summer" of 1919. In fact, the entire year was blood-soaked with at least sixty destructive white insurrections from January 22 to December 27, terrorizing Black communities from Syracuse, New York, to Bogalusa, Louisiana, and from Washington, D.C., to Chicago. The rage against Chicago's Black community became so violent that scores of federal troops seized control of the city to halt open warfare between armed white and Black groups. W.E.B. Du Bois urged his brethren to arm themselves against the lynchers: "We might as well die today as tomorrow." In Georgia, a white mob burned one man at the stake; in Louisiana, a throng tied a man to an automobile and dragged him to death; and in Alabama, whites hung an African American from a bridge. In Arkansas, a Black veteran of the First World War (a frequent target of white rage) was "chained to a tree and shot forty or fifty times" for failing to yield a sidewalk to a white man. In Mississippi, three thousand whites, with the blessing of a Baptist minister, roasted John Hartfield, who they accused of assaulting a white woman. In the fall of 1919, one English visitor to the United States remarked that he could not forget "the feverish condition of the public mind."

While nothing could match the astounding level of white violence in 1919, nothing else could equal the insidious and horrific murder of Mary Turner the year before near Valdosta, Georgia. Turner had made the mistake of protesting the lynching of her husband and six other African American sharecroppers. To repay her audacity, whites hung her upside down, soaked her in gasoline, and then incinerated her. As she burned, one of the rioters sliced open her womb with a butcher knife, ripped out her unborn infant, and threw it to the ground. Another eager white man then crushed its skull under his heel. Statues of Mary Turner, not Confederate generals, should have been raised in the town squares of the South.

Reborn in 1915, the Ku Klux Klan of the 1920s became the most venomous, but also the most American, of institutions. Immensely popular and painfully public, the new Klan's appeal can be fathomed only as an expression of intense white racial anxiety. For at least ten years, it may have been one of the most influential and powerful organizations in the United States. While its claim to having as many as six million members is likely an exaggeration, it nevertheless proved enormously popular, as Linda Gordon powerfully recounted: parades of tens of thousands of white-robed members marched through the nation's capital at least three times between 1925 and 1928 to ensure that "we shall always enjoy WHITE SUPREMACY in this country." Its membership was largely Northern and Western, not Southern. Indiana became its epicenter, where the organization elected eleven of the state's thirteen congressmen. The Klan spent most of its energy railing against Catholics, Jews, and immigrants, although it hardly neglected African Americans. Equal parts political party, religious denomination, Masonic society, Rotary Club, and Fuller Brush Company, the new Klan became an avenue of social advancement for groups consciously or unconsciously suffering status anxiety—creating a path into the middle class.

For a time, Klan subsidiaries (Klaverns) published 150 newspapers

A Ku Klux Klan parade on Pennsylvania Avenue in Washington, D.C., led by men from Connecticut and Rhode Island, September 13, 1926.

and magazines, established two colleges, and founded a motion picture company. The Klan presented itself as anti-elitist and anticorruption, battled the liquor interests (while privately drinking their fill), and won the support of forty thousand Protestant ministers and a majority of the nation's police and sheriff departments outside New York and Boston—which possessed large Irish populations. It decisively influenced the election of seventy-five congressmen, eleven governors, sixteen U.S. senators, and countless state and local officials. Its reach proved nearly unprecedented, and its influence terrible. For example, Hatton Summers, the head of the U.S. House Judiciary Committee, was a Klan member who quashed efforts to pass antilynching legislation. At least two U.S. Supreme Court justices belonged, the appropriately named Hugo Black and Edward Douglass White. The Klan's power saturated the Democratic Party to the point that its 1924 national convention became known as the "Klanbake." Even Harry Truman and Gutzon Borglum, sculptor of Mount Rushmore, were members. Perhaps more shocking, the Klan had produced its own version of women's rights, drawing into its fold Quaker feminists. It claimed three million female members, and as later conservative women would assert, Klan women believed that political activism was a woman's responsibility. As the Hoosier Daisy Douglas Brushwiller lyrically proclaimed: "I am the Spirit of Righteousness. They call me the Ku Klux Klan. / I am more than the uncouth robe and hood / With which I am clothed. / YEA, I AM THE SOUL OF AMERICA."

That very soul had become contested ground, its meaning achieving a level of uncertainty previously unknown to white Americans. The drama, anxiety, and perceived perilous social trends, especially Catholic and Jewish immigration, elicited violent reactions among middle-class whites and sparked fear and rage at the most elite social levels, shockingly even among Emancipationist advocates. John Jay Chapman (1862–1933), a reformer, author, scholar, public intellectual, and graduate of Harvard University and its law school, had the deepest abolitionist roots. On his mother's side, he directly descended from Founding Father John Jay and the early abolitionist William Jay, while his paternal grandmother was the famed

Boston abolitionist Maria Weston Chapman, whom he respected and admired. In 1918, as the reputation of the antislavery movement sank to new depths, he published a perceptive and brilliant study of William Lloyd Garrison and never abandoned his commitment to African American civil rights. He courageously traveled to Coatesville, Pennsylvania, in 1912, on the one-year anniversary of the incineration of Zachariah Walker, to offer a stinging and public rebuke of the ugly lynching that involved the heart of the city's white community. In 1921 he opposed Harvard University's revolting Jim Crow policies. President Abbott Lawrence Lowell had ordered the exclusion of Black students from freshman dormitories, which Chapman denounced as a blatant "political move intended to conciliate southern sentiment. It is done in order to keep alive at Harvard the idea of white supremacy." In an essay that appeared in the Boston and New York press, Chapman's criticism clearly had more than the Harvard community in mind. "I am speaking here of the North and especially of Massachusetts," he wrote. "Such negroes among us as can receive a college education must be offered one which is without stigma. . . . This shall be a sign to them [white students] that the negro is engrafted in our American civilization."

John Jay Chapman (1862–1933) was an editor, author, historian, and defender of African American rights who nonetheless retained a lifelong commitment to white Protestantism. He eagerly cooperated with the KKK to attack what he saw as threatening Catholic and Jewish power. Alfred Quinton Collins, oil on canvas, c. 1895.

Chapman never betrayed his or his family's Emancipationist commitment to African Americans, but neither did he disavow the idea of "Anglo-Saxonism" that underpinned the white supremacy he had censored at Harvard. While a student at the university, he had read Charles Darwin's 1871 *Descent of Man* and hailed it as the most important book he had ever encountered—"I mean," he wrote his mother, "in its limitless consequences." He also admired Herbert Spencer, the English biologist and sociologist who coined the phrase "survival of the fittest" and contended that helping the "good-for-nothing at the expense of the good, is an extreme cruelty." This philosophy Spencer labeled "social Darwinism," and Chapman viewed it as a corollary to Darwin's ideas that "permeated & govern men's minds." Darwin's influential work, as Chapman well understood, divided the world between the "Caucasian race" and "the Melanian races," with the larger-brained Caucasians representing "civilization" and the Melanian (darker-skinned) people embodying "savagery." Chapman never abandoned this understanding of human civilization, and when he traveled to England with his new bride in 1899, he pondered the fate of England and America and decided that "the prestige of the Anglo Saxon race is today in America."

The First World War and the death of his son Victor in the Lafayette Escadrille in 1916—the first American airman to die in the war—unhinged Chapman. Although from the war's outset he had urged American intervention on President Woodrow Wilson, the consequences left him deeply disturbed and desperately searching for the origins of the cultural traumas he perceived. Writing in 1917 to Theodore Roosevelt, who also would lose a son in the war, Chapman denounced the Catholic Church as "a political machine" that threatened domination of the United States. His anti-Catholicism merged with anti-Semitism in the fall of 1920. Chapman read Henry Ford's vile accusations in his newspaper, the Dearborn *Independent,* and in *The International Jew: The World's Foremost Problem,* a book Ford promoted that feverishly swallowed the prewar Russian forgery the *Protocols of the Elders of Zion.* Ford's anti-Semitic campaign drenched the country—his newspaper reached a circulation of 300,000, and the book sold half a million copies, influencing what was taught in schools and even what clothes children should wear to emphasize "Americanness." His revolting campaign, imagining devious Jewish tactics, only fortified the popular delusion that Jews were making boundless efforts at world domination in a "World Plan for the subjugation of the Gentiles."

That as sophisticated an author and intellectual as Chapman could accept such vile poison only points to the intensity of the psychic crisis gripping white Americans who perceived the nation's Protestant, Anglo-Saxon foundation as crumbling. Nor was Chapman ignorant of or isolated from Jewish Americans. He had known and worked with Jewish New Yorkers since his early days in the Bowery, where he taught Jewish children and worked with many Jewish actors who performed the plays he wrote. Astonishingly, he remained close friends with Meyer Daniel Rothschild (1858–1943), a New York precious stone importer, and also with the political reformer and insurance company owner Isaac H. Klein (1861?–1919). Rothschild had praised Chapman's heroic oration at Coatesville in 1912—"It is bound to find an echo in many hearts"—and continued his friendship with Chapman into the 1920s. In a 1920 remembrance of Klein, Chapman had compared him to Abraham Lincoln, believing that he possessed "a burst and a blaze of natural power and natural goodness . . . which no one could resist. Wherever he went and whomever he met, benevolence rushed out of him." As early as 1897, Chapman glorified Jewish civilization. The "history of the Jews is the most remarkable," he wrote, "the most notable thing, on the globe. Their sacred books and chronicles and traditions and history make the annals of every other nation mere rubbish—and I feel this same power in the Jews I know. They are the most humane and the strongest people morally, mentally and physically. They persist." And in a startling, but largely imaginary, coda, he also declared, "I'm glad I'm a Jew."

But Chapman's personal relationships with Jews and his actual, if distant, Jewish connections through his mother's family failed to temper the intense anxiety he suffered in the 1920s over what he saw as the Jewish-Catholic threat to Anglo-Saxonism. He informed Rothschild of Henry Ford's reprinting of the fraudulent *Protocols of the Elders of Zion* and sent copies to his own mother. Rothschild's denunciation of Ford's and Chapman's anti-Semitism failed to alter his friend's views in the slightest. "Please tell me frankly," Rothschild wrote to him in the fall of 1920, "what you conceive the 'Jewish peril' to be?" Chapman believed his own anti-Semitic campaign, along with Henry Ford's, would "save us from not only the Jews but the Catholics, for they are only 2 forms of the same danger." What danger? As Chapman informed Louis Marshall, president of the American Jewish Committee, "the solidarity of any race among us represents a danger to the republic. Every man in America must become an individual and drop all race allegiances. Now the Jews claim the right to push their own race solidarity; and yet they will not suffer others to push against it." Jews, Chapman held, reject any criticism. They "consider themselves blameless and misunderstood." Moreover, he contended, Jews controlled key sectors of the press to defend themselves. "The *New York Times* is an organ of Jewish propaganda," he claimed, and was decidedly prejudiced against "gentiles." Anglo-Saxon "gentiles" could affirm race solidarity, but no one else.

With each passing year, Chapman became increasingly fearful of what he imagined as the spreading influence and control of the Catholic-Jewish conspiracy. "The Jews are pushing a world movement," he warned. "One cannot doubt that it is controlled from a centre and that its design is to rule the world—as far as possible—by a clique." The U.S. Supreme Court (where Louis Brandeis served) and the viceroy of India, and places from the Holy Land to Russia, were "all in a ring," which Chapman discovered after reading Ford's edition of the *Protocols of the Elders of Zion*. In 1924 he warned Ernest Hamlin Abbott, fellow Harvard graduate and editor of *Outlook Magazine* (which he took over from his father, the famous minister Lyman Abbott), that "events in the great world are flopping about in a cataclysmic way, e.g., the machine of the Roman Church is in the control of the Jews." With such power, he advised the doubting architect Ralph Adams Cram, the church could claim a "monopoly of education and . . . impose her system on all humanity. I never heard of any one who doubts that." This "decay" at the center of the nation had started a generation or two earlier, and so Chapman called for a "new gang" to rise up to oppose the scoundrels. That "new gang" would be led by Henry Ford, a man who "typifies intellectual courage and [even] with all his peculiarities and limitations is a star of great magnitude." Should Ford fail to rescue the nation, Chapman believed, real Americans could fall back on the Ku Klux Klan to do so.

In April 1925 Chapman went public with his conspiratorial fears. His inflammatory essay "Strike at the Source" appeared in the *Forum,* one of New York's leading journals (much like the *Atlantic Monthly*), which began publishing in 1886 and continued until 1950. Thomas Wentworth Higginson, Albion Tourgée, Charles Dudley Warner, Hamlin Garland, Thomas Hardy, Jules Verne, Theodore Roosevelt, and Woodrow Wilson, as well as W.E.B. Du Bois, all had written for the *Forum.* Chapman likely chose the journal because of its elite status and because he knew its editor, George Henry Payne, who had been Theodore Roosevelt's campaign manager in 1912. The threat posed by the Catholic Church, he argued, continued the Reformation conflict between "Authority" on the one hand and "the Private Mind" on the other. The church's encyclicals proved that "the Catholic faith conflicts with democracy." More important, he warned, the papacy sought total control of North America, the way it dominated South America. It labored to cover the land with "her colleges, nunneries and seminaries of all kinds. Her attack on public schools has been prolonged, persistent, organized and effective." Moreover, "her influence in public libraries, bookshops, publishing houses, editorial offices, in the radio and movie business, has become notorious." Fortunately, according to Chapman, "the Ku Klux Klan have taken up the cry against the Roman machine." One need not accept the whole Klan agenda, he believed, to recognize that when it came to the Catholic Church, it, as Henry VIII said of Thomas Cranmer, "hath the right sow by the ear."

Chapman's *Forum* outburst produced such a supportive response that he kept an alphabetical notebook to record the scores of letters he received. Letters from "all over the country," he bragged to a friend, poured into his hands. He compared his own persuasive powers to those of Wendell Phillips and especially Henry Ford, who, Chapman believed, broke the taboo against speaking out against Jews. Because of his essay, he claimed, the *Forum* had gained one thousand new subscribers. The Masonic monthly the *New Age,* which had 270,000 subscribers, reprinted his essay, as did two Klan journals. A Klan group in West Virginia ordered five thousand reprints. One Klansman advised Chapman that his essay "has created a veritable sensation," and the editor of the Klan's *National Kourier* sent him praise after each of his anti-Catholic rants. To repay the Klan for its support—and ignoring its sordid history and revolting conduct—Chapman published a poem in the *Kourier,* "Cape Cod, Rome and Jerusalem."

> But see, a sail—nay more—from every land
> The cloud, the ocean, convoyed by a crew
> Of Master Pirates who have work in hand:
> Old Europe's nation-wreckers heave in view!
> And lo, to aid them, on our margin stand,
> Our citizens,—the Jesuit and the Jew.

While Chapman received an occasional rebuke for his screeds, the vast majority of his correspondents offered nothing but admiration for his "courage." In 1924 Katherine S. Day, the great-granddaughter of the minister Lyman Beecher (father of Harriet Beecher Stowe), praised his stand against Catholics and his defense of "our heritage." With a red pencil, Chapman underlined her suggestion that he establish a "Protestant National Welfare Council" to fight the "anti-republican Roman hierarchy." Joining the anti-Catholic fusillade, the editor of the liberal Unitarian *Christian Register* expressed admiration for Chapman's refusal to "allow the Roman Catholic Church to run away with its propositions, all of which are contrary to the foundations and the very soul of democracy and freedom."

But perhaps Chapman made his most damaging mark in winning the praise of the influential Yale-trained advocate of eugenics, Madison Grant, whose 1916 *Passing of the Great Race* would become a bible to Adolf Hitler. Indeed, the Nazi regime's inhuman medical experiments and drive for racial purity owed everything to Grant and other American advocates of "racial purity" at the beginning of the twentieth century, when the United States became the "global leader in race law." In fact, as one international law expert concluded, when the Nazi regime formulated its infamous 1934 Nuremburg race laws, "they began by asking how the Americans did it." Grant's writings convinced many states to pass sterilization statutes and to outlaw racial intermarriage. In 1924 Grant expressed to Chapman that "I agree with everything you say" in his New York *Herald* essay "The Speechless Protestants," which denounced Harvard's desire to name a Catholic to its governing board. But Chapman's *Forum* essay, a year later, electrified Grant because "the Catholic Church under Jesuit leadership, the Jews and the Communist Labor Party are all international organizations and as such are hopelessly irreconcilable to the principles of nationalism upon which modern Christendom is founded."

The eugenics movement that catapulted Madison Grant and others to national prominence had begun with the work of the English statistician and polymath Sir Francis Galton (1822–1911). Galton, who coined the term in 1883, applied traditional breeding techniques for farm animals to humans, explaining with apparently reasonable logic that if breeding could improve livestock, why not humans? The popular American scholar Edward A. Ross (1866–1951) spent most of his career advancing eugenics to combat what he saw as the Asian menace, arguing that eugenics would prove the surest way to human perfectibility by breeding "a people as gifted and well-dispositioned as the best five percent among us. 'Of such is the kingdom of heaven.'" Ross maintained that "a truly angelic society could be built upon earth" through eugenics, "an unselfish concern for the future of our race." Ross, Grant, Lothrop Stoddard, scores of other eugenicists—and ultimately Germany's Nazi regime—all adopted Galton's notion that by "preventing the more faulty members of the flock from breeding . . . a race of gifted men might be obtained." While their ideas may have appeared generous and idealistic, they were in fact a pervasive and lethal modernization of the white supremacism of John H. Van Evrie. Like their nineteenth-century predecessor, the eugenicists employed the latest advances in "science" to control and objectify African Americans as a subspecies of humans designed by god and nature to do the white man's work. And like Van Evrie, they displayed a genius for disseminating their toxic ideas, which infiltrated and permeated every aspect of social interaction until the Nazi eugenocide took American racial ideals to their logical conclusion.

Galton's ideas about eugenics had spread quickly across the Atlantic, where anxieties about immigration incited not only the Klan but widespread popular support for breeding through sterilization and segregation. In what amounted to a national obsession, as the disability historian Dennis Downey observed, Americans perceived eugenics as indispensable to "biological improvement and race survival." Hundreds of colleges offered courses on eugenics and related subjects, and faculty members regularly poured out eugenics studies for academic and mass consumption, presenting the concept to the public as "the science of better breeding." Medical schools came under tremendous pressure to include eugenics in physician training curricula, and if a college resisted, as Massachusetts's Tufts University Medical School did, the National Council on Medical Education and Hospitals compelled it to "conform with prevailing patterns of discrimination." During the 1950s, even after the Nazi horrors, some educators still advanced eugenics. The *American Biology Teacher,* a professional journal, condemned society for protecting "those who cannot do so for themselves." One journal contributor rejected pity for the physically and mentally disabled as misguided and a threat to the human race. And the mass institutionalization of what early twentieth-century Americans called the "feeble-minded"—the intellectually disabled—came about entirely from the eugenics effort to remove them from the national gene pool. Massive state facilities were constructed to warehouse the physically and intellectually disabled, many of which became overcrowded and underfunded sterilization centers, what one visitor to Pennsylvania's Pennhurst State School and Hospital called "Dachau without the ovens."

Eugenics, masquerading as an idealistic effort to improve the human race, became—as the physician, sexologist, and department head at the Bronx Hospital Dispensary, William Robinson, confessed—an effort to "weed out the defective, the degenerate, the vicious, the criminal." In 1917 Robinson called for programs of "practical eugenics" to limit births and insisted the state must sterilize the "feeble-minded, degenerate and criminal." Sterilization must be applied to those with epilepsy and any other chronic disease, especially to career criminals. Moreover, Robinson believed, "all mental or moral insane, all feeble-minded, all cruel degenerates, congenital criminals and congenital prostitutes, and all paupers who, after the means of prevention have been given them, continue to breed children whom they cannot support and which become a public charge, should be prevented from propagating their kind." Rapists, he believed, should be castrated. One can readily see the Nazi attraction to American eugenicists and race law.

Robinson and better-known eugenicists like Grant, Ross, and Stoddard provided a much-needed boost to white supremacy, offering scientific legitimacy to the suppression of African Americans. They revived Van Evrie's ideas, maintaining that Black and white had separate creations and developed independently of each other. The terms they employed to describe African Americans were remarkably similar to Van Evrie's; he had labeled African Americans as examples of "subgenation," while modern eugenicists referred to them as a "subgenera." Van Evrie had believed in democracy for all whites, but the modern eugenicists went beyond his racial democracy to favor elite rule over all "inferiors" of whatever color. As Madison Grant contended, eugenicists sought to eliminate all "those who are weak or unfit." Prescott Hall, a Harvard-educated lawyer, founder of the Immigration Restriction League, and eugenicist, focused public attention on the "untold miseries" the nation allegedly suffered by the introduction "for purposes of national gain of an alien people, to wit, the African negro."

Similarly, the Harvard-trained Yale University geographer Ellsworth Huntington (1876–1947)—president of the Association of American Geographers and of the American Eugenics Society—instructed his students that the "highest" human type came from "relatively cool, dry regions." Like Emerson before him, he affirmed that the "ideal climate" for human development was that of England and the European continent. A close second was the northern United States and the Pacific Northwest, with New Zealand falling "little if any behind." Climate, he declared, favored the white race, and those who had settled North America were "among the most competent of all the races that the world has yet seen." To Huntington, it seemed inescapable that such a people would not fail "to dominate the world." The lowest human forms, on the other hand, emerged from "warm and relatively inaccessible regions such as tropical Australia, South America and Africa." Regrettably, Huntington explained to his students, the slave trade managed to bring only the "disagreeable, dangerous, or otherwise undesirable" elements from Africa to the United States. Huntington, hailed as the world's "leading geographer," and his influential *Principles of Human Geography* lived on long after his death in 1947, seeing its sixth edition in 1964.

Edward A. Ross, who coined the phrase "race suicide," which Theodore Roosevelt popularized, is regarded as the father of American sociology. He argued throughout this era that the "Teuton" sat at the top of the racial hierarchy, which fully justified the white man's higher status and higher material reward. Meanwhile, all other races wallowed in lethargy and self-indulgence, "beaten members of beaten breeds." A racial determinist, Ross repudiated the democratic ideals of the previous century, rejecting the idea that "social intercourse" and education could "lift up a backward folk to the level of the best."

His "modern" sociology, in fact, progressed not an inch beyond the academic prattle of Josiah Knott and Louis Agassiz, and he even reintroduced skull size and construction to explain white superiority. The Chinese, he said, were a "mediocre and intellectually servile race," while Jews as a race were "thrifty and always ready for a good stroke of business," willing to join with their "worst enemy if it pays. [The Jew] is calculating, enterprising, migrant and ambitious." Just as Van Evrie had proclaimed in the previous century, Ross maintained that because of "climate selection," African Americans thrived in tropic-like zones and so were destined to do the white man's work in the South. Race took center stage in Ross's sociology, with racial

domination as its essential element: "The superiority of a race cannot be preserved without *pride of blood* and an uncompromising
attitude toward the lower races." In his 1936 autobiography, Ross
expressed some regret for the racial theories he had promoted thirty
years earlier. He dropped his anti-Asian rhetoric and confessed that
as far as Blacks were concerned, "their faces are a script I have not
yet learned to read." In fact, however, Ross had not changed his
ideas at all. To him, Africa remained "the dark continent," and the
"black will have to work and if he will not work of his own accord,
he will be made to." Turning his vile attention to South America,
he exclaimed that the sun made the Chilean man into a "dangerous rapist" and Chilean women into prostitutes and whores. A trip
to Russia restored his faith in the "spirited Caucasians," a race of
"the handsomest people my eyes have ever lighten on, blood kin, I
suspect, to the Greeks of classic antiquity. The bronzed eagle-face
with firm chin and straight nose is the normal type." John H. Van
Evrie could not have expressed it any more clearly.

But not even Ross could match the power, influence, and author-
ity of America's chief eugenicist and white supremacist, Lothrop
Stoddard. Remembered primarily for his 1920 book *The Rising
Tide of Color Against the White World,* five years later he also penned
Re-Forging America: The Story of Our Nationhood, which he hoped
would become the official national textbook. This Harvard-trained
Ph.D. merged history, eugenics, elitism, caste, and anti-Communism
in a toxic brew that battled to defend white supremacy against the
Jew, the lower classes, the intellectually inferior, and the mongrelized "colored horde." The First World War terrified Stoddard—he
labeled it the "White Civil War"—and in *The Rising Tide of Color* he
mimicked W.E.B. Du Bois, declaring that "the conflict of color" is
"the fundamental problem of the twentieth century." He hysterically
warned against "the subjugation of white lands by colored armies"
but advised that the threat to white supremacy would more likely
emerge from migration, which threatened to "irretrievably" swamp
the white world. White supremacy stood at a critical point, shaken
by the war and by what Stoddard saw as Du Bois's 1915 "threat" that
African Americans would destroy the "color line. For colored folk

have much to remember and they will not forget." While the "African," Stoddard believed, represented a vastly inferior being who was easily dominated by whites around the world, America's "failure" to "disarm" Blacks threatened the nation's safety and security. The truth of the matter, he warned, was that "the white world to-day stands at the crossroads of life and death. . . . A fever has rocked the white frame and undermined its constitution. . . . Worst of all, the instinct of race-solidarity has partially atrophied." The pivotal moment had arrived, he exclaimed, as "the tide ebbs. The swimmer must put forth strong strokes to reach the shore. Else—swift oblivion in the dark ocean."

In 1922, inspired by Stoddard's dire warnings, an essayist for the St. Louis *Post Dispatch* cautioned that the United States faced the double threat of "alien pressure" from without and "degeneracy and retrogression within." Worldwide colored forces were gaining strength, especially after the Russo-Japanese War of 1904–5 and the First World War. Caucasians could ill afford another "civil war" that "hacked savagely at [their] own throat," while the "east" looked on and gloated. The nation must, he demanded, "establish in law the national color line which now exists in fact." Separation must exist, interracial marriage must be banned, and African Americans must "work out their own destiny apart." Borrowing from Van Evrie, Stoddard explained that the abolition of slavery represented "the worst thing that ever happened to the negro and the best for the whites. As a slave, a negro was a valuable domestic animal, and as such, was assured of good care by his owner." His conduct in freedom proved "that he is not equal to our swift, complicated civilization." Thus, if the white race hoped to survive, "we must first of all purge ourselves of the germs of the disease."

Some newspapers dismissed Stoddard's assertions as "on the level of Ku Klux Klan intelligence," but his popularity knew few bounds when it came to issues of race and immigration. By 1927, when his attempt at a national history, *Re-Forging America: The Story of Our Nationhood,* appeared, Stoddard deemphasized the threat posed by immigration and now regarded "our great negro problem" as the nation's most compelling issue. He dropped his customary xenophobia, since in 1924 the nation had largely closed "the gates to mass-immigration," and turned his attention to "the dilemma of color, at once the most chronic and the most acute of American issues." To set a racial standard for the nation to recapture, he looked back in history and saw America's first fifty years as its racial "golden age," when most Americans shared the same "blood, speech, and culture." To his mind, if the "Nordic race" should become eclipsed, "with it would pass that which we call civilization." A new dark age would descend on the earth, blotting out "our racial inheritance." Sharing a full democratic society with "brown, yellow, black, or red men" amounted to committing "suicide pure and simple, and the first victim of this amazing folly will be the white man himself."

Stoddard's book sought to provide essential historical background for this most intractable and dangerous crisis. Its origins lay with the abolitionists, deluded extremists who, in demanding the immediate end of slavery, had depicted innocent Southerners as "inhuman monsters" and advanced the intolerable notion of "race-equality." Such radicalism had incited the South and thrown the white nation into "a supreme death-grapple between the two sections of Anglo-Saxon America." This intolerable "Moloch" resulted in a war that devoured "the flower of the race," leaving the country with dangerous "racial losses." It crippled the nation's genetic stock, leaving it vulnerable and the South "bankrupt and impoverished." Reconstruction, "the crowning disaster of the Civil War period," then unleashed "4,000,000 emancipated negroes" who could not care for themselves and wandered in "vagabondage," constituting a "dangerous social problem." The nation had averted disaster only through the energy and diligence of "great secret societies" such as the "'Knights of the White Camellia' and the 'Invisible Empire' of the Ku Klux Klan." To restore order and the "rightful" place of whites in society, these groups out of necessity terrorized "superstitious negroes" and killed the dangerous ones, along with their carpetbagger allies, to "defend the pure white South from the insane plans of Northern fanatics and racial polluters." The damaging and toxic legacy of this period, Stoddard explained, produced the current racial crisis. Americans needed a national policy to preserve white domination and racial purity. The only avenue to national survival lay in what Stoddard called "bi-racialism," the complete and utter segregation of the races. The "color-line" must be rendered permanent and impenetrable to ensure national "self-preservation." Separation must be comprehensive and universal, extending from where the races are born, to where they work, eat, travel, and go to church. "Finally," he concluded, "when they die, they are embalmed by different undertakers and are buried in separate cemeteries." Under any other construction of society, he warned, "*our* America would be foredoomed to pass away." As the capstone to his racial edifice, Stoddard proclaimed, "Nothing is more certain than that the Fathers of the Republic intended America to be a 'white man's country.'"

7

Lost Cause Victorious,
1920 to 1964

If we overlook the original sin of the slave trade, there was much to be said for slavery as a transitional status between barbarism and civilization.

—Samuel Eliot Morison and Henry Steele
Commager, *Growth of the American Republic*, 1930

The first page of Thomas Maitland Marshall's 1930 *American History* textbook began with the brazen headline "THE STORY OF THE WHITE MAN." A professor of history at Washington University in St. Louis, Marshall possessed the requisite training and expertise to teach American history to the nation's young. He informed fledgling students that the white man had begun to read "five thousand years ago" and to "record important events." He outlined which ancient nations had helped propel the "advancement of the white man." Nothing else mattered. Indeed, rarely had anything else ever mattered so much to the teaching of American history.

The "eugenocide" that permeated so much of American society during the 1920s formed the cultural background for history education in the next forty-five years. As a result of the toxic ravings of Lothrop Stoddard and Madison Grant and of influential academics like Ellsworth Huntington and Edward A. Ross, along with the reborn Klan, educators hardened the idea that African Americans represented alien and inferior beings well suited, if not designed by God and nature, for the institution of slavery into a basic social assumption. Subsequent popular histories and schoolbooks at all grade levels, with few exceptions, continually reaffirmed this idea in classrooms across the United States. Until the mid-1960s, American history instruction from grammar school to the university relentlessly characterized slavery as a benevolent institution, an enjoyable time, and a gift to those Africans who had been lucky enough to be brought to the United States. As the Pulitzer Prize–winning historian James Truslow Adams asked rhetorically in his shocking 1934 history of slavery and the Civil War, "Would a [Paul] Robeson prefer beating a tom tom to thrilling audiences throughout the world with his beautiful voice? Would the colored washer woman I had in the North give up her comfortable house and her car . . . for the ancestral grass hut in the jungle? . . . Would a Du Bois prefer to be head man to an African chief instead of a Harvard graduate, scholar and writer?" During the 1930s Newton D. Baker, who had been Woodrow Wilson's secretary of war, served as a trustee of the philanthropic Carnegie Corporation that funded Gunnar Myrdal's 1944 study of the United States and race, *An American Dilemma*. To Baker, however, "history" had shown that previous Americans had been utterly courageous in their willingness to "receive" slaves and "make useful laborers of them. How many white civilizations," he crowed, "could have dared to receive so many wild savages, who were practically uncaged animals, and spread them around . . . passes human comprehension. What has been done for the Negro in a hundred years is an unparalleled achievement."

Not only had "negroes" allegedly benefited from slavery, but *whites* allegedly bore the heavy burden of slavery, a greater curse to "the white people of the South . . . [than] it was to the negroes." In his history of the Civil War, Adams insisted that "for white America, I believe there is no question that slavery and all that flowed from it has been an unmitigated curse." Princeton University's Thomas Jefferson Wertenbaker lamented the tragedy of slavery for its impact on poor whites, forcing many to flee north and others to wallow in abject poverty, as they could not compete with slave labor. In his mind, white children growing up alongside slave children learned only evil from them. Who actually suffered the most from slavery? asked the *Industrial History of the United States,* written by a Boston high school teacher and in print from 1922 to 1941. "The white man's burden" proved beyond any doubt, the author wrote, that "there seems to be but one answer possible. The South as a whole suffered, but chiefly the white South." And a trio of influential academics, led by the historian Walter Prescott Webb, wrote in their history for elementary schools that the antebellum South was home to only one true race: "white people." People of African descent existed outside the real America in a kind of ancillary—and subservient—parallel existence. Nonetheless, they lived better than Northern factory workers, as another text recorded, and were "properly fed, clothed, and sheltered" in "fairly comfortable homes." Students learned from their history textbooks, as Adams had insisted, that without question "it was better for the negro to be a civilized slave . . . than to be a savage in the jungles of Africa."

Most texts of the 1920s diminished the importance of slavery's introduction into Virginia in 1619, ignoring the irony of the simultaneous establishment of slavery and representative government. Instead, they saw slavery as having both "good and evil" influences. School histories emphasized what slavery allowed the "planter class" to accomplish: establishment of large tobacco, rice, and indigo plantations, "which their help was able to work the year round." Because of the South's climate and the nature of these crops, students learned, slavery had been the most appropriate labor force for the South. Some men like Thomas Jefferson may have had reservations about the institution, but as one 1928 textbook detailed, they could not free their slaves because the "poor and ignorant" Africans "would become vagabonds and nuisances and a burden on the communities in which they lived." Early Americans faced a terrible dilemma, according to these authors. They may have found the idea of slavery objectionable, but those Southerners who wished to see slavery end could find no practical way to afford the loss of their labor. Moreover, "Free negroes were not wanted in a community." If whites freed their slaves, "there was no way to get rid of them. It was a knotty problem," Webb and his colleagues confessed. Economics, however, resolved this "southern dilemma," as the cotton gin made slavery essential to the South.

When it came to slavery's economic impact on American history, few could compete with the history-writing team of Charles Austin and Mary Ritter Beard. Mary Beard published six of her own books, including the 1946 *Woman as Force in History.* Charles Beard, best known for his *Economic Interpretation of the Constitution of the United States* (1913), helped explain eighteenth-century Southern interest in a stronger central government through the Constitution because of its ability to better suppress possible slave insurrections. When crafting their 1921 textbook *History of the United States,* the Beards stressed a united Northern and Southern "zeal for profits." Yankee traders, they explained, earned enormous wealth in the slave trade, while Southerners reaped unprecedented profits from a system that eliminated the conflict between capital and labor. Furthermore, they advised students, "slavery was no crime" and was "an actual benefit to the slaves." Like other texts of the period, theirs insisted that masters treated their slaves well, just like any other "domestic animal," as the surest way "to make them most profitable." Yet the Beards reminded students that the life of a "savage, fresh from the jungles of Africa," could be brief, thus requiring continual replacement, which only enriched all concerned in the traffic. As the South's "one-crop" system came to dominate, the "ignorant and uncivilized" African proved the ideal farmworker since he proved to be "hard to train" for any other occupation. Some in the South objected to the "peculiar institution," but as an eight-hundred-page 1930 junior high school text explained, such men could afford to be critics since they had no financial interest in the institution. Approval or disapproval of slavery, the Beards explained, "was a question of the pocketbook. . . . The matter of slavery was determined largely by the supposed *interest* of the white man."

Textbooks in the 1920s and '30s emphasized the benefits that Africans derived as American slaves and in turn how slavery "paid" white Southerners. One 1930 account, quoting Massachusetts's John Adams, noted that the enduring and profitable nature of slavery was an example of how "men's *interests* govern their *opinions.*" Presumably, this motive compelled slave owners to treat their property with kindness and generosity. Only one text, published in 1934 by three

Chicago historians and teachers, challenged that view by emphasizing the slave foundations of both New England and the South,
reviling the institution as "one of the dark pictures in the history of
colonial civilization." But nearly all other textbooks published from
1919 to the 1960s depicted slaves as happy, joyful, and "fond of singing and dancing," especially at work, their "weird croonings brought
from savage Africa." Textbook after textbook described slaves as
living in comfortable cabins, with plenty of nourishing food, and
spending their evenings singing around campfires. Lucy Wilson,
who disdained slavery, nevertheless in her 1929 text instructed
students that masters "treated their slaves gently and cared for them
in their old age." Slaves kept vegetable gardens, raised chickens,
and lived carefree and happy, "sure of food, shelter, clothing, and
medical care." Free African Americans, not slaves, lived in "poor and
unsanitary quarters," argued the influential Henry Steele Commager
and two academic colleagues in their 1934 history.

A few histories used in the 1930s confessed that the life of a slave
could be difficult, perhaps even "very unhappy." But as Columbia
University's Harold Rugg advised junior high school students, their
lives were "no worse than that of some employees in the mills and
factories in the north." He assured readers that depictions of the
injustice of slavery came not from real life but from antislavery
propaganda, such as Harriet Beecher Stowe's *Uncle Tom's Cabin,* a
reviled target of history educators. Rugg, whose many textbooks
dominated American classrooms, had sold over five million by 1940.
He frequently came under attack for his alleged lack of patriotism
and New Deal sympathies, earning the sobriquet "Harold the Red."
In 1940 the American Legion burned his books in Ohio, and the
Daughters of the American Revolution urged schools to ban them
entirely. By 1945, sales had dropped to twenty thousand a year (a
figure that any university professor today would lust for). Not even
his harshest critics ever offered a word of rebuke about his portrayal
of African Americans. In his teacher's guide, Rugg emphasized that
while the United States might be a nation of immigrants, only white
ones mattered, as he divided the world between "us" and "our dark-
skinned citizens." "Negroes," he detailed in *Introduction to American*

Civilization, had been in America for 250 years, but only as cotton-picking slaves. After the Civil War, "most of them did what they had always done—planted cotton and worked on farms."

The iconoclastic Beards damned Stowe's novel as "unfair to the South." Other histories recommended that students instead read Joel Chandler Harris's "charming picture of Uncle Remus and the little white lad who listened entranced to the tales of Br'er Rabbit," who "reveals a happier relationship between the two races." Some authors insisted that only when "the negroes were lazy" did whites force them to work. Mary Gertrude Kelty's elementary school text insisted that "slaves did less work in a day than free laborers do." More important, she instructed students that since Blacks would not work on their own, they had to be enslaved. To rivet the idea of the happy slave into a student's mind, such books often included either full-color or black-and-white images of happy slaves dancing or playing fiddles and banjos by their cabin doors. Even authors who mentioned the sufferings of the Middle Passage and the breakup of slave families would also include an image of the happy banjo-playing slave.

When it came to depicting happy banjo-playing slaves, few could top Fremont P. Wirth's *The Development of America.* The most widely used classroom history during the 1940s, especially in Black schools in the South, it remained "virtually unmatched in popularity and sales volume" for years and was adopted by high schools in at least twelve different states from 1936 to 1957. A professor at the Nashville Peabody College for Teachers—founded in 1875 and now part of Vanderbilt University—the Illinois-born Wirth (1890–1960) served as president of the National Council for the Social Studies and published ten textbooks, histories, and supplementary publications from 1930 to 1960. His account of the development of slavery in the United States, unlike most others, included the Portuguese origins of the slave trade and English participation. Slavery, he wrote, was a "necessary evil," essential after the invention of the cotton gin, and could not be ended because of fear of endangering "the safety of the white race." While he juxtaposed the palatial estates of the masters with the slave's rude cabin, he assured students that slaves

"Slaves at home, after the day's work was over. Negroes always have been fond of singing and dancing; and the banjo has been a favorite musical instrument with them." Hanson Booth, illustration from Fremont P. Wirth, *The Development of America* (1937), p. 352.

lived comfortably and ate well, "similar to an army mess hall." Slave horsemen received fine clothing to impress guests, while field hands required only rude clothing, and "pickaninnies wore little more than a long shirt" or nothing at all. They sometimes endured objectionable treatment, Wirth confessed, but the navy and the merchant marine also whipped sailors. "Slavery, however, had a bright side," he explained. Slaves enjoyed good medical care, perhaps as many as

20 percent could read, they rarely endured harsh punishment, and all received "a decent burial in the 'God's acre' of the plantation." In short, Wirth imagined slavery as a "patriarchal system in which master and slave felt themselves members of one family."

While few readers today recall Wirth's books, the same can hardly be said of the works of two twentieth-century titans of the historical profession, Samuel Eliot Morison and Henry Steele Commager. Most students of American history from the 1930s to the 1970s in some way were touched by either one. Morison crafted some of the most influential studies of American colonial history ever written, including a biography of Columbus, a two-volume history of the European exploration of the New World, a maritime history of Massachusetts, an account of Puritan intellectual life, a biography of John Paul Jones, and a multivolume history of Harvard University, where he was the last professor to commute to work on horseback. He also compiled the fifteen-volume *History of United States Naval Operations in World War II,* published between 1947 and 1962. In all, he published more than two dozen titles and countless essays and pamphlets—a heroic achievement by any standard. For his part, Commager, who spent most of his career at Columbia University and Amherst College, published a similar number of books—and hundreds of essays and reviews—including documentary collections and historical studies, from a biography of the abolitionist Theodore Parker to a study of the Enlightenment in Europe and America and an intellectual history of the United States. While at Columbia, he also mentored graduate students who would become the country's leading constitutional scholars.

In 1930 the two authors jointly published *The Growth of the American Republic,* a college-level textbook—sometimes used in high schools—that saw its fifth edition in 1962. In the 1950s, it still earned from $10,000 to $12,000 a year in royalties—perhaps equivalent to $100,000 in modern currency—making it one of the nation's most successful schoolbooks ever. In its discussion of slavery, it referred to the contradiction of a people who claimed allegiance to "natural rights" yet also held slaves, but in other respects it did not differ from the most malignant discussions in legions of other texts.

"As for Sambo, whose wrongs moved the abolitionists to wrath and tears," they wrote, "there is some reason to believe that he suffered less than any class in the South from its 'peculiar institution.' The majority of slaves were adequately fed, well cared for, and apparently happy. Competent observers," the two held, placing their considerable prestige behind their words, "reported that they performed less labor than the hired man of the northern states." Relying on the account of slavery in Edward Channing's 1921 U.S. history rather than on any of the more than two hundred published slave narratives, much less plantation records, Morison and Commager assured students that masters cared for their property and that the "faithful darky" repaid his owner with grateful loyalty. "Topsy and Tom Sawyer's nigger Jim were nearer to the average childlike, improvident, humorous, prevaricating, and superstitious negro than the unctuous Uncle Tom" of Harriet Beecher Stowe's creation. Southern whites, they assured their readers, loved the negro "in his place" and never displayed any "physical revulsion" for a slave's color, since "white children were suckled by black mammies, and played promiscuously with the pickaninnies." They presented slavery as a welcomed "transitional status" between African barbarism and American civilization, from which the slave—or as Morison preferred to call him, "Sambo"—could only benefit.

Morison, despite retaining his obtuse views on race, eventually allowed subsequent editions of his work to be purged of some of its more offensive statements—although its retrograde view of Reconstruction remained. Commager claimed to reject American racism and also anti-Semitism for good measure. But he felt no compulsion to alter *Growth of the American Republic,* and when Black students confronted him at his Columbia University office, he refused to budge and rejected their demands to revise his book. Moreover, he saw no harm in Theodore Parker's belief in Anglo-Saxonism and Black inferiority, and he informed the historian George Fredrickson that there was "nothing objectionable" in Parker's views. Commager later explained that history depended on the literate and thus bore the stamp of those who left sufficient records for others to use in assessing the past. It was, he admitted, "the slave-owner's version of slavery which came down to us and which was widely accepted as history." Commager appeared to change his tone in 1942, when he teamed with his Columbia colleague Allan Nevins to publish *America: The Story of a Free People.* Their account emphasized that "the most important fact about American slavery was that it was Negro slavery: most of the features that characterized it were connected with race rather than with status. The whole institution was designed largely to regulate the relationship of black and white rather than of master and slave." Their book then drew the obvious parallel between the South's justifications for slavery and the "doctrine of white supremacy formulated after the Civil War." The change in tone, however, more likely resulted from a change in collaborator than from any alteration of Commager's views.

In 1950, when Commager published his influential intellectual history of the United States after 1880, *The American Mind,* he could find no room in that "mind" for African Americans except as a proverbial "problem" for whites. A similar 1943 work by Merle Curti, who for a time also taught at Columbia, found the "Mind of the Negro" difficult to assess since he claimed they left "no written record." Those who had escaped north and published memoirs could not be trusted since, he wrote, their books had been "edited" by abolitionists. While he contradicted this assessment with praise for the narratives of Sojourner Truth and Frederick Douglass, in the end he had no idea how to include African Americans in the nation's intellectual history, except through the gaze of whites. Curti cited a "negro song" meant to represent the African American perspective in the nation's intellectual life:

> Niggers plant de cotton.
> Niggers pick it out
> White man pocket money
> Nigger goes without.

Commager's *The American Mind,* however, made no effort to include African Americans. He preferred to discuss Charles A. Beard, the now largely forgotten James Branch Cabell, Sarah Orne

Jewett, and Elinor White. His American mind could not encompass a W.E.B. Du Bois or an Alain Locke, much less survey the Harlem Renaissance and its explosion of literature and art. Even in 1965, when Yale reprinted Commager's study, it continued to ignore Paul Laurence Dunbar, Langston Hughes, Zora Neale Hurston, Richard Wright, and his own contemporary James Baldwin. For Commager and subsequent experts in American intellectual history into the 1970s, the American mind remained as white as the paperback cover of his book, "negroes" remained only "a problem," and their African ancestors amounted to nothing more than unknowable primitives.

From the 1940s to the '60s, characterizations of slave life in the nation's textbooks hardly changed—and in some cases became more demeaning and distorted. With few exceptions, Northern presses continued to blanket the country with accounts of slavery for all grade levels that characterized Blacks as so ignorant that the *only* labor they could perform was Southern agricultural work, and as being incapable of learning "to do the many different tasks on a northern farm." "Accustomed" to hot climates, "'mammies' and the 'pickaninnies' seem to be having a good time," the 1942 *Our Land and Our People* instructed junior high school students. In the 1930s and '40s, Ralph V. Harlow, who would go on to write the only biography of John Brown supporter Gerrit Smith, assured high school students that slaves accepted their status, remaining "happy, irresponsible, and reasonably contented with their lot. Their work was no harder than that of the independent small farmers, and they were secure in the knowledge that the ordinary necessities of life—shelter, clothing, and food would be provided by their own-ers." Rather than the whip, offers of "a good barbecue" and "two outfits of clothing each year" encouraged slaves to work. Moreover, slaves labored outdoors, which was "at least healthful." Another text published the same year provided a similarly comforting account of slavery and illustrated "typical" plantation life with a scene from the 1936 musical film *Showboat,* featuring Paul Robeson.

Schoolbooks published during World War II bore titles that stressed the democratic ideals that the nation's soldiers defended on battlefields around the world. Between the covers, however, only whites exercised the rights and responsibilities of democracy. While Africans displayed remarkable progress through the institution of slavery, school histories emphasized, their presence "ultimately produced a problem that led to the American Civil War." John D. Hicks (1890–1972), best remembered for his history of the Populist movement, became the era's most successful professor at the University of California at Berkeley. His history lectures regularly attracted over five hundred students and, as the university still proudly proclaims, "reached a larger audience through 'Hicks histories,'" which included his 1943 *A Short History of American Democracy.* It was, the university explained, "impossible to estimate the number of students whose knowledge of American history has been built on the 'Hicks histories,' but it is certainly an immense number." What they learned from Hicks's textbooks duplicated what appeared in countless others across the educational spectrum: that slaves lived well and "with fair contentment," their lives vastly superior to any they could have led in Africa. Slavery, to Hicks, became little more than a series of picnics, barbecues, and episodes of singing and dancing, with slaves enjoying a "keen sense of humor." They rarely fretted over their lives and often felt "deeply devoted to their master and his family," and in return "white children loved their mammies." Hicks depicted slaves' religion as "extremely picturesque, and their moral standards sufficiently latitudinarian to meet the needs of a really primitive people. Heaven to the Negro was a place of rest from all labor, the fitting reward of a servant who obeyed his master and loved the Lord." When it came to "social relations" and marriage, Hicks drove home the most damaging assessment of African Americans in any midcentury school history:

> More or less formal marriages among slaves were encouraged by some masters, although cohabitation without marriage was regarded as perfectly normal, and a certain amount of promiscuity was taken for granted. Slave women rarely resisted the advances of white men, as their numerous mulatto progeny abundantly attested.

The post–World War II world saw few changes in such characterizations of slavery, as young students continued to learn that slaves lived comfortably and received kind treatment from their owners, who formed enduring attachments with their property. "Negroes are, by nature, cheerful people," a 1951 junior high school textbook explained, "and the slaves did much to make their own life enjoyable." Occasionally a slave family experienced the sale of a relative, but this proved "rare, and cannot be regarded as typical of slavery in the South." As in the early twentieth century, those books appearing in the 1950s categorically repudiated any version of slavery that stressed harsh or unjust conditions, although some condemned the slave trade. Once slaves arrived on American shores, life brightened. Even authors who declined to explicitly defend slavery dismissed condemnations of the institution as stemming from the corrupting influence of Harriet Beecher Stowe's *Uncle Tom's Cabin.* As zealously as any Lost Cause advocate, *Northern* authors in the 1950s and '60s depicted race relations in the Old South as having been as "happy as the one pictured by Joel Chandler Harris." Slaves lived joyfully, comfortably, and without the worries of "unemployment and old age." Slave children could play with white kids in the "great house," in the evening they sang and danced, and on special occasions they attended picnics or went on " 'coon' and 'possum' " hunts. In one high school text used from 1950 to 1968, the authors—a professor at Pennsylvania's Dickinson College and a prolific high school teacher from Melrose, Massachusetts—wrote that whipping a slave was preferable to imprisonment or reductions in food allocations, since that would have "meant the loss of their labor." The slave was content and, as elementary school students learned, economically necessary, since without slave labor no rice or cotton production would have been possible. As a fifth-grade textbook used in California from 1953 to 1965 explained, planters justifiably declared that "we must have slaves if we are going to raise all the cotton the world needs." Additionally, authors emphasized that slaves learned valuable trades such as sewing, weaving, carpentry, and nursing. As late as the mid-1960s, school histories cited Thomas Jefferson as evidence that "typical" thoughtful masters "provided for their slaves as carefully as they did for members of their own families and in turn won the love of their slaves."

.   .   .

Two of the nation's most successful textbook authors, Columbia University's David Saville Muzzey (1870–1965) and Stanford University's Thomas A. Bailey (1902–83), rejected their colleagues' understanding of slavery and its role in American history. Resisting, in part, the overwhelming tide of pro-Southern nostalgia, both men believed that the South had defended "a damnable cause." Professional reviews of Muzzey's first textbook indicted him for his "hatred of slavery" and for referring to the "disgrace and curse of human bondage," an opinion that one educator remarked "seems at least unnecessary." Following Muzzey, Bailey instructed students that the "inhumanity" of slavery flew in the face of the nation's emerging democratic principles. Although representing two distinct generations of authors and living on opposite coasts, they were linked through Muzzey's 1911 *An American History*, which Bailey read as a high school student and, as he later explained, shaped his understanding of American history and the way he would craft his own books.

David Saville Muzzey's New England roots stretched back to the seventeenth century. Born into a prominent Lexington, Massachusetts, family, he was a descendant of Isaac Muzzey, who gave his life in defense of American liberty on April 19, 1775. He graduated from Harvard in 1893 and studied at New York City's Union Theological Seminary, as well as the University of Berlin and the Sorbonne, then earned a Ph.D. at Columbia, where he remained until retiring in 1940. His 1911 textbook *An American History*, in various versions and editions, would dominate American classrooms for the next *fifty* years. As late as 1964, Muzzey's books remained popular across the country: 30 percent of Indiana high school history teachers, for instance, still taught one of the many versions of his book—an unprecedented achievement for any author.

Unlike most authors, Muzzey devoted an entire chapter to slavery and abolition, insisting that the subject "played the most

David Saville Muzzey (1870–1965) was the nation's most successful textbook author. High schools across the country, from 1912 to the 1960s, employed his damaging textbooks. Although he despised slavery, he asserted Black inferiority and considered Reconstruction to have been as great a crime as slavery. Photograph, 1912.

important part in the history of our country." He discussed the colonial development of slavery, the torments of the Middle Passage, and the inhuman conditions of the "peculiar institution," and offered no foolish or damaging assessments of the joys of slave life. While he claimed that American colonists did not demand slaves and blamed the introduction of slavery on Great Britain, he also censured rapacious New England merchants who eagerly sought the trade's profits. Moreover, all the colonists had believed in the legality of slavery, at the same time that they acted so jealously "for the protection of their own rights and freedom." In the book's 1929 edition, he explained that however much George Washington and "the enlightened men of the South deplored the existence of slavery . . . they found themselves part of an industrial system which seemed to demand the negro slave for its very existence." In words that would offend many readers, especially in the South, he wrote that slavery presented "a sad picture of violence, greed, and stunted moral sense." The nation's forefathers had tolerated slavery "for the sake of the profits it yielded." Their failure to end the practice, he declared in no uncertain terms, ultimately led to civil war.

Muzzey's repudiation of slavery had few equals during the first half of the twentieth century and appeared as aggressive as any account in the Emancipationist tradition of the late nineteenth century. But a careful study of his work also reveals a commitment to white supremacy as fierce as any in the books of Fiske, Burgess, Dunning, and Wilson. As for Native Americans, Muzzey always referred to them as "savages" who had reached only the stage of "lower barbarism," much like, he wrote, the "Mississippi negro of today." As for African Americans, they were, he assured high school students, a race "centuries behind whites in civilization." His textbook's assessment of Reconstruction expressed deep sympathy for the Ku Klux Klan and insisted that "the races must always be kept distinct socially, the dominance of the white man can and must be the dominance of the elder and stronger brother who educates, and encourages the weaker." For Muzzey, the presence of "savages" and "negroes" in the country constituted the central "race problem" for white Americans. His views on race are too often still dismissed as simple failures to transcend the "prevailing attitudes" of his time. He abhorred slavery, but his presentation of American history both reaffirmed and deepened the country's damaging commitment to white supremacy.

Thomas A. Bailey's ever-popular *The American Pageant,* continuously in print since 1956, reached its fifth edition in 1975. His lively and opinionated work, like Muzzey's, touched generations of American high school and college students. It also followed his predecessor's well-trod path regarding slavery and race. Growing up near San Jose, California, Bailey spent his career at Stanford University as a respected diplomatic historian, living in a protected and comfortable white world where, he confessed in his autobiography, African Americans were "so rare in our area as to be a curiosity." His father, a curiosity of a different sort, had regaled the young Bailey with Van Evrie–like eruptions against Abraham Lincoln, who, he charged, had prosecuted a "bloody war" against the South "over a 'passel of niggers.'" Nevertheless, to Bailey, U.S. history stood out over the world's landscape like the majestic redwoods he had grown up with, making "substantial contributions" to every phase of human activity.

The United States had been a marvelous success story, and Bailey intended to explain just how that happened.

The American Pageant, like Muzzey's *An American History*, rejected any Lost Cause sympathy for Southern slavery and cautioned its readers at the outset that the simultaneous founding of representative government and slavery in Virginia in 1619 represented an "ill-omened beginning." Bailey heaped blame on England for forcing slavery on the American colonies, as Muzzey and generations of earlier authors had done, although he—and all others—never clarified exactly how England compelled American colonists to buy humans from slave traders. He noted that African Americans comprised about 20 percent of the colonial population, labeling them "the mudsills of society," and that "the inhumanity of Negro slavery was magnified by the ringing phrases of the Declaration of Independence." While he emphasized the integral role slavery had played in the South and the lack of freedom and opportunity free Blacks endured in the North—"fettered freedom," he called it—the only images of Blacks he included in his book were demeaning, emphasizing Black subservience; and like his mentor, he always referred to Native Americans as "redskins." Bailey rejected the standard justifications for slavery as nothing more than "white washing." If bondage had been so Christian and beneficial to the slave, such a "blessing," he asked, why "did its victims universally pine for freedom, and why did so many take to their heels as runaways?" Bailey's *The American Pageant* condemned slavery as a corrupt and immoral system, but one that had produced a degraded and inferior people with "loose morals, sexual and otherwise." As with slavery, Bailey adhered to Muzzey's commitment to white supremacy, something that would become painfully manifest in his account of Reconstruction.

Between Muzzey's 1911 *An American History* and the early 1940s, only about seven other elementary and high school textbooks offered positive assessments of the antislavery movement. As in the first and subsequent editions of Muzzey's work, these schoolbooks followed the Emancipationist tradition of characterizing the antislavery movement as a moral force that sought to "rid the country of the disgrace and curse of human bondage." Most of these texts focused on the career of William Lloyd Garrison, although some also included references to early leaders like Benjamin Lundy and later activists such as Lucretia Mott, Wendell Phillips, and Harriet Beecher Stowe. Surprisingly, Muzzey mentioned Garrison's campaign on behalf of Northern free Blacks, who suffered mightily from racial prejudice. With captivating style, he distinguished between antislavery moderates who proclaimed that slavery represented "the calamity of the South and not its crime" and men like Garrison, who denounced slavery as a calamity "*because* it was a crime." Most textbooks failed to list the sources that their authors relied on, but Muzzey's more sympathetic approach to the abolitionists did list them, and he undoubtedly benefited from the sources he used to understand antislavery motivations and aims. For his sympathetic account of the abolitionists, he relied on the multivolume 1885 biography of Garrison by his children, as well as on the antislavery writings of Samuel Joseph May, John Greenleaf Whittier, and James Gillespie Birney. He also had read the scholarship of Harvard's Albert Bushnell Hart and, surprisingly, W.E.B. Du Bois. Yet he and nearly all other authors presented the antislavery movement as an effort of white men and women, completely ignoring the fact that African Americans had protested slavery, as Boston's Black abolitionists had clarified, long before Garrison. While he accurately portrayed the outrage the movement incited throughout the South *and* the North, his readers would have had to conclude that the abolitionists had been largely responsible for radicalizing Southern attitudes. Muzzey placed the abolitionists along a radical continuum, with Garrison at one end and John C. Calhoun at the other. In his view, "the mutual provocation of the abolitionists and the ardent defenders of the slavery system" bore responsibility for the Civil War.

For scores of other textbooks from 1919 through the 1950s, the abolitionists represented not the best of the democratic tradition but a threat to it. For a few, they amounted to irrelevant agitation at a time when the real story was the nation's splintering political system. For some others, antislavery agitation diverted attention from the more "reasonable" plans of the American Colonization Society. During the 1920s, the Beards expressed disdain for the abolitionists' "imperious and belligerent demand for instant emancipation" and their contempt for "any other views" not their own. Garrison, one popular Michigan author explained, may have been passionate, but he was also "one-sided" and "prejudiced," mistakenly denouncing "slavery and slave holders in the same scathing terms. He was unable to understand that while slavery was wrong many slaveholders were good men." To that Yankee author, apparently, there could be sin but no sinners. To others, Garrison was simply a "rabid abolitionist" who believed he followed God's will but gave no thought to what that would cost the South. Abolitionists' theories "sobered the South," a Colorado history professor emphasized, "their glibness enraged it," and their "unconstitutional schemes for abolishing it portrayed their ignorance of the case; God was on their side, but for the most part they did not know why." Throughout the 1920s, textbook after textbook bitterly condemned the abolitionists, finding them insolent, intolerant, and guilty of insulting and infuriating Southerners. As a *two-volume* elementary schoolbook explained in 1927, the abolitionists epitomized "dangerous fanatics and troublemakers." They provoked but did not persuade, spreading misunderstanding not wisdom, and inciting fear rather than instilling confidence. For many, Harriet Beecher Stowe's *Uncle Tom's Cabin* almost single-handedly brought on the Civil War.

During the 1920s, at least twenty different textbooks lacerated the antislavery movement as a volatile, uncompromising outrage that had provoked slave rebellions, unjustly and unnecessarily inflamed Southern opinion, and ultimately plunged the country into a horrific civil war. Carl Russell Fish, a University of Wisconsin history professor, characterized Wendell Phillips, the silver-tongued voice of the movement, as a prime example of antislavery insolence who "was often hissed and mobbed." That Garrison and his colleagues' "violent agitation" was to blame for inciting the Nat Turner rebellion became an article of faith, as did their threatening slaveholders with "absolute poverty." One author even accused the pacifist Quaker poet John Greenleaf Whittier of "flinging out warlike verses." Other schoolbooks argued that prior to Garrison, Americans had expressed little concern for slavery, but after he began his agitation, the nation seethed with an anger that could not be quenched except by war. In Northern eyes, because of Garrison and Stowe, the North could see the South only "as wicked and cruel." A 1926 textbook written for young Catholic schoolchildren accused Stowe of creating an entirely false picture of slavery, compelling the North to reject Daniel Webster's principle that "it would be better to save the Union with slavery than to destroy it for the sake of giving freedom to the Negro."

The rampage against the antislavery movement only intensified during the 1930s and '40s as economic disruption, fascism, and war raged around the world. Authors may have seen a parallel between the abolitionists and the socialists, Communists, and New Deal radicals who populated their own political terrain, perceiving both groups as disruptive and threatening cultural forces. Portrayed as radical, extreme, and unbalanced, the antislavery movement's obsession with denouncing slavery as a sin, authors emphasized, amounted to a belief that "it was better to break up the Union than to allow the people of the South to own slaves." Garrison remained the archetypal agitator in nearly every textbook of the era, and his newspaper, *The Liberator,* became the primary organ for spreading his impractical, dangerous, and thoughtless "ideals." But as Ephraim Douglass Adams, Thomas A. Bailey's mentor at Stanford, contemptuously stated, Garrison's paper was so inferior that "men and women" had to give him money to keep it afloat since it "never paid as a publication." Nonetheless, because of him and his fellow agitators, the more time passed, the more national divisions widened and deepened. Everyone wanted peace, writers contended, but the abolitionists wanted insurrections and their relentless propaganda created a grievously mistaken "sympathy and pity for slaves." Any textbook that mentioned the memoir of Frederick Douglass—and few ever bothered—did so not to provide direct evidence of slavery's injustice and barbarism, but to display how such propaganda further incited destructive antislavery agitation. In at least one instance, unsatisfied with blaming Garrison for causing the Civil War, an author made up a quote to depict him as so insane as to endorse "the immediate enfranchisement of our slave population." Much to the chagrin of textbook authors, Garrison did argue for racial equality, but his actual statement endorsed the vote only for free Blacks.

In the late 1930s the influential but controversial Columbia University professor Harold "the Red" Rugg, in his popular text *America's March Toward Democracy,* offered a confused account of the abolitionists, merging Quakers, Benjamin Lundy, the Grimké sisters, "liberty-loving women," and the political abolitionist James Gillespie Birney into a force that opposed only "slave keeping," while Garrison and others sought to incite slave insurrections. He provided testimony from the South Carolina author William Gilmore Simms to prove that slaves actually enjoyed their lot. Other textbook authors of the decade attacked political antislavery leaders like Charles Sumner and Massachusetts governor John A. Andrew as "extremists." But whether Quaker, female, political, or literary-minded, "all of these were pitiless in their attitude toward the slaveholders." Several accounts insisted that abolitionists sent pamphlets into the South "calling upon the slaves to revolt against their masters." All abolitionist propaganda, as one 1935 text asserted, proved not only destructive but entirely unnecessary, as "civilized mankind" showed every indication of "gradually moving away from" slavery. Samuel Eliot Morison and his colleague Henry Steele Commager assured students that slavery ended "in spite of the abolitionists, rather than because of them; and in the worst way." As James Truslow Adams emphasized in the mid-1930s, the North had "no special interest in the negro," and the Northerner had never been "as kind to him as has the Southerner and has more greatly disliked close contact with him." Ultimately, Adams insisted, Northerners had no cause to interfere with slavery, because life in the nineteenth-century South "was the most charming which our country has known."

Textbooks published during World War II maintained the assault on the antislavery movement, instructing students that slave masters "treated their slaves kindly and took a deep interest in their welfare. As a rule," explained a fifth-grade text published by two teachers and a professor of social science, "the slaves loved the people of the plantation and stood by them even after slavery was ended." Northern ministers, authors, speakers, and journalists "said many unkind and untrue things about the owners of slaves." Worse still, abolitionists demanded freedom for slaves "without compensation to the owner." Such injustice "caused much hatred but did little good." Writers inevitably associated abolitionists with violence and slave owners with love for and devotion to their property. Berkeley's influential John D. Hicks repudiated any academic who published a sympathetic account of the movement, and he dismissed the few favorable biographies of Garrison as excessive and distorted. Columbia's Allan Nevins and Henry Steele Commager diminished the importance of the abolitionists, shifting student attention to politicians and the Free Soil movement, assuring readers that abolitionists had had little relevance. As one popular junior high school text in use from 1937 to 1951 explained, the abolitionists were unsophisticated and failed to understand that the problem "was not so simple a matter in regions where slaves were numerous." Southerners' loss of personal wealth because of emancipation amounted to a problem only slightly less staggering than the "serious problem of what to do with the freed Negroes." In the end, it always came down to race.

As the anti-Communist obsession gripped the nation during the 1950s and '60s, textbooks warned against radicals like Garrison, Stowe, and Elijah P. Lovejoy, the antislavery editor in Alton, Illinois, gunned down by an anti-abolitionist mob in 1837, who poked "their noses into other people's business" and tried to "regulate affairs" in the South. Such meddlesome reformers, a team of teachers and a college president detailed in 1956, only inflamed the public and distorted the real picture of the Old South and in so doing "helped to bring about a war between the North and the South." Garrison remained the primary malcontent, unmindful of the "social problems" that emancipation would cause, and only made enemies of sensible, conservative antislavery advocates who could not tolerate his denunciation of the U.S. Constitution as "an agreement with HELL." Such attacks, writers insisted, only forced the South to more stridently defend the institution of slavery. Other texts, especially for younger students, omitted all references to the abolitionist movement, as one 1958 teacher's manual had done, or simply referred to anonymous groups that "made speeches against slavery" and "stirred up differences between the American people." A fifth-grade history, used in California during the late 1950s and early '60s, referred only to Northerners who "did not believe that men and women should be bought and sold." But the same text also asked, if cotton production lost its slave labor, "who would do the work?"

Stanford's Thomas A. Bailey, who had examined his era's conflicting scholarship on slavery and abolitionism, instructed the tens of thousands of students who read his book that only leaders like Daniel Webster and Abraham Lincoln possessed rational antislavery views. But Garrison, "the Massachusetts Madman," threatened the nation's peace and unity with his violent and unrestrained fanaticism. For Bailey, Garrison and his ilk remained only one step removed from the "bearded, iron-willed, and narrowly ignorant" John Brown. Brown's stare, Bailey assured his readers, "could force a dog or a cat to slink out of a room." In Bailey's and in virtually every other textbook of the period, the Connecticut-born Brown emerged as an unbalanced and violent fanatic who, as a 1958 high school history curtly concluded, "regarded himself as a heaven-sent agent to free negroes and punish slaveholders." His only success, they all maintained, was in proving to the South that it could have no safety in the Union. Near the end of his book, Bailey concluded his discussion of African Americans with praise for the Supreme Court's 1954 decision to end "separate and equal" schools. Amazingly, he never bothered to name the case that helped transform the country's race relations, much less identify the Black lawyers like Thurgood Marshall or the NAACP Legal Defense Fund that orchestrated the *Brown v. Board of Education* challenge. To Bailey, the Court's action, not the antislavery movement, represented the appropriate example for social action. Reflecting his times, he remarked that the case showed the world that "Communist agitators" lied when they claimed that the United States intended to hold "the Negro perpetually in the ditch."

·   ·   ·

Heroism, patriotism, and preservation of the Union understandably remained central concerns of the majority of the nation's schoolbooks, which partially accounts for their repudiation of the abolitionist movement. But their recitation of the causes of the Civil War also displayed steady movement toward reconciling Northern and Southern perspectives. Northern authors that identified slavery as the war's central cause did so by explaining that the South left the Union because of the Lincoln administration's hostility to it, coupled with a legitimate belief in the "right" to secession. Most assessments followed Ralph V. Harlow's emphasis that two distinct societies had developed since the founding in 1776 and that the North, "impelled by the desire to make the whole country alike, began to attack" areas that allowed slavery to thrive. David Saville Muzzey, who rejected any "right to secession," also shifted responsibility for the war northward. "The actual cause of the secession of the South was the hostility of the North to the institution of slavery, culminating in the election to the presidency of a man pledged to the exclusion of slavery from all the territories of the United States." Fremont Wirth's popular account, published in New York City and Atlanta, insisted that slavery had little to do with secession, since he claimed that "preservation of that institution was not a political issue in 1860." Just as Harlow had first written in 1925, Wirth assured his readers that secession resulted from a long struggle for political power between two sections of the country with conflicting economic interests. The South, identifying with the nation's original patriots, protested that they bore "a burden of taxation in excess of any imposed by the British government prior to the Revolution." At the same time, Wirth blamed the Republican Party's insistence upon excluding slavery from the territories as a prime threat to the South's "economic interests," in that way masking slavery as a cause of the war.

James Truslow Adams, who had ancestors who fought on both sides of the Civil War, considered the North morally hypocritical for working twelve-year-old children harder in factories than masters worked their slaves in the South. His 1935 high school textbook argued that "the South felt it had a better moral basis for the war than the North . . . who asked only to be allowed to secede in peace from a Union which they believed had become hostile to their own welfare." The North, according to Adams, could maintain the Union only "by the coercion of millions of unruly citizens in a neighboring group of states." Citing the warning of Southern Unionists, Adams instructed his readers that "a Union based on bayonets instead of hearts would cease to have any value." In the midst of World War II, such authors remained wedded to the idea of noble Southern heroism, that the South possessed a right to secede and a right to its slaves, and that it never would be secure under a Northern-dominated government.

Such Northern views complemented the arguments of decidedly pro-Southern textbooks that clung to a defense of "constitutional rights" and opposition to a dangerously centralizing federal government that threatened state sovereignty. Such texts disclaimed any hint that the protection of slavery had anything to do with causing the Civil War. For Southern and Northern authors steeped in the Lost Cause history of John W. Burgess, William A. Dunning, and Woodrow Wilson, as well as novelists Thomas Nelson Page, George W. Cable, and, worst of all, Thomas Dixon, Republicans represented a sectional party dedicated to thwarting the South. As one account used in schools from 1928 to 1937 assured its readers, Northern abolitionism masked a "liberal view of the Constitution in order to increase the power of the federal government" and cripple the idea of state sovereignty "so dear to the South." North Carolina–born William E. Dodd, the head of the University of Chicago's history department, along with two Texans, Walter Prescott Webb and Eugene C. Barker, crafted their book for young students during the 1920s and '30s to dismiss slavery as a cause of the Civil War. Instead, they directed student attention to the "heroism and courage displayed by the South" during the war, which they claimed "excited the sympathy and admiration of the world." The South ultimately lost not because of slavery but because of the region's reliance on agriculture, which left it comparatively poor, while the North became economically diversified and "piled up wealth." Rather than slavery, they argued, the "South's devotion to a single occupation" had spelled its doom.

While most textbooks offered only passing mention of the Emancipation Proclamation, with Muzzey's long-lived history providing the most detailed account, only about a half-dozen books stretching back to the 1920s bothered to mention that the Proclamation authorized the recruitment of African American soldiers, and none detailed the services they rendered or referred to those who served in the Union navy. One text, written by Marguerite S. Dickson, a New York City teacher, and used in Concord, Massachusetts, praised the Emancipation Proclamation as guaranteeing that freedom "should be the blessing of all men, black or white." She also referred to the recruitment of Black soldiers during the war but immediately stepped back from its significance by assuring students that "the slaves were not so ready to leave their masters" and continued to care for their plantations. Typical, Muzzey's history also failed to discuss African American military service, and for the powerful team of Morison and Commager and the vast majority of school textbooks, emancipation was an unintended consequence of a war fought only by Billy Yank and Johnny Reb.

Educators may have ignored Blacks' role in the Civil War, but they compensated for that neglect by focusing on what they saw as their ludicrous and villainous participation in Reconstruction. From the 1920s to the late '50s, an unrelenting stream of racial repudiation and condemnation flowed through the nation's classrooms. Even Catholics, who published schoolbooks that assured young students that the "Mother Church folds her arms about all her children and questions not their color or their race," nonetheless described Reconstruction as the rise of "ignorant and vicious Negroes [who] filled offices which once had been occupied by brilliant Southern statesmen." Catholics, who suffered so relentlessly from the disgraceful prejudice of men like John Jay Chapman and endured the Klan's systematic assaults, nonetheless crafted schoolbooks that instructed their children that in order to regain their rightful place and power, Southern white men formed "a sort of police" called the Ku Klux Klan. Franciscan sisters taught students that the Klan eventually lost control and had to be repressed. But because the Emancipation Proclamation had unleashed thousands of negro "good-for-nothing tramps who refused to work" and who lived by "begging and stealing," the improvised "police" had played a vital role in restoring the true South. As another Catholic text instructed students, eventually "the Confederate leaders recovered the right to vote and things turned for the better."

At least fifty-one textbooks used in American classrooms from the 1920s to the '60s endlessly repeated the standard historical and political narrative of Reconstruction that had been created by James Shepherd Pike in the 1870s. Without fail, and regardless of how textbooks portrayed slavery, abolitionists, and the Civil War, educators instructed American youth that Northern carpetbaggers and their Southern scalawag partners had used "illiterate negroes," "negroes ignorant of politics and self-government," to seize office and plunder the "prostrate" South. In one Michigan history professor's account—which remained in print from 1920 to 1937—not only were the "evils of carpetbagger rule in the South . . . almost beyond description," but far worse, "Negroes" began to make outlandish demands for racial equality. Fortunately, as *The Making of Our Country* advised students, the Klan emerged to fight "Negro misrule" and restore whites to power, thus allowing the "New South" to emerge. The iconoclastic Charles and Mary Beard had forged their careers out of the desire to have cooperation replace competition as society's governing force, to assist humanity in its quest to free itself from "injustice, ignorance, and folly," and to end the power of the "few" who "live upon the toil of the many." Yet they promoted a history of Reconstruction that depicted the South's former planter elite—"the finest talents of the South"—as its prime victims, driven from power by "their former bondsmen under the tutelage of Republican leaders." Unconcerned with lynching or racial repression, much less the actions of the KKK, the Beards focused on the emergence of Northern capitalists as the ultimate beneficiaries of the presumed misguided repression of Southern agriculture as embodied by the former slave masters. The Beards had good reason to damn the rise of the capitalist elite during the Gilded Age, and they expressed some regret for the suppression of Black rights in the South. But they still presented African Americans as culturally deprived, "imported from the forests of Africa," and "handicapped or not by innate disabilities for life in America." They ended their discussion with the stunning and approving evaluation that "neither the hopes of the emancipators nor the fears of their opponents were realized."

Educators depicted the South as having "gracefully" yielded to its fate at the end of the war only to be rewarded with "negro rule." The "low and ignorant," manipulated by carpetbaggers who guarded the freedpeople "like sheep," profited from the "sorrows and humiliations of the Southern [white] people." In legions of textbooks, the Republican Congress, led by radicals like the "vindictive" Charles Sumner and the "narrow-minded, radical, Northern sectionalist" Thaddeus Stevens—whom James Truslow Adams labeled the "dictator" of the House of Representatives—punished "the best men of the South" with "Negro suffrage" to enable an "era of shameless plundering." Even Columbia's Henry Steele Commager joined with Lost Cause academics to renounce the Thirteenth, Fourteenth, and Fifteenth amendments to the Constitution as having nothing to do with liberty and freedom but instead designed to serve as the Radicals' legal tools to control the South. As a result, "Negroes" came to believe that the "South belonged to them," and with "laziness, dishonesty, and crime," as one history declared, managed to loot the Southern states. Only organized power through the Klan could, the standard accounts instructed students, restore economic and political success, permit the real South to "manage its own affairs," and as two Stanford University professors announced in 1931, "re-establish white control." In history after history, the Klan emerged as the one force that stopped the pillaging of the South and effectively ended the horrific experience of "negro rule." America, educators insisted, had been saved by the Klan.

David Saville Muzzey's account of Reconstruction proved so demeaning and derogatory, his defense of the Klan so outrageous, that in the late 1930s the NAACP singled it out for condemnation. To Muzzey, the freedpeople at the end of the war had acted as if "the Day of Jubilee had arrived" and they would receive their former masters' lands. Carpetbaggers, according to Muzzey, then turned the former slaves against the only people "who could really help them . . . their old masters." Elected Black officials, especially in South Carolina—again displaying the influence of James Shepherd Pike—commenced an "orgy of extravagance, fraud, and disgusting incompetence." Why, Muzzey asked his students to contemplate, would the North "put upon the South the unbearable burden of Negro rule supported by the bayonet?" Some acted out of idealism, others sought power, and still more wanted to punish the South for secession. The unpardonable inauguration of negro suffrage, he roared, was the "crime of Reconstruction," which stood "the social pyramid on its apex" and set the "ignorant, superstitious, gullible slave in power over his former master." That crime, Muzzey concluded, inaugurated the era of bitterness that seethed "to the present day." At the same time, Morison and Commager's *Growth of the American Republic* echoed Muzzey's condemnation of Reconstruction. They imagined former slaves cheering that they will never have to work again with some horrific lines of "poetry" clipped from Stephen Vincent Benét's 1928 *John Brown's Body:*

> Every nigger's gwine to own a mule,
> Jubili, Jubilo!
> Every nigger's gwine to own a mule,
> An' live like Adam in de Golden Rule,
> An' send his chillun to de white-folks' school!
> In de year of Jubilo!

Morison and Commager taught that Southern whites suffered more from Reconstruction than from losing the Civil War, and far more than the former slaves. Poor seventy-year-old Thomas Dabney, they wrote, once a proud planter, suffered such deprivation that he had to do "all the family wash for years after the war." Worse still, old George Fitzhugh, the grand ideologue of slavery, became so destitute that he "lived in a poor shanty among his former slaves." One wishes that the authors had intended such tragic farce as mockery.

In authors' accounts of Reconstruction, logic took a back seat to endless assertions of Black incompetence, laziness, demoralization (because they no longer "enjoyed" the control that slavery offered), ignorance, and helplessness. At the same time, textbook authors insisted that the lazy freedpeople, who did little but aimlessly roam and steal, posed an outrageous threat that required the Black Codes passed by most of the former Confederate states in the first years after the war. These codes proved essential, the 1950 text *Making of Modern America* maintained, because the freedpeople "did not know how to use their newly gained freedom" and had to be forced to work. Grammar school children learned that African Americans "were so ignorant and inexperienced that they hardly knew what to do with their liberty." Besides, what could be expected of a people so "densely ignorant as well as dishonest," so devoid of civilization, that "many of them did not know their own names"? As Ralph V. Harlow's *Story of America* proclaimed, African Americans proved no more "fitted to take on the responsibilities of citizenship than so many eight-year-old children." A high school teacher in Pittsburgh authored a U.S. history that provided among its "study questions" one that asked students to ponder whether "the negro's experience in slavery in the South [was] better for him than the kind of freedom he would have enjoyed in Africa." The author wished to show students that once Reconstruction ended, Black and white had been able to "settle down on a peaceful basis" and that Blacks, who possessed "no civilization" comparable to whites, could then progress under proper tutelage. He cited the case of Booker T. Washington to prove that segregated schools and hard work, without any demand for "social equality when they could not use it properly," would lead to success.

At least twenty different school histories, published for Northern or Southern students from the 1930s to the late '50s, went beyond the standard denigration of the freedpeople as ignorant, lazy, criminal tools of carpetbaggers to praise the Ku Klux Klan for its actions in rescuing the white South. For elementary school students, the New Yorker Mary Gertrude Kelty's *The Story of the American People,* which relied on James Shepherd Pike's diatribe, expressed sorrow for the level of suffering whites endured until rescued by "the famous

Ku-Klux Klan." At last, she proclaimed, the South was left "to handle the negro problem in its own way." Whether their authors were Ph.D.-trained scholars or high school teachers, schoolbooks taught the youngest to the oldest students that only the Klan had been able to end the tyranny of Black rule imposed on the South by Radical Republicans and their carpetbag tools. If the Klan's actions at times proved brutal and wrong, well, "so were the things the carpetbaggers were doing." For such an era of "unparalleled dishonesty," the Klan understandably spread throughout the South to cow "ignorant Negroes," defeat Negro militias, reestablish home rule, and restore, as John D. Hicks declared in 1943, the "Democratic, or 'white man's' Party." As the University of Chicago's Marcus Wilson Jernegan and two high school teachers asked, how did the South defeat the oppressive Reconstruction regime? The answer they and so many others gave to their students was simple: the Ku Klux Klan. Its members, Jernegan and his colleagues wrote, took "an oath to frighten the Negroes in order to prevent them from exercising their political rights and to help abolish carpet-bag and scalawag rule."

"Riders of the Ku Klux Klan. They worked at night." This still image from D. W. Griffith's 1915 silent film *The Birth of a Nation* appeared as an illustration in Southworth and Southworth, *The Story of Our America* (1951), p. 351.

Klan members played on the supposed "superstitious" nature of "the negro" and during the night approached Black homes in white robes and hoods shouting, "Beware! The Great Cyclops is angry!" Others condemned President Grant's attempt to suppress the Klan as an obstacle to ending the "tragic era." Perhaps the most shocking of all was the 1951 junior high school textbook authored by Gertrude and John Van Duyn Southworth, who not only reviled "negroes who were abusing their power," but used as an illustration a scene from D. W. Griffith's incendiary 1915 film *Birth of a Nation* to legitimize and romanticize the Klan.

In 1956, as Martin Luther King, Jr., was rising to become the country's leading civil rights advocate, Thomas A. Bailey's *American Pageant* assaulted Reconstruction as a series of enactments written "with a pen made from a sword," then rammed "down Southern throats." He depicted it as an unconstitutional attempt to impose Black and Republican rule on the South, using "carpetbaggers and scalawags" who in turn would "use Negroes as political tools." The result, he wrote, "would be amusing were it not so pathetic and tragic." The "footloose Negro" had done little, while poor whites were compelled to work. Without "the Negro," he complained, whites had to pull their own plows. Moreover, he lamented, one "of the cruelest calamities ever to be visited upon the much-abused Negro was jerking him overnight from bondage to freedom, without any intermediate steps of preparation." The wretched "simple-minded," "bewildered," "fancy-free" negroes then became a "menace," stealing, drinking, and acting arrogantly toward whites. African Americans in the South, in his description, were so "hapless" and incompetent, so unable to exist in freedom, that after the Civil War scores of them simply lay down and died. Other textbooks of the late 1950s followed Bailey's lead—and the dominating professional scholarship of the previous thirty years—to characterize the freedpeople as fools dreaming of "fritters a-fryin'" while being protected by the Four-teenth and Fifteenth amendments. In time, however, with the help of the Klan, as another 1956 schoolbook explained, *"the Southern whites [struck] back,"* regained their power, and "found ways to get around the fifteenth amendment," ultimately allowing the South to repair "the damage caused by the war."

. . .

Back in 1903, the Georgia-born, Columbia University–trained historian of slavery and the South Ulrich B. Phillips had declared that the "history of the United States has been written by Boston and largely written wrong." By the time he published his influential *American Negro Slavery* in 1918, his earlier complaint had become painfully obsolete. His instructors at Columbia, along with colleagues at Johns Hopkins and Princeton, had assumed leadership in recrafting the American understanding of slavery and the Old South, the Civil War, and Reconstruction. But professional historians hardly acted alone. Northern publishers for decades had been simultaneously bringing out different editions of popular textbooks, one for students in the North and another for the South. Edward Channing had bitterly complained about the revisions made to his 1910 *Elements of United States History* for Southern students, rendering it, to his mind, a bucket of lies. But the Southern market could easily bypass Northern books in favor of imprints provided by the irrepressible United Daughters of the Confederacy (UDC) and state histories, as well as books like John S. Tilley's 1951 *Facts the Historians Leave Out: A Youth's Confederate Primer.* Muzzey's book, for one, condemned Reconstruction and "negro rule," and endorsed the Klan, yet in the South it came under withering attack for labeling secession a "rebellion" and referring to Lincoln as the South's "savior." According to the UDC, Muzzey's book demonstrated the necessity for home-grown textbooks. Unpredictably, Southern white women then took the lead in guaranteeing that the Lost Cause would be the only version of the past to appear in textbooks south of the Mason-Dixon Line.

Mildred Lewis Rutherford (1851–1928), the Queen of Athens, Georgia, the UDC's official historian, principal of the city's Lucy Cobb Institute, and vice president of the Stone Mountain memorial project, wielded unchallenged authority when it came to Southern education. Even the United Confederate Veterans bowed to her

Mildred Lewis Rutherford (1851–1928) was a historian for the United Daughters of the Confederacy. Rutherford, *Four Addresses* (1916), frontispiece.

authority and instructed all Southern libraries to adopt her "measuring rod" when purchasing books. For unacceptable ones that were already in their collections, librarians should scrawl "unjust to the South" on their title pages. In 1921 Rutherford declared that 81 percent of the nation's schools and colleges utilized "textbooks untrue to the South." Moreover, she complained, most academic histories "magnify and exalt the New England colonies" and "barely mentioned Jamestown," in this case a fully justified charge. In 1917 she went after Harvard's Albert Bushnell Hart, whose *Slavery and Abolition* had come out eleven years earlier, rejecting his version of slavery and the Civil War and exclaiming, "I lived in those early days and I know whom of I speak." For Rutherford, the stakes could not have been higher: "In a few years there will be no South to demand a history, if we have history as it is now written." As far as she could tell, most historical works depicted the white South as "sunken in brutality and vice, a race of slave drivers who disrupted the Union in order to perpetuate human slavery."

In 1912, to preserve and help disseminate what she saw as a truer account of the Old South, Rutherford and the UDC recruited students to interview surviving former slave owners and record their recollections. This, Rutherford held, "would be REAL history."

One student honored by the UDC presented an essay based on such interviews and received a gold medal for proving that slavery had been "the happiest time of the Negroes' existence," a version of history that shortly would become orthodoxy in most textbooks used across the country. For Rutherford, as textbooks written by the North's best scholars already parroted, "slavery taught the Negro self-control, obedience and perseverance—yes, taught him to realize his weaknesses and how to grow stronger. . . . [Slavery] was fast elevating him above his nature and his race." She refuted all charges of white racial prejudice in the South, correctly pointing out that David Saville Muzzey's textbook dripped with race prejudice. Then, engaging in a bout with alternate reality worthy of John H. Van Evrie or a modern politician, she declared that the "South was more interested in the freedom of the slaves than the North."

Modern historians have repeatedly emphasized the influence of Southerners like Woodrow Wilson, U. B. Phillips, and William E. Dodd in manufacturing the Lost Cause interpretation of Civil War history, but in fact the most influential exponents of this interpretation, such as William A. Dunning and John W. Burgess, were either Northern-born or Northern-trained, and the most influential advocates emerged out of New York's Columbia University. And the very first manifestation of Lost Cause literature came not from the South but from the Philadelphia-born composer, teacher, and illustrator Septimus Winner. Ironically, *Northern* influence can even be seen in the South's most determined voice of the Lost Cause, Mildred Lewis Rutherford. Not only did she reprint Rushmore G. Horton's and John H. Van Evrie's 1866 *A Youth's History of the Great Civil War,* but she absorbed the text's damaging view of slave conduct during the Civil War and of Lincoln's motivations and aims. Among the eleven core principles she employed to gauge the acceptability of a textbook, she included Northern responsibility for the war, its coercive policies, and the Republican Party's avowed hostility to the South. She united William Lloyd Garrison and Abraham Lincoln in their desire for abolitionism and especially invoked Van Evrie's assertions that Lincoln became a dictator to invade the South and that he smashed the Constitution in his quest to destroy slavery. She even employed Garrison's rhetoric—inaccurately—to blame Lincoln and Republicans for their desire to burn the Constitution, believing it "is a compact with death and a league with hell."

Rutherford refused to change her views, but most Southern historians and their textbooks rejected her caustic view of Lincoln. Long before the 1920s ended, they accepted what most Northerners had come to believe, that Lincoln's Reconstruction policies—had he lived—would have been favorable to the South and that his assassination represented "a severe loss to the whole country." One grammar school textbook, used between 1912 and 1924 and authored by three Texans—which took fifty-two pages to even mention New England—condemned his assassination as a "horror both in the North and the South." Lincoln would have prevented the chaos and crime of Reconstruction, they argued, because he would have implemented a "simple and broad-minded plan." The book was little different from the scores of similar texts used across the North, characterizing the world that the colonists had encountered as a land of "wild beasts and wild men." Like so many others, the text said little about the introduction of slavery, then described the typical plantation as a well-ordered machine, a "self-supporting community" where slaves became blacksmiths, carpenters, and shoemakers. Slave masters, the authors wrote, accepted the "grave responsibility of slavery" and turned an inferior race into a "better fed and better clothed" people "than the laboring class" of "many other lands." For all their sacrifices, Southerners were rewarded with the outrages of the abolitionists, shocking zealots who called for the immediate end of slavery "without compensation to the owners." As most other texts explained, secession and independence represented necessary measures under the dire threat of a repressive North that had ingeniously turned a political dispute into a moral crusade. To prove that the war had little to do with emancipation, the authors explained that—just as virtually every Northern text would do—"the great majority of negroes remained quietly and faithfully at work on the plantation."

The South's distrust of Northern textbooks eventually spurred creation of its own publishing industry, a goal espoused by Southern leaders like J.D.B. De Bow since the 1850s. Dallas, Texas's Southern Publishing Company, which also took responsibility for printing the Klan's *Fiery Cross* newsletter, was especially influential. If states could locate no acceptable general U.S. history, at the right price, they could turn instead to state histories, reliably written by Southern authors who would always refer to the "War Between the States," not to the American Civil War. During the 1920s, for instance, the state of South Carolina's superintendent of education hired Mary Simms Oliphant to revise and update her grandfather William Gilmore Simms's 1840 *History of South Carolina* to include the Civil War, Reconstruction, and the First World War. Simms's granddaughter, like the vast majority of U.S. history textbook authors, saw slavery as a benevolent institution that trained a people that "had never even heard of Christ. Their masters had taught them how to till the soil and how to live a useful life." She, like most Southern authors, also regretted Lincoln's death and defended Andrew Johnson, who, she asserted, only tried to implement Lincoln's policies. Her view of Reconstruction differed not in the least from that of David Saville Muzzey, and like him she defended the Klan as essential to protect "the white man against the negro" and to "fight the evil-doing radicals."

The same strategies, books, and interpretations continued to rule Southern education throughout the 1950s and '60s, with the help of the Daughters of the American Revolution, who sought out "subversion" wherever they imagined it lay. The Commonwealth of Virginia from 1957 to 1964 relied especially on the South Carolina historian Francis Butler Simkins's *Virginia: History, Government, Geography* published, not in the South, but by New York's Charles Scribner's Sons. Echoing Rutherford and Northern authors, Simkins described slavery as a blessing to the benighted African, an illiterate people who "knew nothing of Christianity" and became civilized through their experience as American slaves. Bending to more modern sentiments, Simkins and his coauthors assured readers that modern Virginians did not approve of slavery, yet the institution "made it possible for Negroes to come to America and to make contacts with civilized life, and to play an important part in the development of

Virginia." As Yankee textbooks remarked at the same time, who else did whites have to do their work? Besides, they "learned to work and play on the plantations," and "in his new home, the Negro was far away from the spears and war clubs of enemy tribes. . . . He had better food, a better house, and better medical care than he did in Africa. And," as Northern authors had been writing for decades, "he was comforted by a religion of love and mercy." George Washington had set the example in the eighteenth century, Simkins declared, with his calm, peaceful Mount Vernon, where his "negroes" lived in comfort with "sweetened tea, broths, and sometimes a little wine."

When it came to sectional strife, Virginia children learned that "white people of the North and West did not want Negroes among them whether they were free or slave." To salve the consciences of the descendants of slave owners, Simkins explained that Southern Black freedom, even if desired, proved impossible because of Northern racism. But Virginians would never have proved so irresponsible as to unleash "a large, free Negro population," he wrote, because "without supervision of white masters" Blacks would "fall into crime and poverty." As his Northern counterparts had been arguing since the 1890s, Simkins denounced the abolitionists' unreasoned and incendiary demands for emancipation as not merely unjust but intended to incite rebellions. Abolitionists had misled the North, he wrote; Harriet Beecher Stowe had irresponsibly created a false image of Southern slavery, which Simkins denounced as a wicked way for her "to use her imagination." Because of such outrages, Virginia and the South could no longer find safety in the Union, and in a chapter boldly entitled "Virginia Defends Herself," he described how Virginia left the Union to ward off a Northern invasion, an interpretation of the coming of the war nearly identical to that of Rushmore G. Horton and John H. Van Evrie. And following the majority of Northern and Southern authors, Simkins asserted that the "horrors" of Reconstruction had come about because the "moderating" force of President Lincoln had been removed, which then allowed the Republican Congress to obtain its revenge with the tyranny of "negro suffrage." That interpretation of the most consequential years in American history, with only a few exceptions, had been propounded by the majority of Northern schoolbooks in use since 1900.

Northern and Southern schoolbooks followed larger cultural forces in their effort to forge sectional reconciliation. At the celebrated 1913 Civil War soldiers' reunion, old blue and gray enemies had shaken hands and exchanged words instead of bullets across the stone walls of Gettysburg. In 1931 even the Connecticut team of schoolteacher and principal Mabel Casner and Yale's American Studies founder Ralph Henry Gabriel saw the event as proof that the wounds of war had healed. Moreover, the criminal acts of Reconstruction, especially Black enfranchisement, had been reversed, and the Union had been saved. Some Northern textbooks, especially those for younger students, avoided all discussion of the post–Civil War years, skipping from Lincoln's sad assassination directly to construction of the first transcontinental railroad, Buffalo Bill, and Colorado gold. One 1957 fifth-grade textbook devoted only two pages to Reconstruction, explaining that white men in the South lost the vote and that "carpet baggers secured power by means that were not fair . . . and bad feelings" resulted. But "little by little conditions improved . . . [and] negroes learned to take care of themselves." Another junior high school history, published from 1939 to 1946, simply followed its account of the Civil War with a chapter on the "New South." It offered few specifics but provided the telling conclusion that "difficulties which had long vexed the nation" had been settled, while others endured. "Slavery was dead," it declared, "but the negro still remained."

As the history of textbooks reveals, Americans came to see a path to national reconciliation through their shared devotion to white supremacy. While the North had won the Civil War, the white South had won the subsequent peace, which opened up a likely avenue to reunification. Emphasizing the renewed national bonds, Casner and Gabriel recorded in their history a poem by the Yale-educated New Yorker Francis Miles Finch: "Love and tears for the Blue; Tears and love for the Grey." But in any nation or place, for such new unity to endure, a symbol is required to weld it and rivet the new identity. By 1920, Americans found that symbol in the man who came to embody heroism, genius, and dedication to cause: Virginia's Robert E. Lee. Even a Yankee like Massachusetts's Charles Francis Adams, Jr.—who commanded an African American regiment during the war—praised Lee as a man who reflected "honor on our American manhood." Statues, monuments, and street names dedicated to the commander of the Army of Northern Virginia blanket the former Confederate states, but most Americans are unaware that states outside the South similarly honored the former Confederate commander. Two schools in California are named for him, as are creeks and campgrounds in, of all places, Pennsylvania, and even the state of Washington named an elementary school for Lee. During the 1940s, the United Daughters of the Confederacy organized a branch in Seattle and regularly honored his birthday, and the Trenton, New Jersey, *Evening Times* heralded him as a better general than his fellow Virginian George Washington. Most surprising of all, Boston, the seat of the antislavery movement, named a steamship for him in the 1920s, and in 1930 the city's "Southern Club" regularly held a dance party, "Robert E. Lee Night," in his honor at the Copley Plaza Hotel.

We can well expect textbooks crafted by Southerners or for students in the South to enshrine Robert E. Lee into a national pantheon, teaching students, beginning in the first grade, that he had become "the most beloved of all the great men Virginia has produced." As early as 1895, however, Northern culture and its textbooks also began elevating General Lee to iconic status as a national, not sectional, hero, ironically embodying the idea of loyalty. Philadelphia's Lucy Langdon Williams Wilson found Robert E. Lee to be "nearly perfect as a man can be." Others thought Lee possessed every quality Lincoln lacked, "perfection of figure, erectness of carriage, and a pleasing countenance." Henry Steele Commager, as late as 1980, instructed students who truly wished to understand the Civil War to read the monumental, four-volume, Pulitzer Prize–winning biography of Robert E. Lee by Douglas Southall Freeman. They would gain "an awareness of having lived with a great man—and to have seen him through the eyes of another great man."

In the 1950s Lee emerged as the most brilliant of the nation's warriors, "a cultivated gentleman, and a man of the greatest nobility of character." Schoolbooks instructed students that all soldiers adored him and that "Northerners admired and respected him." Authors presented him as a "tragic hero" who hated slavery but could never "bring himself to bear arms against his beloved state, Virginia." A California textbook used in the late 1950s and early '60s, *Exploring the New World,* followed the pattern set at the close of the nineteenth century, seeking sectional reconciliation on slavery and the Civil War. Its authors wished to avoid cultural strife in the midst of the Cold War (and the reality of slavery and racism) and promoted national unity by asserting that during the Civil War everyone (white) was brave, everyone (white) fought for principle, and Gen. Robert E. Lee represented all that was noble, gallant, and heroic in American society. "His name is now loved and respected in both North and South," they explained. "We know that he was not only a gallant Southern hero but a great American." As so often happens, however, just as the nation's textbooks sealed sectional bonds with the apotheosis of the South's most noble and heroic figure, the white supremacist foundations of American history textbooks began to crack, ultimately paving the way to a new democratic synthesis.

8

Renewing the Challenge

This is the nation's golden hour,
Nerve every heart and hand,
To build on Justice, as a rock,
The future of the land.

—Frances Ellen Watkins Harper, "Words for the Hour"

The history we teach is the product of the culture we create, not necessarily of the actual history we made. The great abolitionist Wendell Phillips once observed that "most men see facts, not with their eyes, but with their prejudices." The Pulitzer Prize–winning historian Leon Litwack sadly confirmed Phillips's observation by indicting past members of his breed as the one group of scholars most responsible for the "mis-education of American youth" and for doing the most to warp "the thinking of generations of Americans" on the issue of race and African Americans. While painfully true, the burden of responsibility for misshaping the American past and the Black role in it is shared equally by nearly all educators. As we have seen, teachers, scholars, and writers of every stripe, from Noah Webster, Emma Willard, and Horace Mann to David Saville Muzzey, Thomas A. Bailey, and Samuel Eliot Morison reinforced the elements of white supremacy that their peers and fellow citizens so richly valued.

Slavery's demise fortified what the poet, novelist, and literary critic Robert Penn Warren labeled the North's "treasury of virtue," its reassuring historical memory of the Civil War. But the abolition of slavery, as subsequent educators and authors made abundantly clear, had no impact on white perceptions of Black inferiority; nor did it lessen demand for Black subservience. Wendell Phillips had warned the North immediately after the Civil War that while the country had abolished the slave, "the master remains." But the lesson learned by his fellow Yankees was that while slavery had ended, "the negro remains." The experience of Reconstruction, as seen through the malignant eyes of Maine's James Shepherd Pike, reaffirmed for Northern whites beyond any shadow of a doubt the principles of Black inferiority they had absorbed all their lives. As a result, Northerners who had been skeptical supporters of experimenting with Black political power in the South irreversibly concluded that the African American's very nature made it mandatory that whites must always rule. Reconstruction, although intended to be a transforming democratic experience, ironically only increased the North's desire to erect walls of racial segregation. In Detroit during the 1930s, a white developer actually constructed an *eight-mile wall* to separate an existing Black community from a new all-white neighborhood that the Federal Housing Authority (FHA) had at first refused to help fund because of its proximity to African Americans. While Southerners used the powers of the police state to enforce residential segregation, Northern communities—with the help of the FHA—"redlined" their comparatively smaller African American populations into ghettos and adopted restrictive covenants to prevent the integration of white neighborhoods. Moreover, banks refused to offer loans to African Americans, regardless of financial status. During the Second World War, white Detroiters protested and then attacked new housing constructed specifically for African Americans, perceiving such efforts as dangerous social and economic threats. Additionally, from 1865 to 1934, the federal government distributed 246 million acres of Western lands—taken from Native Americans—to 1.5 million white families. Forty-six million adults today, as the *New York Times*'s Nikole Hannah-Jones reminds us, are descendants of those privileged white families and beneficiaries of the wealth it created. Nor could Black soldiers returning from World

War II fully share in the benefits of the G.I. Bill, which helped create so many white suburbs and allowed whites to gain transforming college educations.

Sign at the Sojourner Truth U.S. federal housing project, Detroit, February 1942.

From the 1890s to the 1960s, the overwhelming number of school textbooks reiterated the theme of Black incapacity and the unquestioned necessity to affirm white power. While authors sometimes discussed Northern efforts after the Civil War to establish schools throughout the South, reserving special praise for the work of the New England–based Peabody Education Fund, they belittled the universal Black enthusiasm for their creation. From the 1940s to the '60s, Berkeley's John D. Hicks taught students that anything beyond vocational training for African Americans was a waste of time. He mocked their "pathetic eagerness" for education, asserting that they showed "no great proficiency beyond the elementary stages." Thus did Northern white children learn that "Negroes were unfit to rule." It had been a terrible mistake, textbooks proclaimed, "to prevent the intelligent white people from governing" after the Civil War. Authors assured their readers that "men of intelligence and property will not submit to the rule of the ignorant very long." As Washington University's Thomas M. Marshall concluded, "White robes and fiery crosses . . . had the desired results."

Until World War II, Southern white domination of African Americans proved ruthless and, in countless ways, far worse than anything inflicted during the era of slavery, as Douglas Blackmon painfully recounted in his devastating 2009 study, *Slavery by Another Name*. And during the same time, as in those wretched days before the Civil War, the North would again benefit from Southern oppression. Whether by the cotton that filled their mills or later by the coal that fueled their furnaces and factories, Northerners profited from the exploitation of Black labor. Accordingly, they uncritically accepted the South's social and economic order, tirelessly declaring that Southern whites knew best how to "manage the negro." During the First World War, when the "Great Migration" began, sending over six million African Americans northward, and eastern and southern Europe sent millions more immigrants into Northern cities, insistence on segregation and white domination took on near hysterical proportions. The enormous popularity of eugenics before World War II bore witness to the intensity of the white psychic crisis such changes incited. Thus the reborn Ku Klux Klan proved far more popular outside the South than within it. Correspondingly, well into the 1960s, history textbooks relentlessly demeaned African Americans and refused to include real images of them, preferring imaginary ones. By establishing a common national understanding of the character of African Americans, textbooks created an illusory version of the past that served the separate and mutual interests of Northern and Southern whites alike. They also helped achieve the vision of national unity that John H. Van Evrie had imagined eighty years earlier.

.   .   .

At the same time, however, gradual *and* dramatic transformations of the national understanding of the past occurred as Americans began to redefine themselves and their society. The unbroken African American quest for full equality that began in the eighteenth century, expanded in the nineteenth, and blossomed in the twentieth, coupled with the impact of the Second World War and the postwar Communist challenge, began to alter white Americans' racial perceptions. Over time these forces compelled the nation to confront the hypocrisy of continuously affirming democratic principles while simultaneously refusing to acknowledge the justice of extending them to Black Americans. When President Lyndon Johnson addressed a joint session of Congress on March 15, 1965, to insist on passage of a new voting rights act, no previous president had ever thought of, much less demanded, such action from the nation:

> It is the effort of American Negroes to secure for themselves the full blessings of American life. Their cause must be our cause too. Because it's not just Negroes, but really it's all of us, who must overcome the crippling legacy of bigotry and injustice.
> And we shall overcome.

Many of the seventy million Americans watching that nationally televised speech felt electric shivers of hope surge through their bodies. Dr. Martin Luther King, Jr., wept with anticipation. "We have overcome today," he later proclaimed in Selma, Alabama. Others felt confusion or rage. Ten days after the speech, the thirty-nine-year-old white Detroit civil rights worker Viola Liuzzo was brutally assassinated near Montgomery, Alabama. Nevertheless, Johnson's historic speech marked a critical turning point, compelling Americans to rethink national identity. The arc of change proved very long, and only in the 1970s did textbooks begin to reflect a shifting society and question how Americans had previously understood their past and themselves.

No change, however, was possible without the persistent African American quest for equality and full justice. From the antislavery movement to the Equal Rights League, which fought for civil rights from 1864 to 1921, to the National Afro-American Council, the

New England Suffrage League, the National Suffrage League, the National Negro American Political League, the National Association of Colored Women, the Niagara Movement, and finally the National Association for the Advancement of Colored People, African Americans maintained a vigorous and consistent battle for full civil rights. Beginning during the Civil War, they also sought full educational opportunities. Despite the false and derogatory assessments of textbooks and white propagandists, at their first opportunity African Americans in the Reconstruction South sought "access to knowledge" with an intensity that fifteen thousand Black and white Northern educators could not begin to satisfy.

The Niagara Movement, an African American civil rights organization founded in 1905 and led by W.E.B. Du Bois and Boston's radical publisher William Monroe Trotter, similarly made education a central focus of its efforts. One of the prime objectives of its "Declaration of Principles" was the establishment of free and compulsory education for *all* children, especially in the South, "where the Negro-American are almost wholly without such provisions." Writing ten years later, Du Bois heralded quality education as central to the civil rights struggle, rejecting vocational training as an effort that "would fasten ignorance and menial service" on Blacks for yet another generation. True education, he held, was essential to the creation of the next generation of the world's "leaders, thinkers, and artists."

But activists like Du Bois and Trotter sought even broader educational goals, hoping to transform American historical memory and in that way change what Americans valued as their history and saw as their future. In 1905, when the Niagara Movement's original seventy-five members from twenty-three states joined, they took the "Garrison Pledge." In memory of William Lloyd Garrison, they pledged to follow his example and work to realize the "great ideal of human liberty which ever guided & inspired him." Borrowing from his inaugural *Liberator* editorial in 1831, the pledge proclaimed that members would "be as harsh as truth & uncompromising as justice." Dedicated to honor past "friends of freedom," Niagara members invoked Garrison as an enduring symbol of freedom. They reminded the public of his central role in the destruction of slavery, at a time when textbooks and popular historical memory vilified him as a radical and intolerant agitator who helped bring on the Civil War. Driving home the significance of Garrison's legacy, the founding of the Niagara Movement took place during the centennial of Garrison's birth, which African Americans elaborately celebrated and employed as a reminder of the Emancipationist tradition's democratic promise. Trotter even established his newspaper, the *Guardian,* in the same Boston office where Garrison had published the *Liberator.* With a bust of Garrison always on his desk to remind him of the long struggle for freedom, Trotter proclaimed his *Guardian* as the nation's "greatest race paper."

Several of the leaders whom Du Bois saw as essential to the future of the race, the "talented tenth," forged a Harvard University– Washington, D.C., education nexus. "The best and most capable of their youth," Du Bois proclaimed in 1903, "must be schooled in the colleges and universities of the land. . . . All men cannot go to college but some men must." Roscoe Conkling Bruce, son of Mississippi's first elected Black U.S. senator, Blanche K. Bruce, was one of those men. Graduated from Harvard in 1902, from 1907 to 1921 he served as Washington, D.C.'s assistant superintendent of education for "colored schools." Bruce's relationship with his fellow Black Harvard graduates was strained at best. While a Harvard student, he had spied on his more radical Black colleagues, especially Trotter, for Booker T. Washington, and in 1915 he earned the rebuke of the district's Black newspaper, the Washington *Bee,* which reviled him as "the most despised man in Washington." But Bruce kept the confidence of the district's white school board members, even when Black parents and three hundred of the system's teachers called for his removal.

The textbooks and curriculum that Bruce helped oversee in the first decade of the twentieth century for his 17,703 Black students proved no different than those used in white schools across the North. One U.S. history text that the district adopted even condemned the institution of slavery. Under Bruce's leadership, students read Milton, Shakespeare, Carlyle, and Emerson, learned math, physics, biology, and geography. The famed M Street High School offered French, German, Latin, and Greek, while Central High School focused on ancient and Roman history, as well as European and American. The Eurocentric curriculum offered to Black students may have been no different from that provided to whites, but it also contained the same faults. In the case of U.S. history, teachers could not take the story beyond 1860, avoiding conflict with Lost Cause advocates, even though the district's board included the Black activist and feminist Mary Church Terrell.

But Bruce, whatever his shortcomings, also possessed an unswerving dedication to African American history and culture and worked to expand that curriculum. He brought Harvard's Albert Bushnell Hart to the district to assist educators in acquiring "methods of teaching history and government at various ages." More important, he supported and enthusiastically praised two of his teacher-administrators. The journalist, lawyer, and activist John Wesley Cromwell served as principal of the Alexander Crummell School, and Carter G. Woodson, the second African American to earn a Ph.D. from Harvard's history department, taught in the district's schools and briefly served as principal of the Armstrong Manual Training School. Bruce urged his teachers to use the studies that both had published, Cromwell's 1914 *The Negro in American History: Men and Women Eminent in the Evolution of the American of African Descent,* and Woodson's 1915 *The Education of the Negro Prior to 1861.* Bruce believed that curriculum should include the careers of Presidents Washington and Lincoln and political figures such as Daniel Webster, even Wendell Phillips and William Lloyd Garrison, as well as poets such as Whittier, Longfellow, and Lowell. But "What about Toussaint L'Ouverture?" he proclaimed. "Was he not a great soldier?" And what about "Paul Laurence Dunbar and what of Frederick Douglass? I say that unless our schools utilize . . . the careers and personalities of colored men and women as well as of white[,] our children will be overwhelmed by the prestige of the white man and their own initiative impaired." The student, Bruce insisted, should be touched by the "spirit of Alexander Crummell," the Episcopal minister, philosopher, reformer, and pan-Africanist.

Woodson and Cromwell, Bruce declared in 1915, valued "what men and women of Negro blood have actually done," and they give "our children and youth a sense of pride . . . an honorable self-confidence, a faith in the future and its possibilities."

Carter G. Woodson (1875–1950) founded "Negro History Week," the *Journal of Negro History,* and in 1915 the Association for the Study of Negro Life and History. He is honored as the father of modern African American history. Like W.E.B. Du Bois, he studied under Albert Bushnell Hart at Harvard. Photograph, c. 1915.

Perhaps Bruce's greatest accomplishment was his support for Carter G. Woodson, a creative and innovative scholar trained by Albert Bushnell Hart, who helped transform the field of American history. At Woodson's death in 1950, Du Bois remarked that had he been white, there is little doubt that he would have been a professor at a major university. But when he completed his degree in 1912, "there was not the slightest thought that a black man could ever be on the faculty of Harvard or of any other great school." Born the son of former slaves, Woodson rose from the West Virginia coal mines to graduate from Kentucky's Berea College, then earned graduate degrees from the University of Chicago and Harvard. After teaching in the district's schools, Woodson spent most of his career at Howard University, where he was the dean of the College of Arts and Sciences. But Woodson is rightly honored, if not revered, as the founder of what is now known as the Association for the Study of African American Life and History, the *Journal of Negro History* (now the *Journal of African American History*), and for launching in 1926 the celebration of "Negro History Week," which in 1976 officially became February's Black History Month. Equally important, he established the Associated Publishers (AP) to bring out the latest Black history, biography, folklore, and literature. In 1922 the AP published his high school textbook *The Negro in Our History* and in 1928 his *Negro Makers of History for Young Readers*, as well as other authors' adult poetry and fiction. His tireless efforts not only boosted racial pride but helped transform the definition of American history.

Since nearly all Southern states employed centralized approval procedures for the adoption of school textbooks, one could easily imagine that the publications of scholars like Woodson would never pass white muster. Yet from Maryland to South Carolina and west to Oklahoma, public school systems eagerly adopted his books for their segregated schools. Atlanta, New Orleans, Birmingham, St. Louis, and even Tulsa all adopted Black history textbooks for their separate school systems. Rural areas in Alabama, North Carolina, and Texas followed suit. Some schools even made Black history compulsory, and students who failed their "Negro history" class at Atlanta's Booker T. Washington High School could not graduate. By 1933, at least 50 of the South's 174 segregated high schools offered Black history courses, and nearly all of Mississippi's Black schools offered them as electives. Even in the 1920s, "Negro Schools" could adopt collections of Black-authored poetry and a biography of Toussaint L'Ouverture. Never, of course, had any thought been given to requiring white students to take such classes, something that would have breached the national wall of white supremacy. Ironically, the only resistance came from Black teachers, whom Woodson believed opposed the trend because of their own "mis-education." Yes, understandably, they may have hesitated to teach Black history, fearing potential white community reaction or not wanting to raise expectations that had no chance of being realized.

Fears of a white backlash seemed realistic as Woodson took direct aim at the accepted history of Reconstruction. Virtually every textbook and all scholarship of the 1920s reviled fictive "Negro rule" as the cause of corruption and the presumed disastrous experiment of

Reconstruction. But Woodson rejected that assessment: as "a matter of fact," he wrote, "most of the local offices in these commonwealths were held by white men," and those African Americans who did hold office had the same qualifications as white ones. He refuted the idea that Black legislators "were illiterates, ignorant of the science of government." Both Blanche K. Bruce and John Mercer Langston, he informed readers, had graduated from Oberlin College, and Langston had become a lawyer. "Most Negroes who sat in Congress during the eighties and nineties," he advised readers, "had more education than Warren G. Harding, now President of the United States."

Woodson's *The Negro in Our History,* meant for students and the general public, included dozens of images of slave life and of prominent individuals, Black and white, male and female, who helped shape the African American experience. It also focused on the development of African civilizations, not dismissing them as barbaric, as every other text had done. Rather than perpetuating the hopelessness that suffused white accounts of Africa, Woodson presented African civilizations as equal to their contemporaries and as "temples of significance comparing favorably with those of the Greeks and Romans." No assessment like that could have been found in any American schoolbook or work of scholarship.

Woodson, Du Bois, and their contemporaries were painfully aware of the depth of the challenges they faced, as the "inferiority of the Negro is drilled into him in almost every class he enters and in almost every book he studies." As Woodson explained in *The Mis-Education of the Negro,* African American history had been reduced to the "benevolent" influence of slavery, the love of slaveholders, and characterizations of abolitionists as meddlesome fanatics who disrupted an institution that masters eventually would have modified on their own. Men like Garrison and John Brown had brought on the Civil War, and making the "Negro" a citizen during Reconstruction had been a tragic mistake, worsened by inciting the displeasure of the master class, which "will never tolerate him as an equal; and the Negro must live in this country in a state of recognized inferiority." All this, Woodson explained, aimed at control: "If you can control a man's thinking you do not have to worry about his action. When you determine what a man shall think you do not have to concern yourself about what he will do. If you make a man feel that he is inferior, you do not have to compel him to accept an inferior status, for he will seek it himself."

Resisting the impact of such white supremacist aims in education became a central focus of the NAACP, just as it had been critical to the earlier Niagara Movement. The association's Committee on Public School Textbooks warned in 1932 that "American children are being taught a conception of the character, capacity, history and achievements of the Negro utterly at variance with the facts, and calculated to arouse against him feelings of aversion and contempt." Seven years later the NAACP damned American public schools as a "breeding ground of bigotry and prejudice." It cautioned parents, Black and white, that "the very textbooks which their children study in school are often germ carriers of the most vicious propaganda against . . . the Negro citizen." The association's 1939 report on textbooks went on to damn D. W. Griffith's 1915 film *Birth of a Nation*—which still infected schoolbooks as late as 1951—for offering up a "never-ending storehouse of pictures based on the old South with its crooning black mammies, obedient colored servants, and psalm-singing workers who tip their hats graciously to white southern planation lords." But American academics and textbook authors, along with the overwhelming majority of white Americans, largely ignored the NAACP's rebuke and continued to reproduce the same demeaning stereotypes that diminished Black humanity and elevated white supremacy.

When W.E.B. Du Bois's *Black Reconstruction in America, 1860–1880* appeared in 1935, Ralph J. Bunche declared that "Dr. Du Bois has unloosed his brilliant and bitter eloquence" to completely rewrite one of the most consequential eras in American history. Bunche, who would go on to earn a Ph.D. in political science from Harvard and the Nobel Peace Prize in 1950, explained that until the publication of Du Bois's work, nearly all Americans understood the emancipation of the slave and enfranchisement of "the Negro" as "gestures against nature." In choosing to write about Reconstruction, Du Bois could directly assault the central features of white supremacy and its power over the education of Americans. As Du Bois declared in the book's last chapter, "The Propaganda of History," America's children learned that *"all Negroes were ignorant";* that "all Negroes were lazy, dishonest and extravagant"; and that "Negroes were responsible for bad government during Reconstruction." Moreover, because of assumed Black incapacity, corruption, and carpetbagger exploitation, the South could only have been redeemed by the Ku Klux Klan. In short, he wrote, Americans understood Reconstruction as a tragedy for whites, "a disgraceful attempt to subject white people to ignorant Negro rule." Those responsible for crafting the American understanding of its history, he explained with disgust, had far more interest in inflating the white "national ego" than in rendering the truth of the past.

William Edward Burghardt Du Bois (1868–1963) remains the nation's most important African American scholar, historian, sociologist, journalist, activist, and public intellectual. He is usually remembered for his civil rights activism and socialism, but his scholarship, especially on Black social history and the slave trade, and his great tome on Reconstruction, helped transform modern African American history. Cornelius Marion Battey, photograph, 1918.

Du Bois explained to his readers that if the slaves of 1860 had been white, the Radical Republican Thaddeus Stevens would be remembered as "a great statesman," Massachusetts senator Charles Sumner would be hailed as a great democrat, and the German-American transplant, Civil War general, and Missouri senator Carl

Schurz would be sanctified as a "keen prophet, in a mighty revolution of rising humanity." The "ignorance and poverty" of the former white slaves "would have been explained by history, and the demand for land and the franchise would have been justified as the birthright of natural freemen." But they were not white, and the idea of race dictated the landscape. Reconstruction thus became understood and taught as the supremacy of "barbarism" over "civilization." Instead of justice, "we have in fifty years, by libel, inuendo and silence, so completely misstated and obliterated the history of the Negro in America and his relation to its work and government that today it is unknown. This may be fine romance, but it is not science. It may be inspiring, but it is certainly not the truth. And beyond this, it is dangerous. . . . It has more than that, led the world to embrace and worship the color bar." He surveyed American textbooks and all scholarship on Reconstruction and was "aghast at what American historians have done to this field." It represented "one of the most stupendous efforts the world ever saw to discredit human beings, an effort involving universities, history, science, social life, and religion," all to render African Americans permanently inferior and subservient.

Black scholars like Bunche and Rayford W. Logan quickly reviewed Du Bois's work in professional journals. Logan, best remembered for his book on African Americans at the end of the nineteenth century, *Betrayal of the Negro,* had attended Roscoe Conkling Bruce's schools in Washington, D.C., gone on to Williams College, and in 1936 earned a Ph.D. from Harvard. He considered Du Bois's Marxist class analysis too heavy-handed in recasting the era, but he also considered it every bit as legitimate as Charles Beard's popular 1913 critique of the Founding Fathers, *Economic Interpretation of the Constitution of the United States.* Surely, Logan concluded, Du Bois correctly saw Reconstruction as giving rise to "a new capitalism and a new enslavement of labor."

Most white historians, however, ignored Du Bois's assault on America's understanding of Reconstruction. Those who did comment, such as Arthur C. Cole, an influential historian of the Civil War and Reconstruction, found *Black Reconstruction in America* "provocative" but overwrought and dismissed its refutation of white scholarship as "not especially effective." Avery Craven, one of the era's most distinguished American historians, belittled Du Bois as "only the expression of a Negro's bitterness against the injustice of slavery and racial prejudice." He charged that Du Bois had based his work on "abolition propaganda and the biased statements of partisan politicians. . . . With the insistence on Negro human qualities goes the naive assumption of complete fitness for citizenship, the franchise and office holding." By distorting facts and relying on antislavery "propaganda in the name of history," Craven charged, Du Bois had "probably done little toward averting the 'fire and blood' solution of the race question or securing that 'perfect and unlimited equality with any white man' he desires." In commenting on the book of another African American scholar, Craven croaked about "the virtual impossibility for a Negro scholar to write 'sanely' on Southern history." The *American Historical Review*, the pivotal journal in the field of history, refused to review Du Bois's book. After publishing one of his early essays on Reconstruction in 1910, as Columbia University's Eric Foner observed, it was "the last article by a black writer in that august journal until the publication seventy years later of John Hope Franklin's presidential address, which also dealt with Reconstruction."

But Du Bois's book was not entirely ignored or demeaned by white scholars and teachers, and it opened up an avenue of change that bore fruit decades later. Howard K. Beale, a Harvard-trained historian who taught at the University of North Carolina and at the University of Wisconsin, just five years after publication of *Black Reconstruction in America* called for the rewriting of the history that Du Bois had so thoroughly condemned. In the majestic pages of the *American Historical Review*, Beale drew his colleagues' attention to Du Bois, "whose race and social philosophy give his work, *Black Reconstruction*, freshness." Beale, like nearly all other scholars, found Du Bois's Marxism unappealing, but he also declared that his book had "presented a mass of material, formerly ignored, that every future historian must reckon with." Rare for his profession, Beale was progressive on race issues. He recognized Du Bois's career as

pivotal to ending the nation's emphasis on Black industrial education, the legacy of Booker T. Washington, and to finally accepting
full education for all to create "a new and better social order." He
understood that *"whites resent an intelligent, educated Negro because
he refutes their basic philosophy of racial inferiority."* Because of the
work of Du Bois and those he influenced, such as Beale, by 1969
the professional historian's account of Reconstruction had become
completely transformed, shorn of its offensive stereotypes and Lost
Cause domination. Even the profession's standard textbook of the
Civil War and Reconstruction confessed that some whites in the
South "caught a vision of democracy across racial lines" and never
mentioned James Shepherd Pike.

At the time Du Bois challenged the nation's distorted and vicious
memory of Reconstruction, the fifty-three-member American Committee for Democracy and Intellectual Freedom, led by Columbia
University anthropologist Franz Boas, repudiated American racism—
especially in education. As chair of the committee, Boas worked with
an eminent group of American academics, including Ruth Benedict,
a Boas student who also would become a distinguished anthropologist; Robert A. Milliken, the Nobel Prize–winning physicist; and
literary scholars Frank Luther Mott and Ralph Barton Perry. The
committee condemned eugenics, anti-Semitism, and all forms of
racism, especially that aimed at Blacks. They singled out American
textbooks in all fields of study for falsely propagating notions of race
and inheritable social characteristics. They surveyed 160 high school
texts in civics, history, geography, and biology, finding that at least 32
of them openly taught white racial superiority. Of all the textbooks
that employed the term *race,* the committee discovered that a higher
percentage of books used in New York City (78.2 percent) misused
the term than those used in Virginia (71.4 percent). As a result,
the committee urged the nation's scientists, school administrators,
teachers, and publishers to revise textbooks that taught false views of
race, insisting that the term should be eliminated from curriculum
and textbooks. Even Charles A. Beard, who had advanced white
supremacy in his own histories—and which the committee had
censured—backed its demands. While the major publishers Farrar &

Rinehart, Harcourt, Brace & Co., and Houghton Mifflin endorsed the committee's goals, all other presses ignored them.

The advent of the Second World War, especially the wretched Nazi appropriation of American ideas of eugenics, began to challenge the country's white racial paradigms. Harlem congressman Adam Clayton Powell, Jr., saw in it the start of "Civil War II," warning white Americans that the "New Negro" no longer would tolerate white supremacy. The wartime Double V campaign pledged to fight racism abroad and racism at home, and the outbreak of white assaults on Black communities around the country underscored Powell's proclamation. The father of twentieth-century education theory, John Dewey, spoke out against racism during the era. As early as 1909, he had cooperated with Du Bois, Ida B. Wells-Barnett, and African American educators to reject the idea of an "inferior race." At a meeting of the National Negro Conference in New York, he had warned that denying educational opportunities to any group "is not merely doing an injustice to that particular race and to those particular individuals, but it is doing an injustice" to the entire nation. In 1938 and again in 1941, with war raging around the world, Dewey denounced American racism. Such attitudes, he asserted, belie any "profession of democratic loyalty." The example of Germany, Dewey declared, proved that without "basic humanities . . . democracy is but a name." That same year the white president of Virginia's Hampton University, Malcolm Shaw MacLean, took the opportunity to equate American racial oppression with Nazism. If anything could destroy American democracy, he warned, "it will be our failure to stamp out any semblance of hatred, suspicion, and oppression based on" racism. For good measure, he suggested to his Northern white colleagues that they would "profit greatly by employing Negro professors. I can," he continued, "visualize totalitarian administrators cringing in horror from such a proposal, but in a democracy it makes the most obvious common sense."

The 1940s also saw the advent of one of the most consequential critiques of American culture ever penned. As one scholar observed in 1945, "No one can pretend to examine or discuss intelligently the 'minorities' problem in this country without constant reference to Gunnar Myrdal's epochal *An American Dilemma.*" For perhaps the first time, Howard University sociologist E. Franklin Frazier explained with astonishment, a white scholar had assessed African Americans as "simply people," without the usual abysmal stereotypes. More important, another analyst explained, Myrdal had exposed the "Negro Problem" as fundamentally "a white man's problem." As Myrdal revealed in the book's introduction, "at bottom" the American problem was a "moral dilemma," an "ever-raging conflict between" the "American creed" and white Americans' failure to apply it to African Americans. Two years after its publication, the Chicago *Bee* observed that Myrdal's book had sparked unprecedented national interest in the "race question," produced an avalanche of literature on "Negro-white relations," and inspired Americans to "find out what the 'American Dilemma' is all about." While the South ignored the book and a few Northern critics—Black and white—expressed their disdain, newspapers from New York to Chicago glowed with praise for it. *Time* and *Life* magazines exclaimed that not since Alexis de Tocqueville had the United States benefited from such a "sharp-eyed foreigner." W.E.B. Du Bois simply labeled it "monumental" and "unrivaled."

Most important of all, *An American Dilemma* helped transform the nation's legal structure as well as its race relations by famously appearing in note eleven of the 1954 *Brown v. Board of Education* Supreme Court decision. But since so many of the issues that Myrdal tackled in the nearly fifteen hundred pages of his study remain with us, it is understandable that the seventy-fifth anniversary of its publication in 2019 yielded a major conference in New York to assess its impact. Nor is it surprising that professional analysts in a variety of disciplines still revisit the massive two-volume work to better grasp the power of white supremacy today.

Myrdal, a professor of economics at the University of Stockholm, had received a one-year lectureship at Harvard University in 1937 and came to the attention of the educator and president of the Carnegie Corporation, Dr. Frederick Keppel. Ironically, board of trustees member Newton D. Baker, a white supremacist, had first suggested in 1935 that the corporation consider "the general questions of negro education and negro problems." Baker was looking for academic justification for the continued suppression of African Americans, but Keppel saw in Myrdal one of the few scholars capable of conducting a "comprehensive study" of African Americans without the taint of American racial prejudice. While other trustees thought Myrdal naïve—and even Myrdal wondered why the corporation had sought him out—that very quality most appealed to Keppel. His lack of experience, his racial naïveté, made him best suited to conduct an impartial assessment of American race relations.

Keppel's confidence was well placed. Myrdal assembled a talented team of researchers and writers but also plunged into the research himself. He investigated a number of Ph.D. dissertations that examined Black life and culture and found that they all affirmed white prejudice and contained nothing that would "make any white American citizen feel uncomfortable." He discovered that "value-free social science" in America was a fraud, did nothing to foster clarity, and only diminished it. Symbolic of his approach, he not only toured the South to learn firsthand the nature of white attitudes, but he gained the assistance of the nation's leading Black scholars to assess his findings, including E. Franklin Frazier, Ralph J. Bunche, Charles S. Johnson, Alain Locke, and W.E.B. Du Bois, and he even consulted with the Urban League and the NAACP.

Unwieldy, insufficiently focused, and astonishingly comprehensive, *An American Dilemma* (1944) probed the heart of American culture. Over five years of research and writing led Myrdal to the very same truth that John H. Van Evrie had declared ninety years earlier: that white American democracy depended on Black subordination for social stability. No matter how poor, uneducated, or untrained, all whites could take comfort that they remained superior to African Americans. That view, Myrdal concluded, served as a "much needed rationalization." Equality of opportunity, part of what Myrdal called the "American creed," sustained community and individual hope, but steeped in contradiction, it excluded people of color and remained a cherished expression of "personal liberty." While Myrdal grossly underplayed Northern white supremacy, he observed that even New Englanders possessed "a well-furnished component of race prejudice." Moreover, thirty American states had outlawed interracial marriage, and the rest "universally condemned it," which conflicted with the nation's democratic ethos. Much to his credit, the entire second volume of the project meticulously assessed African American life and culture, exploring Black leadership, its history of resistance to white supremacy, and the Black church and press, and it provided a detailed statistical analysis of levels of Black wealth, education, labor, and social life. The result, Myrdal concluded, was that African Americans struggled to survive in an "irrational, inefficient, and cruel American caste system"—while the rest of the nation was "continuously struggling for its soul."

Wartime realities also spurred a collaboration of the two major historians' professional organizations with the National Council for the Social Studies. Their report, which came out the same year as Myrdal's *An American Dilemma,* assessed school curriculum and changes necessary to improve history teaching. They all agreed that any "attempt to treat large groups of Americans as second class citizens would destroy the unity of the nation," something clearly intolerable, as war would rage for another year. The study urged "more tolerance" and greater "appreciation of the contributions of all kinds of people who make up our country." Reliable, accurate history, the committee declared, was essential to that outcome. Those who knew the lives of "Gallatin, Ericsson and Pulitzer, Booker T. Washington and St. Gaudens, will be less inclined to ascribe all virtue and intelligence to a single racial group."

Sound advice, but when it came to recommending subjects that should be taught in American schools, whiteness still ruled. America might be celebrated as the "homeland of a mixed people," but all the recommended historical figures and events were white, and slavery came up only when the report suggested the teaching of the 1857 *Dred Scott* Supreme Court decision. Committee members deemed "recreation, sport, and social life" essential to a student's education, but not the history of slavery, nor any contributions of African Americans. The committee considered Samuel Adams, George Washington, Jefferson Davis, and Robert E. Lee as representative Americans, but not Frederick Douglass, Harriet Tubman, or even Booker T. Washington. Despite the promising rhetoric, for American educators, history remained a mirror, not a microscope, reflecting only the images of the report's authors. Even in 1947, when John Hope Franklin published his pathbreaking textbook, *From Slavery to Freedom: A History of Negro Americans,* he felt compelled to remind white readers that American history also had been shaped by the African American "presence." Indicative of the state of white consciousness, he had to assure readers that "the negro" was "as truly American as another member of other ethnic groups that make up the American population."

The Supreme Court's *Brown* decision only *began* the process of deconstructing and disassembling Jim Crow culture, and as we have seen, the teaching of American history throughout the 1950s and into the '60s still reflected the white supremacist views of fifty years earlier. As late as 1969, the novelist and critic James Baldwin bemoaned that American culture denied identity to African Americans, still viewing them as inferior beasts without civilization or culture, "and that we came out of the jungle and were saved by the missionary." In 1966, 72 percent of white Americans disdained Martin Luther King, Jr., seeing him as an un-American threat, a figure that increased to 75 percent two months before his assassination. Despite President Johnson's sincere aims and his cooperation with King, his FBI under J. Edgar Hoover waged an intense campaign to silence and discredit the civil rights leader and his movement to preserve white power. Hoover went on to declare war on the Black Panther Party and helped orchestrate the 1969 assassination of party deputy chairman Fred Hampton in Chicago.

To explain the persistence of white supremacy, we must understand that the civil rights struggle did not expose a "regional sickness," as the political scientist Jeanne Theoharis has written, but rather a "national malady." Reflexively, when we see references to the civil rights struggle, the South's persistent social and institutional suppression of African Americans comes immediately to mind, by comparison leaving the North to appear as Robert Penn Warren's "treasury of virtue." In fact, Martin Luther King, Jr., received an education in the depth of white racial hatred when he traveled to

Chicago in 1966 and was stoned by raging white mobs. The South had no monopoly on racial protests, which actually stretched from Boston to Los Angeles. Carrying enormous symbolic weight, the first lunch counter sit-in took place not in Greensboro, North Carolina, in 1960, but two years earlier, in Wichita, Kansas. Congress crafted federal laws, especially the 1964 Civil Rights Act, to ignore Northern segregation: it kept federal dollars flowing into New York and other major Northern cities through the claim that segregation existed because of personal choice rather than by law. The Boston branch of the NAACP during the 1960s objected to the intolerable segregation of Boston schools, including curriculum disparities and discrimination in hiring. White school administrators rejected the NAACP's protests as "insulting." Boston officials, the civil rights activist Ruth Batson recalled, then advised the association that "our kids were stupid and this was why they didn't learn." The Boston School Committee exclaimed that "we have no inferior education in our schools. What we've been getting is an inferior type of student."

The NAACP and the Urban League renewed the campaign against racist textbooks, and in 1965 the league met with representatives of the publishing industry to insist on revisions. They backed up their effort with local protests against the "racist poison in the school books." Young readers' books suffered, with only 6.7 percent of them in the 1960s including any Black figures. Even in the late 1960s, schoolbooks and children's literature remained a white world, what James Baldwin referred to as the "great stumbling block" to social change. William F. Brazziel, who taught at Virginia State College and the University of Connecticut, condemned the nation's publishers for the "psychological lynching" of African American children by their insistence on preserving a white world with damaging stereotypes in their books.

Resistance to change raged as intensely in California as in Mississippi, Virginia, Georgia, or South Carolina. In 1964 a team of highly respected academics surveyed the texts used in California's elementary schools. The committee found them obsolete and profoundly damaging, serving to increase racism by reinforcing "notions among white people of their superiority and among Negroes of their inferiority." With California's Black parents demanding change, by 1967 John Hope Franklin and several colleagues published a new eighth-grade textbook, *Land of the Free,* that challenged the long legacy of white supremacy. Predictably, whites exploded in anger. They denounced the book for including "troublesome" Blacks like Martin Luther King, Jr., W.E.B. Du Bois, Rosa Parks, and even Crispus Attucks, who appeared to be too close to modern Black radicals for whites to accept. As Franklin revealed in his autobiography, one white Pasadena group reviled his textbook as Communist propaganda, "hostile to religious concepts." The group said it overemphasized "Negro participation in American history, projects negative thought models, criticizes business and free enterprise, plays politics, foments class hatred, slants and distorts facts, [and] promotes propaganda and poppycock." In 1968 *Time* magazine listed *Land of the Free* as one of 334 books that should be banned. In 1971 the state of California refused to renew its agreement for the work, localities refused to use it, and the book died.

. . .

The advent of the 1960s saw little change in the way textbooks presented the history of slavery, and most of those aimed at younger students either ignored the subject or softened its impact to absurd levels. A fifth-grade history turned slavery into a middle-class experience, with slave men working the fields and slave women cleaning house and cooking. One high school text used in Indiana in the 1960s had been first published in 1945 and remained in use until at least 1969. It not only diminished slavery's importance but falsely claimed that Thomas Jefferson had freed his slaves before his death. Editions of David Saville Muzzey's *Our Country's History* used throughout the 1960s differed little from earlier versions of his text. He warned that slavery's introduction had had "fateful consequences" for the nation but offered no sustained examination of the institution and certainly not its impact on the formation of the Constitution.

The presentation of slavery's history took a dramatic turn in 1963 with publication of *The National Experience: A History of the United States* by a team of the country's leading historians: C. Vann Woodward, Kenneth Stampp, Arthur M. Schlesinger, Jr., Edmund S. Morgan, Bruce Catton, and John Morton Blum. They placed American slavery in a broader New World context, comparing conditions with slaves in the Caribbean. The text emphasized that slaves, with the exception of those struggling on the South's large cotton and sugarcane plantations, tended to live a relatively normal lifespan. The authors failed to exploit the abundant available slave testimony and ignored the horrid conditions on Louisiana sugar plantations, but they also abandoned all the damaging "happy slave" accounts that so blighted previous texts. Instead, they emphasized the regime of labor that sought the most work at the lowest cost, but without crippling conditions. Above all, the textbook declared, slavery persisted because of the "fears, ambitions, and aspirations of Southern white men." The image of the "contented slave" had been replaced by recognition of the "superior power of the white caste and the effectiveness of its elaborate technique of control." Slavery, the authors assured readers, was an "efficient and profitable labor system" and an enormous "capital investment." It produced field hands as well as talented craftsmen and even factory workers. Despite what previous authors had written about the South's willingness to end the institution on its own without the "needless" provocation from men like William Lloyd Garrison, "the master class had no compelling economic reason for wanting to abolish slavery." Although the authors underplayed the issue of racial subordination, in the end they confessed that slavery "deprived a whole race of the chance to develop its potentialities and of the freedom that white men treasured so highly."

The way textbooks, and scholarship, described the history of slavery would not be the same after 1963. Although older textbooks and state histories with demeaning and romanticized accounts of slavery remained in wide use throughout the South, the new generation of textbooks fled from images of the contented slave, the "brutish Africans," and the loving master. The new professional history, which had begun a profound transformation during the 1940s, began to seep deeply into schoolbooks, emphasizing the contradiction of a nation founded simultaneously on slavery and on the rights of man.

From the late 1960s to the '80s, textbook accounts of slavery underwent a profound transformation, personalizing the enslaved and even depicting free Southern African Americans as living precariously between slavery and freedom. Without excuses or evasions, by 1967 textbooks began depicting American history as revolving around race, observing that slavery's history started with Columbus, and damning the institution as "a blight upon mankind since the dawn of history." Slaves lived not happily but in a "suffocating smog of insecurity," never knowing when families would be obliterated to pay off the master's debts. One 1967 text backed up the stark reality of slave life by pairing photographs of the master's idealized plantation mansion with the slave's shack. In the 1970s, textbooks even began appearing for the intellectually handicapped, and they too stressed the injustice of slavery and pointed out that for the slave, America decidedly was "not a land of freedom and opportunity." The slave lived a barren existence, "often cold and hungry," with no "freedom and no rights." Other authors began emphasizing the ideological development of white supremacy to justify enslavement. Images of Africa began to change as well, conforming more with the reality offered by Carter G. Woodson than that of Noah Webster, stressing civilization and extensive trade and contacts with Europe. By the 1980s, textbook authors routinely included images and discussions of Frederick Douglass, Phillis Wheatley, and Benjamin Banneker in their accounts. Suddenly, African Americans appeared as fully human, even a people resisting their oppression, not "a problem" or an archetype.

With the civil rights movement surging toward its climax in the mid-1960s, schoolbook accounts of the antislavery movement followed a trajectory parallel to that of the history of slavery. The textbooks of the early 1960s offered approving statements for "moderate" individuals such as the Quaker Benjamin Lundy but still denounced William Lloyd Garrison as "fanatical and extreme." They emphasized Northern opposition to abolitionism and taught students that abolitionism not only proved a failure but damaged other antebellum reform movements. Moreover, as one 1961 text stressed, abolitionism bore primary responsibility for driving "a wedge between North and the South." Its authors, one of whom became a leading scholar of American intellectual history, offered praise for the American Colonization Society, which they believed offered a wise and "moderate" plan to solve the slave problem. Textbooks for younger students either avoided any mention of the antislavery movement or offered only a sentence or two about individuals who "made fiery speeches and wrote rousing newspaper articles" that worried Southerners. Why should people object to slavery, one 1963 account asked, when slaves received good care "and always had jobs"? Moreover, their "faithful service" was always rewarded with "gifts and sometimes . . . freedom."

As with the history of slavery, the 1963 *National Experience* initiated a reconsideration of abolitionism that reflected the change in professional historians' understanding of the movement. Garrison received far less attention, with emphasis shifting to his colleagues Theodore Dwight Weld, Wendell Phillips, Gerrit Smith, and Lewis and Arthur Tappan of New York. Students now learned that the overwhelming number of abolitionists rejected violence and focused on moral suasion to change opinions. Rather than being a wedge that destroyed the Union, the movement became a force that "helped to persuade the great majority of Northerners that slavery was morally wrong and therefore could not be accepted as a permanent institution." Rather than causing the national crisis, the abolitionists had helped prepare the North for "the terrible struggle that lay ahead." But in 1963 the reconsideration stopped short when it came to John Brown. Bruce Catton, the popular historian of the Civil War who won a Pulitzer Prize in 1954, crafted the text's section on Brown and depicted him as a dishonest charlatan who "regularly failed to pay his debts." If not entirely mad, Catton described him as "a monomaniac about religion and slavery, a psychopathic individual." After his escapade at Harpers Ferry, Catton remarked, Virginia should have declared him insane and committed him to an asylum. Instead they executed him and "made him a martyr." To Catton's mind, Brown's raid convinced the South that all the North meant to declare war on slavery and the South.

· · ·

Later textbooks followed *The National Experience*'s lead and gradually expanded discussion of the movement—returning to the emphasis of the Emancipationists in the 1880s—and offered a wider spectrum of antislavery leaders, including Lucretia Mott and Frederick Douglass. Books published in 1967 and 1968 took the unprecedented step of introducing students to the Black abolitionists William Whippier and especially David Walker, who were now included in the circle of Black insurrectionists that featured Denmark Vesey and Nat Turner. By the 1970s, the antislavery movement appeared in elementary and high school textbooks as a *biracial* effort, with one schoolbook including a photograph of Harriet Tubman but *not* William Lloyd Garrison. Northern prejudice and its impact on free Black lives emerged as never before, especially the painful issue of separate schools and white intolerance for the education of African Americans—clearly not a subject relegated to the distant South. Harriet Beecher Stowe's *Uncle Tom's Cabin* no longer received denunciations as a dangerous exaggeration, and students now learned that however unpopular Garrison had been before the Civil War, afterward he had become "an American hero."

Until the 1980s, most textbooks ignored the African American role in the Civil War, even those that praised Lincoln's adoption of the Emancipation Proclamation. During the 1960s, Robert E. Lee retained his "spotless character," and even a text that mentioned the approximately 200,000 African Americans who had served in the military devoted more space to women's role in the war. Until the 1980s, for the vast majority of American history textbooks, the Civil War remained largely a white man's struggle.

The "dark and bloody ground of Reconstruction" painfully stammered through U.S. history textbooks, becoming transformed only as acceptance of the civil rights movement grew. From the 1950s to the early '60s, Lost Cause white supremacy dominated teaching of the post–Civil War era, as even elementary schoolbooks asserted Black incompetence and the former slaves' unsuitability for freedom. "The Negroes had a hard time getting used to being free," one fifth-grade text used in early 1960s California explained, "they hardly knew what to do." The text said nothing about the era's pivotal civil rights legislation and constitutional amendments but instead focused on how much "negroes" needed education and the leadership of Booker T. Washington.

Astonishingly, David Saville Muzzey's fifty-year-old account still dominated schoolroom instruction in the early 1960s. To the former Columbia University professor and other authors of the period, Reconstruction proved that "vengeance rather than justice" had followed the war. Radical Republicans like Thaddeus Stevens embodied Northern "vengeance," unable to understand that the South's repressive Black Codes had been "necessary measures of social protection" for whites. The last editions of his textbook had been purged of some of the more outrageous assertions from the 1940s and '50s, but Muzzey and other authors still found Northern efforts to transform the South after the war, even the Freedmen's Bureau, as only tempting "Negroes away from work [and] into politics." The Fourteenth Amendment and other civil rights legislation were little more than obvious plots to extend Republican political control over the South. As for the heinous actions of the Ku Klux Klan, Muzzey clung to his assertions that Northern corruption and "Negro rule" forced whites to take "the law into their own hands." For the years 1877 to 1954, he offered not a word about Blacks, and he even refused to name the landmark Supreme Court case that overturned segregation.

But the civil rights and Black power movements of the 1950s and '60s, along with academic and popular authors—Black and white, across a broad spectrum of American culture—altered America's understanding of itself and its past. Spurred by the Nazi racial horrors and the impact of Gunner Myrdal's *An American Dilemma*, American scholars began to investigate prejudice as a psychological and sociological phenomenon. Gordon W. Allport, who served in Harvard's department of psychology from 1930 to 1967, shook national thinking about the psychology of whites with his 1954 *The Nature of Prejudice*. Allport, reaching for objectivity, argued that prejudice is both "self-gratifying" and "blind conformity" to "prevailing folkways." He found varying levels of racial prejudice among whites, depending on the phrasing of survey questions, but in his study about 30 percent of high schoolers readily admitted that African Americans belonged to an inferior race. Greater familiarity with the history of white supremacy, especially the work of John H. Van Evrie (which was available to him at Harvard), would have helped Allport see the deeper role that race played in creation of white identity. In a revealing interview, he quoted a five-year-old white girl who had expressed her unhappiness that a neighboring African American family had moved away. "Now," she cried, "there is no one that we are better than."

This renewed interest in the dynamics of racial prejudice, along with profound white ignorance of the reality of Black life in America, led to an astounding story in 1960 and 1961. John Howard Griffin, a Dallas journalist, wanted to know what it was like to be an African American in the South. With medication, skin stain, a heat lamp, and a shaved head, Griffin became "a Negro" and traveled by foot, cab, bus, and train from New Orleans to Atlanta. "How else except by becoming a Negro could a white man hope to learn the truth?" he wrote. His astounding diary account of his brief stay on the other side of the color line appeared in 1961 as *Black Like Me,* with a film version in 1964. His first night as a "Negro" in New Orleans taught him all he needed to know about the world whites created: "Tonight they looked at me but did not see me." But what they did see clearly insulted and revulsed whites, who seethed that a Black person would have the temerity to ask for anything—water, or even a reply. The ordeal of Jim Crow life penetrated Griffin's every breathing moment. Finding the very necessities of life—food, water, even a bathroom— became trials forever dictated by white demands, by white insistence that Black people not interfere in white lives, and by the "hate stare." As he reported in the autumn of 1960, the year before publication of his book, "My revulsion turned to grief that my own people could give the hate stare, could shrivel men's souls, could deprive humans of rights they unhesitatingly accord their livestock."

The interviews he gave and the brief essays he published concerning his experiment *prior* to the book's appearance gave him a more complete view of his fellow whites' attitudes. The Klan burned a cross near his home, and others hung him in effigy from a streetlamp. Griffin and his family, even his parents, fled to Mexico in fear of their lives. "I like to see good in the white man," he remarked to *Time* magazine. "But after this experience it's hard to find it in the Southern white." His explosive and revealing adventure riveted national attention on the African American ordeal, although at least one New York critic dismissed the notion that one had to become Black to understand "the evils of oppression and discrimination." But Dan Wakefield, the novelist, journalist, and screenwriter, found Griffin's book a "brief, unsettling, and essential document of contemporary American life." Thanks to Griffin's brave account, Wakefield observed, white Americans could learn how their prejudice forced African Americans to spend much of their life "searching for the basic things that all whites take for granted." Wakefield, who reviewed Griffin's book for the *New York Times*, had written his own account of race relations in the South after traveling there over a five-year period. He gave a national perspective to what Griffin had left as a regional tragedy. Quoting the novelist James Baldwin, Wakefield wrote that segregation might be official in the South, but it was unofficially the rule in the North. "Negro inferiority underlies the life of Northern ghettos as well as the life of any Southern town." Racism and Jim Crow did not magically end at the Mason-Dixon Line, as Yale's C. Vann Woodward reminded his academic colleagues in 1962, with "racial inhumanity in the South" and "benevolence, liberality and tolerance in the North." Those outside the South still lived the myth of Robert Penn Warren's "treasury of virtue." Even the great nineteenth-century French observer Alexis de Tocqueville had warned that Black freedom never equaled white anywhere, "and he cannot meet him upon fair terms in life or in death."

For whites who wished to comprehend the extent of their own domination, African Americans had left a long and eloquent record, which then exploded during the era of the Harlem Renaissance. It continued unabated during the 1950s and '60s with novels like Ralph Ellison's *Invisible Man.* The National Book Award winner, which "illuminated the blackness of my invisibility," would become a landmark in American literature and a mainstay in high school and college courses. Ellison explored the "inner eyes" of those who shaped African Americans into a "phantom in other people's minds." "If you're white, you're right," he bitterly and ironically observed in discussing what color of paint sold best. Claude Brown's 1965 *Manchild in the Promised Land*—which would sell four million copies by 2002, when Brown died—followed Ellison's insider view with shocking starkness in the Harlem of the 1940s and '50s. Both books focused national attention on Northern Black life shaped by white expectations, restrictions, and demands. The grisly, pained, even vulgar reality that Brown constructed explored how the Great Migration had taken Southern African Americans on a journey, not from slavery to freedom, but from "the fire into the frying pan." His autobiographical account allowed white readers to see how their expectations constricted Black life every bit as much as Griffin's account of the South did. When Brown began his own quest for education and escape, whites and Blacks both thought that "this Negro must be dreaming. Doesn't he know that Negroes are supposed to just be porters?"

But Claude Brown's book, along with the writings of Malcolm X and Eldridge Cleaver, had changed the terrain whites stood on. "The white youth of today," Cleaver insisted in his 1968 *Soul on Ice,* "to escape the onus of the history their father made . . . must face and admit the moral truth concerning the works of their fathers. That such venerated figures as George Washington and Thomas Jefferson owned hundreds of black slaves, that all of the Presidents up to Lincoln presided over a slave state, and that every President since Lincoln connived politically and cynically with the issues affecting the human rights and general welfare of the broad masses of the American people."

At the same time, Black and white authors directly challenged the "rise of democracy" themes that so pervaded academic and textbook history. The Mississippi-born journalist and historian Lerone Bennett, Jr., rejected white accounts of Black Americans' African heritage just as Alexander Crummell had done a century before. Despite recounting the African American role in the nation's history in his ever-popular *Before the Mayflower: A History of the Negro in America,* he bemoaned the reality that white Americans would not admit to the history that stared them in the face. African Americans remain "strangers in their own house . . . still permanent exceptions to the melting pot theory." Not only did whites refuse to see them as melting into the mainstream of American life, but "most Americans are determined that they shall not get in the pot." Forty years later, he would challenge professional historians and popular culture again by rejecting the legacy of Abraham Lincoln as the emancipator and recognizing his lifelong fascination with colonization.

The dominant white narrative came under assault from a variety of perspectives. The Trinidadian historian, journalist, and Marxist C.L.R. James, whose *Black Jacobins* was first published in 1938, saw new light in 1963 to advance Black power. "Vengeance! Vengeance!" became the Haitian war cry, James wrote of Toussaint L'Ouverture and his Haitian revolutionaries. As if a direct threat to the white world, James explained that the Haitian Revolution destroyed much because Haitians "suffered much." Their soldiers "carried a white child on a pike as a standard," he proudly exclaimed. Three years later the Yale historian David Brion Davis published the first volume of his history of slavery and Western society, a monumental effort that won him a Pulitzer Prize in 1967. By 1975 his *Problem of Slavery in Western Culture* had seen its sixth printing, and by 2006 it would be joined by three additional massive volumes tracing the history of human bondage. For the European settlers of North America, Davis reminded readers, "the negro" symbolized "gloom, evil, baseness, wretchedness, and misfortune." He even quoted one seventeenth-century Frenchman who asserted that it "might be properly said, that these Men came out of Hell, they were so burnt, and dreadful to look upon." The result of Davis's enormous effort to comprehend the impact of slavery in the New World, as another Yale historian, David Blight, reminds us, is that "tyranny is a central theme of American history, that racial exploitation and racial conflict have been part of the DNA of American culture."

As David Brion Davis transformed our understanding of the role of slavery in the Western world, in 1968 Winthrop Jordan published his massive and influential 651-page *White Over Black,* a history of white attitudes about African Americans from 1550 to 1812. The nation's founders had claimed "America as a white man's country," and Jordan explained that the impulses to white supremacy had been as "deep and powerful" as any in the new nation. With authority—and evidence—displayed by few other American historians, Jordan taught that the founders of America all perceived their whiteness as essential to their identity and success. "Retention of whiteness would be evidence of purity and of diligent nurture of the original body of white folk. Could a blackened people look back to Europe," he asked, "and say that they had faithfully performed their errand?" Whiteness was essential.

Clearly, textbooks alone could not spur so dramatic a national reassessment. But such academic and popular writings compelled a rethinking of the American past. Correspondingly, textbook presentations of Reconstruction began shedding the false and repressive nostalgia for Southern white rule. *The National Experience* led with its reinterpretation of the era as an unsuccessful effort to end Southern white supremacy, not a welcome defeat of "negro rule and carpetbag corruption." Newer textbooks began following Carter G. Woodson's earlier reminders that "negro rule" had been a myth and that those few Blacks who did serve in government proved "able and talented men." Unlike Muzzey's and previous accounts, the Klan appeared, not as innocent Halloween figures but as a violent terrorist organization. During Reconstruction, Radical Republicans had certainly wanted the South to pay for its disloyalty, but students now learned that it aimed to establish new conditions of freedom and equality. Its failure had resulted not from Black incompetence but from white resistance North and South, which sought national reconciliation "at the expense of the Negroes." A few texts in the late 1960s clung to the older interpretation, but the majority in use during the 1970s and '80s dropped the traditional defense of white rule and instead focused on the effort to establish Black rights and a process of creating full freedom. Rather than faceless stereotypes, textbooks now put names to actual Black leaders, such as Blanche K. Bruce, P.B.S. Pinchback, and Frederick Douglass. One text in 1971 even drew student attention to the work of W.E.B. Du Bois. The history of Reconstruction had been transformed from a mistaken loss of white power to the "great tragedy" of the nation's failure to "obtain a lasting equality in citizenship for the negro." While the first Reconstruction had failed to establish equality, students now learned that the civil rights struggles of their own era amounted to a "Second Reconstruction" that could fulfill the promise of the first.

By the nation's bicentennial, mainstream American historians finally admitted to the central paradox of the nation's history. As the Yale historian Edmund S. Morgan observed, the "rise of liberty and equality in this country was accompanied by the rise of slavery." Moreover, he admitted, "it may be said that Americans bought their independence with slave labor." But confessing to an obvious truth, one that had been commonplace in the schoolbooks of the 1870s and '80s, did not amount to a complete rethinking of the integration of our African heritage into the narrative of our history. Discussions of African Americans still too often amounted to only "white attitudes towards Blacks." Even as late as 1991, those who helped shape public thinking about the American past proved quite willing to confess to the profoundly racist nature of the American experience and at the same time insist that the nation be seen as a melting pot in which all became one. Even the liberal historian Arthur M. Schlesinger, Jr., denigrated what he labeled as "intensified ethnic and racial militancy." Those who clung to their ethnicity, in Schlesinger's eyes, "denounce the goal of assimilation to challenge the concept of 'one people.'" To authorities like Schlesinger, the American melting pot must still be filled with a pale broth, not a colorful stew. By 1990, the history that students stepped into had begun to look more like that sought by Martin Luther King, Jr., than John H. Van Evrie. But the moral arc of the universe that the great civil rights leader had summoned took longer than he had ever imagined to bend toward justice.

Epilogue

Thus in Thy good time may infinite reason turn the tangle straight, and these crooked marks on a fragile leaf be not indeed.

—W.E.B. Du Bois, *The Souls of Black Folk*

Confederate flags swayed during the January 6, 2021, assault on the U.S. Capitol and on American democracy. Such emblems sometimes can be diverting symbols, tempting viewers to shrug off racial oppression as something as extinct as the Confederacy and Southern slavery. In this case, far from it. The gallows with its wretched noose erected outside the Capitol spoke louder. In 2008, while many wistful Americans had hailed Barack Obama's election as the end of the *ancien régime*, almost an equal number woke up the following morning in shock. The election of an African American president became the harbinger of profound change, one that jeopardized white identity and supremacy. The number of white Americans feeling overwhelmed, disparaged, and dispossessed only increased with each passing day. As the *New Yorker* magazine writer and Harvard historian Jill Lepore observed in 2010, many whites felt the shocking sensation that Obama's "election had ripped a tear in the fabric of time." As if affirming Newton's Third Law of physics, that for every action there is an equal and opposite reaction, national politics immediately responded with the election of the great white demagogue. Anxious whites rose up in 2016 to elect someone who would reempower them, even if only symbolically. White men in America believed that "their voice wasn't being heard," Vanderbilt University professor of sociology and medicine Jonathan Metzl observed. "Trump gave them their voice back." In the fall of 2016, as the former president of the Organization of American Historians Earl Lewis related, the prospect of a Donald Trump victory had inspired those whites suffering from a perceived sense of lost dignity, status, and respect with new hope. They saw in him a renewal of white supremacy *and* Black subordination. Trump would, as one white New Yorker informed an African American woman who grabbed the last seat in a subway car, put people like her "back in the f___ing fields!"

Such sentiments are only the most obvious expressions of white anxiety and fear over their perceived declining racial status and power. The fictional idea of differing races, with genetically determined levels of ambition and material success, still dominates white perception of color inequality. Moreover, that view is so ingrained in the white mind, as Metzl discovered, that many Americans prefer suffering and death to a change in public policy that might benefit people of color, "Mexicans, welfare queens" and "nonwhite others." Such a frame of mind—a culturally determined identity—helps shape white behavior across the nation. What the Chicago-born historian Howard K. Beale wrote in 1934 concerning Northern white attitudes remains just as true today. "Northerners accept a few Negro children into a white school without question," he observed, but "where there are large numbers of Negroes in any one school, the problem becomes acute and the Northerner finds that he, too, has prejudices."

The manifestation of such beliefs can be seen in the record of racial demographics from Boston to Minneapolis to Chicago. To avoid association with African Americans, white families either remove themselves to city enclaves or to the suburbs. If too many people of color reside in their neighborhood, those whites who can afford the expense will send their children to private schools. Chicago demographics tell the tale. As of 2020, 175,680 school-age white children live in the city, yet only 37,198 attend public schools, representing just 10.9 percent of the city's public school population.

There are, however, 122,116 African American public school students (35.8 percent), 159,163 students of Hispanic ethnicity (46.7 percent), and 4,488 students designated as multicultural (1.3 percent). Out of a total of 652 city schools, Chicago has 227 that are 90 percent African American, an additional 103 that are 90 percent Hispanic or mixed, and a total of 539 that are at least 60 percent students of color. But this is not a new trend. By the 1990s, the segregation of Northern schools had returned to levels not seen since 1968. As Jonathan Kozol's *Shame of the Nation* revealed, school systems like Chicago's exist in states from Massachusetts to California. Even in predominantly white sections of New York City, if a school possesses too many African American students, white parents will remove their children. Moreover, precious few whites would ever have it known that they permitted their children to attend a school named for Martin Luther King, Jr. As Kozol sadly concluded in 2005, the nation had returned to "apartheid schools." This determination to preserve whiteness and the wellsprings of its cultural authority is just as revealing as the desperate attack on January 6.

.   .   .

During the 1990s, concerted efforts to rectify the racial imbalance in the teaching of American history found the entire subject politicized by conservative enemies of what became popularly known as "multiculturalism." Such concerns, one study asserted, would "lead to greater divisions among students . . . and less respect for individualism, not the reverse." The study even charged that giving more attention to Harriet Tubman than to Harriet Beecher Stowe was an act of "present mindedness" that failed to "teach the past as it actually happened," but rather as some "wish it had happened." Thus, since American culture has always diminished the importance of African Americans, we must continue to do so, to be true to history "as it actually happened." Also in the 1990s, UCLA's National Center for History in the Schools convinced the publishing house Houghton Mifflin to produce a series of textbooks for students in kindergarten through eighth grade and offered a detailed set of standards for history teaching. The volume for fifth graders devoted about fifty pages to the history of slavery, relying on slave testimony to give an intimate account of the slave experience. Both efforts produced a firestorm of anger across the country, as the far-right extremist Pat Buchanan denounced UCLA's effort as the treasonous act of the "bead-wearing sandaled crowd of leftover sixties radicals who had no faith in America and enjoyed teaching children to malign their country." Others denounced the suggested standard guidelines as an effort to "poison the minds of American children against the history and heritage of this country." Even Kansas's U.S. senator Robert Dole rejected UCLA's education standards as nothing short of a "war on traditional American values." While the center's website remains, it no longer offers an American history textbook.

Some analysts saw the controversy as pointless sound and fury that ignored the changes that had already occurred to history curriculum across the country. But real issues remained, as did the cultural warfare. The American Textbook Council, founded in 1989, waged total war on advocates of new history school curriculum. Gilbert T. Sewall, the council's peripatetic director, became a vocal and inflexible opponent of curriculum change, considering its advocates as little more than special pleaders for groups "aggrieved by past events in American or world history." Without specifying which groups he scorned, Sewall disparaged advocates of multiculturalism as reducing history to "one-dimensional cases of exploitation and victimization." In 2000, according to the ATC's director, the pendulum had swung so far to the left for the sake of "diversity" that it crowded out the basic "facts" of American history, the "old master narratives" of "faith in progress and patriotic pride." History, according to Sewall, had been reduced to condemnations of a nation that had fallen short of its ideals,

led by a patriarchy that deserves censure for its past treatment of female, non-white, and Native Americans, for trade in black human labor, and for its exploitation of the wilderness landscape and of immigrants. Young readers will encounter minority heroism and suffering. They may learn about a nation's shameful past, learning about events in such a way as to undercut civic confidence and trust. . . . They may conclude, with the Middle Passage, that the nation's record is indelibly tainted from the start.

Such "history," Sewall lamented, would erase "national memory" and appreciation for the "nation's achievements." He did not deny that Native Americans and African Americans played a role in the nation's past, just that equating the slaughter of Native Americans and the enslavement of Africans with John Winthrop's "City on a Hill" is "off the mark." English language, common law, religion, and literary traditions, he declared, "contributed to American society in unique ways, without being part of a blending." By the advent of the new century, Sewall bemoaned, history had become a "multicultural romance." For history to retain its accuracy, the ATC held that whiteness must remain supreme.

Ironically, textbooks that incorporate aspects of the African American past into U.S. history can still perpetuate white supremacy. Schoolbooks by evangelical publishers, for example, continue to refer to the slaves who first arrived in Virginia in 1619 as "indentured servants." While admitting that the introduction of these "workers" would eventually cause "tremendous social division and moral tension for succeeding generations of Americans," a 2001 textbook described slaves' lives as those of well-cared-for adjuncts of white families. This description differs little from that of the 1950s and similarly ignores the Middle Passage. Students would learn, however, that African kings were as greedy as white slave traders, "all of whom allowed their love of profit to outweigh their love for their fellow man." The consequences, the *United States History for Christian Schools* explained, would be harshest for "the black races but for the white race as well." While admitting that flogging was common, the text asserted that whites treated their servants "well enough" to allow them to work. It claimed that slave owners, out of "humanitarian motives," took their property to church and taught slaves to read and write. A similar 2018 textbook by the same publisher described the slave trade with reasonable accuracy and even included a quote from Olaudah Equiano's 1789 autobiography. Both texts, however, avoided any meaningful discussion of the institution of slavery and its impact on Black families. They diverted and isolated African Americans from the mainstream of the nation's past and characterized slavery as the cause of "tremendous social division and moral tension for succeeding generations of Americans." Thus, the central issue was not the tragedy and impact of Black enslavement but the political quandary for whites.

The evangelical texts accurately emphasized religious and evangelical influences on the antislavery movement. Just as in the first sixty years of the twentieth century, however, both texts saw William Lloyd Garrison as a damaging extremist and even a dangerous atheist because of his criticism of the Bible as a pro-slavery document. Both editions employed the same botched Garrison quote about the impact of slavery on the Constitution and even accused him of printing fabrications of atrocities and slaves' lives to smear Southern masters. The 2018 text did mention that women participated in the antislavery movement but alluded only to Sarah and Angelina Grimké of South Carolina. Frederick Douglass received a mention, but only as yet another uncompromising radical. John Brown, with "his gang," amounted to a crazed agent of the devil and a mass murderer who enjoyed the support of the "plush parlors of Boston's elite." Abolitionism, these textbooks taught, advocated unconstitutional acts that, if successful, would have ended slavery prematurely, thus harming "the economy for the whole nation." Besides, the 2018 textbook asserted, slaves "would have trouble finding jobs because they would not have been given the skills to have good paying jobs." After a final repudiation of abolitionism, the author spent two pages exonerating the Bible, which, he wrote, "provides no support for American slavery." This would have come as a shock to antebellum Southern ministers like Virginia's Thornton Stringfellow, who bellowed against abolitionists for *denying* that the Bible affirmed slavery, declaring that "God himself" proclaimed the law of slavery.

In the history of the Civil War and Reconstruction, the Lost Cause endures as a "brother's war" fought over states' rights, and slavery was merely "another issue over which the sections parted company." The two editions by evangelical publishers treated the war as a result of extremists on both sides who pushed the sections into a war fought by courageous white soldiers over the "Union v. Independence." The 2018 edition asked the student—presumably a Southern one— how they would respond to William Tecumseh Sherman's Georgia campaign as a "Christian congressional representative." It didn't ask the student how they would react to the April 12, 1864, Fort Pillow slaughter. Slavery, freedmen, and Black soldiers had no place in a war fought by such dedicated patriots. In a highlighted sidebar of terms for the student to remember, "states' rights" appears first. Reconstruction, little different from that portrayed during the first sixty years of the twentieth century, depicted vindictive Northerners as imposing an unjust peace on a devastated South. Robert E. Lee, as in the 1950s, remained a national icon, reflecting true Christian character, an "irreplaceable son" of Virginia who always prayed for his enemies. While the books did not defend the Klan, given the "horrors" visited on the South, its rise represented an understand-able reaction. Much to its credit, the newest edition did discuss the education program of the Freedmen's Bureau, cited Frederick Douglass on the condition of the freedpeople, and rejected the Klan and lynch law. Nonetheless, it presented Reconstruction and Black enfranchisement as an unjust imposition on the South.

Slavery and the Civil War remain flashpoints in the nation's cultural landscape, pivotal aspects of national memory and rem-nants of sectional identity. In a 2016 booklet, the academic editor of the John C. Calhoun papers, Clyde N. Wilson, expressed his devotion to the white South and insisted on the "right to honor our Confederate forebears because they are ours. . . . They not only won a place in the hearts of us, their descendants. They also won the lasting admiration of everyone in the civilized world who values an indomitable spirit in defense of freedom." There is no question about the "us" he refers to or precisely whose "freedom" he believes his Confederate forebears defended. Wilson reflects the long legacy of a mythical past that depicts the Confederacy as having nothing to do with slavery—a word that somehow vanished from his screed—and everything to do with opposition to "invasion and conquest . . . to crush and punish disobedience to government, to create a powerful centralized state, and to keep the South as a captive source of wealth for Northern business and politicians."

While extreme, Clyde Wilson's allegiance to an imagined past, one that affirms Southern white political power, reflects larger, more pervasive cultural trends and a firm reluctance to weaken the supremacy of whiteness. Not until 2019 did the state of Texas—which along with California has a centralized purchasing process that drives the textbook publishing business—agree to drop its insistence that schoolbooks ignore slavery as the primary cause of the Civil War. A comparison of California and Texas textbooks revealed a willingness to emphasize the brutality of slavery, but the Texas editions deemphasized the Founding Fathers' complicity in the institution of slavery and its role in forming the Constitution. The depiction of Reconstruction remains highly problematic, avoids any serious discussion of the suppression of African Americans, and gives individual teachers (with questionable training) the responsibility to detail the full picture of the era. But neither is this problem strictly regional. The New York children's book author Joy Masoff downplayed the brutality of slavery in her elementary school history of Virginia and didn't even include the word in the book's index. She did introduce the issue of racism to her readers but avoided any discussion of white supremacy and left the cause of the Civil War unclear. But she managed to inform young Virginians that "if states' rights were going to be taken away, they [Virginians] did not want to be part of the U.S. anymore." Relying on a white supremacist website for her information, Masoff erroneously and embarrassingly claimed that "thousands" of African American soldiers fought for the South. Duplicating elementary school texts from the early 1960s, she glorified Robert E. Lee, simplified Reconstruction beyond recognition, and never even alluded to the Klan or lynching.

. . .

In 2010, with the backing of the U.S. Department of Education, several educational organizations joined with the American Historical Association to offer a new framework for history education "in a democracy." The framework the organizations created stressed the importance of the American Revolution, the formation of the Constitution, the Civil War, and the "struggles over slavery and civil rights." It clearly gave importance to vital traditional features of the nation's past, but also urged educators to fully emphasize "what racial, ethnic, religious, and national groups formed this nation," what racial tensions arose, and what issues remain unresolved.

Many scholars and authors have responded positively to the call. Columbia University's Eric Foner enhanced his textbook *Give Me Liberty! An American History* with suggested readings, supportive websites, a glossary of terms, organizations, and important events. Significantly, diversity is the book's central theme, helping students to recognize that American history developed out of a complex interaction of "Europeans, American Indians and Africans." Traditional textbooks, challenging to write and for students to read and increasingly costly to publish, may have a limited future, as online texts and resources are free and readily available. For several years, Stanford University Press has offered teachers and students at all levels an invaluable, free, two-volume American history text online, along with teaching materials, tests, documents, syllabi, and primary source readings. It is easy to use, well written, and searchable and represents a continuously evolving collaborative effort. Richly illustrated, its account of Reconstruction makes clear the book's value to modern educators: "A notion of white supremacy and Black inferiority undergirded it all."

Online sources can offer educators and students at all levels an astonishing range of options and invaluable texts and resources, all free and easily accessible. The University of North Carolina at Chapel Hill's Documenting the American South includes all known memoirs of former slaves; among the richly diverse Digital Commonwealth: Massachusetts Collections Online is the Boston Public Library's antislavery collection of over 40,000 items, including original correspondence of William Lloyd Garrison and his abolitionist collaborators; at the prolific Internet Archive one can access 28 million books and texts, along with millions of recordings and 3.5 million images. The invaluable and easily searchable Digital Library of the HathiTrust contains over 17 million items and includes Cornell

University's Making of America Digital Library of 267 monograph volumes and over 100,000 journal articles with nineteenth-century imprints. Columbia University's Amistad Digital Resource collection spans the full range of African American history and offers African American history curriculum for K–12 schools with supplemental documents, recordings, and images that can be riveting. The digital collections of the New York Public Library's Schomburg Center for Research in Black Culture include an amazing array of illustrations, photos, manuscripts, and books. Finally, educators can benefit from the indispensable and easily accessible collections of the National Archives and the Library of Congress, especially its digital newspaper collection. Additionally, the *New York Times*'s 1619 Project, created by the Pulitzer Prize–winning reporter Nikole Hannah-Jones in 2019, seeks to place the history of slavery and its consequences at the very center of our national narrative. Within its first year, it proved a revelation for many students, and was adopted by 3,500 classrooms in all fifty states. In 2021, the *New York Times* and Random House brought out a significantly expanded version of the project in book form. The cities of Chicago and Washington, D.C., have both assigned the project to all its schools, while Buffalo, New York, has made it mandatory for seventh through twelfth grades.

Academic and professional organizations, often in conjunction with the National Endowment for the Humanities, have developed substantial teacher-training programs and websites to aid in the democratization of education. This is an especially acute issue for elementary school teachers, most of whom lack any history train-ing and fear classroom discussions concerning slavery, race, and the nation's painful legacy of injustice, especially regarding African Americans. The Zinn Education Project, named for the Boston University professor Howard Zinn, has offered a wide variety of resources and training programs since 2008. It has brought together elementary and high school teachers with some of the country's leading scholars for programs in a full range of social justice issues from slavery and Reconstruction to the civil rights movement. In its survey of 165 schoolteachers, the program discovered that many educators, regardless of geographic location, avoid teaching the history of Reconstruction. So, in 2022, the project released a comprehensive website dedicated to the teaching of Reconstruction. Similarly, the Gilder Lehrman Institute of American History for the last twenty-seven years has offered teacher-training seminars with eminent American history professors covering the full range of American history. Additionally, the Southern Poverty Law Center's Learning for Justice program, the independent Facing History and Ourselves, Historians Against Slavery, and the Massachusetts Historical Society all offer detailed programs, texts, lesson plans, and digital resources for school teachers. Eighteen students from Massachusetts's Lowell High School developed an impressive website, We Are America, to highlight national diversity and "start a local conversation on identity and belonging."

These models are vital and inspiring, but they alone cannot transform an educational system mired in political strife, throttled by mandated curriculum, staggered by inadequate teacher training, and in some places crippled by a lack of Internet access and computer equipment. At the same time, as Stanford University's Sam Wineburg reminds us, reliance on online tools by poorly trained teachers poses its own considerable risks. Many who lack historical knowledge and sophistication remain bewildered by available choices or fall victim to the endless array of dangerous websites that support white supremacy or denounce the Holocaust as a "hoax." Online education remains a risky business. The failure to properly train teachers can have devastating results. Young students have been traumatized by humiliating "slave auctions," and in 2021 three Wisconsin middle school teachers compelled their sixth graders to devise a system of slave punishment using "Hammurabi's code" from ancient Mesopotamia. Parents objected to this damaging and preposterous assignment, and the teachers resigned. Clearly, multicultural gains and improved curriculum are at risk, leaving history teaching, as the *Washington Post* reported in 2018, "an explicit promulgation of white privilege."

For parents—or school administrators—who object to any emphasis on African Americans and the role of race in American history, modern technology offers an escape. By 2003, over one million children received their education at home, and by 2019—before the coronavirus pandemic—about 2.5 million were homeschooled, some 3 to 4 percent of school-age children. Since then the number of such children has at least doubled. This has offered some parents the opportunity to revert to the textbooks of the nineteenth century, especially Samuel Goodrich's "Peter Parley's" tall tales. With nearly every pre-1923 text available free through a home computer—or through print-on-demand outlets—parents, students, and even teachers can easily avoid the central conflicts of American history and enjoy a national narrative that allows European whites to again possess the past—and perhaps the future.

Even with reliable Internet resources and textbooks, the 2018 report of the Southern Poverty Law Center, *Teaching Hard History: American Slavery,* painfully detailed that the teaching of the nation's slave past is failing. Its survey of seventeen hundred social studies teachers found that a "bare majority" of those who claimed competence to teach the history of slavery did not have the proper resources to do so. And most either cannot or will not connect the legacy of slavery to the present. Only *8 percent* of the thousand or more high school students surveyed by the SPLC could identify slavery as the central cause of the Civil War. Astonishingly, 48 percent identified "tax protests" as primarily responsible for the strife. Thus we should not be puzzled that Americans cannot make the connection between this past and our present. The process becomes nearly impossible when students come to the classroom, as one Connecticut teacher noted, with the idea that all issues related to slavery and race are "fixed now." Even with textbooks that cover the history of slavery, the *Teaching Hard History* report revealed that many teachers—90 percent of those surveyed—refused to teach it.

Textbooks, clearly, have a long, contentious, and disappointing history. An 1898 report compiled by a committee of New England high school and college educators admitted that most schoolteachers considered a textbook "an evil, to be tolerated" and "deliverance from which one should earnestly pray." About ten years earlier Harvard's resolute Albert Bushnell Hart had directed his own survey of schoolbooks and history instruction. It foreshadowed the 1898 report, revealing that most students refused to read any textbooks, with one confessing that he had picked up his "only for amusement." Hart also discovered that while the teaching of history had increased after the Civil War, instruction focused more on ancient and European history rather than on American history and had been confined to only one or two grades. Half of the ninety schools that Hart's survey queried about history curriculum omitted American history entirely. On average, schools only devoted one-tenth of student time to learning history. Moreover, that portion of education devoted to American history—however complete the textbooks—stressed the period before 1789, allowing educators to avoid all issues related to slavery and the rights of African Americans. Since students at best received only inconsistent and scattered instruction in history, they would have little or no chance to reinforce whatever lessons they had learned. This abysmal record of American history teaching left too many students with little more than popular prejudices and mythology to guide their judgments.

If nothing else, we have been consistent in our approach to education. Diane Ravitch, one of the nation's most influential educational policy analysts, assessed history instruction during the 1980s and found that little had changed since the 1880s. She and her associates surveyed 7,812 students to evaluate their knowledge of history. On average, only 54.5 percent answered the most rudimentary questions accurately, what Ravitch labeled a failing grade. When asked to select which fifty-year block included the American Civil War, only 32.2 percent correctly chose the 1850–1900 period. Over 60 percent of students thought the war had taken place before 1850. In 2005 a Senate subcommittee discovered that only 10 percent of high school seniors displayed any proficiency in U.S. history; all others were only at the most basic level, and 57 percent fell below standards.

Many factors account for such consistently dreadful results. For most of our past, education administrators assumed that no special training was required to teach history or social studies. Thus most teachers' fund of historical knowledge was limited to the information that appeared in their textbooks. From the 1950s to the '90s—if not to the present—athletic coaches too often received responsibility for teaching U.S. history. In one Texas school in 1958, nine of fourteen social studies teachers were athletic coaches. Cornell University professor and former president of the American Historical Association Mary Beth Norton recalled that her high school history instructor also served as the track coach. As the U.S. Department of Education determined in the 1990s, most of the nation's high school teachers possessed *no* history training—not even a college minor concentration—and up to 88 percent of states did not require a history teacher to have any history classes in their educational background. The new century brought no improvement. An analyst in 2003 found that history represented the subject that young students "know *least*," and that too often instructors had "never seriously studied" what schools paid them to teach. The popular historian and Pulitzer Prize winner David McCullough similarly testified before a U.S. Senate subcommittee in 2005, lamenting that school history teachers simply "don't know the subject" and that the textbooks they used seemed designed "to kill any interest that a student might have in history." As the influential historian James O. Horton wrote in 2006, during the 1990s a school "history teacher is spelled *C-o-a-c-h*." Thus, he found part of the answer as to why so many college students believed that Jefferson Davis had been president of the United States during the Civil War.

Another answer lies in the fact that some school districts stopped teaching American history or offered only one year of such instruction, with world history disappearing altogether. In the 1980s and '90s, textbooks still failed to stress the African American role in the Civil War. To compensate, some instructors substituted the compelling but somewhat fanciful 1989 film *Glory* for actual instruction, although the film may have required parental permission for students to view it. Many high school students never sat in any high school history class, and some who did and protested what they viewed as objectionable characterizations of African Americans received a rebuke from their instructors and the label "troublemaker." The result, as one modern white pioneer in African American history discovered, is that students come to hate history, "which they perceive as a prepackaged product, a long piece of stale bologna, sliced thin and served up cold." Indeed, an analysis of textbook content during the 1980s revealed that only 8 percent of individuals mentioned were African American. Even those teachers and textbooks that included African Americans in instruction did so "segregated from basic American history." In the following decade, the popular author of *Lies My Teacher Told Me,* James W. Loewen, found that all the textbooks he analyzed deliberately diminished the impact of American racism, and "not one" allowed African Americans "to speak for themselves about the conditions they faced."

The impact of all these factors can be seen in classrooms across the nation. From 2011 to 2021, teachers in Vermont, New York, New Jersey, Ohio, Virginia, Tennessee, Mississippi, and Florida compelled Black students to stand in front of their white classmates posing as slaves to be auctioned off to the highest bidder. Such "curricular violence," as one Black Vermont parent wailed, is hardly unique. For ten years, students in a New Jersey fifth-grade class had to create slave auction advertisements. In Watertown, New York, the teacher in a fourth-grade class ordered a Black boy and girl to stand in front of their white classmates with their hands behind their backs just as "in slave times," and the winning bidder became their "master." The teacher then announced that if the "slaves" tried to escape "they would be chased down and violence would be done to them." An investigation of the incident revealed "lasting emotional harm" to the two students. When a similar event took place in an Ohio fifth-grade class, a mother objected, but her complaints were dismissed; she was told that "this activity was a part of the state's required curriculum." In Florida, a teacher assured his students that the N-word "just means ignorant." Minnesota fifth graders, in a lesson plan right out of the 1920s, learned that African Americans regretted the end of slavery because "the enslavers took care of them and gave them food and clothing." In Rhode Island, students received absolutely no exposure to the history of slavery until high school, and even then it amounted to a one-paragraph text. In Oregon, a teacher advised a group of biracial students who had acted up at lunchtime that "you're lucky I'm not making you pick cotton and clean my house." A Texas teacher advised his students that if the South had won the Civil War, all the Black students in class would now be slaves.

In 2020 the *New York Times* reported that the medical students and residents in a Duke University survey remained convinced that African Americans have thicker skin and less sensitive nerve endings—the same vile garbage spewed across the United States by Harvard University's biologist and ethnologist Louis Agassiz in the nineteenth century. A New Jersey high school in 2018 compelled a Black high school student to cut off his dreadlocks, "yet another reminder of a system that polices blackness at every turn." In May 2019, when a large group of African American seventh graders visited the Boston Museum of Fine Arts, staff informed them that in the museum they could have no food, no water, and "no watermelon."

A Rutgers University psychologist found that 101 Black teenagers in Washington, D.C., collectively reported 5,600 offensive racial instances in a two-week period—and this occurred during the Obama presidency. The influential *New York Times* journalist Charles Blow explained that when he was young, "I was led to believe Blackness was inferior. . . . We had been trained in it, bathed in it, acculturated to hate ourselves. . . . At every turn, at every moment, I was being baptized in the narrative that everything white was right, good, noble, and beautiful, and everything Black" was not. The bitter influence lay everywhere, even in the "blue-eyed white Jesus hanging over your bed," he wrote. The experience of Black high school students in a Boston suburb in 2020 reinforced Blow's own account. A local branch of the NAACP along with the students protested school curriculum and the punishments handed out to Black students. "I am not going to lie," one of the female high school students exclaimed, going to high school "made me hate being Black."

Despite the monumental outburst of thoughtful, accurate, and determined scholarship since the mid-1960s, the way we teach history in the public schools remains as lifeless as John Brown's body. But slavery and race, as the Ohio State University scholar Hasan Kwame Jefferies observed in his introduction to *Teaching Hard His-*

tory, "isn't in the past. It's in the headlines." However it's taught in schools, history is far from a dead thing. "We carry it within us," James Baldwin memorably remarked in his essay "The White Man's Guilt." We "are unconsciously controlled by it in many ways, and history is literally present in all that we do. It could scarcely be otherwise, since it is to history that we owe our frame of reference, our identities, and our aspirations."

Notes

Introduction

xii *Exploring the New World:* Some of this discussion is borrowed from Donald Yacovone, "Textbook Racism: How Scholars Sustained White Supremacy," *Chronicle of Higher Education,* April 8, 2018. The Horace Mann quote in the epigraph is from *Thoughts, Selected from the Writings of Horace Mann* (Boston: Lee & Shepard, 1872), 113.

xiii At the same time, however: O. Stuart Hamer, et al., *Exploring the New World* (1953; reprint, Chicago: Follett, 1962), 261–62, 264–67.

xiv But this is not a book: James Baldwin, "American Dream and American Negro," *New York Times Magazine,* March 7, 1965, in Baldwin, *Collected Essays* (New York: Library of America, 1998), 717; James Estrin, "Understanding Race and History Through Photography," *New York Times,* March 24, 2017; Charles H. Wesley, *Negro History in the School Curriculum* (Washington, D.C.: Howard University Press, 1925), 4; Jonathan Zimmerman, *Whose America? Culture Wars in the Public Schools* (Cambridge, Mass.: Harvard University Press, 2002), 48 quoted.

xv If nothing else, this exploration: Kristina DuRocher, *Raising Racists: The Socialization of White Children in the Jim Crow South* (Lexington: University Press of Kentucky, 2011), 39–40 and passim; Larry E. Tise, *Proslavery: A History of the Defense of Slavery in America, 1701–1840* (Athens: University of Georgia Press, 1987), 16–18. In his introduction to several of John H. Van Evrie's incendiary pamphlets, John David Smith made the standard accusation that Southerners bore primary responsibility for the creation and perpetuation of racism and ideas of Black inferiority. John David Smith, ed., *Anti-Abolition Tracts and Anti-Black Stereotypes* (New York: Garland, 1993), 1:xii–xiv; Toni Morrison, *Playing in the Dark: Whiteness and the Literary Imagination* (Cambridge, Mass.: Harvard University Press, 1992), 38.

xv History textbooks proved a perfect vehicle: George H. Callcott, *History in the United States, 1800–1860, Its Practice and Purpose* (Baltimore: Johns Hopkins University Press, 1970), 58–59; Ambrose Caliver, *Secondary Education for*

Notes

Negroes, Bulletin no. 17, U.S. Department of the Interior (1933; reprint, New York: Negro Universities Press, 1969), 2–15; Keith Whitescarver, "School Books, Publishers, and Southern Nationalists: Refashioning the Curriculum in North Carolina's Schools, 1850–1861," *North Carolina Historical Review* 79 (January 2002): 28–49; Thomas D. Snyder, ed., *120 Years of American Education: A Statistical Portrait* (Washington, D.C.: U.S. Department of Education, 1993), 55, table 19.

xvi Those numbers would only grow: Gerard Giordan, *Twentieth-Century Textbook Wars: A History of Advocacy and Opposition* (New York: Peter Lang, 2003), 16–20; Charles W. Eagles, *Civil Rights, Culture Wars: The Fight over a Mississippi Textbook* (Chapel Hill: University of North Carolina Press, 2017), 1–4, 12–14.

xvi Until recent days, Americans have always emphasized: Amos Dean, *The True Method of Studying and Teaching History: A Paper Read Before the American Association for the Advancement of Education* (Albany, N.Y.: Weed, Parsons, 1857), 5–7; Francis Newton Thorpe, *In Justice to the Nation: American History in American Schools, Colleges, and Universities* (Philadelphia: n.p., 1886), 5; Herbert Baxter Adams, *The Study and Teaching of History. Phi Beta Kappa Address* (Richmond, Va.: Whittet & Shepperson, 1898), 3–13.

xvii Far from mere aggregations: Barry Joyce, *The First U.S. History Textbooks: Constructing and Disseminating the American Tale in the Nineteenth Century* (Lanham, Md.: Lexington Books, 2015), 3–6; Fannie Fern Andrews, *Memory Pages of My Life* (Boston: Talisman Press, 1948), 35; William M. Davidson, *A History of the United States* (Chicago: Scott Foresman, 1902), i; Mabel B. Casner and Ralph Henry Gabriel, *The Rise of American Democracy* (New York: Harcourt Brace, 1943), v; William Appleman Williams, *History as a Way of Learning* (New York: New Viewpoints, 1973), 8–11; Michael Kammen, ed., *The Past Before Us: Contemporary Historical Writing in the United States* (Ithaca, N.Y.: Cornell University Press, 1980), 23.

xvii In part, we are right to see: Adam Fairclough, *Teaching Equality: Black Schools in the Age of Jim Crow* (Athens: University of Georgia Press, 2001), 11; Robert Lerner, Althea K. Nagai, and Stanley Rothman, *Molding the Good Citizen: The Politics of High School History Texts* (Westport, Conn.: Praeger, 1995), 1–2; Thomas A. Bailey, *The American Pageant: A History of the Republic* (Boston: Little, Brown, 1956); Thomas A. Bailey, *The American Pageant: Recollections of a Stanford Historian* (Stanford, Calif.: Hoover Institute Press, 1982), 180, 192–93.

xviii Thomas Maitland Marshall's *American History:* Thomas Maitland Marshall, *American History* (New York: Macmillan, 1930), 1:76–78, 147, 285, 341–42.

xix At the advent of the twentieth century: Joseph Moreau, *Schoolbook Nation: Conflicts over American History Textbooks from the Civil War to the Present* (Ann Arbor: University of Michigan Press, 2003), 210; Edward Channing, *A Students' History of the United States* (New York: Macmillan, 1898), vii; Wesley, *Negro History in School Curriculum,* 8; Arthur M. Schlesinger, Jr., *The*

Disuniting of America: Reflections on a Multicultural Society (New York: W. W. Norton, 1998), 58–59, quoting his father; James O. Horton and Lois E. Horton, eds., *Slavery and Public History: The Tough Stuff of American Memory* (New York: New Press, 2006), 40, quoting Rhodes; Arthur C. Perry and Gertrude A. Price, *American History*, 2 vols. (New York: American Book, 1914), 1:133.

xx The real problem to solve: Ira Berlin, foreword to Bethany Jay and Cynthia Lynn Lyerly, eds., *Understanding and Teaching American Slavery* (Madison: University of Wisconsin Press, 2016), xv; Horton and Horton, *Slavery and Public History*, 39, quoting Otis; Rachel Wheeler, "Un/Becoming America: Finding a New Vocation for Historians," *Perspectives on History* 57 (April 2019): 20; David W. Blight, "Blind Justice," *New York Times Book Review*, February 10, 2019, 10.

xx Without teachers, we are lost: Henry Adams, *The Education of Henry Adams*, ed. Ernest Samuels (1918; reprint, Boston: Houghton Mifflin, 1974), 300; Amos Bronson Alcott, *The Doctrine and Discipline of Human Culture* (Boston: James Monroe, 1836), 19.

1. The Contours of White Supremacy

3 Samuel Train Dutton was superintendent: Samuel T. Dutton, *The Morse Speller* (New York: Morse, 1896), 114; "Educator's Personally," *Journal of Education* 89 (April 17, 1919): 439; "Samuel Train Dutton," *League of Nations Magazine* 5 (April 1919): 272; [Samuel T. Dutton et al.] New England Association of School Superintendents, *Outline Course of Study in United States History and Civics* (Brookline, Mass.: NEASS, 1891), 5–11; Samuel T. Dutton, *Social Phases of Education in the Schools and the Home* (New York: Macmillan, 1900), 217–18; Ruth Miller Elson, *Guardians of Tradition: American Schoolbooks of the Nineteenth Century* (Lincoln: University of Nebraska Press, 1964), 68.

4 Many historians and commentators: Hasan Kwame Jeffries, "Preface," Southern Poverty Law Center, *Teaching Hard History: American Slavery* (Montgomery, Ala.: SPLC, 2018), 5; Arthur M. Schlesinger, Jr., *The Disuniting of America: Reflections on a Multicultural Society* (New York: W. W. Norton, 1998), 18–19; James W. Loewen, *Lies My Teacher Told Me: Everything Your American History Textbook Got Wrong* (New York: Simon & Schuster, 2007), 37–38.

5 Slavery, however, did not require: David Whitford, "A Calvinist Heritage to the 'Curse of Ham': Assessing the Accuracy of a Claim About Racial Subordination," *Church History and Religious Culture* 90 (2010): 31–32; Tise, *History of the Defense of Slavery*, 16–18.

5 Rather than Southern slavery: Peter Novick, *That Noble Dream: The Objectivity Question and the American Historical Profession* (Cambridge, U.K.: Cambridge University Press, 1988), 225; Susan Neiman, *Learning from the*

Germans: Race and the Memory of Evil (New York: Farrar, Straus & Giroux, 2019), 293, quoted.

6   The Rev. Henry M. Field: Henry M. Field, *Capacity of the Negro—His Position in the North. The Color Line in New England,* in Brook Thomas, ed., *Plessy v. Ferguson: A Brief History with Documents* (Boston: Bedford Books, 1997), 101–19, quoted 119.

6   North and South cherished white supremacy: Van E. Gosse, "Patchwork Nation: Racial Orders and Disorder in the United States, 1790–1860," *Journal of the Early Republic* 40 (Spring 2020): 45–46; Nell Irvin Painter, *The History of White People* (New York: W. W. Norton, 2010), 383; George Fredrickson, *White Supremacy: A Comparative Study of American and South African History* (New York: Oxford University Press, 1981), xviii–xix, quoted; Matthew Frye Jacobson, *Whiteness of a Different Color: European Immigrants and the Alchemy of Race* (Cambridge, Mass.: Harvard University Press, 1998), 4–5.

7   African American blood: Kelly Miller, *An Appeal to Conscience* (1918; reprint, New York: Arno Press, 1969), 73; John Wood Sweet, *Bodies Politic: Negotiating Race in the American North, 1730–1830* (Baltimore: Johns Hopkins University Press, 2003), 60–61; Eve LaPlante, *Salem Witch Judge: The Life and Repentance of Samuel Sewall* (New York: HarperOne, 2007), 223–31; Lawrence W. Towner, "The Sewall-Saffin Dialog on Slavery," *William and Mary Quarterly* 21 (January 1964): 43; Samuel Sewall, *The Selling of Joseph* (Boston: Bartholomew Green and John Allen, 1700), in Samuel Sewall, *The Diary of Samuel Sewall, 1674–1729,* ed. M. Halsey Thomas, 2 vols. (New York: Farrar, Straus & Giroux, 1973), 2:1118; Sewall, *Diary,* April 3, 1711, 2:657.

8   Prior to North American colonization: Henry Louis Gates, Jr., and Donald Yacovone, *The African Americans: Many Rivers to Cross* (Carlsbad, Calif.: SmileyBooks, 2013), 17–22; Jean Devisse, "A Sanctified Black: Maurice," in David Bindman and Henry Louis Gates, Jr., eds., *The Image of the Black in Western Art* (Cambridge, Mass.: Harvard University Press, 2010), 2, part 1:139–94; Ibram X. Kendi, *Stamped from the Beginning: The Definitive History of Racist Ideas in America* (New York: Nation Books, 2016), 15, 30–37; Winthrop D. Jordan, *White over Black: American Attitudes Toward the Negro, 1550–1812* (Baltimore: Penguin Books, 1969), 56–62, 67–69.

8   But the hundred years: Margaret Ellen Newell, "Indian Slavery in Colonial New England," in Alan Gallay, ed., *Indian Slavery in Colonial America* (Lincoln: University of Nebraska Press, 2009), 37–38, 56–59; Francis J. Bremer, *John Winthrop: America's Forgotten Founding Father* (New York: Oxford University Press, 2003), 312–15; Whitfield, "Calvinist Heritage," 27; Alden T. Vaughan, *Roots of American Racism: Essays on the Colonial Experience* (New York: Oxford University Press, 1995), 7, 15–17.

9   the phrase "Jim Crow society": Steve Luxenberg, *Separate: The Story of Plessy v. Ferguson, and America's Journey from Slavery to Segregation* (New York:

W. W. Norton, 2019), 4; Jordan, *White over Black,* 71, 79–80; Fredrickson, *White Supremacy,* 101–2; Sweet, *Bodies Politic,* 147–50, 180–81; Brian Purnell, Jeanne Theoharis, and Komozi Woodard, eds., *The Strange Careers of the Jim Crow North: Segregation and Struggle Outside the South* (New York: New York University Press, 2019), esp. 1–42.

9 As would become a mainstay: Sweet, *Bodies Politic,* 109–10, quoted, 154–58.

10 The European "Enlightenment": Winthrop, *White over Black,* 222–23, 248, 253.

10 As we are well aware: Stephen Jay Gould, *The Mismeasure of Man* (New York: W. W. Norton, 1981), 32–35; Benjamin Franklin, *Observations Concerning the Increase of Mankind* (Boston: S. Kneeland, 1755), 6, 8, 14–15; Sweet, *Bodies Politic,* 171.

11 The Revolution's success: Sweet, *Bodies Politic,* 253, 262–67, 312–15; Jacobson, *Whiteness of a Different Color,* 25–26.

12 The North's Christian churches: Sweet, *Bodies Politic,* 180–81, 348–49; Jordan, *White over Black,* 276; Mary Locke, *Anti-Slavery in America: From the Introduction of African Slaves to the Prohibition of the Slave Trade, 1619–1808* (1901; reprint, Gloucester, Mass.: Peter Smith, 1965), 40, 192–93; Paul J. Polgar, *Standard-Bearers of Equality: America's First Abolition Movement* (Chapel Hill: University of North Carolina Press, 2019), 211–29; Joanne Pope Melish, *Disowning Slavery: Gradual Emancipation and Race in New England, 1780–1860* (Ithaca, N.Y.: Cornell University Press, 1998), 39–40; John Saillant, *Black Puritan, Black Republican: The Life and Thought of Lemuel Haynes* (New York: Oxford University Press, 2003); Harvey Amani Whitfield, *The Problem of Slavery in Early Vermont, 1777–1810* (Barre: Vermont Historical Society, 2014).

13 The nineteenth-century North: *Dictionary of American Biography* (New York: Scribner's, 1928): 1:93–94; Nehemiah Adams, *The Sable Cloud: A Southern Tale, with Northern Comments* (Boston: Ticknor & Fields, 1861), 5; *At Eventide: Discourses* (Boston: D. Lothrop, 1877).

13 But Adams is best remembered: Adams, *A South-Side View of Slavery* (1854; reprint, Boston: Ticknor & Fields, 1860), 2–3, 10–21.

14 Adams, quite likely, had read: Ibid., 36–37, 48–49, 58–65, 70–75, 99–123.

14 One might dismiss Adams: George M. Fredrickson, *The Black Image in the White Mind: The Debate on Afro-American Character and Destiny, 1817–1914* (New York: Harper & Row, 1971), 155–56; Horace Bushnell, *Discourse on Christian Nurture* (Boston: Massachusetts Sabbath School Society, 1847), 15; Bushnell, *The Census and Slavery: A Thanksgiving Discourse Delivered in the Chapel at Clifton Springs, New York, November 29, 1860* (Hartford, Conn.: L. E. Hunt, 1860), 13.

15 By the time Bushnell wrote *Christian Nurture:* Forrest Wood, *Black Scare: The Racist Response to Emancipation and Reconstruction* (Berkeley: University of California Press, 1968), 2–3; Fredrickson, *Black Image in White Mind,* 100–101; Sweet, *Bodies Politic,* 317–24, 341, 399–407; Alexis de Tocqueville,

Democracy in America, ed. J. P. Mayer (Garden City, N.Y.: Doubleday, 1969), 342–43; Eugene H. Berwanger, "Negrophobia in Northern Proslavery and Antislavery Thought," *Phylon* 33 (1972): 267–68.

15 Nineteenth-century writers and analysts: Fredrickson, *Black Image in White Mind,* 100; "The Anglo-Saxon Race," *North American Review* 72 (July 1851): 34–71. I am much indebted to Nell Irvin Painter's *The History of White People* (New York: W. W. Norton, 2010), 139–40, 151, 162–64, 174–75, for her keen insights into Emerson and American identity.

16 Emerson hoped to recast America: Ralph Waldo Emerson, *English Traits,* ed. Howard Mumford Jones (1856; reprint, Cambridge, Mass.: Harvard University Press, 1966), 21–22, 30, 42–43; Painter, *History of White People,* 181–83, 186; William S. McFeely, *Frederick Douglass* (New York: W. W. Norton, 1991), 166.

17 White supremacy not only marked: Martin Klammen, *Whitman, Slavery, and the Emergence of Leaves of Grass* (University Park: Pennsylvania State University Press, 1995), 23–30, 36–38, 94–95; David S. Reynolds, *Walt Whitman's America: A Cultural Biography* (New York: Alfred A. Knopf, 1995), 440–86.

18 Mark Twain, who made his home: Charles Dudley Warner, "Equality," *Atlantic Monthly* 45 (January 1880): 19–32.

18 Such a definition of equality fit: The discussion of Henry Adams is based on my essay "Tricksterism, Anti-Semitism, and White Supremacy in *The Education of Henry Adams*: A Centennial Reassessment," *Left History* 23 (Spring–Summer 2020): 59–86.

19 Famously, Adams's account detailed: Henry Adams, *The Education of Henry Adams,* ed. Ernest Samuels (Boston: Houghton Mifflin, 1974), 100.

20 Preoccupied with class decline: Henry Adams, *The History of the United States During the First Administration of Thomas Jefferson* (1891–98; reprint, New York: Antiquarian Press, 1962), 1:377–98, esp. 378, where Adams wrote that L'Ouverture's influence in the United States proved "as decisive as that of any European ruler"; Adams, *Education of Henry Adams,* 42, 44, 45, 256, 268; also see Henry Adams to Charles Francis Adams, Jr., June 22, 1869, in J. C. Levenson et al., eds., *The Letters of Henry Adams,* 6 vols. (Cambridge, Mass.: Harvard University Press, 1982), 2:38–39, 39n2, where Adams related his contempt for Phillips to his brother.

21 For Adams, African Americans played: Henry Adams to Charles Milnes Gaskell, August 22, 1877, in *Letters of Henry Adams,* 2:316; Henry Adams to Charles Milnes Gaskell, January 23, 1894, ibid., 4:156; Michael O'Brien, *Henry Adams and the Southern Question* (Athens: University of Georgia Press, 2005), 13–14, 43–72; Brooks D. Simpson, *The Political Education of Henry Adams* (Columbia: University of South Carolina Press, 1996), 25–26.

21 While Henry Adams represented one way: Many of Lovecraft's writings are contained in H. P. Lovecraft, *The New Annotated H. P. Lovecraft: Beyond Arkham* (New York: Liveright, 2019). This discussion of Lovecraft is based on Wes House, "We Can't Ignore H. P. Lovecraft's White

Supremacy," *Literary Hub*, September 26, 2017; John Gray, "H. P. Lovecraft Invented a Horrific World to Escape a Nihilistic Universe," *New Republic*, October 24, 2014; Lovecraft, "On the Creation of Niggers," H. P. Lovecraft papers, Brown University, https://repository.library.brown.edu/studio /item/bdr:425397/; "The Horror of Red Hook," HPLovecraft.com, http:// www.hplovecraft.com/writings/texts/fiction/hrh.aspx. For an attempt at an update, see Aja Romano, "Lovecraft Country's First Trailer Teems with Monsters, Genre Subversion, and Social Allegory," *Portside: Material of Interest to People on the Left*, May 3, 2020.

23 Horace Mann (1796–1859): Donald Yacovone, *Samuel Joseph May and the Dilemmas of the Liberal Persuasion, 1797–1871* (Philadelphia: Temple University Press, 1991), 77, 212n21; Jonathan Messerli, *Horace Mann: A Biography* (New York: Alfred A. Knopf, 1972), 183–84, 446–47; "Speech by Horace Mann, April 1833," *Colonizationist Journal of Freedom* (April 1834): 12–18.

24 This icon of American education: Horace Mann, *Lectures in Education* (Boston: Ide & Dutton, 1855), 145; Horace Mann, *Slavery: Letters and Speeches* (Boston: B. B. Mussey, 1851), 81, 83.

25 Massachusetts, usually thought of: A J Aiséirithe and Donald Yacovone, eds., *Wendell Phillips, Social Justice, and the Power of the Past* (Baton Rouge: Louisiana State University Press, 2016), 10–11.

25 The Colonization Society, born in the halls: Henry Louis Gates, Jr., and Donald Yacovone, eds., *Lincoln on Race and Slavery* (Princeton: Princeton University Press, 2009), lii–lviii; Eric Burin, *Slavery and the Peculiar Solution: A History of the American Colonization Society* (Gainesville: University Press of Florida, 2005), 34–35, 45–47; Fredrickson, *Black Image in White Mind*, 17; Matthew Mason, *Apostle of Union: A Political Biography of Edward Everett* (Chapel Hill: University of North Carolina Press, 2016), 68–69, 285; Edward Everett, "Colonization and Civilization of Africa," in Everett, *Orations and Speeches on Various Occasions* (Boston: Little, Brown, 1865), 329–330; Edward Everett, *Address at the Anniversary of the American Colonization Society, January 18, 1853* (Boston: Massachusetts Colonization Society, 1853); Francis P. Blair, Jr., *The Destiny of the Races of This Continent: An Address before the Mercantile Library Association of Boston . . .* (Washington, D.C.: Buell & Blanchard, 1859).

26 Caleb Cushing (1800–79): Caleb Cushing, *An Oration Pronounced at Boston Before the Colonization Society of Massachusetts, on the Anniversary of American Independence* (Boston: Lyceum Press, 1833), 2–9; David Roediger, *The Wages of Whiteness: Race and the Making of the American Working Class* (London: Verso, 1991), 140–42.

27 No one better embodied American nationalism: Daniel Webster, *Speech of the Hon. Daniel Webster, on Mr. Clay's Resolutions . . . March 7, 1850* (Washington, D.C.: Gideon, 1850).

27 Like most of his fellow citizens: Speech of Daniel Webster in American Colonization Society, *Thirty-fifth Annual Report, January 20, 1852* (Washington,

D.C.: C. Alexander, 1852), 26–29; Samuel F. B. Morse, *An Argument on the Ethical Position of Slavery in the Social System, and Its Relation to the Politics of the Day* (New York: Society for the Diffusion of Political Knowledge, 1863), 16.

28 The Philadelphian Septimus Winner: On minstrelsy, see Eric Lott, *Love & Theft: Blackface Minstrelsy and the American Working Class* (New York: Oxford University Press, 1993).

28 No mere sentimentalist: Michael K. Remson, *The Songs of Septimus Winner* (Lanham, Md.: Scarecrow Press, 2003); "Septimus Winner," Library of Congress, https://www.loc.gov/item/ihas.200185362/; Septimus Winner Papers, Historical Society of Pennsylvania, http://www2.hsp.org/collections/manuscripts/w/Winner1536.html; Septimus Winner, "Ellie Rhee," https://www.civilwarpoetry.org/union/songs/ellie.html; "Carry Me Back to Tennessee," Duke University Libraries, https://library.duke.edu/digitalcollections/hasm_b1043/; Septimus Winner, *Cognitions of a Crank* (Philadelphia: Drexel Biddle Press, 1903), 37.

31 Composers, ministers, social leaders: On the history of the *Roberts* case, see Stephen and Paul Kendrick, *Sarah's Long Walk: The Free Blacks of Boston and How Their Struggle for Equality Changed America* (Boston: Beacon Press, 2004); Leonard W. Levy and Douglas Jones, "Jim Crow Education: Origins of the 'Separate but Equal' Doctrine" in Leonard W. Levy, *Judgments: Essays on American Constitutional History* (Chicago: Quadrangle Books, 1972), 316–31.

32 After the Civil War, while Congress began: Eric Foner, *Reconstruction: America's Unfinished Revolution, 1863–1877* (New York: Harper & Row, 1988), 529–31; Charles Postel, *Equality: An American Dilemma, 1866–1896* (New York: Farrar, Straus & Giroux, 2019), 276–79, quoted.

33 But the Supreme Court did not: Charles A. Lofgren, *The Plessy Case: A Legal-Historical Interpretation* (New York: Oxford University Press, 1987), 178–80; Timothy J. Hall, *Supreme Court Justices: A Biographical Dictionary* (New York: Facts on File, 2001), 206–9.

34 The *Plessy* case had resulted from: Lofgren, *Plessy Case,* 178; Brook Thomas, ed., *Plessy v. Ferguson: A Brief History with Documents* (Boston: Bedford Books, 1997), 43–45, 50–51.

34 Born in South Lee, Massachusetts: Hall, *Supreme Court Justices,* 206–9; Clare Cushman, ed., *The Supreme Court Justices: Illustrated Biographies, 1789–1993* (Washington, D.C.: Congressional Quarterly, 1993), 256–60; Charles A. Kent, ed., *Memoir of Henry Billings Brown* (New York: Duffield, 1915), 1–2.

35 Honoring and defending the white race: Luxenberg, *Separate: Story of Plessy,* 23, 136, 234; Kent, *Memoirs of Henry Billings Brown,* 22–23, 133.

35 It's richly ironic that the judge: Lofgren, *Plessy Case,* 3; Philip Hutchinson, "The Harlan Renaissance: Colorblindness and White Domination in Justice John Marshall Harlan's Dissent in *Plessy v. Ferguson*," *Journal of African*

American Studies 19 (December 2015): 429–34; Springfield *Republican*, May 20, 1892, in Thomas, *Plessy v. Ferguson*, 131.

36 William James, the nineteenth century's: William James, "Louis Agassiz," *Science* 5 (new series) (February 19, 1897): 285–89; David Starr Jordan, "Louis Agassiz, Teacher," *Scientific Monthly* 17 (November 1923): 401–11; Molly Rogers, *Delia's Tears: Race, Science, and Photography in Nineteenth-Century America* (New Haven, Conn.: Yale University Press, 2010), 18–19; Gould, *Mismeasure of Man*, 43; Thomas G. Aylesworth, "The Heritage of Louis Agassiz," *American Biology Teacher* 27 (October 1965): 597–99; Louis Menand, *The Metaphysical Club: A Story of Ideas in America* (New York: Farrar, Straus & Giroux, 2001), 97–100.

37 Louis Agassiz (1807–73): Louis Agassiz, "The Diversity of Origin of Human Races," *Christian Examiner* (July 1850), pamphlet, 1–36; Edward Lurie, "Louis Agassiz and the Races of Man," *Isis* 45 (September 1954): 227–42.

38 What changed Agassiz wasn't science: Lurie, "Louis Agassiz and the Races of Man," 233–42; Rogers, *Delia's Tears*, 117–18, 128–30; Gould, *Mismeasure of Man*, 44–45.

39 In 1850 Agassiz returned to South Carolina: Rogers, *Delia's Tears*, 238–40, 279; Gould, *Mismeasure of Man*, 48.

2. *"The White Republic Against the World"*

40 Smart, ambitious, and blessed: George Fredrickson, *Black Image in the White Mind: The Debate on Afro-American Character and Destiny, 1817–1914* (New York: Harper & Row, 1971), 92; Professor Michael E. Woods of the University of Tennessee is writing Van Evrie's biography: *The Business of Bigotry: John H. Van Evrie and the Rise of a Racist Publishing Empire*.

41 Van Evrie, who popularized the terms: The term *master race* first appeared in Southern and Northern papers in the early 1830s, perhaps first in the Richmond (Va.) *Enquirer*, February 4, 1832, also in the *Liberator*, April 7, 1832, and in the Lynchburg *Virginian*, February 4, 1836. References to "white supremacy" appear only after publication of Van Evrie's work, for instance see Buffalo *Morning Express and Daily Democracy*, August 6, 1856, *Massachusetts Spy*, August 13, 1856, St. Paul (Minn.) *Daily Pioneer*, May 21, 1857, and became common currency in Democratic newspapers. Van Evrie is absent from Eric Foner's massive *Reconstruction* (1988) and Mark W. Summers, *The Ordeal of the Reunion: A New History of Reconstruction* (Chapel Hill: University of North Carolina Press, 2014). At least one important historian completely misunderstood the nature of the nineteenth-century Democratic Party and the importance of race: see Mark E. Neely, Jr., *Lincoln and the Democrats: The Politics of Opposition in the Civil War* (New York: Cambridge University Press, 2017), 83–84, 98–99; Paul F. Boller, Jr., *American Thought in Transition: The Impact of Evolutionary Naturalism, 1865–1900* (Washington,

D.C.: University Press of America, 1981), 208–10. As Boller stated, Americans read Van Evrie more than his opponents. More recently, Richard S. Newman recognized Van Evrie's appeal in both urban and rural areas of Pennsylvania. See his "The Age of Emancipatory Proclamations: Early Civil War Abolitionism and Its Discontents," *Pennsylvania Magazine of History and Biography* 137 (January 2013): 51–53; Fredrickson, *Black Image in White Mind,* 191; *Weekly Wisconsin Patriot,* February 27, 1858. On Lincoln's awareness of Van Evrie, see Abraham Lincoln, "Fragment: Notes for Speeches," October 1, 1858, Teaching American History, https://teachingamericanhistory.org/library/document/fragment-notes-for-speeches/.

42 A somewhat elusive character: "In Search of America's 'first professional racist' in Rochester," *Talker of the Town,* February 22, 2019; "Remembering Those Who Came Before Us," rememberingancestors.blogspot.com/2009/11/anson-colman.html; Silas Emmett Lucas, *Genealogy of the Dodson, Lucas, Pyles, Rochester, and Allied Families* (Birmingham, Ala.: self-pub., 1959), 217; S. Austin Allibone, *A Critical Dictionary of English Literature . . . ,* 3 vols. (Philadelphia: J. B. Lippincott, 1897), 3:2506; Weekly *Ohio State Journal,* March 1, 1843; I want to thank Professor Michael Woods for this reference. U.S. Mexican War Pension Index, FamilySearch.org. Van Evrie's death on May 17, 1896, was noted by the *New York Times,* May 20, 1896. Before his rise in New York City, he sometimes spelled his name Vanevery, and in a variety of other ways; John H. Van Evrie to John C. Calhoun, March 4, 1846, in Clyde N. Wilson et al., eds., *The Papers of John C. Calhoun,* 28 vols. (Columbia: University of South Carolina Press, 1959–2003), 20:660–62.

42 Moving to New York City: William S. McFeely, *Frederick Douglass* (New York: W. W. Norton, 1991), 149–53; David W. Blight, *Frederick Douglass: Prophet of Freedom* (New York: Simon & Schuster, 2018), 190; "In Search of America's 'First Professional Racist' in Rochester," *Talker of the Town,* February 22, 2019; Washington *Daily Union,* July 22, 1854; Frederick Douglass, "Is the Negro a White Man—Dr. Van Evrie and the New York Day Book," *Frederick Douglass's Paper,* September 14, 1855; New York *Day-Book,* quoted in the *National Anti-Slavery Standard,* September 1855.

43 New York City in the 1850s: Hellmut Lehmann Haupt, *The Book in America: A History of the Making and Selling of Books in the United States,* 2nd ed. (New York: R. R. Bowker, 1951), 120–21; John Strausbaugh, *City of Sedition: The History of New York City During the Civil War* (New York: Twelve, 2016), 11–19, 31; Chronicling America, National Endowment for the Humanities, Library of Congress, https://chroniclingamerica.loc.gov/search/titles/; *Trow's New York City Directory* (New York: J. F. Trow, 1859–60), 34–35.

44 Van Evrie set up shop: *Trow's New York City Directory,* 34, 408.

44 In a pattern that should be familiar: Van Evrie's appeal is reminiscent of the Trump White House approach to politics, as when President Trump declared: "The forgotten man and women of our country will be forgotten no longer. Everyone is listening to you now." *The White House, 1600 Daily,* April 4,

2019; Fredrickson, *Black Image in White Mind,* 63, 92–93; David Roediger, *The Wages of Whiteness: Race and the Making of the American Working Class* (London: Verso, 1991), 135–37; Martin Klammer, *Whitman, Slavery, and the Emergence of Leaves of Grass* (University Park: Pennsylvania State University, 1995), passim.

46   The New York *Day-Book:* Mark E. Neely, Jr., *Lincoln and the Democrats: The Politics of Opposition in the Civil War* (New York: Cambridge University Press, 2017), 99–102; Baltimore *Sun,* December 19, 1857.

46   Van Evrie quickly turned the *Day-Book:* Van Evrie quoted in Chestertown (Md.) *Transcript,* February 22, 1868; *Frank Leslie's Illustrated Newspaper,* March 17, 1860; *Daily Chicago Herald,* March 24, 1860; Charleston *Courier,* October 12, 1861; Howard C. Perkins, "The Defense of Slavery in the Northern Press on the Eve of the Civil War," *Journal of Southern History* 9 (February–November 1943): 503–9.

46   While some modern historians: Camden (N.J.) *Democrat,* December 17, 1864; Columbus (Ohio) *Crisis,* February 28, 1866; Eric Conrad, "Whitman and the Proslavery Press: Newly Recovered 1860 Reviews," *Walt Whitman Quarterly Review* 27 (2010): 227–28; David S. Reynolds, *Walt Whitman's America: A Cultural Biography* (New York: Alfred A. Knopf, 1995), 470 quoted; Boston *Evening Transcript,* February 1, 1861.

47   The same praise came from newspapers: "Black & White Races of Men," *De Bow's Review* 30 (old series) (April 1861): 446–56; *De Bow's Review* 5 (new series) (January 1868): 109; Augusta (Ga.) *Daily Constitutionalist,* September 9, 1865; Fredericksburg (Va.) *New Era,* September 19, 1865; Maryland *Union,* July 9, 1868.

47   But Van Evrie's reach proved far broader: Van Evrie, Horton & Co. to D.D.T. Moore, January 12, 1872 in *Moore's Rural New Yorker,* January 20, 1872; *Kansas Weekly Herald,* September 15, 1855; *London Critic* 22 (March 2, 1861): 283–84; "Africa Laid Open," *New Monthly Magazine* (London) 130 (February 1864): 150; New York *Weekly Anglo-African,* March 9, 1861; Orestes Brownson, "Literary Notices and Criticisms," *Bronson's Quarterly Review,* April 1861, 264–67; Perkins, "Defense of Slavery in the Northern Press," 506–9.

48   The *Day-Book* and Van Evrie, Horton & Co.: Catalogue in rear of Rushmore G. Horton, *A Youth's History of the Great Civil War in the United States, from 1861 to 1865* (New York: Van Evrie, Horton, 1866); New Haven (Conn.) *Columbian Register,* June 21, 1862; New York *Observer,* November 24, 1859; *Metropolitan Record and New York Vindicator,* February 2, 1861.

49   Van Evrie dreamed of becoming: John H. Van Evrie to John C. Calhoun, March 4, 1846, *Papers of John C. Calhoun,* 20:660–62.

49   At midcentury, when Van Evrie began: Michael E. Woods, *Arguing Until Doomsday: Stephen Douglas, Jefferson Davis, and the Struggle for American Democracy* (Chapel Hill: University of North Carolina Press, 2020), 7; James Lander, *Lincoln & Darwin: Shared Visions of Race, Science, and Religion*

(Carbondale: Southern Illinois University Press, 2010), 98–99, 138; Neely, Jr., *Lincoln and the Democrats,* 79; Thomas J. Balcerski, *Bosom Friends: The Intimate World of James Buchanan and William Rufus King* (New York: Oxford University Press, 2019), 8–9, 82; Richard Hofstadter, *The American Political Tradition: And the Men Who Made It* (New York: Random House, 1948), of course, labeled John C. Calhoun with that ingenious epithet, 68–92; Fredrickson, *Black Image in White Mind,* 63; Jean Baker, *Affairs of Party: The Political Culture of Northern Democrats in the Mid-Nineteenth Century* (Ithaca, N.Y.: Cornell University Press, 1983), 180; Mobile *Register,* February 25, 1869; New York *Observer,* November 24, 1859; Washington *Review and Examiner,* December 6, 1865; John H. Van Evrie, *The Six Species of Men, with Cuts Representing the Types of the Caucasian, Mongol, Malay, Indian, Esquimaux and Negro. With Their General Physical and Mental Qualities, Laws of Organization, Relations to Civilization, &c.* (New York: Van Evrie, Horton, 1866, 1868), 24; [John H. Van Evrie] By a Unionist, *Abolition and Secession: Cause and Effect: Together with the Remedy for Our Sectional Troubles* (New York: Van Evrie, Horton, 1862), 7–8; Van Evrie, *Subgenation: The Theory of the Normal Relation of the Races: An Answer to "Miscegenation"* (New York: John Bradburn, 1864), 68; Baltimore *Sun,* December 19, 1857.

50 He also sought to exploit American xenophobia: J. H. Van Evrie, *Negroes and Negro "Slavery"* (Baltimore: John D. Toy, 1853), 26–27.

50 The Democratic Party offered: Woods, *Arguing Until Doomsday,* 153; Lander, *Lincoln and Darwin,* 230–31; Van Evrie, *Negroes and Negro "Slavery";* Raleigh *Weekly North Carolina Standard,* November 28, 1855; New Orleans *Daily Picayune,* October 26, 1856.

51 The 1854 case of Capt. James Smith: *National Anti-Slavery Standard,* November 18, 1854, and June 23, 1855; Washington, D.C., *Daily Globe,* December 20, 1854; Van Evrie, "A Man Sentenced to Death for Importing Negroes from Africa," Washington, D.C., *Sentinel,* November 14, 1854.

52 White supremacy bound together: St. Paul *Daily Pioneer,* May 21, 1857; Joshua A. Lynn, *Preserving the White Man's Republic: Jacksonian Democracy, Race, and the Transformation of American Conservatism* (Charlottesville: University of Virginia Press, 2019), 2–5, 57; Woods, *Arguing Until Doomsday,* 166–67, 172–73; Baker, *Affairs of Party,* 191–92, 348–49; Stephen A. Douglas Speech at Chicago, July 9, 1858 in Robert W. Johannsen, ed., *The Lincoln-Douglas Debates of 1858* (New York: Oxford University Press, 1965), 33–35; Caroline E. Vose, "Jefferson Davis in New England," *Virginia Quarterly Review* 2 (October 1926): 557–68.

53 By the time Van Evrie's career began: Woods, *Arguing Until Doomsday,* 143–44, 153; Baker, *Affairs of Party,* 178–79; American Colonization Society, *Thirty-fifth Annual Report, Jan. 20, 1852* (Washington, D.C.: A. Alexander, 1852), 26–29; Fredrickson, *Black Image in White Mind,* 155–56.

53 Thus as we have seen, many Northern: Horace Bushnell, *The Census and Slavery: A Thanksgiving Discourse, Delivered in the Chapel at Clifton Springs,*

N.Y., November 29, 1860 (Hartford, Conn.: L. E. Hunt, 1860), 13; "Address of Frederic P. Stanton," *Proceedings of the Annual Meeting of the American Colonization Society* (January 20, 1852), 14–19; P. J. Staudenraus, *The African Colonization Movement, 1816–1865* (New York: Columbia University Press, 1961); William Lloyd Garrison, *Thoughts on African Colonization* (Boston: Garrison and Knapp, 1832).

53 Van Evrie, however, saw no "negro problem": [Van Evrie], *Abolition and Secession*, 5–6.

54 As he explained in his *Six Species of Men:* This and the following paragraph are based on Van Evrie, *Free Negroism* (New York: Van Evrie, Horton, 1862), 28–29; Van Evrie, *The Six Species of Men*, 12–15; Van Evrie, *Abolition and Secession*, 4–6.

55 But most important, he believed that African Americans: Van Evrie, *White Supremacy and Negro Subordination* (New York: Van Evrie, Horton, 1867), 39, 290–93, 300–2; Fredrickson, *Black Image in White Mind*, 93–94, 187–88.

55 The rise of abolitionism had convinced: Van Evrie, *Negroes and Negro "Slavery,"* 5–6, 11–16, 21–22.

56 The Civil War posed an existential crisis: *American Publishers' Circular and Literary Gazette*, January 26, 1861, 40; New Oregon (Ia.) *Plaindealer*, March 15, 1861; Benjamin Wood, *Speech of Benjamin Wood of New York, on the State of the Union, in the House of Representatives, May 16, 1862* (New York: Van Evrie, Horton, 1862); Neely, *Lincoln and Democrats*, 80–81.

58 At first, his efforts backfired: *Saturday Review of Politics, Literature, Science and Art* 11 (May 4, 1861): 454–55; *The South* (Baltimore), August 26, 1861, quoting the Philadelphia *Ledger;* New York *Commercial Advertiser*, April 18, 1861; April 17, 1861, George Templeton Strong, *Diary*, ed. Allan Nevins and Milton H. Thomas, 4 vols. (New York: Macmillan, 1852), 3:121–23. Van Evrie also did not share the doubts that several prominent Copperheads possessed regarding democracy and elite rule. He remained true to democracy and egalitarianism, but for whites only. Joanna Dunlap Cowden, *Heaven Will Frown on Such a Cause as This: Six Democrats Who Opposed Lincoln's War* (Lanham, Md.: University Press of America, 2001), 4, 10, 135; Ernest A. McKay, *The Civil War and New York City* (Syracuse, N.Y.: Syracuse University Press, 1990), 276–77.

58 When the Lincoln administration temporarily shut down: Columbus (Ohio) *Crisis*, December 5, 1861; Howard C. Perkins, "The Defense of Slavery in the Northern Press on the Eve of the Civil War," *Journal of Southern History* 9 (February–November 1943): 505; [Van Evrie], *Abolition and Secession*, 20–24.

59 Rather than blaming the South: [Van Evrie], *Abolition and Secession*, 3, 6–7, 11–12; Eugene H. Berwanger, "Negrophobia in Northern Proslavery and Antislavery Thought," *Phylon* 33 (1972): 269.

59 When the Lincoln administration first threatened: Detroit *Free Press*, March 15, 1868; "Omnium," *The Old Guard* 1 (September 1863): 239, cited in Wood, *Black Scare*, 73–74; Van Evrie, *Free Negroism*, 3–6; Van Evrie,

Subgenation: The Theory of the Normal Relation of the Races. An Answer to "Miscegenation" (New York: John Bradburn, 1864), 65; [Van Evrie], *Abolition and Secession,* 10, 14; Wood, *Black Scare,* 20; *The Old Guard,* 7 (December 1867): 957; Washington *Review and Examiner,* December 6, 1865. The Camden (N.J.) *Democrat,* December 17, 1864, praised the *Old Guard* as a solid Democratic organ that "ought to be in every Democratic family."

60 In addition to agitating the racial waters: Forrest G. Wood, *Black Scare: The Racist Response to Emancipation and Reconstruction* (Berkeley: University of California Press, 1968), 22–23; Bridgeport (Conn.) *Republican Farmer,* May 27, 1864; Wisconsin *Daily Patriot,* June 29, 1864.

61 Equally important, Van Evrie's views energized: "Immorality in Politics," *North American Review* 98 (January 1864): 105–27; Wood, *Black Scare,* 36; Samuel F. B. Morse, *The Letter of a Republican, Edward N. Crosby . . .* (New York: SDPK, 1863), 7–8; Samuel F. B. Morse, *An Argument on the Ethical Position of Slavery in the Social System, and Its Relation to the Politics of the Day* (New York: SDPK, 1863), 10; Kenneth Silverman, *Lightning Man: The Accursed Life of Samuel F. B. Morse* (New York: Alfred A. Knopf, 2003), 394–98; Charles Godfrey Leland, "What Shall We Do with Our South?," *Knickerbocker* 58 (September 1861): 189–93; *Knickerbocker* 66 (August 1865): 161–62; Samuel F. B. Morse, no. 6, *Emancipation and Its Results* (New York: SDPK, 1863), 25–32.

61 At the close of 1863: Henry Louis Gates, Jr., *Stony the Road: Reconstruction, White Supremacy, and the Rise of Jim Crow* (New York: Penguin Press, 2019), 136–41. Wood, *Black Scare,* 53–79, has the fullest report of the hoax, although he did not appreciate the extent of Van Evrie's reach with his response to the pamphlet. Jennifer Weber, *Copperheads: The Rise and Fall of Lincoln's Opponents in the North* (New York: Oxford University Press, 2006), 160–61, 209; John Strausbaugh, *City of Sedition: The History of New York City During the Civil War* (New York: Twelve, 2016), 299–300.

62 Whether duped or not: Van Evrie, *Subgenation,* iii–iv.

62 He repeated his view that humans: Van Evrie, *Six Species of Men,* 7–11; Leslie M. Harris, *In the Shadow of Slavery: African Americans in New York City, 1626–1863* (Chicago: University of Chicago Press, 2003), 112–13, 191, 194; Ira Berlin and Leslie Harris, eds., *Slavery in New York* (New Press and New-York Historical Society, 2005), 139, 141.

64 As he wrote elsewhere, Van Evrie: Van Evrie, *Subgenation,* 8–9, 13–15; Van Evrie, *White Supremacy and Negro Subordination; or, Negroes A Subordinate Race, and (so-called) Slavery Its Normal Condition* (New York: Van Evrie, Horton, 1867), 44–47; Van Evrie, *Six Species of Men,* 12–15; Melissa Stein, *Measuring Manhood: Race and the Science of Masculinity, 1830–1934* (Minneapolis: University of Minnesota Press, 2015), 89–91.

64 In a dangerous move: Van Evrie, *Subgenation,* 5–8, 39–41; Boston *Congregationalist,* February 8, 1861; Van Evrie, "Inequality of Human Races," *Old Guard* 7 (February 1869): 81–90, quoted 82.

65 Congressional Reconstruction generally aimed: Foner, *Reconstruction*, xxv, and *The Second Founding: How the Civil War and Reconstruction Remade the Constitution* (New York: W. W. Norton, 2019); Van Evrie, *The Abolition Conspiracy to Destroy the Union; or, A Ten Years' Record of the Republican Party; The Opinions of William Lloyd Garrison, Wendell Phillips, Abraham Lincoln, William H. Seward . . .* (New York: Van Evrie, Horton, 1863, 1866), 3–4; *Old Guard* 7 (December 1869): 957.

66 The momentous, unprecedented: Lawrence Goldstone, *Inherently Unequal: The Betrayal of Equal Rights by the Supreme Court, 1865–1903* (New York: Walker & Co., 2011), 17, quoting the *Enquirer;* Wood, *Black Scare,* 134; Eric Foner, "There Have Been 10 Black Senators Since 1865," *New York Times,* February 16, 2020; Fredrickson, *Black Image in White Mind,* 185; Lyde Cullen Sizer, *The Political Work of Northern Women Writers and the Civil War, 1850–1872* (Chapel Hill: University of North Carolina Press, 2000), 227, 234–37.

67 No solid foundation for a transformation: Wood, *Black Scare,* 85–86; Joanne Pope Melish, *Disowning Slavery: Gradual Emancipation and "Race" in New England, 1780–1860* (Ithaca, N.Y.: Cornell University Press, 1998), 120–22; Charles Postel, *Equality: An American Dilemma, 1866–1896* (New York: Farrar, Straus & Giroux, 2019), 188; Massachusetts Colonization Society, *Twenty-Seventh Annual Report* (Boston: MCS, 1868), 7.

68 To Van Evrie, these examples: Van Evrie, *White Supremacy,* v–vii, 21–23, 32, 48–57, 156–57, 168; Van Evrie, *Six Species of Men,* 20–21, 24; Van Evrie, *Abolition Is National Death; or, The Attempt to Equalize Races the Destruction of Society* (New York: Van Evrie, Horton, 1866), 22–25. For the preposterous idea that the Nile Valley had been populated by whites, Van Evrie may have relied on the German Egyptologist Karl Richard Lepsius (1810–84) or Bayard Taylor, both of whom asserted that whites—or a white offshoot—had populated the Nile Valley. Timothy Kendall, "Racism and the Rediscovery of Ancient Nubia," www.pbs.org/wonders/Epr1/1 retel 1.htm; Bayard Taylor, *A Journey to Central Africa; or, Life and Landscapes from Egypt to the Negro Kingdoms of the White Nile* (New York: G. P. Putnam, 1854), 236–37.

69 At the onset of 1868: Van Evrie, "Tricks of President-Making," *Old Guard* 6, issue I (January 1868); Foner, *Reconstruction,* 340–41.

69 While he continued to rail against: Van Evrie, "What Next?," *Old Guard* 6, issue XII (December 1868): 881–84; Van Evrie, " 'The Situation': What the South Has Not Lost by the War," *Old Guard* 5 (December 1867): 879–86; Mobile *Register,* February 25, 1869.

70 While Van Evrie's break with: Trenton (N.J.) *Daily True American,* January 8, 1868; Detroit *Free Press,* March 15, 1868; Vinton (Ohio) *Democratic Enquirer,* August 15, 1867; Maryland *Union,* July 9, 1868.

71 A month after President Grant took office: Van Evrie, "To President Grant," *Old Guard* 7 (April 1869).

71 After 1868, freed of any need to: Jack P. Maddex, *The Reconstruction of Edward A. Pollard: A Rebel's Conversion to Postbellum Unionism* (Chapel Hill:

University of North Carolina Press, 1974), 4–5, 26–27, 51–55, 60; Edward A. Pollard, *The Lost Cause: A New Southern History of the War of the Confederates,* enlarged ed. (New York: E. B. Treat, 1868), 753–59.

72 Van Evrie took his fight for the "larger contest": Van Evrie published another novel, William H. Peck's *The Confederate Flag on the Ocean: A Tale of the Cruises of the Sumter and Alabama* (New York: Van Evrie, Horton, 1868); Winchester (Tenn.) *Home Journal,* April 4, 1867; "Cooke, John Esten," *Encyclopedia Virginia,* www.encyclopediavirginia.org/Cooke_John_Esten_1830–1886; John Esten Cooke, *Wearing of the Gray,* ed. Emory M. Thomas (Baton Rouge: Louisiana State University Press, 1997), xiv–xvii; John Esten Cooke, *The Heir of Gaymount* (New York: Van Evrie, Horton, 1870), 56.

73 Even more important, Van Evrie emerged: Van Evrie, Horton to D.D.T. Moore, January 12, 1872, in *Moore's Rural New Yorker,* January 20, 1872; "Black and White Races of Men," *De Bow's Review* 30 (old series) (April 1861): 446–56; Boston *Evening Transcript,* January 31 and February 1, 1861; Philadelphia *Press,* February 1, 1861; New York *Commercial Advertiser,* January 14, 1861; Buffalo *Morning Express,* February 4, 1861; New York *Observer,* February 7, 1861; Washington, D.C., *Constitution,* January 31, 1861; Baltimore *Sun,* February 12, 1861; Wisconsin *Daily Patriot,* November 17, 1863; Bridgeport (Conn.) *Republican Farmer,* May 27, 1864; *Saturday Evening Post,* April 17, 1869; *Harper's Weekly* 3 (July 23, 1859): 479; *American Quarterly Church Review and Ecclesiastical Register* 16 (July 1864): 316; Kansas *Weekly Herald,* September 15, 1855; San Francisco *Pacific,* July 30, 1868.

74 As his advertising made clear: Augusta (Ga.) *Daily Constitutionalist,* September 9, 1865; Fredericksburg (Va.) *New Era,* September 19, 1865; Oxford (Mich.) *Falcon,* January 30, 1869; Westminster (Md.) *Democratic Advocate,* December 14, 1865; New Orleans *Times Picayune,* February 10, 1861; Washington, D.C., *Constitution,* January 31, 1861; Winnsboro (S.C.) *Tri-Weekly News,* March–December 1866.

74 In a stunning revelation: This advertisement appeared in the Milledgeville (Ga.) *Southern Recorder,* February 16, 1869. I want to thank Michael Woods for bringing this to my attention. I also found one in *Old Guard* 6 (April 1868): 322. A long list of endorsements ran often in newspapers like the Port Tobacco (Va.) *Times,* the Charles County *Advertiser,* February 24, 1859, and the New York *Evangelist,* December 25, 1856. American newspapers were replete with advertisements for the machine he offered.

75 Beyond his newspapers: Hartford (Conn.) *Courant,* January 24, 1861; *Metropolitan Record and New York Vindicator,* February 2, 1861; *American Publisher's Circular and Literary Gazette,* January 26, 1861, 40; Plymouth (Ind.) *Weekly Democrat,* June 26, 1862; Eaton (Ohio) *Democratic Press,* November 19, 1863.

75 Such views only intensified: Detroit *Free Press,* March 15, 1868; Trenton (N.J.) *Daily True American,* January 8, 1868; Clearfield (Penn.) *Republican,*

January 17, 1866; Iowa *Plaindealer,* July 26, 1867; Vinton (Ohio) *Democratic Enquirer,* January 9, 1868; Bedford (Penn.) *Gazette,* May 3, 1867 to June 5, 1868; Dayton (Ohio) *Daily Empire,* May 18, 1867.

76 Through pamphlets, newspapers, books: Horton, *Youth's History;* Rushmore G. Horton, *The Life and Public Services of James Buchanan. Late Minister to England and Formerly Minister to Russia,* . . . (New York: Derby & Jackson, 1856), iii–v, 150–53; "Editor's Table," *Old Guard* 5 (November 1867): 877.

76 The guns at Appomattox had hardly quieted: Much of the theme for the Horton text had been worked out in Van Evrie's many publications, especially *The Abolition Conspiracy to Destroy the Union; or, A Ten Years' Record of the "Republican" Party; The Opinions of William Lloyd Garrison, Wendell Phillips, Abraham Lincoln, William H. Seward* . . . (New York: Van Evrie, Horton, 1863, 1866); "Editor's Table," *Old Guard* 5 (November 1867): 877.

77 "This book has been written in the cause": Horton, *Youth's History,* iii–v; Richard Hofstadter, *The Paranoid Style in American Politics, and Other Essays* (Chicago: University of Chicago Press, 1965); David Brion Davis, "Some Themes of Counter-Subversion: An Analysis of Anti-Masonic, Anti-Catholic, and Anti-Mormon Literature," in *From Homicide to Slavery: Studies in American Culture* (New York: Oxford University Press, 1986), 137–54; David Brion Davis, ed., *The Fear of Conspiracy: Images of Un-American Subversion from the Revolution to the Present* (Ithaca, N.Y.: Cornell University Press, 1971).

77 In their version of history: Horton, *Youth's History,* iii–iv, 29–38, 45–46, 75–77, 92–93.

78 In Horton's telling, the North then sent: Horton, *Youth's History,* 291, 309.

79 The book attracted much attention: Chicago *Republican,* September 10, 1866; Harrisburg (Penn.) *Patriot,* January 25, 1883; Bennington (Vt.) *Banner,* October 2, 1879.

79 Van Evrie appeared to abandon: Kalamazoo (Mich.) *Gazette,* May 16, 1878, reported that he still edited *The Day-Book;* Richmond (Va.) *Times Dispatch,* May 17, 1908; Anne E. Marshall, "Mildred Lewis Rutherford (1851–1928)," in *New Georgia Encyclopedia,* April 16, 2019; Mildred Lewis Rutherford, *Truths of History* . . . (Athens, Ga.: self-pub., c. 1920), 10, 28. See also Rutherford, *The South Must Have the Rightful Place in History* (Athens, Ga.: self-pub., 1923); C. R. Wharton, *The Lone Star State: A Social History* (Dallas: Southern, 1932).

80 Van Evrie's *White Supremacy and Negro Subordination:* Merrill Peterson, *Lincoln in American Memory* (New York: Oxford University Press, 1994), 253–54. Also see the Dixie Project, Christogenea.org, and https://daily stormer.su/aryan-narrations-white-supremacy-and-negro-subordination-vi/.

80 Van Evrie found his final resting place: "Dr. John H. Van Evrie," Find a Grave, www.findagrave.com/memorial/60784257/john-h-van_evrie; Rochester *Democrat and Chronicle,* December 31, 1922; David W. Blight, *Frederick Douglass: Prophet of Freedom* (New York: Simon & Schuster, 2018), 754–55.

3. From "Slavery" to "Servitude"

82 Joseph Emerson, the head: Joseph Emerson, *Letter to a Class of Young Ladies Upon the Study of the History of the United States* (Boston: Crocker & Brewster, 1828); Elizabeth Palmer Peabody, *First Steps to the Study of History: Being Part First of a Key to History* (Boston: Hilliard, Gray, 1832), 1–9, passim; Marie Elizabeth Ruffin Carpenter, *The Treatment of the Negro in American History School Textbooks* (Menasha, Wis.: George Banta, 1941), 69.

84 In 1827 only Massachusetts and Vermont: Bessie Louise Pierce, *Public Opinion in the Teaching of History in the United States* (1926; reprint, New York: Da Capo Press, 1970), 6–14; R. M. Elson, *Guardians of Tradition*, 5–8; Barry Joyce, *The First U.S. History Textbooks: Constructing and Disseminating the American Tale in the Nineteenth Century* (Lanham, Md.: Lexington Books, 2015), 43–44; George H. Callcott, *History in the United States, 1800–1860: Its Practice and Purpose* (Baltimore: Johns Hopkins University Press, 1970), 25–26, 61.

85 Especially for the first two generations: William Swinton, *First Lessons in Our Country's History . . . Aiming to Combine Simplicity with Sense* (New York: Ivison, Blakeman, Taylor, 1872); Thomas Howland Mumford, *The Child's First History of America* (New York: D. Appleton, 1856).

85 Noah Webster's 1832 *History of the United States:* Callcott, *History in the United States,* 56–58, 179–80; Noah Webster, *History of the United States* (Louisville, Ky.: Wilcox, Dickerman & Co., 1832), v, 13–45. Webster's remarks about Africans are repeated in Amos G. Beman to Noah Webster, April 27, 1843, cited in Donald Yacovone, "Editor's Introduction," *Massachusetts Historical Review* 4 (2002): ii–iii.

86 The sense of white American identity: R. M. Elson, *Guardians of Tradition,* 65–67, 87–88; Callcott, *History in the United States,* 167–68.

87 Many textbooks simply used: Michael Kraus, *A History of American History* (New York: Farrar & Rinehart, 1937), 215–39; "George Bancroft," Naval History and Heritage Command, https://www.history.navy.mil/research/library/research-guides/z-files/zb-files/zb-files-b/bancroft-george.html.

88 With astonishing detail and sparkling generalizations: George Bancroft, *History of the United States of America from the Discovery of the Continent to 1789,* 6 vols. (New York: D. Appleton, 1882–84), 1:126–40; John Shaw, *A Ramble Through the United States, Canada, and the West Indies* (London: J. F. Hope, 1856), 307, cited Bancroft, but Egbert Guernsey, *History of the United States of America, Designed for Schools* (1847; reprint, New York: Daniel Burgess, 1854), 92, did not; also see Joyce, *First U.S. History Textbooks,* 120–21.

88 In the era before the Civil War: Joyce, *First U.S. History Textbooks,* 238–40; Gregory M. Pfitzer, *History Repeating Itself: The Republication of Children's Literature and the Christian Right* (Amherst: University of Massachusetts Press, 2014), 18–19, 33–35, 53; Callcott, *History in the United States,* 89;

Daniel Roselle, *Samuel Griswold Goodrich, Creator of Peter Parley: A Study of His Life and Work* (Albany: State University of New York, 1968), vi, 53–54, 85–89; Samuel Griswold Goodrich, *Peter Parley's Own Story* (New York: Sheldon, 1864), 31; Carpenter, *Treatment of Negro in Textbooks*, 68.

90 Goodrich's biographer asserted: Samuel Griswold Goodrich, *The First Book of History for Children and Youth*, 16th ed. (Philadelphia: DeSilver, Thomas, 1836), 73–82; Roselle, *Samuel Griswold Goodrich*, 75–76; New Orleans *Courier* quoted by *Liberator*, March 26, 1852; *De Bow's Review*, cited in Pierce, *Public Opinion in the Teaching of History in the United States*, 138–42.

91 "I have taken advantage of every convenient occasion": For this and the following paragraph, Callcott, *History in the United States*, 183; Goodrich, *Peter Parley's Own Story*, 310–12; Roselle, *Samuel Griswold Goodrich*, 129–40; [Goodrich], *The First Book of History for Children and Youth*, 82; Joyce, *First U.S. History Textbooks*, 92–93, 176–78.

92 Goodrich's work, in the end: Goodrich, *Peter Parley's Own Story*, 251–53; Samuel Griswold Goodrich, *A Pictorial History of the United States . . . for Use of Schools and Families* (Philadelphia: E. H. Butler, 1866), passim.

92 Perhaps Goodrich's popularity in the South: Samuel Griswold Goodrich, *Peter Parley's Geography for Beginners* (1844; reprint, New York: Huntington & Savage, 1847), 30–43, 126–27, 130–38.

93 Another New Englander, Salma Hale: Samuel Abbott Green, "School Histories and Some Errors in Them," *American Educational Monthly* 9 (June 1872): 249–53; Joyce, *First U.S. History Textbooks*, 176; Salma Hale, *History of the United States from Their First Settlement to . . . 1817*, 2 vols. (1827; reprint, New York: Harper & Bros., 1841), 1:28–30, 177, 2:282.

94 For most authors, avoidance: Marcius Willson, *History of the United States, for the Use of Schools* (New York: Mark H. Newman, 1845), 172, 331, 376. The book was updated in 1848, but included no new publication date.

94 As the nation approached the 1850s: Guernsey, *History . . . Designed for Schools*; Frank Hasbrouck, ed., *The History of Dutchess County, New York* (Poughkeepsie, N.Y.: S. A. Matthieu, 1909), 1:718–19; Christopher D. Ellithorp, "Egbert Guernsey," *American National Biography*, www.anb.org.

95 His *History of the United States*: Guernsey, *History . . . Designed for Schools*, vi–vii. 44–68; John Bonner, *A Child's History of the United States*, 2 vols. (New York: Harper & Bros., 1855), 1:17–21, 76. On official American policy toward Native Americans, see Roger L. Nichols, *Massacring Indians: From Horseshoe Bend to Wounded Knee* (Norman: University of Oklahoma Press, 2021).

96 Although Guernsey failed to provide: Guernsey, *History . . . Designed for Schools*, 77, 92, 148–49, 166–67, 398, 454–55; see Bancroft, *History of United States*, 1:126–31. G. P. Quackenbos, *Illustrated School History of the United States and the Adjacent Parts of America* (New York: D. Appleton, 1859), 446–47, took the same approach on Clay. He also went further and declared that

Calhoun's death deprived the Senate "of one of its most brilliant ornaments and the country of a pure and enlightened statesman."

97 But by the time he revised his text: Guernsey, *History . . . Designed for Schools,* 451–59.

97 Samuel Griswold Goodrich's brother: Charles A. Goodrich, *A History of the United States of America . . .* (1852; reprint, Boston: Hickling, Swan & Brewer, 1858), 6, 32, 264, 274, 310.

99 But in the mid-1850s: Bonner, *Child's History,* 1:129–48; Benson J. Lossing, *A Pictorial History of the United States for Schools and Families* (New York: F. J. Huntington–Mason Bros., 1854), 55, 282, 311; David D. Van Tassel, "Benson J. Lossing: Pen and Pencil Historian," *American Quarterly* 6 (Spring 1954), 32–44, quoted 40.

101 As Northern publishers and authors: Keith Whitescarver, "School Books, Publishers, and Southern Nationalists: Refashioning the Curriculum in North Carolina's Schools, 1850–1861," *North Carolina Historical Review* 79 (January 2002): 45, 29 quoted; Joyce, *First U.S. History Textbooks,* 253 quoted; Ronald J. Zboray, *A Fictive People: Antebellum Economic Development and the American Reading Public* (New York: Oxford University Press, 1993), 196–97; J. W. Morgan, "Our School Books," *De Bow's Review* 3 (April 1860): 434–40.

101 What Southern critics sought: Morgan, "Our School Books," 434–40; Joyce, *First U.S. History Textbooks,* 233.

102 But no general history of the United States: Joyce, *First U.S. History Textbooks,* 253–54; Bartholomew R. Carroll, *Catechism of the United States History* (Charleston, S.C.: McCarter & Dawson, 1859), vi, 27, 41–42, 203, 241–49.

103 The one book that might have met: William Gilmore Simms, *History of South Carolina from Its First European Discovery . . .* (1840; reprint, New York: Redfield, 1859). His granddaughter, Mary C. Simms Oliphant, updated the text in the 1920s to include the Civil War and the era of Jim Crow through the First World War. Simms and Oliphant, *The History of South Carolina,* rev. ed. (Columbia, S.C.: State, 1927); Mary Ann Wimsatt, "William Gilmore Simms," *American National Biography,* www.anb.org; David Brion Davis, *Homicide in American Fiction, 1798–1860* (Ithaca, N.Y.: Cornell University Press, 1957), 137–43, 185–90, quoted 41.

104 Simms also crafted a brief "memoir": William Gilmore Simms, "Memoir," in John B. Moreau, comp., *The Army Correspondence of Colonel John Laurens . . . with a Memoir by William Gilmore Simms* (New York: Bradford Club, 1867), 9–54, and John Laurens to Henry Laurens, February 2, 1778, 117; Benjamin Quarles, *The Negro in the American Revolution* (1961; reprint, Chapel Hill: University of North Carolina Press, 1996), 63–64; Don Higginbotham, *The War of American Independence: Military Attitudes, Policies, and Practice, 1763–1789* (New York: Macmillan, 1971), 395.

104 Simms intended his history of South Carolina: Simms, *History of South Carolina from First Discovery,* 5–20, 85, 95, 101.

105 With verve and style: Ibid., 105–7, 154; Henry Louis Gates, Jr., and Donald Yacovone, *The African Americans: Many Rivers to Cross* (Carlsbad, Calif.: SmileyBooks, 2013), 41–43.

105 Although we often think of female textbook authors: "Blanche Berard," Find a Grave, https://www.findagrave.com/memorial/127109426/blanche-berard; *Army and Navy Journal,* March 20, 1897, 522; Augusta Blanche Berard, *School History of the United States* (Philadelphia: H. Cowperthwaite, 1855).

106 Berard's history, like so many other: Berard, *School History,* 72–109, 191–94.

107 Few textbook authors, male or female: Ezra Brainard, *Mrs. Emma Willard's Life and Work in Middlebury* (Middlebury, Vt.: Middlebury College, 1918), 3; Anne Firor Scott, "Emma Willard: Feminist," *Women's Studies Newsletter* 7 (Fall 1979): 5–7; Nina Baym, "Women and the Republic: Emma Willard's Rhetoric of History," *American Quarterly* 43 (March 1991): 1–23; Alma Lutz, *Emma Willard: Daughter of Democracy* (Boston: Houghton Mifflin, 1929), 120–21; Nancy Iannucci to author, October 24, 2019, email from the Willard School's historian and archivist.

107 Willard, who had been publishing: Baym, "Women and the Republic," 5; Joyce, *First U.S. History Textbooks,* 44–45, 246–48; Joseph Moreau, *Schoolbook Nation: Conflicts over American History Textbooks from the Civil War to the Present* (Ann Arbor: University of Michigan Press, 2003), 39.

108 Willard was not only the nation's: Emma Willard, *Abridged History of the United States; or, Republic of America* (New York: A. S. Barnes, 1846), v–vii; Alma Lutz, *Emma Willard: Pioneer Educator of American Women* (Boston: Beacon Press, 1964), 124–25; Deborah Bingham Van Broekhoven, " 'Let Your Names Be Enrolled': Method and Ideology in Women's Antislavery Petitioning," in Jean Fagan Yellin and John C. Van Horne, eds., *Women's Political Culture in Antebellum America* (Ithaca, N.Y.: Cornell University Press, 1994), 198; Emma Willard, *Via Media: A Peaceful and Permanent Settlement of the Slavery Question* (Washington, D.C.: Charles H. Anderson, 1862), 1–9.

109 Willard's 1846 textbook: Willard, *Abridged History,* 311–12 and passim.

110 Her expanded text of the early 1850s: Emma Willard, *History of the United States; or, Republic of America* (New York: A. S. Barnes, 1851, 1852), iii–vi, 1–88.

110 Willard spent little time recounting: Ibid., 118–19.

111 Asserting that England had forced: For this and the following paragraph, ibid., 118–20, 267, 451–55, 466–68; Joyce, *First U.S. History Textbooks,* 246–48.

112 In the momentous dawning of 1860: For this and the following paragraph, William Lloyd Garrison to Helen E. Garrison, June 29, 1840, in Louis Ruchames, ed., *The Letters of William Lloyd Garrison: A House Dividing Against Itself, 1836–1840* (Cambridge, Mass.: Harvard University Press, 1971), 2:654–59; Mary Botham Howitt, *An Autobiography,* ed. Margaret Howitt, 2 vols. (London: W. Isbister, 1889), 2:33, quoted; Mary Howitt, *Our Cousins in Ohio* (New York: Collins & Brother, 1851?), 22–25.

114 Howitt's two-volume history: Mary Howitt, *A Popular History of the United States of America,* 2 vols. (New York: Harper & Bros., 1860), 1:1–62.

114 Her book was one of the few: Ibid., 1:178, 241–42, 375–76, 397.

115 With her unprecedented criticisms: Ibid., 2:50, 319, 376.

115 Through the years of the Civil War: For this and the following paragraph, Charles A. Goodrich and William H. Seavey, *History of the United States of America, for the Use of Schools* (Boston: William Ware, 1867); S. G. Goodrich, *Pictorial History,* 65, 436–48.

4. The Emancipationist Challenge, 1867 to 1883

117 Textbooks quickly incorporated: Bonner, *Child's History;* Judith Ann Giesberg, "'To Forget and Forgive': Reconstructing the North in the Post–Civil War Classroom," *Civil War History* 52 (September 2006): 282–302.

118 In the first years after the war: Goodrich and Seavey, *History . . . for the Use of Schools,* 21; Swinton, *First Lessons,* 30. While condemning white conduct toward Native peoples, David B. Scott's *A School History of the United States* (New York: Harper & Bros., 1870) similarly described Native people as rude and uncivilized, 15.

118 The revised 1867 textbook: Goodrich and Seavey, *History . . . for the Use of Schools,* 32, 152, 226.

119 Students now obtained a glorious view: Ibid., 231–32, 275, 282, 287, 310. In one exception, the book mentioned in small type, to be ignored by "lower grades," the appearance of Black troops at Port Hudson, Louisiana, but not what happened at this important battle or anything about the level of Black participation in the war. Swinton, *First Lessons,* 160–95.

120 Even into the 1870s: Scott, *School History,* 41, 275–77, 309–13, 316–20; Alexander Johnston, *History of American Politics: Handbooks for Students and General Readers* (New York: Henry Holt, 1882), also emphasized the role of the cotton gin (86–93).

120 John J. Anderson, a New York City grammar school principal: John J. Anderson, *An Introductory School History of the United States* (New York: Clark & Maynard, 1867), 112–13, 123–24, 126–52; John J. Anderson, *A Grammar School History of the United States* (1868; reprint, New York: Clark & Maynard, 1882), 151–52, 157–84. Harvard University's copy of Anderson's grammar school textbook was inscribed by a Connecticut student named Louis Tuttle, who made it clear that he wished to be known as "L.T."

121 But textbook authors could not explain: Eric Foner, *Nothing but Freedom: Emancipation and Its Legacy* (Baton Rouge: Louisiana State University Press, 1983), 1–2, 39–45.

122 Understandably, many in the North: Frederick Douglass, "In What New Skin Will the Old Snake Come Forth," May 10, 1865, in John W. Blassingame et al., eds., *The Frederick Douglass Papers: Series One: Speeches, Debates, and*

Interviews, 1864–80, vol. 4 (New Haven, Conn.: Yale University Press, 1991), 82–83.

123 Just so there would be no misunderstanding: Delany quoted in W.E.B. Du Bois, *Black Reconstruction in America, 1860–1880* (1935; reprint, Cleveland: World, 1964), 233; Charles Sumner, "Enfranchisement and Protection of Freedmen," December 20, 1865, in Charles Sumner, *Complete Works,* 20 vols. (New York: Negro Universities Press, 1969), 13:56–58, 61, 82, 85; Charles Sumner, "Equal Right of Colored Persons to be Protected by the National Courts," December 4, 1865, in Sumner, *Complete Works,* 13:16–18.

124 Sumner was well informed: Caroline E. Janney, "Free to Go Where We Liked: The Army of Northern Virginia After Appomattox," *Journal of the Civil War Era* 9 (March 2019): 4–28; Leon F. Litwack, *Been in the Storm So Long: The Aftermath of Slavery* (New York: Vintage Books, 1979), 338–40; also see Rene Hayden et al., eds., *Freedom: A Documentary History of Emancipation, 1861–1867,* Series 3, *Land and Labor* (Chapel Hill: University of North Carolina Press, 2013), vols. 1 and 2.

125 African Americans who went south: Jermain Wesley Loguen to Robert Hamilton, July 25, 1865, in New York *Weekly Anglo-African,* August 5, 1865, in C. Peter Ripley et al., eds., *The Black Abolitionist Papers: The United States, 1859–1865* (Chapel Hill: University of North Carolina Press, 1992), 5:353–56.

126 A concerned Northern public: "Obituary," *Harvard Crimson,* December 4, 1874; John Richard Dennett, *The South as It Is, 1865–1866* (New York: Viking Press, 1965), vii–viii, 41, 190–91; Introduction to John Richard Dennett, *The South as It Is,* ed. Caroline E. Janney (Tuscaloosa: University of Alabama Press, 2010), viii–x; James M. McPherson, *The Abolitionist Legacy: From Reconstruction to the NAACP* (Princeton: Princeton University Press, 1975), 37–40.

126 In the year following the end of the war: *Nation,* August 10, 1865; "Slavery and the Slavocracy," *Nation,* August 17, 1865. Other freedmen rescued and cared for the man so viciously maimed and, astonishingly, he later turned up at the Freedmen's Bureau office in Washington, D.C.

127 Frederick Douglass recognized: For this and the following paragraph, "Will the Free Negro Race at the South Die Out?," *Nation,* September 14, 1865, August 20, 1868, February 18, 1869; E. L. Godkin, "Wendell Phillips as a Whipper-In," *Nation,* February 8, 1866; "One Excuse for Conservatives," *Nation,* September 13, 1866; "Universal Suffrage and Universal Amnesty," *Nation,* November 29, 1866; "Equal Suffrage Universal," *Nation,* April 11, 1867; "The Negro's Claim to Office," *Nation,* August 1, 1867; James Brewer Stewart, *Wendell Phillips: Liberty's Hero* (Baton Rouge: Louisiana State University Press, 1986), 247.

128 While the antislavery vanguard: For this and following paragraph, Giesberg, "'To Forget and Forgive': Reconstructing the North in the Post–Civil War

Classroom," 290; David Blight, "How Competing Visions of American History Shaped Our National Narrative," *Washington Post,* June 28, 2020, 20, and especially his *Race and Reunion: The Civil War in American Memory* (Cambridge, Mass.: Harvard University Press, 2001); Sanford Niles, *School History of the United States* (St. Paul, Minn.: D. D. Merrill, 1890), 4; [Samuel T. Dutton et al.,] New England Association of School Superintendents, *Outline Course of Study in United States History and Civics* (Brookline, Mass.: NEASS, 1891), 5–10. On the workings of national or historical memory, also see my "Race, Radicalism, and Remembering Wendell Phillips," in A J Aiséirithe and Donald Yacovone, eds., *Wendell Phillips, Social Justice, and the Power of the Past* (Baton Rouge: Louisiana State University Press, 2016), 272–330.

129   Elisha Mulford's *The Nation:* Colin Brown, "Elisha Mulford (1833–85) and His Influence: 'A Fame Not Equal to His Deserts'?" *Pennsylvania Magazine of History and Biography* 108 (January 1984): 25–39, 43, 47–48; Mark E. Neely, Jr., "Romanticism, Nationalism, and the New Economics: Elisha Mulford and the Organic Theory of the State," *American Quarterly* 29 (Autumn 1977): 417–20; Mitchell Snay, *Fenians, Freedmen, and Southern Whites* (Baton Rouge: Louisiana State University Press, 2010), 148–49, 170; Elisha Mulford, *The Nation: The Foundations of Civil Order and Political Life in the United States* (New York: Hurd & Houghton, 1870), 360–61.

130   In many ways, Mulford's 1870 work: Charles Sumner to Caleb Cushing, September 8, 1870, in Beverly Wilson Palmer, ed., *The Selected Letters of Charles Sumner,* 2 vols. (Boston: Northeastern University Press, 1990), 2:518–19; Brown, "Elisha Mulford (1833–85) and His Influence," 31, 38–41; Neely, Jr., "Romanticism, Nationalism, and the New Economics," 409, 417–20; Joseph Moreau, *Schoolbook Nation: Conflicts over American History Textbooks from the Civil War to the Present* (Ann Arbor: University of Michigan Press, 2003), 61; Mulford, *Nation,* 6–17, 321, 340.

130   For Mulford, the country owed: Mulford, *Nation,* 62, 73, 100, 127.

131   Mulford believed that a true nation: Ibid., 226, 321–22, 340.

132   After the postwar civil rights legislation: "Samuel Eliot," *American National Biography,* www.anb.org; Samuel Eliot, *History of the United States from 1492 to 1872* (Boston: Brewer & Tileston, 1874), 396–75, 469. In 1856, he also had published *Manual of United States History from 1492 to 1850* (Boston: Brewer & Tileston, 1856).

132   Other texts censured the Supreme Court: Johnston, *History of American Politics,* 86–87, 92–93, 122–23, 172; John R. G. Hassard, *History of the United States of America: For the Use of Schools* (1878; reprint, New York: Catholic Publication Society, 1881), 54, 274–75, 307–9.

133   While we know that predominantly white: John W. Cromwell, *Address of the Difficulties of the Colored Youth, in Obtaining an Education in the Virginias* (Philadelphia: Colored Education Convention, 1875), 4; Adelaide M. Cromwell, *Unveiled Voices, Unvarnished Memories: The Cromwell Family in Slavery*

and Segregation, 1692–1972 (Columbia: University of Missouri Press, 2007), 1, 38–47, 76, 81–84, 98–105. For instance, see John W. Cromwell, *The Negro in American History* (Washington, D.C.: American Negro Academy, 1914).

134 Attendance proved a daunting challenge: Cromwell, *Address of the Difficulties of the Colored Youth,* 10–12.

134 That same year, however: Thomas Wentworth Higginson, *Young Folks' History of the United States* (Boston: Lee & Shepard, 1875). On Higginson, see Tilden G. Edelstein, *Strange Enthusiasm: A Life of Thomas Wentworth Higginson* (New York: Atheneum, 1970) and Howard N. Meyer, ed., *The Magnificent Activist: The Writings of Thomas Wentworth Higginson* (New York: Da Capo, 2000); Joseph Moreau, *Schoolbook Nation: Conflicts over American History Textbooks from the Civil War to the Present* (Ann Arbor: University of Michigan Press, 2003), 14; Gregory M. Pfitzer, *History Repeating Itself: The Republication of Children's Historical Literature and the Christian Right* (Amherst: University of Massachusetts Press, 2014), 167.

135 Having met at Ohio's Oberlin College: Carol Faulkner, *Women's Radical Reconstruction: The Freedmen's Aid Movement* (Philadelphia: University of Pennsylvania Press, 2004), 36–42; Caroline F. Putnam to Samuel May, Jr., February 8, 1885, Samuel May, Jr., Papers, 1825–1903, box 1, MS N–536, Massachusetts Historical Society.

135 Higginson's exceptional text: Higginson, *Young Folks' History,* 54, 87, 92, 104, 117, 264–65, 268–69.

136 In detailing the political history: For this and the following paragraph, ibid., 272, 281–88. On the Garner case, see Steven Weisenburger, *Modern Medea: Family Story of Slavery and Child-Murder from the Old South* (New York: Hill & Wang, 1998). She is also the inspiration for Toni Morrison's Pulitzer Prize–winning novel *Beloved.*

138 Thereafter Higginson's narrative: Higginson, *Young Folks' History,* 281–88, 305–17, 329.

138 In Selma, Alabama: *Catalog of Burrell School, Selma, Alabama* (Selma: self-pub., 1875–76), 11–15; Joe M. Richardson, *Christian Reconstruction: The American Missionary Association and Southern Blacks, 1861–1890* (Athens: University of Georgia Press, 1986), 101–2, 164, 226–27, 241, 289; Hayden et al., eds., *Freedom: A Documentary History of Emancipation,* 2:617–18; *National Journal of Education,* March 16, 1880, 182; "Burrell Schools," Waymarking.com, https://www.waymarking.com/waymarks/WM3QE8_Marker_Burrell_Schools.

139 John J. Anderson's text: Anderson, *Grammar School History,* 21, 39, 136–41, 150–59, 184, 186.

140 But the textbook employed: Southland College, *Catalogue of Southland College and Normal Institute* (Helena, Ark.: M. Cullaton, 1882), 10, 180–82; for a brief history of Southland see https://encyclopediaofarkansas.net/entries/southland-college-361/.

140 Josiah W. Leeds's *A History of the United States:* Josiah W. Leeds, *A History of the United States of America . . . Designed for General Readers and for Academies*

(Philadelphia: J. B. Lippincott, 1877), 12, 27–28, 76; Josiah W. Leeds scrap-books, 1872–1907, special collections, MS.Coll.1102, Haverford College.

140 Leeds carefully wove slavery: Edmund S. Morgan, *American Slavery, American Freedom: The Ordeal of Colonial Virginia* (New York: W. W. Norton, 1975), 126–29, 216–18, 281–82; David Eltis and David Richardson, *Atlas of the Transatlantic Slave Trade* (New Haven, Conn.: Yale University Press, 2010), 18–19; Leeds, *History . . . Designed for General Readers,* 103–5, 240, 251–53, 269–71.

141 Leeds's textbook then recorded: Leeds, *History . . . Designed for General Read-ers,* 269–71, 370–73, 402–9, 427–28. On the early Quakers, see Jack D. Marietta, *The Reformation of American Quakerism, 1748–1783* (Philadelphia: University of Pennsylvania Press, 1984). For the Germantown petition against slavery, see "Germantown Friends' Protest Against Slavery, 1688," Library of Congress, https://www.loc.gov/resource/rbpe.14000200/?st=text. On English abolitionists, see Adam Hochschild, *Bury the Chains: Prophets and Rebels in the Fight to Free an Empire's Slaves* (Boston: Houghton Mifflin, 2005). On Elihu Burritt, see Merle Curti, *The Learned Blacksmith: Elihu Burritt* (New York: Garland, 1971). On Lundy and Garrison, see Henry Mayer, *All on Fire: William Lloyd Garrison and the Abolition of Slavery* (New York: St. Martin's Press, 1998).

142 In 1891 Southern Black schools: Elizabeth Zoe Vicary, "Edward Austin Johnson," in *African American National Biography,* eds. Henry Louis Gates, Jr., and Evelyn Brooks Higginbotham, 8 vols. (New York: Oxford University Press, 2008), 4:565–66; Mark Robert Schneider, *"We Return Fighting": The Civil Rights Movement in the Jazz Age* (Boston: Northeastern University Press, 2002), 262. On Shaw University, see https://docsouth.unc.edu/highlights/shaw.html; Edward A. Johnson's text appeared in two separate 1891 editions: *A School History of the Negro Race in America, 1619 to 1890* (Raleigh, N.C.: Capital, 1891) and also a self-published edition.

144 Black children should have the opportunity: Johnson, *A School History of the Negro Race in America,* iii–v, 9–11.

144 As tangible evidence of Black ability: For this and the following paragraph, ibid., 9–14, 27–39, 56–73, 84–87, 80–196; Johnson also published *History of Negro Soldiers in the Spanish-American War, and Other Items of Interest* (Raleigh, N.C.: Capital, 1899). On Nell, see his *The Colored Patriots of the American Revolution,* with an introduction by Harriet Beecher Stowe (Boston: Robert F. Wallcut, 1855).

145 A core set of textbooks published: William Cullen Bryant and Sydney How-ard Gay, *A Popular History of the United States,* 5 vols. (New York: Scribner, Armstrong, 1876–99), 4:315–20, 332–35, 435–36, 504, 544–45, 5:358–81. The popular work was written mostly by the former abolitionist Sydney Howard Gay and by 1899 reached five massive volumes totaling over three thousand pages. Volume four alone reached 648 pages. Rockford (Ill.) *Daily Register,* June 26, 1888; *New York Times,* December 9, 1875; San Francisco

Call Bulletin, February 20, 1876; Chicago *Daily Tribune,* August 3, 1878; *North American Review* 127 (November–December 1878): 509–11; Seattle *Daily Intelligencer,* June 4, 1879; Lawrence J. Friedman, *Gregarious Saints: Self and Community in American Abolitionism, 1830–1870* (Cambridge, U.K.: Cambridge University Press, 1982), 265; Eric Foner, *Gateway to Freedom: The Hidden History of the Underground Railroad* (New York: W. W. Norton, 2015), 182, 228–30.

146 Such popular texts and schoolbooks: On Stephens and Swails and their work in the South after the war, see my *A Voice of Thunder: A Black Soldier's Civil War* (Urbana: University of Illinois Press, 1998), especially 99–113 and 257n16; Thomas Holt, *Black over White: Negro Political Leadership in South Carolina During Reconstruction* (Urbana: University of Illinois Press, 1977), 74, 76–78, 109; and Gordon C. Rhea, *Stephen A. Swails: Black Freedom Fighter in the Civil War and Reconstruction* (Baton Rouge: Louisiana State University Press, 2021). For those who went south to help build freedom the literature is vast, but the best place to start is Willie Lee Rose, *Rehearsal for Reconstruction: The Port Royal Experiment* (New York: Vintage Books, 1964); Robert C. Morris, *Reading, 'Riting, and Reconstruction: The Education of Freedmen in the South, 1861–1870* (Chicago: University of Chicago Press, 1976); Russell Duncan, *Freedom's Shore: Tunis Campbell and the Georgia Freedmen* (Athens: University of Georgia Press, 1986); Joe M. Richardson, *Christian Reconstruction: The American Missionary Association and Southern Blacks, 1861–1890* (Athens: University of Georgia Press, 1986); James D. Anderson, *Education of Blacks in the South, 1860–1935* (Chapel Hill: University of North Carolina Press, 1989); Paul A. Cimbala, *Under the Guardianship of the Nation: The Freedmen's Bureau and the Reconstruction of Georgia, 1865–1870* (Athens: University of Georgia Press, 1997); Carol Faulkner, *Women's Radical Reconstruction: The Freedman Aid Movement* (Philadelphia: University of Pennsylvania Press, 2004).

146 "That to man may be given his birthright": Hezekiah Butterworth, "The Banner That Welcomes the World," *Advocate of Peace* 55 (May 1893): 99; Hezekiah Butterworth, "The Pestalozzian Celebration," *Journal of Education* 42 (December 1895): 417–18; *Watchman and Reflector,* May 28, 1874; "Review," *Journal of Education* 43 (April 1896): 267; "Our Book Table," *Journal of Education* 48 (October 1898): 274; Aberdeen (S.D.) *Daily News,* September 6, 1905; Riverside (Calif.) *Daily Press,* September 5, 1905; "Hezekiah Butterworth," *Journal of Education* 62 (September 1905): 326–27; Hezekiah Butterworth, *Young Folks' History of America* (Boston: Estes & Lauriat, 1882). Most secondary sources incorrectly cite the number of ZigZag books as sixteen, but in fact there are eighteen.

147 Little has been written about Butterworth: U.S. Census, 1840 and 1850; "Obituary," *New York Times,* September 6, 1905; Edwin M. Bacon and Richard Herndon, eds., *Men of Progress* (Boston: New England Magazine, 1896), 27; *National Cyclopedia of Biography,* vol. 2 (New York: James T.

White, 1899), 111; Hezekiah Butterworth, *A ZigZag Journey in the Sunny South* (Boston: Estes & Lauriat, 1886).

148 At first, his text said little: Butterworth, *Young Folks' History,* 72, 156, 340–44.

148 Rare for a children's text: For this and the following paragraph, ibid., 344–51.

149 After 1820 the entire nation fell: Ibid., 354–57.

149 After describing the hopeless condition: Ibid., 356–58.

150 As Higginson had done: Ibid., 383–87. Butterworth's account of Brown is also similar to the earlier one in William Cullen Bryant and Sydney Howard Gay, *A Popular History of the United States . . . ,* vol. 4 (New York: Charles Scribner's Sons, 1881), 429–31.

150 Butterworth possessed a marvelous ability: Butterworth, *Young Folks' History,* 388–404, 431–32.

151 Lincoln's Emancipation Proclamation was: Ibid., 435–36, 490–523.

152 One year after publication of Butterworth's book: Charles Carleton Coffin, *Building the Nation: Events in the History of the United States from the Revolution to the Beginning of the War Between the States* (New York: Harper & Bros., 1883), 5–6.

152 Coffin was born in rural Boscawen: "Charles Carleton Coffin," *Granite Monthly* 8 (April 1885): 99–106; William Elliot Griffis, *Charles Carleton Coffin, War Correspondent, Traveler, Author, and Statesman* (Boston: Estes & Lauriat, 1898), 34–43, 63–67, 264–65; J. Cutler Andrews, *The North Reports the Civil War* (Pittsburgh: University of Pittsburgh Press, 1955), 81–84; Charles Carleton Coffin, "First Lecture. Secret History of the Rebellion in the Civil War," n.d., Coffin papers, MSS 40, 17, New England Historic Genealogical Society.

154 During the 1850s, Coffin had worked: "Charles Carleton Coffin," *Granite Monthly,* 99–106; Griffis, *Charles Carleton Coffin,* 37–43, 69–75; Andrews, *North Reports the Civil War,* 81–84; John M. Taylor, "Following the Flag for the *Boston Journal*: The Career of Carleton Coffin," *Civil War Times Illustrated* 21 (September 1982): 40–45; George M. Adams, "Hon. Charles Carleton Coffin," *New England Historic Genealogical Register* 50 (July 1896): 291–92; Boston *Journal,* March 16, 1896; Charles Carleton Coffin, *Four Years of Fighting: A Volume of Personal Observation with the Army and Navy* (Boston: Ticknor & Fields, 1866).

155 Coffin well earned his fame: Coffin, *Four Years of Fighting,* iii, 1–7, 343–47, 416.

156 As he drank in the scene: Ibid., 343–47.

156 No wonder education mattered so much: Boston *Traveler,* September 10, 1857; Salem *Observer,* July 28, 1860; Boston *Daily Advertiser,* September 11, 1884; *Congregationalist,* October 4, 1876; "Reading for Teachers in the High School," *Journal of Education* 43 (January 16, 1896): 42; "American Institute Notes," *Journal of Education* 40 (July 19, 1894): 80–81; Tacoma (Wash.) *Daily News,* March 10, 1892; Adams, "Hon. Charles Carleton Coffin," 294; *Journal of Education* 38 (December 7, 1893): 363, and 42 (October 10, 1895): 250.

157 Coffin designed *Building the Nation:* Charles Carleton Coffin, *The Story of Liberty* (New York: Harper & Bros., 1878), 7; Charles Carleton Coffin, "About Cotton and Other Things," *Congregationalist,* April 24, 1878.

158 Fortified by unrivaled experience: Coffin, *Building the Nation,* 15, 17–20.

159 Coffin used the example of the Connecticut Yankee: Ibid., 74–77, 148, 282–90.

160 Having devoted a chapter to American race hatred: Ibid., 285–90, 305–13.

161 But as *Building the Nation* emphasized: Ibid., 387–415.

161 Given the irrepressible Southern desire: Ibid., 460–67.

5. Causes Lost and Found, 1883 to 1919

163 By the time Douglass mourned: David W. Blight, *Frederick Douglass: Prophet of Freedom* (New York: Simon & Schuster, 2018), 743, quoting Frederick Douglass, "The Lessons of the Hour" (speech), January 9, 1894, Iowa Department of Cultural Affairs, https://iowaculture.gov/history/education/educator-resources/primary-source-sets/reconstruction-and-its-impact/lessons-hour; William Gillett, *Retreat from Reconstruction, 1869–1879* (Baton Rouge: Louisiana State University Press, 1979), 188–89, 191, quoting the *Herald, The Independent,* and Gideon Welles.

164 Although the North always had disdained: Robert Penn Warren, *The Legacy of the Civil War: Meditations on the Centennial* (New York: Random House, 1961), 59.

164 James Shepherd Pike's: James Shepherd Pike, *The Prostrate State: South Carolina Under Negro Government* (New York: D. Appleton, 1874), 3–12; Foner, *Reconstruction,* 525–26; James M. McPherson, *The Abolitionist Legacy: From Reconstruction to the NAACP* (Princeton: Princeton University Press, 1975), 41; Robert F. Durden, "The Prostrate State Revisited: James S. Pike and South Carolina Reconstruction," *Journal of Negro History* 39 (April 1954): 87–88; Robert F. Durden, *James Shepherd Pike: Republicanism and the American Negro, 1850–1882* (Durham, N.C.: Duke University Press, 1957), 9–18.

165 Frederick Douglass led a small contingent: Durden, "The Prostrate State Revisited," 93; McPherson, *Abolitionist Legacy,* 42–43, 215; Portland (Me.) *Daily Press,* May 12, 1872; Chicago *Daily Tribune,* July 19, 1876, which carried details of Small's remarks in Congress; Columbia (S.C.) *Daily Phoenix,* July 29, 1874; Wilmington (Del.) *Daily Gazette,* October 21, 1876; Red Wing (Minn.) *Grange Advance,* March 4, 1874; Woodstock (Vt.) *Spirit of the Age,* January 29, 1874.

166 Pike had actually begun his assault: Durden, "The Prostrate State Revisited," 89–91; Heather Cox Richardson, *The Death of Reconstruction* (Cambridge, Mass.: Harvard University Press, 2001), 104–12, 202–3.

167 *The Prostrate State,* presumably based: Pike, *Prostrate State,* 61–63.

167 Instead of being victimized by: Ibid., 3–12, 29, 35, 58.

168   The world had turned upside down: Ibid., 15–19; Helen F. Giles, *How the United States Became a World Power* (New York: Charles E. Merrill, 1930), 1–14. Giles's book was also edited by Edgar Dawson, a history professor at Hunter College.

169   While the white North gloried: Steve Luxenberg, *Separate: The Story of Plessy v. Ferguson, and America's Journey from Slavery to Segregation* (New York: W. W. Norton, 2019), 361–62; David W. Blight, *Frederick Douglass: Prophet of Freedom* (New York: Simon & Schuster, 2018), 424–25; James Brewer Stewart, *Wendell Phillips: Liberty's Hero* (Baton Rouge: Louisiana State University Press), 98.

169   The 1898 report of the New England: New England History Teacher's Association, *Textbooks in American History: A Report Presented by the Committee on Textbooks, Oct. 15, 1898* (Boston: NEHTA, 1898), 9–10. Committee members included William McDonald from Bowdoin College, Charles F. A. Currier from MIT, Edward G. Bourne from Yale, Caroline Close from English High School in Cambridge, Mass., and J. Eston Phyee, a high school teacher in Hartford, Conn.; Marie Elizabeth Ruffin Carpenter, *The Treatment of the Negro in American History School Textbooks* (Menasha, Wis.: George Banta, 1941), 9–10.

170   The "science" that the NETA believed: Henry Steele Commager, "John Fiske: An Interpretation," *Proceedings of the Massachusetts Historical Society* 66 (October 1936–May 1941): 332–45; Michael Kraus, *A History of American History* (New York: Farrar & Rinehart, 1937), 371–79; Cynthia Eagle Russett, *Darwin in America: The Intellectual Response, 1865–1912* (San Francisco: W. H. Freeman, 1976), 48–54; Samuel Swett Green, *Reminiscences of John Fiske* (Worcester, Mass.: Charles Hamilton, 1902), 5.

170   In 1884 Fiske published: John Fiske, *The Destiny of Man, Viewed in the Light of His Origin* (Boston: Houghton Mifflin, 1884), 71–72, 86–92; Joseph Moreau, *Schoolbook Nation: Conflicts over American History Textbooks from the Civil War to the Present* (Ann Arbor: University of Michigan Press, 2003), 150.

171   Fiske's 1895 textbook: John Fiske, *A History of the United States for Schools* (Boston: Houghton Mifflin, 1895), 1–10, 71–73, 309–10.

172   Fiske offered no judgment: Ibid., 330–31, 351–53, 363–64.

173   Avoiding censure and blame: Ibid., 396–97, 413; G. P. Quackenbos, *Illustrated School History of the United States and the Adjacent Parts of America* (New York: D. Appleton, 1871), 460–61; Andrew C. McLaughlin and Claude Halstead Van Tyne, *A History of the United States for Schools*, 2 vols. (New York: D. Appleton, 1916), 2:49, 371–73; James Monteith, *Youth's History of the United States: Designed for Intermediate Classes in Public and Private Schools* (New York: A. S. Barnes, 1882), 15, 64–67, 304–23. A chronological list of questions and answers used in the North and the South said nothing about Black military service in the war; [North Carolina], *School Laws of North Carolina, as Ratified April 12, 1869* (Raleigh: M. S. Littlefield, 1869),

5, 35–37. For Southern views, see John A. Chapman, *School History of South Carolina* (Newberry, S.C.: Newberry, 1893), 214; Lida A. Field, *A Grammar School History of the United States* (New York: American Book, 1897), 330–31; W. N. McDonald and J. S. Blackburn, *A Southern School History of the United States of America* (Baltimore: George Lycett, 1869), 442, 458. McDonald and Blackburn did mention the battle at Fort Pillow on April 12, 1864, but entirely ignored Black participation and asserted that "quarter was, however, granted to those who asked for it."

173 All this set the stage: Fiske, *History of United States,* 343–45, 396–97; Hilary A. Herbert et al., *Why the Solid South: or, Reconstruction and Its Results* (Baltimore: R. H. Woodward, 1890), 1; Woodrow Wilson, *Division and Reunion, 1829–1889* (New York: Longmans, Green, 1893), 238; Henry E. Chambers, *A Higher History of the United States for Schools and Academies* (New York: University, 1889), 417–20; Alma Holman Burton, *The Story of Our Country: A Primary History of the United States* (Chicago: Werner School Book, 1896), 222–23; Oscar H. Cooper, Harry F. Estill, and Leonard Lemmon, *History of Our Country: A Text-book for Schools* (Boston: Ginn, 1898), 387–400; Mary Tucker Magill, *History of Virginia for the Use of Schools* (1873; reprint, Lynchburg, Va.: J. P. Bell, 1914), 292–93; Eva March Tappan, *Our Country's Story: An Elementary History of the United States* (Boston: Houghton Mifflin, 1902), 228; Josephus Nelson Larned, *A History of the United States for Secondary Schools* (Boston: Houghton Mifflin, 1903), 548, 562–75; Franklin L. Riley, J.A.C. Chandler, and J. G. de Roulhac Hamilton, *Our Republic: A History of the United States for Grammar Grades* (Richmond, Va.: Hunter, 1910), 399–400, 408–21; Nathaniel Wright Stephenson, *An American History* (Boston: Ginn, 1913), 466–68; Matthew Page Andrews, *History of the United States* (Philadelphia: J. B. Lippincott, 1914), 320–22; Perry and Price, *American History,* 2:219; McLaughlin and Van Tyne, *History for Schools,* 2:394–400; Eleanor E. Riggs, *An American History* (New York: Macmillan, 1916), 392–93; John Holladay Latané, *A History of the United States* (Boston: Allyn & Bacon, 1918), 424–48; William Backus Guitteau, *The History of the United States: A Textbook for Secondary Schools* (Boston: Houghton Mifflin, 1919), 465–79.

174 Fiske's and Pike's rendering of the war: Moreau, *Schoolbook Nation,* 66–67, 73, 138–39; Mindy Spearman, "Race in Elementary Geography Textbooks: Examples from South Carolina, 1890–1927," in Christine Woyshner and Chara Haeussler Bohan, eds., *Histories of Social Studies and Race: 1865–2000* (New York: Palgrave Macmillan, 2012), 115–34; Richardson, *Death of Reconstruction,* quoting the *New York Times,* 205.

174 Moreover, Fiske's and Pike's views: John David Smith and J. Vincent Lowery, eds., *The Dunning School: Historians, Race, and the Meaning of Reconstruction* (Lexington: University Press of Kentucky, 2013), 1–48, quoted 4; William A. Dunning, *Essays on the Civil War and Reconstruction and Related Topics* (New York: Macmillan, 1897), vii–viii, 250–51, 369.

175 Despite the influence of Fiske, Pike: Moreau, *Schoolbook Nation,* 73; Judith Ann Giesberg, "'To Forget and Forgive': Reconstructing the North in the Post-Civil War Classroom," *Civil War History* 52 (September 2006): 285, 295.

175 For the very youngest students: John Clark Ridpath, *History of the United States, Prepared Especially for Schools* (1876; reprint, Cincinnati: Jones Bros., 1878); Alfred S. Barnes, *A Popular History of the United States* (New York: A. S. Barnes, 1978); Alfred S. Barnes, *A Brief History of the United States: For Schools* (New York: A. S. Barnes, 1872), 50 quoted, 195–97, 242; Lucy Langdon Williams Wilson, *United States History in Elementary Schools* (New York: Macmillan, 1899), 1–3; George H. Boker, "The Black Regiment," in Charles Morris, ed., *Half-Hours with the Best American Authors* (Philadelphia: J. B. Lippincott, 1896), 3:227–29; Mary Sheldon Barnes, *Studies in American History: Teacher's Manual* (Boston: D. C. Heath, 1893), 80, 102, 106, 112–13, 131–32. On May, see my *Samuel Joseph May and the Dilemmas of the Liberal Persuasion, 1797–1871* (Philadelphia: Temple University Press, 1991), 180, passim.

176 At the close of the nineteenth century: 1905 New York State Census, ancestry .com; Atchison (Kans.) *Daily Globe,* December 29, 1887; Brooklyn *Daily Eagle,* December 11, 1906; Dallas *Morning News,* November 23, 1919; Jan Cohn, "The Civil War in Magazine Fiction of the 1860s," *Journal of Popular Culture* 4 (Fall 1970): 370.

178 Writing a book employing only: Helen W. Pierson, *History of the United States in Words of One Syllable* (New York: George Routledge & Sons, 1883), 19–20, 80–102, 107, 113, 129–30, 138–42, 145–47; Niles, *School History,* 228, 250, also discussed the draft riots and the terror attack on the Colored Orphan Asylum.

178 More advanced textbooks used: M. E. Thalheimer, *Eclectic History of the United States* (Cincinnati: Antwerp, Bragg, 1881), iii, 39–40, 78, 87–88, 144; Horace Scudder, *A History of the United States of America . . . for the Use of Schools and Academies* (Philadelphia: J. H. Butler, 1884), iv, 21, 71–72, 93–96, 116–19, 161–62, 170–72, 319–39, 369–74.

179 Mary Elsie Thalheimer's 1881 text: Arkansas *Gazette,* April 5, 1884; Southern Historical Society, *Papers* 12 (1884): 189; William Richard Cutter, *New England Families, Genealogical and Memorial: A Record of the Achievements of Her People in the Making of Commonwealths and the Founding of a Nation,* vol. 2 (New York: Lewis Historical, 1914), 1099; Thalheimer, *Eclectic History,* 296, 318; Scudder, *History of United States,* 400.

180 As the publications of Columbia University's: Louis Menand, *The Metaphysical Club: A Story of Ideas in America* (New York: Farrar, Straus & Giroux, 2001), 6–10, 22; Randall Kennedy, "Introduction: Blacks and the Race Question at Harvard," in Werner Sollors, Caldwell Titcomb, and Thomas A. Underwood, eds., *Blacks at Harvard: A Documentary History of African-American Experience at Harvard and Radcliffe* (New York: New York University Press, 1993), xvii.

181 Channing published a monumental: Michael Kraus, *A History of American History* (New York: Farrar & Rinehart, 1937), 438–52; Channing, *Students' History;* Channing, *The United States of America, 1765–1865* (Cambridge, U.K.: Cambridge University Press, 1896), 256 quoted.

181 His text reflected the then-common perception: Channing, *Students' History,* 140–43, 249–50, 297.

182 With enormous care and detail: Ibid., 423–27, 476–78, 498–501, 537–53.

183 On the issue of slavery, Channing: Ibid., 537–74.

183 Channing's assessments, despite their shortcomings: Kraus, *A History of American History,* 339; Carol F. Baird, "Albert Bushnell Hart: The Rise of the Professional Historian," in Paul Herman Buck, ed., *Social Sciences at Harvard, 1860–1920: From Inculcation to the Open Mind* (Cambridge, Mass.: Harvard University Press, 1965), 129–74. Harvard's Widener Library and the University Archives hold this astonishing collection of Hart's writings.

184 One cannot overemphasize Hart's importance: Albert Bushnell Hart, *Slavery and Abolition, 1831–1841* (New York: Harper & Bros., 1906); Hart, *Essentials in American History* (New York: American Book, 1905); Jacqueline Goggin, *Carter G. Woodson: A Life in Black History* (Baton Rouge: Louisiana State University Press, 1993), 22–29; David Levering Lewis, *W.E.B. Du Bois: Biography of a Race, 1868–1919* (New York: Henry Holt, 1993), 90, 112–13, 127, 197, 229, 294; Kelly Miller, *An Appeal to Conscience* (1918; reprint, New York: Arno Press, 1969), 10; August Meier and Elliott Rudwick, *Black History and the Historical Profession, 1915–1980* (Urbana: University of Illinois Press, 1986), 77–78, 94–100; Baird, "Albert Bushnell Hart," 149; Mary White Ovington, *The Walls Came Tumbling Down* (New York: Harcourt, Brace, 1947), 102–4.

185 Hart understood, as so many: Miller, *Appeal to Conscience,* 10; Baird, "Albert Bushnell Hart," 154; Hart, *Slavery and Abolition,* 79–85, 143–45, 170–75, 180–99, 203, 208–9, 215, 322.

186 His 1905 *Essentials in American History:* Hart, *Essentials in American History,* 347–51, 397–98.

186 As for slavery, Hart contextualized it: Ibid., 99–101, 344–45, 406–7, 460.

186 But Hart's work collided: Ibid., 344–45, 491–510; Woodrow Wilson, *Division and Reunion, 1829–1889* (New York: Longmans, Green, 1893).

187 Dunning's scholarship had rejected: William A. Dunning, *Reconstruction, Political and Economic, 1865–1877,* The American Nation series, vol. 22 (New York: Harper & Bros., 1907), 24–29, 32–34, 57–58, 122, 175.

187 Hart, one of the most influential voices: Dunning, *Reconstruction,* xiii–xiv; Moreau, *Schoolbook Nation,* 84–86.

188 Despite the shortcomings of textbooks: David H. Montgomery, *The Leading Facts of American History* (Boston: Ginn, 1895), 59–60, 196–97; Thomas Hunter, *A Narrative History of the United States, for the Use of Schools* (New York: American Book, 1896), 46; William A. Mowry and Arthur May Mowry,

A History of the United States for Schools (New York: Silver, Burdett, 1896), 97, 267–69.

189 At the beginning of the twentieth century: Thomas Bonaventure Lawler, *Essentials of American History* (Boston: Ginn, 1902), 55–56, 224–25; Davidson, *History of United States,* 69, 147–49, 254; William M. Davidson, *A History of the United States* (Chicago: Scott Foresman, 1906), 69, 148–49, 254; James Alton James and Albert Hart Sanford, *American History* (New York: Charles Scribner's Sons, 1910), 43–44, 130–31; Francis Newton Thorpe, *A History of the American People* (Chicago: A. C. McClurg, 1901), 37, 144–45, 311; Tappan, *Our Country's Story,* 50–51, 129, 173.

189 As William H. Mace explained: William H. Mace, *A School History of the United States* (Chicago: Rand McNally, 1904), 34–35, 219–21; Larned, *History for Secondary Schools,* 75–76, 308–9; Henry William Elson, *School History of the United States* (New York: Macmillan, 1912), 46–47, 130; Charles Kendall Adams and William P. Trent, *A History of the United States* (Boston: Allyn & Bacon, 1903), 28, 67, 250; John Bach McMaster, *A School History of the United States* (New York: American Book, 1897), 33–34; William Estabrook Chancellor, *A Text Book of American History* (New York: Silver, Burdett, 1903), 85.

190 These same histories built on: Giesberg, "'To Forget and Forgive,'" 286–87; Niles, *School History,* 178–79, 184–85, 194–96.

190 For beginning readers: Burton, *Story of Our Country,* 212–15; H. A. Guerber, *The Story of the Great Republic* (New York: American Book, 1899), 122–24; Hunter, *Narrative History,* 221, 249–51, 259, 262–69.

191 From 1896 to 1912: Mowry and Mowry, *History of the United States for Schools,* 269–74; Adams and Trent, *History of the United States,* 281–83, 328; Wilbur F. Gordy, *A History of the United States for Schools* (New York: Charles Scribner's Sons, 1898), 287–89; Thorpe, *History of American People,* 388–97; Lawler, *Essentials of American History,* 237–38; Davidson, *History of United States* (1902), 327–29, 337, 353; Tappan, *Our Country's Story,* 195–96, 199; Chancellor, *Text Book of American History,* 337–39; Larned, *History for Secondary Schools,* 405–11; Mace, *School History,* 300–302; James and Sanford, *American History,* 314–18; Edmond S. Meany, *United States History for Schools* (New York: Macmillan, 1912), 348–49, 364–65; H. W. Elson, *School History,* 214, 286–88.

191 John Brown eventually emerged: Niles, *School History,* 198; Montgomery, *Leading Facts,* 278–79; Larned, *History for Secondary Schools,* 473–74; Adams and Trent, *History of the United States,* 336–37; Mace, *School History,* 329; Tappan, *Our Country's Story,* 206; Davidson, *History of United States* (1902, 1906), 374–76; Lawler, *Essentials of American History,* 286–87, 312–13.

192 These same textbooks agreed: Gordy, *History of the United States for Schools,* 318; Larned, *History for Secondary Schools,* 381–82; Mowry and Mowry, *History of the United States for Schools,* 280–81; Chancellor, *Text Book of American History,* 359; Thorpe, *History of American People,* 436; Davidson, *A History of*

the United States (1902), 379, 423; Adams and Trent, *History of United States,* 306, 312, 320–21, 348; H. W. Elson, *School History,* 329–30.

192 While most textbooks—even some: Tappan, *Our Country's Story,* 218, 225; Mace, *School History,* 338–85, while celebrating emancipation, failed to mention Black Civil War service; Larned, *History for Secondary Schools,* 534; Hunter, *Narrative History,* 320; Niles, *School History,* 200–201, 226–27, 246; Mowry and Mowry, *History of the United States for Schools,* 314; Albert F. Blaisdell, *The Story of American History for Elementary Schools* (Boston: Ginn, 1901), 368; Gordy, *History of the United States for Schools,* 349–50.

193 The history of Reconstruction gave: Leeds, *History . . . Designed for General Readers,* 433–35; Johnston, *History of American Politics,* 196–201; Niles, *School History,* 255–60; Scudder, *History of United States,* 412–16; Chancellor, *Text Book of American History,* 376–86; Davidson, *History of United States* (1906), 461–78; Thorpe, *History of American People,* 468–73. Thorpe, a lawyer and constitutional scholar, also crafted a junior high school textbook that, while far simpler in content, placed emphasis on Black suffrage. Thorpe, *A School History of the United States* (New York: Hinds, Noble & Eldredge, 1900), 216–19.

194 These textbooks retained a surprising level: Boston *Herald,* December 12, 1905; Washington *Bee,* December 23, 1905.

194 Just seven years later: Hilary A. Herbert, *The Abolition Crusade and Its Consequences . . .* (New York: Charles Scribner's Sons, 1912), 46–49, 57–59, 74–75 226.

195 Herbert's white supremacist view: Herbert et al., *Why the Solid South* (1890); Kraus, *A History of American History,* 380–95; Ellis Paxson Oberholtzer, "John Bach McMaster, 1852–1932," *Pennsylvania Magazine of History and Biography* 57 (1933): 1–31; McMaster, *School History.*

195 McMaster's *School History:* McMaster, *School History,* 312–15, 342–59, 379–80.

196 But when it came to Reconstruction: Ibid., 429, 439–40; John Bach McMaster, *The Acquisition of Political, Social, and Industrial Rights of Man in America* (Cleveland: Western Reserve University, 1903), 71–72.

197 In the 1880s, as Hezekiah Butterworth: Moreau, *Schoolbook Nation,* 79–83; Wade H. Morris and Chara Haessler Bohan, "Teaching to a Statue: John B. Gordon, History Textbooks, and the Creation of a Lost Cause Hero," in Tina L. Heafner, Laura K. Handler, and Tracy C. Rock, eds., *The Divide Within: Intersections of Realities, Facts, Theories, and Practices* (Charlotte, N.C.: Information Age, 2021), 133–50; George Frederick Holmes, *New School History of the United States* (New York: University, 1886), 1–92, 164, 229–30; John McCardell, *The Idea of a Southern Nation* (New York: W. W. Norton, 1979), 209–15; Edward A. Eggleston, *A History of the United States and Its People: For the Use of Schools* (New York: D. Appleton, 1888), 359–61; Edward A. Eggleston, *A Household History of the United States and Its People for Young Americans* (New York: D. Appleton, 1896), 352–55; Cooper, Estill,

and Lemmon, *History of Our Country*, iv; McDonald and Blackburn, *Southern School History*, 342–81; Blaisdell, *Story of American History for Elementary Schools*, 358–63; Chambers, *Higher History*, 121, 327; Burton, *Story of Our Country*, 222–23; Monteith, *Youth's History*, 65–70, employed almost identical language: after the war all the soldiers "returned quietly to their houses and occupations." Blaisdell, *Story of American History for Elementary Schools*, 406; Joel Dorman Steele and Esther Baker Steele, *A Brief History of the United States* (New York: American Book, 1885), 2, 172–73, 193–98, 242–44, 281–88. The Steeles' text was first published in 1871.

198 Educators already had insisted that any: M. S. Barnes, *Studies in American History*, 6; Ridpath, *History of United States*, v, 63, 303.

198 The Emancipationist Hezekiah Butterworth: Hezekiah Butterworth, *A ZigZag Journey in the Sunny South* (Boston: Estes & Lauriat, 1886), 20, 78, 180; *New York Times*, June 15, 1903.

200 From the late 1880s to 1919: Lawton B. Evans, *The Essential Facts of American History* (Boston: Benj. H. Sanborn, 1909), 53, 171–72, 257; Harry F. Estill, *The Beginner's History of Our Country* (Dallas: Southern, 1919), 51, 62, 134–41; R. B. Cousins and J. A. Hill, *American History for Schools* (Boston: D. C. Heath, 1913), 53–54, 136; Perry and Price, *American History*, 2:135–46; Eggleston, *Household History*, 104–7; Eggleston, *United States and Its People*, 104–9; Wilson, *Division and Reunion*, 124–26; Edna Henry Lee Turpin, *A Short History of the American People* (New York: Macmillan, 1911), 268; Evans, *Essential Facts*, 348–49; David Henry Montgomery, *The Beginner's American History* (Boston: Ginn, 1899), 144, 211–15; Meany, *United States History*, 70, 139–42.

201 A few authors acknowledged that slavery: Elisha Benjamin Andrews, *History of the United States*, 2 vols. (New York: Scribner, 1894), 1:33, 342–45, 2:3–5; Waddy Thompson, *A History of the United States* (Boston: D. C. Heath, 1919), 285–87; Guitteau, *History of United States*, 63–64, 132, 291. Willis Mason West, *History of the American People* (Boston: Allyn & Bacon, 1918), 504–9; McLaughlin and Van Tyne, *History for Schools*, 1:129. McLaughlin had published his own textbook, which was in its tenth edition in 1905. In that text he also denounced "carpetbaggers" as corrupt and announced that Reconstruction proved that "slavery had been a poor schoolmaster for freedom." Andrew C. McLaughlin, *A History of the American Nation* (New York: D. Appleton, 1906), 470–78, 483; John Spencer Bassett, *A Short History of the United States* (New York: Macmillan, 1913), 428–31, 470–71; Cousins and Hill, *American History for Schools*, 316–17; Chambers, *Higher History*, 354.

202 In this period, when it came to slavery, U.S. histories: For this and the following paragraph, see Holmes, *New School History* (Holmes's book first appeared in 1870); Field, *Grammar School History*, 255–56; Chapman, *School History of South Carolina*, 43; Henry Alexander White, *The Making of South Carolina* (New York: Silver, Burdett, 1906), 22, 49, 69; Riley, Chandler, and Hamilton, *Our Republic*, 60–61, 139–43, 266–67 (*Our Republic*, like

Magill's book), enjoyed a long publishing life and remained in print as late as 1932); Magill, *History of Virginia,* 61, 232–34, 242–44; R. G. Hall, Harriet Smither and Clarence Ousley, *The Student's History of Our Country for Grammar Grades* (1912; reprint, Dallas: Southern, 1914), 256–57; Estill, *Beginner's History,* 258–60; John Esten Cooke, *Virginia: A History of the People* (Boston: Houghton Mifflin, 1884), 123–24, 366–67, 507–8; McDonald and Blackburn, *Southern School History,* 44–45. These authors claimed to have published the first U.S. history for the South.

204 Textbook assessments of the antislavery movement: Eggleston, *United States and Its People,* 292–356; Eggleston, *Household History,* 295–300; Riggs, *American History,* 318–19, 323; Montgomery, *Leading Facts,* 237–38, 266–69; Emerson David Fite, *History of the United States* (New York: Henry Holt, 1916), 288–90; Stephenson, *American History,* 329–33; Perry and Price, *American History,* 2:153; Wilson, *Division and Reunion,* 120–22; M. P. Andrews, *History of United States,* 229–32, 253; E. B. Andrews, *History of United States,* 2:17–20; Evans, *Essential Facts,* 349–54, 358; Turpin, *Short History,* 266–67; Cousins and Hill, *American History for Schools,* 317–26; William E. Dodd, *Expansion and Conflict* (Boston: Houghton Mifflin, 1915), 161–83; McLaughlin and Van Tyne, *History for Schools,* 2:312–20; Latané, *History of United States,* 308–13.

205 The anti-Emancipationist eruption: For specific Southern views, see Susan Pendleton Lee, *A Brief History of the United States . . . Prepared for Use in Public and Private Schools* (Richmond, Va.: B. F. Johnson, 1896), 187, 225; John William Jones, *School History of the United States,* rev. ed. (New York: University, 1901), 188–89; Field, *Grammar School History,* 271; McDonald and Blackburn, *Southern School History,* 388–89; Cooper, Estill, and Lemmon, *History of Our Country,* 288–96, 332; Magill, *History of Virginia,* 245–48; Riley, Chandler, and Hamilton, *Our Republic,* 312–14, 322–23; Hall, Smither, and Ousley, *Student's History . . . for Grammar Grades,* 257–59; Cousins and Hill, *American History for Schools,* 363–64; Wilson, *Division and Reunion,* 202–3. For more general-use texts, see Mowry and Mowry, *History of the United States for Schools,* 278–79; Eggleston, *Household History,* 305; H. W. Elson, *School History,* 323–24; James and Sanford, *American History,* 364, 367; Turpin, *Short History,* 278–79; Chancellor, *Text Book of American History,* 358; McLaughlin and Van Tyne, *History for Schools,* 2:344–45; Charles Morris, *School History of the United States of America* (Philadelphia: J. B. Lippincott, 1916), 319–20; Fite, *History of United States,* 342–43; Guerber, *Story of the Great Republic,* 158–59; Estill, *Beginner's History,* 260–61.

205 We are accustomed to hearing arguments: Cynthia Greenlee, "How History Textbooks Reflect America's Refusal to Reckon with Slavery," *Vox,* August 26, 2019.

206 A few Southern states: Caroline E. Janney, *Burying the Dead but Not the Past: Ladies Memorial Associations and the Lost Cause* (Chapel Hill: University of North Carolina Press, 2008), 172–73; White, *Making of South Carolina,*

223; McDonald and Blackburn, *Southern School History*, 257–58, 394–95; Cooper, Estill, and Lemmon, *History of Our Country*, 339–40; Magill, *History of Virginia*, 251–95; Riley, Chandler, and Hamilton, *Our Republic*, 335–40; Field, *Grammar School History*, 5, 308–9; Lee, *Brief History*, 230–31.

206   But these very same texts went on to detail: White, *Making of South Carolina*, 217–18; Field, *Grammar School History*, 286–98; Lee, *Brief History*, 181–82, 201; Mary Tucker Magill, *Stories from Virginia History for the Young* (Lynchburg, Va.: J. P. Bell, 1897), 153–54, 159; McDonald and Blackburn, *Southern School History*, 342, 382–83; Chambers, *Higher History*, 362–63; Turpin, *Short History*, 27–28, 53–54, 94–95, 191, 231, 279–82; Cousins and Hill, *American History for Schools*, 313–14.

207   From a Southern point of view: Cooper, Estill, and Lemmon, *History of Our Country*, 390–92; McDonald and Blackburn, *Southern School History*, 480–85; Chambers, *Higher History*, 352–53; Alexander H. Stephens, *A Compendium of the History of the United States . . .* (Columbia, S.C.: W. J. Duffie, 1872), 419 quoted, 249, 257, 326–29, 395–407, 479–80.

208   Similarly, Reconstruction always had been: Lee Anna Keith, *The Colfax Massacre: The Untold Story of Black Power, White Terror, and the Death of Reconstruction* (New York: Oxford University Press, 2008); Heather Cox Richardson, *The Death of Reconstruction: Race, Labor, and Politics in the Post-Civil War North, 1865–1901* (Cambridge, Mass.: Harvard University Press, 2001), 17, 28–31, 142–43; Douglas R. Egerton, *The Wars of Reconstruction: The Brief, Violent History of America's Most Progressive Era* (New York: Bloomsbury, 2014), 17–19, 290–93, 296, 304–7; Equal Justice Initiative, *Lynching in America: Confronting the Legacy of Racial Terror* (Montgomery, Ala.: Equal Justice Initiative, 2017), 4.

209   Beginning in the 1890s: Moreau, *Schoolbook Nation*, 57, 166; Wilson, *Division and Reunion*, 268–69; Lawler, *Essentials of American History*, 327–45; Alexander Johnston and Winthrop More Daniels, *A History of the United States for Schools* (New York: Henry Holt, 1897), 367–73, 380–82; Fite, *History of United States*, 416–17; Tappan, *Our Country's Story*, 230; Estill, *Beginner's History*, 275; Field, *Grammar School History*, 364–66; White, *Making of South Carolina*, 290–92; Magill, *History of Virginia*, 293; Montgomery, *Leading Facts*, 328–29; Perry and Price, *American History*, 2:225–29; Jacques Wardlaw Redway, *The Making of the American Nation: A History for Elementary Schools* (New York: Silver, Burdett, 1905), 270.

210   Northern educators and academics: Elisha Benjamin Andrews, *The History of the Last Quarter-Century in the United States, 1870–1895*, 2 vols. (New York: Scribner, 1896), 1:38, 120–24. Also see E. B. Andrews, *History of United States; Evans, Essential Facts*, 440–41; Turpin, *Short History*, 331–36; Meany, *United States History*, 449–56; Henry Eldridge Bourne and Elbert Jay Benton, *A History of the United States* (1913; reprint, Boston: D. C. Heath, 1919), 442.

211   As Pike, Dunning, McMaster: Thomas Dixon, Jr., *The Reconstruction Trilogy: The Leopard's Spots, The Clansman, The Traitor*, ed. Sam Dickson (Newport

Beach, Calif.: Noontide Press, 1994), 32–33, 99–100; Laura Martin Rose [Mrs. S.E.F. Rose], *The Ku Klux Klan; or, Invisible Empire* (New Orleans: L. Graham, 1914), 7–17, 51.

212 In a 1901 history published simultaneously: Jones, *School History,* 410–11; James and Sanford, *American History,* 430–31; Riley, Chandler, and Hamilton, *Our Republic,* 408–21; Hall, Smither, and Ousley, *Student's . . . History for Grammar Grades,* 388–94; Adams and Trent, *History of United States,* 448–54; Mace, *School History,* 388–93; Gordy, *History of the United States for Schools,* 376–83; Thompson, *History of United States,* 407–24, 429–31, 439.

213 In a speech before the Wisconsin Bar Association: Moorfield Storey, *The Negro Question: An Address Delivered Before the Wisconsin Bar Association . . .* (New York: NAACP, 1918), 17–19.

6. Educating for "Eugenocide" in the 1920s

215 The Vermont-born educator Lucy Langdon Williams Wilson: William Gould Vinal, "Mrs. Lucy Langdon Williams Wilson," *Science Education* 42 (December 1958): 456–59; Lucy Langdon Williams Wilson, *History Reader for Elementary Schools* (1898; reprint, New York: Macmillan, 1929), 5–25, 29, 43, 122, 127. Wilson also published a brief history teacher's manual: *United States History in Elementary Schools* (New York: Macmillan, 1899). For the portrait by Eakins, see "Portrait of Lucy Langdon Williams Wilson," at https://www.thomaseakins.org/Portrait-Of-Lucy-Langdon-Williams-Wilson.html; Mary Gertrude Kelty, *Teaching American History in the Middle Grades of Elementary School* (Boston: Ginn, 1928), 532–33; Walter Scott Monroe, *Objectives of United States History in Grades Seven and Eight* (Urbana, Ill.: Bureau of Educational Research, 1926), 36–47, 50; Bessie Louise Pierce, *Civic Attitudes in American School Textbooks* (Chicago: University of Chicago Press, 1930), 90–91.

216 The new century's mounting white anxiety: Donald Yacovone, "Race, Radicalism, and Remembering Wendell Phillips," in A J Aiséirithe and Donald Yacovone, eds., *Wendell Philips, Social Justice, and the Power of the Past* (Baton Rouge: Louisiana State University Press, 2016), 296 quoted; Donald Yacovone, "An 'Eminent Negro Artist': Cloyd Lee Boykin, the Legacy of Boston Abolitionism, and the Era of the Harlem Renaissance," *Massachusetts Historical Review* 20 (2018): 75–117; W.E.B. Du Bois, "The American Negro at Paris," *American Monthly Review of Reviews* 22 (November 1900): 577. The exhibition's images can be viewed at "African American Photographs Assembled for 1900 Paris Exposition," Library of Congress, www.loc.gov/pictures/collection/anedub/dubois.html. Mark Robert Schneider, *"We Return Fighting": The Civil Rights Movement in the Jazz Age* (Boston: Northeastern University Press, 2002); Henry Louis Gates, Jr., and Gene Andrew Jarrett, eds., *The New Negro: Readings on Race, Representation, and African American Culture, 1892–1938* (Princeton: Princeton University Press, 2007).

216 But once again, the more freedom: Moorfield Storey, "NAACP Presidential
      Address," March 30, 1911, Moorfield Storey Papers, N–2197, Box 12, Mas-
      sachusetts Historical Society; "Re-Forging America," Springfield *Republican,*
      February 12, 1928; Pierce, *Civic Attitudes in American School Textbooks,*
      84–87; Waddy Thompson, *The First Book in United States History* (Boston:
      D. C. Heath, 1921), 294.

217 Immigration rendered "true" American identity: For this and the follow-
      ing paragraph, T. Lothrop Stoddard, "White Disunion will Inevitably Lose
      Us our Race Heritage," San Jose *Evening News,* May 1, 1916; I am adapting
      Richard Hofstadter's use of "psychic crisis" in his famed essay, "Cuba, The
      Philippines, and Manifest Destiny," in *The Paranoid Style in American Poli-
      tics and Other Essays* (Chicago: University of Chicago Press, 1965), 145–87;
      George M. Marsden, *Fundamentalism and American Culture: The Shaping of
      Twentieth-Century Evangelicalism, 1870–1925* (New York: Oxford University
      Press, 1980), 153; Alfred L. Brophy, *Reconstructing the Dreamland: The Tulsa
      Riot of 1921. Race, Reparations, and Reconciliation* (New York: Oxford Univer-
      sity Press, 2002).

218 From Coatesville, Pennsylvania: Dennis B. Downey and Raymond M. Hyser,
      *No Crooked Death: Coatesville, Pennsylvania and the Lynching of Zachariah
      Walker* (Urbana: University of Illinois Press, 1991); Philip Dray, *At the Hands
      of Persons Unknown: The Lynching of Black America* (New York: Random
      House, 2002); Charles L. Lumpkins, *American Pogrom: The East St. Louis
      Race Riot and Black Politics* (Athens: Ohio University Press, 2008); Robert
      Whitaker, *On the Laps of Gods: The Red Summer of 1919 and the Struggle
      for Justice That Remade a Nation* (New York: Crown Publishers, 2008), 31,
      37–47, 53–54.

219 While nothing could match: Whitaker, *On the Laps of Gods,* 37–38; Julie
      Buckner Armstrong, *Mary Turner and the Memory of Lynching* (Athens:
      University of Georgia Press, 2011); Reneé Ater, *Remaking Race and History:
      The Sculpture of Meta Warrick Fuller* (Berkeley: University of California Press,
      2011). Fuller executed one of the few memorial sculptures of Turner.

219 Reborn in 1915, the Ku Klux Klan: Linda Gordon, *The Second Coming of
      the KKK: The Ku Klux Klan of the 1920s and the American Political Tradition*
      (New York: Liveright, 2017); Gillian Brockell, "A White Mob Unleashed the
      Worst Election Day Violence in U.S. History in Florida a Century Ago,"
      Washington Post, November 2, 2020, quoted.

220 For a time, Klan subsidiaries (Klaverns): Gordon, *Second Coming of the KKK,*
      quoted 116.

221 That very soul had become contested ground: John Jay Chapman, *William
      Lloyd Garrison* (New York: Moffett Yard, 1918). Chapman published a revised
      edition in 1921; Richard B. Hovey, *John Jay Chapman: An American Mind*
      (New York: Columbia University Press, 1959), remains the standard biog-
      raphy; Downey and Hyser, *No Crooked Death,* 118–19; John Jay Chapman,
      "Harvard and the Negro," in John Jay Chapman Notebooks #10, John Jay

Chapman Papers, MsAm1854, Houghton Library, Harvard University. Also see Nell Irvin Painter, "Jim Crow at Harvard: 1923," *New England Quarterly* 44 (December 1971): 627–34.

223 Chapman never betrayed: John Jay Chapman to Mama [Eleanor Jay Chapman], September 21, 1883 and April 8–9, 1899, John Jay Chapman Papers, MsAm1854, Houghton Library, Harvard University; Charles Darwin, *The Descent of Man, and Selection in Relation to Sex* (1871; reprint, New York: D. Appleton, 1882), 20, 54; Cynthia Eagle Russett, *Darwinism in America: The Intellectual Response, 1865–1912* (San Francisco: W. H. Freeman, 1976), 89.

223 The First World War: John Jay Chapman to Theodore Roosevelt, May 25, 1917, John Jay Chapman Papers, MsAm1854, Houghton Library, Harvard University; Norman Cohn, *Warrant for Genocide: The Myth of the Jewish World Conspiracy and the Protocols of the Elders of Zion* (New York: Harper & Row, 1969), 158–59.

224 That as sophisticated an author: John Jay Chapman to William James, October 23, 1908, "Program for 'The Hermits, a Sylvan Comedy for Children,'" November 5 and 9, 1908, John Jay Chapman Papers, MsAm1854; Meyer Daniel Rothschild to John Jay Chapman, October 5, 1912, Additional John Jay Chapman Papers, MsAm1854.8; and Chapman, "Memoir of Isaac H. Klein," January 11, 1920, John Jay Chapman Papers, MsAm1854.1, all in Houghton Library, Harvard University. For Klein, see "Obituary," New York *Daily Tribune,* July 7, 1919; "Death Index," Klein, www.ancestry.com. Chapman's 1897 remarks are quoted in, Edmund Wilson, "Notes on Gentile Pro-Semitism: New England's 'Good Jews,'" *Commentary* (October 1956): 329–35. While Chapman was not Jewish, his mother's Jay family did have Jewish ancestors through the Iselin family. "Iselin Family Tree 127 Genealogy," WikiTree.com, at www.wikitree.com/genealogy/Iselin-Family-Tree–127.

224 But Chapman's personal relationships: Meyer D. Rothschild to John Jay Chapman, October 9, 1920, John Jay Chapman to Louis Marshall, December 13, 1920, John Jay Chapman, Additional Papers, MsAm1854.1; and John Jay Chapman to Mama [Eleanor Jay Chapman], October 28, 1920, Chapman Papers, MsAm1854, all in Houghton Library, Harvard University.

225 With each passing year: John Jay Chapman to Fernand Bladen, November 11, 1921, John Jay Chapman to Ernest Hamlin Abbott, February 5, 1924, John Jay Chapman to Ralph Adams Cram, November 28, 1924, John Jay Chapman Papers, MsAm1854, Houghton Library, Harvard University.

226 In April 1925 Chapman went public: Frank Luther Mott, *A History of American Magazine, 1885–1905,* 4 vols. (Cambridge, Mass.: Harvard University Press, 1957), 4:511–23; John Jay Chapman, "Strike at the Source," *Forum* 73 (April 1925): 449–57, John Jay Chapman Papers, MsAm1854, Houghton Library, Harvard University.

226 Chapman's *Forum* outburst: John Jay Chapman Notebooks #7, John Jay Chapman to Charles Cist, March 3, 1925, Milton Elrod to John Jay Chapman, May 7, 1925 (Elrod is the Klansman quoted), William A. Hamlett to

John Jay Chapman, May 21, 1925, John Jay Chapman to Mary Winslow, May 31, 1925, John Jay Chapman Papers, MsAm1854, Houghton Library, Harvard University.

227 While Chapman received an occasional rebuke: Albert Bushnell Hart and Paul Fuller both expressed opposition to Chapman's radical views: Albert Bushnell Hart to John Jay Chapman, November 20, 1924, Paul Fuller to John Jay Chapman, December 2 and 12, 1924, Jane Partridge Danziger to John Jay Chapman, December 2, 1924, Katherine S. Day to John Jay Chapman, November 19, 1924, Albert Charles Dieffenbach to John Jay Chapman, January 14, 1925, John Jay Chapman Papers, MsAm1854, Houghton Library Harvard University.

227 But perhaps Chapman made his most damaging: James Q. Whitman, *Hitler's American Model: The United States and the Making of Nazi Race Law* (Princeton: Princeton University Press, 2017), 1–27, 34–38, 45–47, 113 quoted; Jonathan Peter Spiro, *Defending the Master Race: Conservation, Eugenics, and the Legacy of Madison Grant* (Burlington: University of Vermont Press, 2009), xi–xii, 155–66; Jennifer Szalai, "'Unworthy Republic': Takes an Unflinching Look at Indian Removal in the 1830s," *New York Times,* March 24, 2020; Madison Grant to John Jay Chapman, November 17, 1924, and March 27, 1925, John Jay Chapman Papers, MsAm1854, Houghton Library, Harvard University.

228 The eugenics movement that catapulted: Spiro, *Defending the Master Race,* 119–21; Edward A. Ross, *Seventy Years of It: An Autobiography of Edward Alsworth Ross* (New York: D. Appleton–Century, 1936), 233.

229 Galton's ideas about eugenics: Dennis B. Downey and James W. Conroy, eds., *Pennhurst and the Struggle for Disability Rights* (University Park: Pennsylvania State University Press, 2020), 1–6, 18–19, 23–24; Sol Gittleman, "When Bigotry Was a Science," *Tufts Magazine* (Fall 2017): 46–49; Zoe Burkholder, *Color in the Classroom: How American Schools Taught Race, 1900–1954* (New York: Oxford University Press, 2011), 57–58.

229 Eugenics, masquerading as: William Robinson, *Eugenics, Marriage, and Birth Control* (New York: Critic and Guide, 1917), 13–18, 63, 70–71, 79, 81.

230 Robinson and better-known eugenicists: Spiro, *Defending the Master Race,* 155–56, 166, 242–43; Prescott Hall, *Immigration and Its Effects upon the United States* (New York: Henry Holt, 1906), 176.

230 Similarly, the Harvard-trained: Ellsworth Huntington, "A Neglected Factor in Race Development," *Journal of Race Development* 6 (October 1915): 169; Ellsworth Huntington, *The Character of Races as Influenced by Physical Environment, Natural Selection and Historical Development* (New York: Charles Scribner's Sons, 1924), 60; Ellsworth Huntington, *Principles of Human Geography* (New York: J. Wiley & Sons, 1947), 348–49; Ellsworth Huntington, *Tomorrow's Children: The Goals of Eugenics* (New York: J. Wiley & Sons, 1935), 10. For his racial theories of human geography, see Huntington's revolting study *The Red Man's Continent: A Chronicle of Aboriginal America*

(New Haven, Conn.: Yale University Press, 1920). Throughout the era, geography and world history textbooks continued Noah Webster's assessment that the "dark continent" possessed no history and was occupied by "hewers of wood and drawers of water." See Gary Nash, Charlotte Crabtree, and Ross E. Dunn, *History on Trial: Culture Wars and the Teaching of the Past* (New York: Alfred A. Knopf, 1997), 47–51.

231 Edward A. Ross, who coined: For this and following paragraph, Nell Irvin Painter, *The History of White People* (New York: W. W. Norton, 2010), 251–53; Edward A. Ross, "The Causes of Race Superiority," *Annals of the American Academy of Political and Social Science* 18 (July 1901): 67–89; Ross, *Seventy Years of It*, 67–68, 126, 144–45, 152–53, 190, 198, 276–77.

232 But not even Ross could match: Painter, *History of White People*, 318–21; Lothrop Stoddard, *The Rising Tide of Color Against White World Supremacy* (New York: Scribner's Sons, 1920), v–vi, 14, 88, 196–97. Stoddard actually participated in a 1929 public debate with Du Bois in Chicago before a largely African American audience that thundered its support for Du Bois and mocked Stoddard after Du Bois exclaimed, "Who in Hell asked to marry your daughters?" David Levering Lewis, *W.E.B. Du Bois: The Fight for Equality and the American Century, 1919–1963* (New York: Henry Holt, 2000), 235–37.

233 In 1922, inspired by Stoddard's: Paul Y. Anderson, "2 Colored Men in the World for Every White One: How Long Can Whites Dominate the Earth?," St. Louis *Post Dispatch*, October 22, 1922.

233 Some newspapers dismissed Stoddard's: "Re-Forging America," Springfield *Republican*, February 12, 1928; Cybelle Fox and Thomas A. Guglielmo, "Defining America's Racial Boundaries: Blacks, Mexicans, and European Immigrants, 1890–1945," *Journal of Sociology* 118 (September 2012): 345; Lothrop Stoddard, *Re-Forging America: The Story of Our Nationhood* (New York: Charles Scribner's Sons, 1927), vii–viii, xxix–xxx, 44.

234 Stoddard's book sought: Stoddard, *Re-Forging America*, 62, 65–67, 72, 85–88, 258–59, 262, 286.

7. Lost Cause Victorious, 1920 to 1964

236 The first page of Thomas Maitland Marshall's: Marshall, *American History*, 1–2.

236 The "eugenocide" that permeated: James Truslow Adams, *America's Tragedy* (New York: Charles Scribner's Sons, 1934), 69–72; Stephen Steinberg, "An American Dilemma: The Collapse of the Racial Orthodoxy of Gunnar Myrdal," *Journal of Blacks in Higher Education* 10 (Winter 1995–96): 65.

237 Not only had "negroes" allegedly benefited: Bessie Louise Pierce, *Civic Attitudes in American School Textbooks* (Chicago: University of Chicago Press, 1930), 89; Louis Ray Wells, *Industrial History of the United States* (New York: Macmillan, 1922), 258–59; Adams, *America's Tragedy*, 69–71; Thomas

Jefferson Wertenbaker and Donald E. Smith, *The United States of America: A History* (New York: Charles Scribner's Sons, 1931), 56–57; Eugene C. Barker, Walter Prescott Webb, and William E. Dodd, *The Growth of a Nation: The United States of America* (Evanston, Ill.: Row, Peterson, 1928), 407–13; S. E. Forman, *A History of the United States for Schools* (New York: Century, 1920), 273–74. In 1934, Lawrence Reddick found that the sixteen textbooks he surveyed, used in Southern and Western states, all portrayed the life of slaves as easy, simple, and coarse, "but [it] was not hard, for the Negroes were good natured and sang songs during and after work." Lawrence D. Reddick, "Racial Attitudes in American History Textbooks of the South," *Journal of Negro History* 19 (July 1934): 237.

238 Most texts of the 1920s diminished: Charles E. Chadsey, Louis Weinberg, and Chester F. Miller, *America in the Making,* 2 vols. (Boston: D. C. Heath, 1927), 1:44, 48, 84–85, 118, 145, 2:148–51; Marguerite Stockman Dickson, *American History for Grammar Schools* (New York: Macmillan, 1921), 60–61, 316–17; Clarence Manion, *American History* (Boston: Allyn & Bacon, 1926), 54–55, 298; R. O. Hughes, *The Making of Our United States* (Boston: Allyn & Bacon, 1927), 48, 237; Barker, Webb, and Dodd, *Growth of a Nation,* 89, 113, 333–36; Walter Lefferts, *American Leaders,* 2 vols. (Philadelphia: J. B. Lippincott, 1919), 1:94–100.

239 When it came to slavery's economic impact: Charles A. Beard, *An Economic Interpretation of the Constitution of the United States* (1913; reprint, New York: Macmillan, 1961), 29, 174, 213; Charles A. Beard and Mary R. Beard, *History of the United States* (New York: Macmillan, 1921), 16–17, 320–21, 332; Reddick, "Racial Attitudes in American History Textbooks of the South," 231; Smith Burnham, *The Making of Our Country: A History of the United States for Schools* (Chicago: John C. Winston, 1920), 341–45; Paul L. Haworth and Alfred W. Garner, *Our Country's History* (1921; reprint, Indianapolis: Bobbs-Merrill, 1926), 42–43, 142–44; James Albert Woodburn, Thomas Francis Moran, and Howard Copland Hill, *Our United States: A History of the Nation* (New York: Longmans, Green, 1930), 115, 356–57.

239 Textbooks in the 1920s and '30s: Woodburn, Moran, and Hill, *Our United States,* 355–58; Marcus Wilson Jernegan, Harry Ellsworth Carlson, and A. Clayton Ross, *Growth of the American People* (New York: Longmans, Green, 1934), 96–98; William J. Long, *America: A History of Our Country* (Boston: Ginn, 1923), 333; Kristina DuRocher, *Raising Racists: The Socialization of White Children in the Jim Crow South* (Lexington: University Press of Kentucky, 2011), 41; Lucy Langdon Williams Wilson, *History Reader for Elementary Schools* (1898; reprint, New York: Macmillan, 1929), 198–99, 345–49; James Truslow Adams and Charles Garrett Vannest, *The Record of America* (New York: Charles Scribner's Sons, 1935), 39–40, 659; Eugene C. Barker, William E. Dodd, and Henry Steele Commager, *Our Nation's Development* (New York: Row, Peterson, 1934), 266–70.

240 A few histories used in the 1930s: Harold Rugg, *America's March Toward Democracy: History of American Life: Political and Social* (Boston: Ginn, 1937), 241–42; Charles W. Eagles, *Civil Rights, Culture Wars: The Fight over a Mississippi Textbook* (Chapel Hill: University of North Carolina Press, 2017), 29–30; Jonathan Zimmerman, *Whose America? Culture Wars in the Public Schools* (Cambridge, Mass.: Harvard University Press, 2002), 65–80; Harold Rugg and James E. Mendenhall, *Teacher's Guide for "An Introduction to American Civilization"* (Boston: Ginn, 1934), 38, 67–68; Harold Rugg, *An Introduction to American Civilization . . .* (Boston: Ginn, 1929), iv–vii, 368–72, 458–59.

241 The iconoclastic Beards damned Stowe's: Olive Smallidge and Frederic L. Paxson, *Builders of Our Nation* (Boston: Houghton Mifflin, 1934), 41, 476–79; Beard and Beard, *History of United States,* 332; Leon H. Canfield et al., *The United States in the Making* (Boston: Houghton Mifflin, 1937), 31, 325–26; Chadsey, Weinberg, and Miller, *America in the Making,* 428; Mary Gertrude Kelty, *The Story of the American People* (Boston: Ginn, 1931), 124, 136, 459–69.

241 When it came to depicting happy: Fremont P. Wirth, *The Development of America* (New York: American Book, 1937), 19, 40, 350–54; Jack Allen, "An Acquaintance of Yours: Fremont P. Wirth," *Peabody Journal of Education* 47, no. 1 (1969): 57–58; "Historical News and Notices," *Tennessee Historical Quarterly* 2, no. 1 (1943): 88; *Next Steps in Public Education in the South: Proceedings of the Association of Colleges and Secondary Schools for Negroes, 1953* (Tuskegee, Ala.: Association, 1953), 84.

243 While few readers today recall Wirth's: For this and the following paragraph, Samuel Eliot Morison and Henry Steele Commager, *The Growth of the American Republic* (New York: Oxford University Press, 1930), 124–27, 413–17; Edward Channing, *A History of the United States,* 6 vols. (New York: Macmillan, 1908–26), 5:125; James O. Horton and Lois E. Horton, eds., *Slavery and Public History: The Tough Stuff of American Memory* (New York: New Press, 2006), 41; Gregory Pfitzer, *Samuel Eliot Morison's Historical World: In Quest of a New Parkman* (Boston: Northeastern University Press, 1991), 256.

244 Morison, despite retaining his obtuse views: Pfitzer, *Morison's Historical World,* 256; Neil Jumonville, *Henry Steele Commager: Midcentury Liberalism and the History of the Present* (Chapel Hill: University of North Carolina Press, 1999), 145–53; Henry Steele Commager and Raymond H. Muessig, *The Study and Teaching of History* (Columbus, Ohio: Charles E. Merrill, 1980), 43; Allan Nevins and Henry Steele Commager, *America: The Story of a Free People* (Boston: Little, Brown, 1942), 214–15.

245 In 1950, when Commager published: For this and the following paragraph, Henry Steele Commager, *The American Mind: An Interpretation of American Thought and Character Since the 1880s* (1950; reprint, New Haven, Conn.:

Yale University Press, 1965); Merle Curti, *The Growth of American Thought* (New York: Harper & Bros., 1943), 21, 168–69, 428–33, 488–91 (song quoted on 490), 624–25. For the continued failure to include Blacks in the nation's intellectual history in the years immediately following this era, see John Higham and Paul K. Conkin, eds., *New Directions in American Intellectual History* (Baltimore: Johns Hopkins University Press, 1979) and Rush Welter, *The Mind of America, 1820–1860* (New York: Columbia University Press, 1975).

246 From the 1940s to the '60s: The only exception I found was the discussion offered of the harsh seventeenth-century conditions in Virginia by Charles H. Coleman and Edgar B. Wesley, *America's Road to Now* (Boston: D. C. Heath, 1942), 52–57, 123–24, 132, which included terrific woodcut images by Charles Child reminiscent of the work of Hale Woodruff. For this and the following paragraph, Daniel Beeby, Joyce L. Hanna, and Clarence H. McClure, *Our Country* (Chicago: Laidlaw Bros., 1942), 116–17, 158–60; Jesse H. Ames, Merlin M. Ames, and Thomas S. Staples, *Our Land and Our People: The Progress of the American Nation* (St. Louis: Webster, 1942), 368–70; Ralph Volney Harlow, *Story of America* (1937; reprint, New York: Henry Holt, 1943), 54–55, 67–68, 309–310; Casner and Gabriel, *Rise of American Democracy*, 72, 96, 100, 262–63, 334–35. Casner and Gabriel originally published their textbook in 1931 as *Exploring American History*.

246 Schoolbooks published during World War II: May T. Morrison, "John Donald Hicks, History: Berkeley," http://texts.cdlib.org/view?docId=hb9t1nb 5rm&doc.view=frames&chunk.id=div00029&toc.depth=1&toc.id=; John D. Hicks, *A Short History of American Democracy* (Boston: Houghton Mifflin, 1943), 13, 32, 291–92. Astonishingly, Hicks grew up in Missouri among parents and grandparents who refused to tolerate expressions of racism. Apparently his graduate education under Carl Russell Fish stripped him of whatever racial tolerance he had absorbed and gave him his understanding of the Civil War and Reconstruction. John D. Hicks, *My Life with History: An Autobiography* (Lincoln: University of Nebraska Press, 1968), 6, 37, 84–86, 95.

248 The post–World War II world saw: Gertrude Van Duyn Southworth and John Van Duyn Southworth, *The Story of Our America* (New York: Iroquois, 1951), 283–85; Henry W. Bragdon and Samuel P. McCutchen, *History of a Free People* (New York: Macmillan, 1958), 19; Marion Lansing, *Makers of the Americas* (Boston: D. C. Heath, 1955), 147, 153; Leon H. Canfield and Howard B. Wilder, *The Making of Modern America* (Boston: Houghton Mifflin, 1950), 42, 65–66, 243–44; "H. B. Wilder of Melrose, Educator," *Herald Traveler,* January 11, 1970. Wilder coauthored three U.S. history textbooks and left teaching to become the editor-in-chief of social studies at Houghton Mifflin. Howard B. Wilder, Robert P. Ludlum, and Harriet McCune Brown, *This Is America's Story* (Boston: Houghton Mifflin, 1956), 287; Lewis Paul Todd and Merle Curti, *Rise of the American Nation* (New York: Harcourt,

Brace & World, 1961), 310–13, 316–17; Hamer et al., *Exploring the New World,* 260–61.

249 Two of the nation's most successful: Peter Novick, *That Noble Dream: The Objectivity Question and the American Historical Profession* (Cambridge, U.K.: Cambridge University Press, 1988), 229–30; J. Montgomery Gambrill, "Review," *American Historical Review* 17 (April 1912): 677–79, quoted; also see reviews in *Journal of Education* 74 (December 28, 1911): 701; 92 (September 9, 1920): 215–16; 119 (May 18, 1936): 289; Thomas A. Bailey, *The American Pageant: Recollections of a Stanford Historian* (Stanford, Calif.: Hoover Institute Press, 1982), 14.

249 David Saville Muzzey's New England roots: Amy Newark, reference librarian at the Cary Memorial Library, Lexington, Mass., email to author, February 25, 2020; Charles Hudson, *History of the Town of Lexington, Middlesex County, Massachusetts* (Boston: Houghton Mifflin, 1913), 28; "Muzzey at 80," *New York Times,* October 9, 1950; David Quigley, "David Saville Muzzey," *American National Biography,* www.anb.org; Maurice G. Baxter, Robert H. Ferrell, and John E. Wiltz, *The Teaching of American History in High Schools* (Bloomington: Indiana University Press, 1964), 142; Barry Joyce, *The First U.S. History Textbooks: Constructing and Disseminating the American Tale in the Nineteenth Century* (Lanham, Md.: Lexington Books, 2015), 289.

249 Unlike most authors, Muzzey devoted: David Saville Muzzey, *An American History* (Boston: Ginn, 1911), 306–15; Muzzey, *History of the American People* (Boston: Ginn, 1929), 235–37.

251 Muzzey's repudiation of slavery: Muzzey, *American History,* 76, 83, 99; Thomas D. Fallace, "The Racial and Cultural Assumptions of the Early Social Studies Educators, 1901–1922," in Christine Woyshner and Chara Haeussler Bohan, eds., *Histories of Social Studies and Race, 1865–2000* (New York: Palgrave Macmillan, 2012), 49; Herbert M. Kliebard, *The Struggle for the American Curriculum* (New York: Routledge-Falmer, 2004), 243–44.

251 Thomas A. Bailey's ever-popular: For this and the following paragraph, Bailey, *American Pageant: Recollections,* 6–8; Bailey, *American Pageant: A History,* vii.

252 *The American Pageant,* like Muzzey's: Bailey, *American Pageant: A History,* 15–16, 67–68, 71, 87, 141, 228–31, 282, 361–66, 406.

252 Between Muzzey's 1911 *An American History:* Muzzey, *American History,* 316–27; Muzzey, *History of American People,* 238–39, 269–77; Benjamin Quarles, *Black Abolitionists* (New York: Oxford University Press, 1969), 19. The other textbooks that offered positive assessments of the abolitionists after 1919 are Guitteau, *History of United States,* 346–48, 394–95; John P. O'Hara, *A History of the United States* (New York: Macmillan, 1919), 245–47, 283, for Catholic elementary schools; Lefferts, *American Leaders,* 2:144–78, intended for fifth graders; Dickson, *American History for Grammar Schools,* 342–43, 347–49; Forman, *History for Schools,* 268–72, a text reprinted from 1910 to 1925; Woodburn, Moran, and Hill, *Our United States,* 365–75, for junior

high schools; and J. R. Scoppa, *A Century of Growth and Progress* (Chicago: Laidlaw Bros., 1943), 140–46.

253 For scores of other textbooks: Charles A. Beard and William C. Bagley, *The History of the American People* (New York: Macmillan, 1919), 67–68, 364–65; Beard and Beard, *History of United States,* 318–20, 331–32; Burnham, *Making of Our Country,* 346–54; Archer Butler Hulbert, *United States History* (Garden City, N.Y.: Doubleday, Page, 1923), 274, 279–82; Ruben Post Halleck, *History of Our Country for Higher Grades* (New York: American Book, 1923), 235–47; Chadsey, Weinberg, and Miller, *America in the Making,* 1:418–23, 2:152–60; Charles L. Robbins and Elmer Green, *School History of the American People* (New York: World Book, 1925), 265–67, 318.

254 During the 1920s, at least twenty: Jesse Macy, *The Anti-Slavery Crusade: A Chronicle of the Gathering Storm* (New Haven, Conn.: Yale University Press, 1921), 54–61; Carl Russell Fish, *History of America* (New York: American Book, 1925), 330–35; Manion, *American History,* 303–6; Hughes, *Making of United States,* 238–41; Ruben Gold Thwaites, Calvin Noyes Kendall, and Frederick L. Paxson, *The History of the United States for Grammar Schools* (1912; reprint, Boston: Houghton Mifflin, 1924), 283–84; Long, *America,* 332–34, which contained an illustration by N. C. Wyeth; Ralph Volney Harlow, *The Growth of the United States* (New York: Henry Holt, 1925), 389–93; Rolla M. Tryon and Charles R. Lingley, *The American People and Nation* (Boston: Ginn, 1927), 424–28; Paul L. Harworth and Alfred W. Garner, *Our Country's History* (1921; reprint, Indianapolis: Bobbs-Merrill, 1926), 316–38; Barker, Webb, and Dodd, *Growth of a Nation,* 358–61, 427–28, 433; William H. J. Kennedy and Sister Mary Joseph, *America's Story: A History of the United States for the Lower Grades of Catholic Schools* (New York: Benziger Bros., 1926), 249, 265.

255 The rampage against the antislavery movement: Smallidge and Paxson, *Builders of Our Nation,* 467–69, 479; Casner and Gabriel, *Rise of American Democracy,* 441–43; Wertenbaker and Smith, *United States: A History,* 316–18; Kelty, *Story of American People,* 464; Marshall, *American History,* 400; Ephraim Douglass Adams and John C. Almack, *A History of the United States* (New York: Harper & Bros., 1931), 424–35; Jernegan, Carlson, and Ross, *Growth of American Republic,* 483; Charles Garrett Vannest and Henry Lester Smith, *Socialized History of the United States* (New York: Charles Scribner's Sons, 1931), 294–95. Vannest and Smith's "creative" use of sources is refuted by the actual Garrison statement that appeared in the *Liberator* 1 (June 4, 1831): 96.

256 In the late 1930s: Rugg, *March Toward Democracy,* 263–67; Carl Russell Fish, *The American Civil War: An Interpretation* (London: Longmans, Green, 1937), 88; Marshall, *American History,* 386–91; William A. Hamm, Henry Eldridge Bourne, and Elbert Jay Benton, *A Unit History of the United States* (Boston: D. C. Heath, 1932), 348–49; Wirth, *Development of America,* 346–50; Barker, Dodd, and Commager, *Our Nation's Development,* 219–24,

279; Jernegan, Carlson, and Ross, *Growth of American Republic,* 380–83, 420; Canfield et al., *United States in the Making,* 327–33; Harlow, *Story of America,* 342–47; Morison and Commager, *Growth of the Republic,* 404–10; Adams and Vannest, *Record of America,* 264–66, 712; Adams, *America's Tragedy,* v–vi, 17, 64–66.

256 Textbooks published during World War II: Beeby, Hanna, and McClure, *Our Country,* 259–60; Ames, Ames, and Staples, *Our Land and Our People,* 272–74, 381; Coleman and Wesley, *America's Road to Now,* 304–7; Hicks, *Short History of Democracy,* 294–99; Casner and Gabriel, *Rise of American Democracy,* 340–42; Nevins and Commager, *Story of Free People,* 216–19; Clarence H. McClure and William H. Yarbrough, *The United States of America* (1937; reprint, Chicago: Laidlaw Bros., 1945), 375–79, 387.

257 As the anti-Communist obsession gripped: Southworth and Southworth, *Story of Our America,* 287–89; Bertrand M. Wainger, *The American Adventure* (New York: McGraw-Hill, 1957), 280, 341–42; Wilder, Ludlum, and Brown, *This Is America's Story,* 318, 367; Canfield and Wilder, *Making of Modern America,* 244–46; Bragdon and McCutchen, *History of a Free People,* 267–69; Edna McGuire, *The Story of American Freedom* (New York: Macmillan, 1957), 274; Gertrude Stephens Brown, Ernest W. Tiegs, and Fay Adams, *Teachers' Manual, Including a Key, to Accompany "Your Country and Mine"* (Boston: Ginn, 1958), 46–47; Hamer et al., *Exploring the New World,* 261–62.

258 Stanford's Thomas A. Bailey: Bailey, *American Pageant: A History,* 367–73, 397, 406–7, 938; Bragdon and McCutchen, *History of a Free People,* 316. Although sympathetic to abolitionists, David Saville Muzzey could marshal no tolerance for Brown (*History of American People,* 344–45). Among the countless other condemnations of Brown are Barker, Webb, and Dodd, *Growth of a Nation,* 443–44; Manion, *American History,* 357–58; Morison and Commager, *Growth of the Republic,* 407–8; Coleman and Wesley, *America's Road to Now,* 343–44; Canfield et al., *United States in the Making,* 385–87.

258 Heroism, patriotism, and preservation: Chadsey, Weinberg, and Miller, *America in the Making,* 1:450–55; Harlow, *Growth of United States,* 318–22; Muzzey, *History of American People,* 351; Adams and Almack, *History of United States,* 510; Thwaites, Kendall, and Paxson, *History for Grammar Schools,* 318, 323; Wirth, *Development of America,* 373–74.

259 James Truslow Adams, who had: Adams, *America's Tragedy,* v–vi, 61–63; Adams and Vannest, *Record of America,* 320; Ames, Ames, and Staples, *Our Land and Our People,* 393.

260 Such Northern views complemented: Barker, Webb, and Dodd, *Growth of a Nation,* 446–47, 489–90; Morison and Commager, *Growth of the Republic,* 897; Rugg, *March Toward Democracy,* 312–13; Jernegan, Carlson, and Ross, *Growth of American Republic,* 558.

260 While most textbooks offered: Guitteau, *History of United States,* 405–8, 457–58; Dickson, *American History for Grammar Schools,* 411–13; Robbins

and Green, *School History*, 357; Haworth and Garner, *Our Country's History*, 415–17; Chadsey, Weinberg, and Miller, *America in the Making*, 1:466, 2:180, 196; Burnham, *Making of Our Country*, 443–45; Muzzey, *American History*, 469–75; Morison and Commager, *Growth of the Republic*, 527.

261 Educators may have ignored Blacks' role: Franciscan Sisters of the Perpetual Adoration, *The Catholic History of the United States* (Chicago: Scott Foresman, 1923), 6, 343, 337, 344; Kennedy and Sister Mary Joseph, *America's Story*, 309–12.

262 At least fifty-one textbooks: Chadsey, Weinberg, and Miller, *America in the Making*, 2:207–17; Burnham, *Making of Our Country*, 454–60; Robert Allen Skotheim, *American Intellectual Histories and Historians* (Princeton: Princeton University Press, 1966), 87–109, quoted 88; Beard and Beard, *History of United States*, 365–98; Charles A. Beard and Mary R. Beard, *The Rise of American Civilization*, 2 vols. (1927; reprint, New York: Macmillan, 1946), 2:104–8, 259–60.

263 Educators depicted the South: Hulbert, *United States History*, 375–83; Dickson, *American History for Grammar Schools*, 448–65; Long, *America*, 387–401; Jernegan, Carlson, and Ross, *Growth of American Republic*, 543–44; Adams and Vannest, *Record of America*, 359–70; Halleck, *History for Higher Grades*, 409–21; Chadsey, Weinberg, and Miller, *America in the Making*, 477–85; Fish, *History of America*, 368–81; Barker, Dodd, and Commager, *Our Nation's Development*, 347–65; Hicks, *Short History of Democracy*, 421–23; Robbins and Green, *School History*, 382–88; Adams and Almack, *History of United States*, 543–61.

263 David Saville Muzzey's account of Reconstruction: For this and the following paragraph, NAACP, *Anti-Negro Propaganda in School Textbooks* (New York: NAACP, 1939), 12–13; Muzzey, *History of American People*, 402–22; Muzzey, *American History*, (1929) 485–86, (1911) 480–502; Morison and Commager, *Growth of the Republic*, 617, 620–24; Nevins and Commager, *Story of Free People*, 265–66.

264 In authors' accounts of Reconstruction: Barker, Webb, and Dodd, *Growth of a Nation*, 494–517; Thwaites, Kendall, and Paxson, *History for Grammar Schools*, 404–10; Ames, Ames, and Staples, *Our Land and Our People*, 429–41; Canfield and Wilder, *Making of Modern America*, 320–31; Harlow, *Story of America*, 387–96; Hughes, *Making of United States*, 299–300.

265 At least twenty different school histories: Kelty, *Story of American People*, 515–18; Rugg, *March Toward Democracy*, 299–313; Canfield et al., *United States in the Making*, 434–49; Hicks, *Short History of Democracy*, 428–42; Coleman and Wesley, *America's Road to Now*, 380–95; Jernegan, Carlson, and Ross, *Growth of American Republic*, 535–36, 548–550, 558; McClure and Yarbrough, *United States of America*, 422–23; Casner and Gabriel, *Rise of American Democracy*, 406–18; Wirth, *Development of America*, 405–20; Barker, Webb, and Dodd, *Growth of a Nation*, 510–11; Harworth and Garner, *Our Country's History*, 450–63; Scoppa, *Century of Growth and Progress*,

218–27; Manion, *American History,* 404–23; Hughes, *Making of United States,* 291–98; Tryon and Lingley, *American People and Nation,* 485–95; Muzzey, *History of American People,* 402–22; Giles, *How the United States,* 9–11; Charles G. Eichel, Harry Blickstein, and Sigmund Newman, *Pictorial History of America,* 2 vols. (Newman-Dupuy, 1931), 1:12–13, 67; 2:6–7, 11; Southworth and Southworth, *Story of Our America,* 343–52; Wilder, Ludlum, and Brown, *This Is America's Story,* 394–401.

267 In 1956, as Martin Luther King, Jr.: Bailey, *American Pageant: A History,* 459–65, 472–82; Bragdon and McCutchen, *History of a Free People,* 344–62; Wilder, Ludlum, and Brown, *This Is America's Story,* 394–401.

268 Back in 1903: Novick, *That Noble Dream,* 73; Ulrich B. Phillips, *Life & Labor in the Old South* (1929; reprint, Boston: Little, Brown, 1963), iii–vi; Charles Dew, *The Making of a Racist: A Southerner Reflects on Family History, and the Slave Trade* (Charlottesville: University of Virginia Press, 2016), 15–17; Bailey, *American Pageant: Recollections,* 8; Zimmerman, *Whose America?,* 32–34.

268 Mildred Lewis Rutherford: Anne E. Marshall, "Mildred Lewis Rutherford (1851–1928)," in *New Georgia Encyclopedia,* georgiaencylopdia.org/articles/history-archeology; Elizabeth Gillespie McRae, *Mothers of Massive Resistance: White Women and the Politics of White Supremacy* (New York: Oxford University Press, 2018), 41–47; Bessie Louise Pierce, *Public Opinion in the Teaching of History in the United States* (1926; reprint, New York: DaCapo Press, 1970), 158–61; Zimmerman, *Whose America?,* 36–40.

269 In 1912, to preserve and help disseminate: Zimmerman, *Whose America?,* 38–39; Mildred Lewis Rutherford, *The South Must Have Her Rightful Place in History* (Athens, Ga.: self-pub., 1923), 18–19; Rutherford, *Truths of History . . .* (Athens, Ga.: self-pub., 1920?), 11.

270 Modern historians have repeatedly emphasized: Zimmerman, *Whose America?,* 36–38; Greg Huffman, "Twisted Sources: How Confederate Propaganda Ended Up in the South's Schoolbooks," *Facing South,* April 10, 2019; Mildred Lewis Rutherford, *A Measuring Rod to Test Textbooks, and Reference Books in Schools . . .* (Athens, Ga.: United Confederates, 1920); Rutherford, *South Must Have Her Rightful Place,* 1–3.

271 Rutherford refused to change her views: R. G. [Robert Green] Hall, Harriet Smither, and Clarence Ousley, *A History of the United States for the Grammar Grades* (Dallas: Southern, 1920), 46, 91, 97–99, 170–82, 244–47, 266–68, 304–59, 383–88; Adams and Vannest, *Record of America,* 354–58.

271 The South's distrust: Joseph Moreau, *Schoolbook Nation: Conflicts over American History Textbooks from the Civil War to the Present* (Ann Arbor: University of Michigan Press, 2003), 272–73, 283; Michael Newton, *White Robes and Burning Crosses: A History of the Ku Klux Klan from 1866* (Jefferson, N.C.: McFarland, 2014), 134; Simms and Oliphant, *History of South Carolina,* 177–79, 212, 220, 229–35.

272 The same strategies, books: Moreau, *Schoolbook Nation,* 272–73; Zimmerman, *Whose America?,* 105; Francis Butler Simkins, Spotswood Hunnicutt,

and Sidman P. Poole, *Virginia: History, Government, Geography* (New York: Charles Scribner's Sons, 1957), 82–85, 181–89.

273 When it came to sectional strife: Simkins, Hunnicutt, and Poole, *Virginia,* 361–79, 382–84, 400–413, 446–52.

274 Northern and Southern schoolbooks: Mabel B. Casner and Ralph Henry Gabriel, *Exploring American History* (New York: Harcourt, Brace, 1931), 501–5; Beeby, Hanna, and McClure, *Our Country,* 276–77; McGuire, *Story of American Freedom,* 293; Ames, Ames, and Staples, *Our Land and Our People,* 429–41.

274 As the history of textbooks reveals: *Public Symbols of the Confederacy* (Montgomery, Ala.: Southern Poverty Law Center, 2016); Charles Reagan Wilson, *Baptized in Blood: The Religion of the Lost Cause, 1865–1920* (Athens: University of Georgia Press, 2009), 159; Seattle *Daily Times,* January 12, 1941; Trenton (N.J.) *Evening Times,* February 22, 1946; Boston *Daily Globe,* April 29, 1928, and January 19, 1930.

275 We can well expect textbooks crafted: Jones, *School History,* 387; Pierce, *Public Opinion in the Teaching of History,* 164–66, 170–71: John W. Wayland, *How to Teach American History: A Handbook for Teachers and Students* (New York: Macmillan, 1914), 63; Simkins, Hunnicutt, and Poole, *Virginia,* 420–28; Barker, Webb, and Dodd, *Growth of a Nation,* 489–90; Casner and Gabriel, *Rise of American Democracy,* 400–405; Montgomery, *Leading Facts,* 326–27; Wilson, *History Reader,* 372–77; Commager and Muessig, *Study and Teaching of History,* 32.

275 In the 1950s Lee emerged as: Canfield and Wilder, *Making of Modern America,* 311; Lansing, *Makers of Americas,* 308, 312–16; Wilder, Ludlum, and Brown, *This Is America's Story,* 382–83; Hamer et al., *Exploring the New World,* 261–62, 264–67.

8. Renewing the Challenge

277 "This is the nation's golden hour": Frances Ellen Watkins Harper, "Words for the Hour," in *Complete Poems of Frances E. W. Harper,* ed. Maryemma Graham (New York: Oxford University Press, 1988), 103.

277 The history we teach is the product: Wendell Phillips, *The Scholar in the Republic* (Boston: Lee and Shepard, 1881), 6; Leon Litwack, "'Trouble in Mind': The Bicentennial and the Afro-American Experience," *Journal of American History* 74 (1987): 326, in Gary Nash, Charlotte Crabtree, and Ross E. Dunn, *History on Trial: Culture Wars and the Teaching of the Past* (New York: Alfred A. Knopf, 1997), 62.

277 Slavery's demise fortified: Ardelia Lee, "The Detroit Wall: A Tale of How Federal Policy Helped Divide a City," *Daily Detroit,* June 6, 2016; Nikole Hannah-Jones, "What Is Owed," *New York Times Magazine,* June 28, 2020, 30–35, 47, 50–53.

279 From the 1890s to the 1960s: Woodburn, Moran, and Hill, *Our United States* (1935 ed.), 489–509; Hicks, *Short History of Democracy,* 416–17 (the third edition of Hicks's book was published in 1966); Marshall, *American History,* 448–63; Giles, *How the United States,* 1–7. On the Peabody Education Fund, see Franklin Parker, "George Peabody, 1795–1869: His Influence on Educational Philanthropy," *Peabody Journal of Education* 78 (2003): 111–18.

280 Until World War II, Southern white domination: Douglas Blackmon, *Slavery by Another Name: The Re-Enslavement of Black Americans from the Civil War to World War II* (New York: Doubleday, 2008); Patricia Sullivan, *Lift Every Voice: The NAACP and the Making of the Civil Rights Movement* (New York: New Press, 2009), 2; Marie Elizabeth Ruffin Carpenter, *The Treatment of the Negro in American History School Textbooks* (Menasha, Wis.: George Banta, 1941), 14.

280 At the same time, however, gradual: For this and the following paragraph, Lyndon Baines Johnson, "Address to a Joint Session of Congress on Voting Legislation," March 15, 1965, https://www.americanrhetoric.com/speeches/lbjweshallovercome.htm; Stephen Tuck, *We Ain't What We Ought to Be: The Black Freedom Struggle from Emancipation to Obama* (Cambridge, Mass.: Harvard University Press, 2010), 321–23.

281 No change, however, was possible: Ronald E. Butchart, "Race, Social Studies, and Culturally Relevant Curriculum in Social Studies' Prehistory: A Cautionary Meditation," in Christine Wayshner and Chara Haeussler Bohan, eds., *Histories of Social Studies and Race, 1865–2000* (New York: Palgrave Macmillan, 2012), 23–25.

282 The Niagara Movement: "Declaration of Principles," in Cary D. Wintz, ed., *African American Political Thought, 1890–1930* (Armonk, N.Y.: M. E. Sharpe, 1996), 103; W.E.B. Du Bois, "The Immediate Program of the American Negro," *Crisis* 9 (April 1915): 310–12.

282 But activists like Du Bois and Trotter: W.E.B. Du Bois Membership Letter, October 7, 1905, "Garrison Pledge of the Niagara Movement," 1905, William Monroe Trotter to W.E.B. Du Bois, March 26, 1905, W.E.B. Du Bois Papers, series 1A, General Correspondence, University of Massachusetts, Amherst; Suffrage League of Boston, *The Celebration of the One Hundredth Anniversary of the Birth of William Lloyd Garrison* (Boston: Garrison Centenary Committee of the Suffrage League of Boston and Vicinity, 1906); Kerri K. Greenidge, *Black Radical: The Life and Times of William Monroe Trotter* (New York: Liveright, 2020), 60, 120–24.

283 Several of the leaders whom Du Bois saw: W.E.B. Du Bois, "The Talented Tenth," in Booker T. Washington et al., *The Negro Problem: A Series of Articles by Representative American Negroes of Today* (New York: J. Pott, 1903), 45–46; David Levering Lewis, *W.E.B. Du Bois, 1868–1919: Biography of a Race* (New York: Henry Holt, 1993), 73, 133, 165, 206. Du Bois's phrase had been coined by Henry Lyman Morehouse in 1896: see Henry Louis Gates, Jr., "Who

Really Invented the 'Talented Tenth'?," PBS.org, https://www.pbs.org/wnet/
african-americans-many-rivers-to-cross/history/who-really-invented-the-
talented-tenth/; Lawrence Otis Graham, *The Senator and the Socialite: The
True Story of America's First Black Dynasty* (New York: HarperCollins, 2006),
159–60, 211–13, 271–76, 285–89; Adelaide M. Cromwell, *Unveiled Voices,
Unvarnished Memories: The Cromwell Family in Slavery and Segregation,
1692–1972* (Columbia: University of Missouri Press, 2007), 115–17.

283 The textbooks and curriculum that Bruce: A. T. Stuart, "Report of Superin-
tendent Stuart," in *Report of the Board of Education,* District 6 (Washington,
D.C. Board of Education, 1909–10), 35–38; "Report of the Board of
Education," *Annual Report of the Commissioners of the District of Columbia*
(Washington, D.C.: Commissioners, 1911), 199, 210. American history texts
used in the district's Black schools included Mace, *School History,* Mont-
gomery, *Beginner's American History,* Montgomery, *Leading Facts,* and David
Montgomery, *An Elementary American History* (Boston: Ginn, 1904).

284 But Bruce, whatever his shortcomings: "The Teachers' Institute" and "The
Negro's Contribution to Civilization," in *Report of the Board of Education,
Commissioners of the District of Columbia, Annual Reports* (Washington,
D.C.: Commissioners of the District of Columbia, 1915), 2–4, 247, 249–50;
Cromwell, *Unveiled Voices, Unvarnished Memories,* 117–19; Jacqueline Gog-
gin, *Carter G. Woodson: A Life in Black History* (Baton Rouge: Louisiana State
University Press, 1993), 30–31.

285 Perhaps Bruce's greatest accomplishment: W.E.B. Du Bois, "A Portrait of
Carter G. Woodson," *Masses and Mainstream* 3 (June 1950): 19–25; Philip
Nel, *Was the Cat in the Hat Black? The Hidden Racism of Children's Literature, and the Need for Diverse Books* (New York: Oxford University Press,
2017), 185.

286 Since nearly all Southern states employed: Zimmerman, *Whose America?,*
45–47.

286 Fears of a white backlash: Carter G. Woodson, *The Negro in Our History*
(Washington, D.C.: Associated Publishers, 1922), 249–52.

287 Woodson's *The Negro in Our History:* Ibid., 1–14, 11 quoted, 249–52.

287 Woodson, Du Bois, and their contemporaries: Woodson, *The Mis-Education
of the Negro* (Washington, D.C.: Associated Publishers, 1933), 2–3, 22–23,
84–86.

288 Resisting the impact of such white supremacist aims: Zimmerman, *Whose
America?,* 32; NAACP, *Anti-Negro Propaganda in School Textbooks* (New York:
NAACP, 1939), 3–9; Southworth and Southworth, *Story of Our America,* 351.

288 When W.E.B. Du Bois's *Black Reconstruction in America:* "Ralph Bunche:
Autobiographical," Nobel Peace Prize 1950, NobelPrize.org; W.E.B. Du Bois,
Black Reconstruction in America, 1860–1880 (1935; reprint, Cleveland: World,
1962), 711–14, 726; Ralph J. Bunche, "Reconstruction Reinterpreted," *Journal of Negro Education* 4 (October 1935): 568–70.

289 Du Bois explained to his readers: Du Bois, *Black Reconstruction in America,* 718–19, 723–27.

290 Black scholars like Bunche and Rayford W. Logan: Rayford W. Logan, "Review of Black Reconstruction," *Journal of Negro History* 21 (January 1936): 61–63; Kenneth Robert Janken, "Rayford Wittingham Logan," in Henry Louis Gates, Jr., and Evelyn Brooks Higginbotham, eds., *African American National Biography* (New York: Oxford University Press, 2008), 5:297–99.

290 Most white historians, however, ignored: Arthur C. Cole, "Review of Black Reconstruction," *Mississippi Valley Historical Review* 23 (September 1936): 278–80; Avery Craven, "Review of *Black Reconstruction*," *American Journal of Sociology* 61 (January 1936): 535–36; Avery Craven, "Review of Charles H. Wesley, *The Collapse of the Confederacy*," *American Journal of Sociology* 44 (March 1939): 775; E. R. Thomas, "Review of Avery Craven, *The Repressible Conflict, 1830–1861*," *Journal of Negro History* 24 (July 1939): 345–48; W. R. Brock, "Race and the American Past: A Revolution in Historiography," *History* 52 (1967): 49–59; Eric Foner, "Black Reconstruction: An Introduction," *South Atlantic Quarterly* 112, no. 3 (Summer 2013): 409–18.

291 But Du Bois's book was not entirely ignored: Howard K. Beale, "On Rewriting Reconstruction," *American Historical Review* 45 (July 1940): 807–27; Beale, "The Needs of Negro Education in the United States," *Journal of Negro Education* 3 (January 1934): 8–19; James G. Randall and David Donald, *The Civil War and Reconstruction,* 2nd ed. (Boston: Little, Brown, 1969), 626–27. Beale also had trained Yale University's C. Vann Woodward, one of the twentieth century's most influential American historians.

292 At the time Du Bois challenged: American Committee for Democracy and Intellectual Freedom, *Can You Name Them?* (New York: ACDIF, 1939), 1–15; *The Genetic Basis for Democracy: A Panel Discussion on Race and Race Prejudice . . .* (New York: ACDIF, 1939), 1; Zoe Burkholder, *Color in the Classroom: How American Schools Taught Race, 1900–1954* (New York: Oxford University Press, 2011), 58–64.

293 The advent of the Second World War: David W. Southern, *Gunnar Myrdal and Black-White Relations: The Use and Abuse of an American Dilemma, 1944–1969* (Baton Rouge: Louisiana State University Press, 1987), 51–52; John Dewey, "Address to National Negro Conference (1909)" and "The Basic Values and Loyalties of Democracy (1941)," in Eric Thomas Weber, ed., *Essays on Social Justice, Economics, Education, and the Future of Democracy* (New York: Columbia University Press, 2021), 24–26, 55–58; John Dewey, "Education and Democracy in the World of Today (1938)," *Schools: Studies in Education* 9 (Spring 2012): 96–100; Malcolm Shaw MacLean, *Higher Education and the Negro* (New York: American Committee for Democracy and Intellectual Freedom, 1941), 2–12; http://hamptonarchives.org/content/maclean-malcom-shaw.

293 The 1940s also saw the advent: Bessie Z. Jones, "Review of *One Nation*," *New England Quarterly* 18 (December 1945): 545–47; E. Franklin Frazier, "Review of *An American Dilemma*," *American Journal of Sociology* 50 (May 1945): 555–57; Clyde V. Kiser, "Review: *An American Dilemma*," *Milbank Memorial Fund Quarterly* 23 (October 1945): 410–14; Marion B. Campfield, "About Books," Chicago *Bee,* August 10, 1947; Southern, *Myrdal and Black-White Relations,* 71–74, 90; Cecil Boylan, "Along the Bookshelf," Detroit *Tribune,* October 26, 1946.

294 Most important of all, *An American Dilemma: Brown v. Board of Education of Topeka,* 347 U.S. 483 (1954), https://supreme.justia.com/cases/federal/us/347/483/; Paul Green, "The Paradox of the Promised Unfulfilled: *Brown v. Board of Education* and the Continued Pursuit of Excellence in Education," *Journal of Negro Education* 73 (Summer 2004): 268–84; Obie Clayton, Jr., and Shelia Flemming-Hunter, "Introductory Essay: Honoring the 75th Anniversary of the Book *An American Dilemma: The Negro Problem and Modern Democracy* by Gunnar Myrdal," *Phylon* 56 (Winter 2019): 2–7; Randall Kennedy, *Interracial Intimacies: Sex, Marriage, Identity, and Adoption* (New York: Pantheon Books, 2003), 23–24, 85, 88.

294 Myrdal, a professor of economics: "To Study Negro Problem," *New York Times,* August 9, 1938; Steve Schindler, "Case 17. Transforming America's Perceptions of Relations Among its Races: Karl Gunnar Myrdal's An American Dilemma, Carnegie Corporation of New York, 1936," https://cspcs.sanford.duke.edu/sites/default/files/descriptive/an_american_dilemma.pdf; Southern, *Myrdal and Black-White Relations,* 2–5; Sissela Bok, "Foreword to An American Dilemma Revisited," *Phylon* 56 (Winter 2019): 9. Bok is Myrdal's daughter.

295 Keppel's confidence was well placed: William Keith Hancock, *Professing History* (Sydney, Australia: Sydney University Press, 1976), 8–10; Southern, *Myrdal and Black-White Relations,* 19–22.

295 Unwieldy, insufficiently focused: Gunnar Myrdal, *An American Dilemma: The Negro Problem and Modern Democracy,* 2 vols. (New York: Harper & Bros., 1944), 1:xli, 4, 573, 582–84, 668, 2:799.

296 Wartime realities also spurred: For this and the following paragraph, Edgar B. Wesley, *American History in the Schools and Colleges* (New York: Macmillan, 1944), 18–19, 74–81. The NCSS joined with the American Historical Association and the Mississippi Valley Historical Association, which in 1965 became the Organization of American Historians. John Hope Franklin, *From Slavery to Freedom: A History of Negro Americans* (1947; reprint, New York: Random House, 1967), xii.

297 The Supreme Court's *Brown* decision: Lawrence Goldstone, *Inherently Unequal: The Betrayal of Equal Rights by the Supreme Court, 1865–1903* (New York: Walker & Co., 2011), 1–13; James Baldwin, "The Nigger We Invent," *Integrated Education: A Report on Race and Schools* 7 (March–April 1969): 15–16; Jeanne Theoharis, *A More Beautiful and Terrible History* (Boston:

Beacon Press, 2018), 3–4; Trey Popp, "The History Wars," *Pennsylvania Gazette,* March–April 2021, 303–31; Jeffrey Hass, *The Assassination of Fred Hampton: How the FBI and Chicago Police Murdered a Black Panther* (Chicago: Lawrence Hill Books, 2019).

297 To explain the persistence of white supremacy: Theoharis, *A More Beautiful and Terrible History,* 32–33, 43–51; Henry Louis Gates, Jr., *Life Upon These Shores: Looking at African American History* (New York: Alfred A. Knopf, 2011), 374; Kate Torgovnick May, "The Brave but Forgotten Kansas Lunch Counter Sit-in That Helped Change America," *Washington Post,* February 6, 2021.

298 The NAACP and the Urban League: Zimmerman, *Whose America?,* 112–13; Sara L. Schwebel, *Child-Sized History: Fictions of the Past in U.S. Classrooms* (Nashville, Tenn.: Vanderbilt University Press, 2011), 101; Nancy Larrick, "The All White World of Children's Books," *Saturday Review,* September 11, 1965, 84–85; Baldwin, "Nigger We Invent," 16–17; William F. Brazziel, "Negro History in the Public Schools: Trends and Prospects," *Negro History Bulletin* 28 (November 1965): 35–38.

298 Resistance to change raged as intensely: Charles W. Eagles, *Civil Rights, Culture Wars: The Fight over a Mississippi Textbook* (Chapel Hill: University of North Carolina Press, 2017), 8–11, 40–47, 96; James W. Loewen and Charles Sallis, eds., *Mississippi: Conflict and Change* (New York: Pantheon, 1974). From the beginning of their Text, the authors labored hard to integrate Native Peoples and African Americans into their narrative. Alan Wieder, "South Carolina School History Textbooks' Portrayals of Race During Reconstruction," *Journal of Thought* 30 (Spring 1995): 23–25; Chara Haeussler Bohan and Patricia Randolph, "Atlanta's Desegregation-Era Social Studies Curriculum: An Examination of Georgia History Textbooks," in Christine Woyshner and Chara Haeussler Bohan, eds., *Histories of Social Studies and Race, 1865–2000* (New York: Palgrave Macmillan, 2012), 135–38, 147–53; Joseph Moreau, *Schoolbook Nation: Conflicts over American History Textbooks from the Civil War to the Present* (Ann Arbor: University of Michigan Press, 2003), 297–305; John Hope Franklin, *Mirror to America: The Autobiography of John Hope Franklin* (New York: Farrar, Straus & Giroux, 2005), 226–31.

299 The advent of the 1960s saw little change: Ruth Wood Gavian and William A. Hamm, *United States History* (Boston: D. C. Heath, 1960), 318; Gertrude Stephens Brown, *Your Country and Mine: Our American Neighbors* (Boston: Ginn, 1963), 22–27, 128–33; David Saville Muzzey, *Our Country's History* (Boston: Ginn, 1961), 41, 63, 136–37, 207–10.

299 The presentation of slavery's history: John Morton Blum et al., *The National Experience: A History of the United States* (New York: Harcourt, Brace & World, 1963), 50–52, 200–203.

300 The way textbooks, and scholarship: Wieder, "South Carolina School History Textbooks' Portrayals of Race During Reconstruction," 23–25; Simkins, Hunnicutt, and Poole, *Virginia;* Steve Hochstadt, "From 'Birth of a Nation'

to Silent Sam: What History and Popular Culture Can Teach Us About the Southern 'Lost Cause' and Confederate Monuments Today," *History News Network,* January 10, 2019. Among those historians who exerted the most profound influence on the rewriting of American history, especially regarding slavery, race, and abolitionism, are W.E.B. Du Bois, Carter G. Woodson, Benjamin Quarles, John Hope Franklin, Frank Tannenbaum, Herbert Aptheker, Russell B. Nye, Louis Filler, Richard Hofstadter, Kenneth Stampp, and C. Vann Woodward.

301   From the late 1960s to the '80s: Jack Allen and John L. Betts, *History: USA* (New York: American Book, 1967), 6, 19, 34–35, 272–73; Richard C. Brown, William C. Lang, and Mary A. Wheeler, *The American Achievement* (Morristown, N.Y.: Silver Burdett, 1966), 43, 260–61; Jack Abramowitz, *American History* (Chicago: Follett, 1971), 66, 269–72; David Bidna, Morris S. Greenberg, and Jerold H. Spitz, *We the People: A History of the United States of America* (Lexington, Mass.: D. C. Heath, 1971), 72, 75, 88, 187; Robert F. Madgic et al., *The American Experience: A Study of Themes and Issues in American History* (Menlo Park, Calif.: Addison-Wesley, 1971), 81–91; Melvin Schwartz and John R. O'Connor, *The New Exploring American History* (New York: Globe Book Co., 1981), 276–92.

301   With the civil rights movement: Gavian and Hamm, *United States History,* 318–21; Todd and Curti, *Rise of American Nation,* 341–53; Brown, *Your Country and Mine,* 133–34.

302   As with the history of slavery: Blum et al., *National Experience,* 251–54, 316–17.

303   Later textbooks followed: Brown, Lang, and Wheeler, *American Achievement,* 286–88; Allen and Betts, *History: USA,* 221–25; Esther Crabtree, *Understanding Your Country and Canada* (1964, reprint, Boston: Ginn, 1968), 242; Abramowitz, *American History,* 279–82; Madgic et al., *American Experience,* 92–96; Bidna, Greenberg, and Spitz, *We the People,* 190–91; Schwartz and O'Connor, *New Exploring American History,* 300–301.

303   Until the 1980s, most textbooks ignored: Muzzey, *Our Country's History,* 289–317; Blum et al., *National Experience,* 345–53; Brown, Lang, and Wheeler, *American Achievement,* 336–37; Madgic et al., *American Experience,* 125; Schwartz and O'Connor, *New Exploring American History,* 326–27.

303   The "dark and bloody ground": Bernard A. Weisberger, "The Dark and Bloody Ground of Reconstruction Historiography," *Journal of Southern History* 25 (1959): 427–47; Hamer et al., *Exploring the New World,* 266–67.

304   Astonishingly, David Saville Muzzey's fifty-year-old account: Muzzey, *Our Country's History,* 322–38, 652; Gavian and Hamm, *United States History,* 391–401; Todd and Curti, *Rise of American Nation,* 407–21; Brown, *Your Country and Mine,* 143–45.

304   But the civil rights and Black power movements: Gordon W. Allport, *The Nature of Prejudice* (1954; reprint, Garden City, N.Y.: Doubleday, 1958),

vii, 12, 15, 75, 429–43; "Gordon W. Allport," Harvard University, https://
psychology.fas.harvard.edu/people/gordon-w-allport; Irwin Katz, "Gordon
Allport's *The Nature of Prejudice*," *Political Psychology* 12 (1991): 125–57.

305 This renewed interest in the dynamics: John Howard Griffin, *Black Like Me*
(New York: Signet, 1961), 5, 17; John Howard Griffin, "The Living Chains of
Blackness: Journey into the Mississippi Night," *Southwest Review* 45 (Autumn
1960): 285–92.

305 The interviews he gave: *Time*, March 28, 1960; *New York Times*, October 5,
1961; "Black Like Me," Dallas *Morning News*, July 2, 1961; Washington *Post*,
October 30, 1977; Stuart H. Loory, "He Crossed the South's Racial Bound-
ary," New York *Herald Tribune*, October 15, 1961. Loory concluded that
Griffin's brave experiment "does not yield its full promise." Dan Wakefield,
"Traveling Second Class," *New York Times*, October 22, 1961; Dan Wakefield,
Revolt in the South (New York: Grove Press, 1960), 15–16; C. Vann Wood-
ward, "The Antislavery Myth," *American Scholar* 31 (Spring 1962): 312–18.

306 For whites who wished to comprehend: Ralph Ellison, *Invisible Man* (New
York: Random House, 1952), 7, 16, 190; Claude Brown, *Manchild in the
Promised Land* (New York: New American Library, 1965), 298; Robert F.
Worth, "Claude Brown, *Manchild in the Promised Land*, Dies at 63," *New
York Times*, February 6, 2002.

307 But Claude Brown's book: *The Autobiography of Malcom X* (n.p.: Castle
Books, 1965); Eldridge Cleaver, *Soul on Ice* (New York: Dell, 1968), 70.

307 At the same time, Black and white authors: Lerone Bennett, Jr., *Before the
Mayflower: A History of the Negro in America, 1619–1966* (1962; reprint,
Chicago: Johnson, 1966), 370; *Forced into Glory: Abraham Lincoln's White
Dream* (Chicago: Johnson, 2000).

308 The dominant white narrative: C.L.R. James, *The Black Jacobins: Toussaint
L'Ouverture and the San Domingo Revolution* (New York: Vintage Books,
1963), 88; David Brion Davis, *The Problem of Slavery in Western Culture*
(Ithaca, N.Y.: Cornell University Press, 1966), 447; David Blight, "Introduc-
tion," *Teaching Hard History: American Slavery* (Montgomery, Ala.: Southern
Poverty Law Center, 2018), 7. Davis's subsequent studies are *The Problem of
Slavery in the Age of Revolution, 1770–1823* (Ithaca, N.Y.: Cornell University
Press, 1975); *Slavery and Human Progress* (New York: Oxford University Press,
1984); and *Inhuman Bondage: The Rise and Fall of Slavery in the New World*
(New York: Oxford University Press, 2006).

308 As David Brion Davis transformed: Winthrop D. Jordan, *White over Black:
American Attitudes Toward the Negro, 1550–1812* (1968; reprint, Baltimore:
Penguin, 1969), xiii, 548.

309 Clearly, textbooks alone could not: Blum et al., *National Experience*, 356–80;
Allan and Betts, *History: USA*, 317–33; Brown, Lang, and Wheeler, *Ameri-
can Achievement*, 344–61; Crabtree, *Understanding Your Country*, 251–54;
Abramowitz, *American History*, 357–75; Schwartz and O'Connor, *New*

Exploring American History, 330–33; Madgic et al., *American Experience,* 140–70.

310 By the nation's bicentennial: Edmund S. Morgan, *The Challenge of the American Revolution* (New York: W. W. Norton, 1976), 141–42; Mary Beth Norton, "Rethinking American History Textbooks," in Lloyd Kramer, Donald Reid, and William L. Barney, eds., *Learning History in America: Schools, Culture, and Politics* (Minneapolis: University of Minnesota Press, 1994), 27; Arthur M. Schlesinger, Jr., *The Disuniting of America: Reflections on a Multicultural Society* (1991; reprint, New York: W. W. Norton, 1998), 19–21.

Epilogue

311 Confederate flags swayed: Jill Lepore, *The Whites of Their Eyes: The Tea Party's Revolution and the Battle over American History* (Princeton: Princeton University Press, 2010), 8–9; Jonathan M. Metzl, *Dying of Whiteness: How the Politics of Racial Resentment Is Killing America's Heartland* (New York: Basic Books, 2019), 264; Earl Lewis, "History Lesson," *American Historian* (February 2019): 1–2.

312 Such sentiments are only: Metzl, *Dying of Whiteness,* 4–9; Isabel Wilkerson, "America's Enduring Caste System," *New York Times Magazine,* July 5, 2020, 26–33, 49–53; "Science Class Defies Racism with Genetics," *New York Times,* December 8, 2019, 1, 22; Howard K. Beale, "The Needs of Negro Education in the United States," *Journal of Negro Education* 3 (January 1934): 10.

312 The manifestation of such beliefs: Chicago 2020, U.S. Census, Census.gov; "Demographics, Chicago Pubic Schools," www.cps.edu; Jonathan Kozol, *The Shame of the Nation: The Restoration of Apartheid Schooling in America* (New York: Crown, 2005), 18–19, 25.

313 During the 1990s, concerted efforts: Lerner, Nagai, and Rothman, *Molding the Good Citizen,* 85; Gary Nash, Charlotte Crabtree, and Ross E. Dunn, *History on Trial: Culture Wars and the Teaching of the Past* (New York: Alfred A. Knopf, 1997), 115–16, 245–46; *National Standards for United States History: Exploring the American Experience* (Los Angeles: National Center for History in the Schools, 1994). The center's website instead offers Gary Nash's *Forbidden Love: The Secret History of Mixed-Race America* (New York: Henry Holt, 1999).

314 Some analysts saw the controversy: For this and the next paragraph, Jonathan Zimmerman, *Whose America? Culture Wars in the Public Schools* (Cambridge, Mass.: Harvard University Press, 2002), 7–8; "American Textbook Council," https://www.historytextbooks.net/; Gilbert T. Sewall, *History Textbooks at the New Century: A Report of the American Textbook Council* (New York: ATC, 2000), 2–12, 23–25, 28–31; also see Gilbert T. Sewall, *History Textbooks: A Standard Guide* (New York: ATC, 1994).

315 Ironically, textbooks that incorporate: Timothy Keesee and Mark Sidwell, *United States History for Christian Schools* (Greenville, S.C.: Bob Jones University Press, 2001), 31, 219; Joseph Jarrell, *United States History* (Greenville, S.C.: Bob Jones University Press, 2018), 23–24, 217–20.

316 The evangelical texts accurately emphasized: Keesee and Sidwell, *History for Christian Schools,* 224–33; Jarrell, *United States History,* 220–23, 270–71; Thornton Stringfellow, "A Brief Examination of Scripture Testimony on the Institution of Slavery," in Drew Gilpin Faust, ed., *The Ideology of Slavery: Proslavery Thought in the Antebellum South, 1830–1860* (Baton Rouge: Louisiana State University Press, 1981), 144.

316 In the history of the Civil War: Keesee and Sidwell, *History for Christian Schools,* 286, 307–8, 332–45; Jarrell, *United States History,* 278–309, 312–21.

317 Slavery and the Civil War remain: Clyde N. Wilson, *Lies My Teacher Told Me: The True History of the War for Southern Independence* (Columbia, S.C.: Shotwell, 2016), 3–4.

318 While extreme, Clyde Wilson's allegiance: Dominique Mosberger, "Texas Students Will Soon Learn That Slavery Played 'Central Role' in Sparking Civil War," *Huffington Post,* November 11, 2018; Dana Goldstein, "Two States. Eight Textbooks. Two American Stories," *New York Times,* January 12, 2020; Joy Masoff, *Our Virginia, Past and Present* (Weston, Conn.: Five Ponds Press, 2010), 114; Sam Wineburg, *Why Learn History (When It's Already on Your Phone)* (Chicago: University of Chicago Press, 2018), 1–2; Kevin Sieff, "Virginia 4th-Grade Textbook Criticized over Claims on Black Confederate Soldiers," *Washington Post,* October 20, 2010.

318 In 2010, with the backing: *U.S. History Framework for the 2010 National Assessment of Educational Progress* (Washington, D.C.: U.S. Department of Education, 2009), v–vi, 10–11.

319 Many scholars and authors have responded: Eric Foner, *Give Me Liberty! An American History,* 5th ed. (New York: W. W. Norton, 2017), 3, 240–42, 371–72, 420; Alexander Stille, "The Betrayal of History," *New York Review of Books,* June 11, 1998, 15–20; "Reconstruction," *American Yawp,* http://www.americanyawp.com/text/15-reconstruction/. The print edition is Joseph L. Locke and Ben Wright, eds., *The American Yawp: A Massively Collaborative Open U.S. History Textbook* (Stanford, Calif.: Stanford University Press, 2019).

319 Online sources can offer educators: Documenting the American South, University of North Carolina at Chapel Hill, https://docsouth.unc.edu/index.html; HathiTrust Digital Library, https://www.hathitrust.org/about; The Making of America, Cornell University Library, https://collections.library.cornell.edu/moa_new/index.html; Boston Public Library, https://www.digitalcommonwealth.org/institutions/commonwealth:sf268508b; Amistad Digital Resource, https://www.amistadresource.org/; Digital Schomburg, New York Public Library, https://www.nypl.org/about/locations/schomburg

/digital-schomburg; Chronicling America, National Endowment for the Humanities, Library of Congress, https://chroniclingamerica.loc.gov/search /titles/; The 1619 Project, *New York Times,* https://www.nytimes.com/interac tive/2019/08/14/magazine/1619-america-slavery.html; John Murawski, "Disputed *New York Times* '1619 Project' Already Shaping Schoolkids' Minds on Race," *RealClear Investigations,* January 31, 2020; Vinson Cunningham, "Prep for Prep and the Fault Lines in New York's Schools," *New Yorker,* March 2, 2020, 62; "Statement on the Recent 'White House Conference on American History,'" *Perspectives on History* 58 (November 2020): 6.

320 Academic and professional organizations: Bruce VanSledright, *In Search of America's Past: Learning to Read History in Elementary School* (New York: Teacher's College Press, 2002), 15; Zinn Education Project, https:// www.zinnedproject.org/; Gilder Lehrman Institute of American History, https://www.gilderlehrman.org/; Learning for Justice, Southern Poverty Law Center, https://www.learningforjustice.org/classroom-resources; Facing History and Ourselves, https://www.facinghistory.org/; Historians Against Slavery, https://www.historiansagainstslavery.org/main/; Massachusetts Historical Society, https://www.masshist.org/education; We Are America Project, https://www.weareamericaproject.com/; Deborah Menkart, Zinn Education Project, emails to author, January 18, 2018, and April 8, 2021.

321 These models are vital and inspiring: For this and the following paragraph, Keith C. Barton and Linda S. Levstik, *Teaching for the Common Good* (New York: Routledge, 2004), 1; Stern, *Effective State Standards,* 13–15; Wineburg, *Why Learn History,* 4–5; Associated Press, "Wisconsin Teachers Resign Following Complaints over Slavery Lesson," *Boston Globe,* April 15, 2021; James D. Anderson, "How We Learn About Race Through History," in Kramer, Reid, and Barney, *Learning History in America,* 87; Sari Edelstein, "'Good Mother, Farewell': Elizabeth Freeman's Silence and the Stories of Mumbet," *New England Quarterly* 92 (December 2019): 610–14; Michael Blakey, "To Better Understand," *Washington Post,* February 25, 2018. These sources cover this and the previous paragraph.

322 Even with reliable Internet resources: Kate Schuster et al., *Teaching Hard History: American Slavery* (Montgomery, Ala.: Southern Poverty Law Center, 2018), 5, 12–29, 37–38.

322 Textbooks, clearly, have a long: New England History Teachers' Association, *Textbooks in American History. A Report Presented by the Committee on Text-books, October 15, 1898* (Boston: NEHTA, 1898); Albert Bushnell Hart, *History: High and Preparatory Schools. How History Is Taught. How History May Be Taught* (Syracuse, N.Y.: George A Bacon, 1887), 3–11; Frances Newton Thorpe, *In Justice to the Nation: American History in American Schools, Colleges, and Universities* (Philadelphia: n.p., 1886), 5–7.

323 If nothing else, we have been consistent: Diane Ravitch and Chester E. Finn, Jr., *What Do Our 17-Year-Olds Know? A Report on the First National Assessment of History and Literature* (New York: Harper & Row, 1987), 44–49; "U.S.

History, Our Worst Subject," *United States Senate Subcommittee on Education and Early Childhood Development* (Washington, D.C.: Government Printing Office, 2005), 18.

323 Many factors account for such consistently: Walter Prescott Webb, *History as High Adventure* (Austin, Tex.: Jenkins Garrett Foundation, 1969), 157; Mary Beth Norton, "Rethinking American History Textbooks," in Lloyd Kramer, Donald Reid, and William L. Barney, eds., *Learning History in America: Schools, Culture, and Politics* (Minneapolis: University of Minnesota Press, 1994), 26–27; Shelden M. Stern, *Effective State Standards for U.S. History: A 2003 Report Card* (Washington, D.C.: Thomas B. Fordham Institute, 2003), 5, 89; David McCullough, statement in "U.S. History, Our Worst Subject," 6–7; James O. Horton, "Slavery in American History: An Uncomfortable Dialog," in James O. Horton and Lois E. Horton, eds., *Slavery and Public History: The Tough Stuff of American Memory* (New York: New Press, 2006), 42.

324 Another answer lies in the fact: Ravitch and Finn, *What Do Our 17-Year-Olds Know?*, 8; Alice Garrett, "Teaching High School History Inside and Outside the Historical Canon," in Kramer, Reid, and Barney, eds., *Learning History in America*, 73–74; audience response to "History of Racism" Zoom event, February 4, 2021, Southern Connecticut State University; Milton Meltzer, *Nonfiction for the Classroom: Milton Meltzer on Writing, History, and Social Responsibility* (New York: Teacher's College Press, 1994), 46–50; Robert Lerner, Althea K. Nagai, and Shirley Rothman, *Molding the Good Citizen: The Politics of High School History Texts* (Westport, Conn.: Praeger, 1995), 70–76; Loewen, *Lies My Teacher Told Me,* 154–55, 168.

325 The impact of all these factors: Dian Kahn email to author, March 2, 2021; Jim Sabataso, "Rutland School Board Hears About Controversial Lesson," Rutland *Herald,* February 11, 2020; Mariann Cabness, "Watertown School District Reaches Agreement with Attorney General . . . ," *News10.com,* August 10, 2020; "Parents Outraged by Mock Slave Auction Held at New Jersey School," *Ebony,* March 21, 2017; Melanie Pratt, "Teacher Makes Black Student a 'Slave,'" *Praise100.9,* March 6, 2021; "New Job for New York 5th Grade Teacher Fired over Mock Slave Auction Sparks Protest," NBC News, March 3, 2020; Kristina Bergess, "Black Students 'Sold' at Mock Slave Auction," ABC News, April 12, 2011; N'dea Yancy-Bragg, "Mock Slave Auctions, Racist Lessons: How U.S. History Class Often Traumatizes, Dehumanizes Black Students," *USA Today,* March 2, 2021; Chris Thies and Mia Monet, "Slave Letter Writing Activity Sparks Outrage in Mississippi School District," *WLBT3,* March 3, 2021; Jon Greig, "Oregon Teacher Resigns After Telling Biracial Student She's Lucky She's Not Making Her 'Pick Cotton,'" *BLAVITY:News,* June 14, 2019, www.blavity.com.

326 In 2020 the *New York Times* reported: Damon Tweedy, "Racism That Lingers at Medical Schools," *New York Times,* August 2, 2020; Jeneé Osterheldt, "A Vital Haven Where Black Men Feel Safe," *Boston Globe,* December 28,

2018; Nicole Phillip, "It Was Very Humiliating," *New York Times Magazine,* September 27, 2019; Brian MacQuarrie, Gal Tziperman Lotan, and Zoe Greenberg, "Racism Allegations Put MFA in Spotlight," *Boston Globe,* May 23 and 25, 2019.

326 A Rutgers University psychologist: Amy Harmon, "How Much Racism Do You Face Every Day?," *New York Times,* January 20, 2020; Charles Blow, "Six Seuss Books Bore a Bias," *New York Times,* March 5, 2021; Alexander Thompson, "Rally Calls Out Racism in Schools, Demand Change," *Medford Transcript,* September 17, 2020.

326 Despite the monumental outburst: *Teaching Hard History,* 12–13; James Baldwin, "The White Man's Guilt," *Ebony,* August 1965, in Baldwin, *Collected Essays* (New York: Library of America, 1998), 722–23.

Bibliography of Textbooks

Abramowitz, Jack. *American History.* Chicago: Follett, 1971.

Adams, Charles Kendall, and William P. Trent. *A History of the United States.* Boston: Allyn & Bacon, 1903.

Adams, Ephraim Douglass, and John C. Almack. *A History of the United States.* New York: Harper & Bros., 1931.

Adams, James Truslow, and Charles Garrett Vannest. *The Record of America.* New York: Charles Scribner's Sons, 1935.

Allen, Jack, and John L. Betts. *History: USA.* New York: American Book Company, 1967.

Ames, Jesse H., Merlin M. Ames, and Thomas S. Staples. *Our Land and Our People: The Progress of the American Nation.* St. Louis: Webster, 1942.

Anderson, John J. *A Grammar School History of the United States.* 1868; reprint, New York: Clarke & Maynard, 1882.

———. *An Introductory School History of the United States.* New York: Clark & Maynard, 1867.

Andrews, Elisha Benjamin. *The History of the Last Quarter-Century in the United States, 1870–1895.* 2 vols. New York: C. Scribner's, 1896.

———. *History of the United States.* 2 vols. New York: Charles Scribner's Sons, 1894.

Andrews, Matthew Page. *History of the United States.* Philadelphia: J. B. Lippincott, 1914.

Bailey, Thomas A. *The American Pageant: A History of the Republic.* Boston: Little, Brown, 1956.

Barker, Eugene C., William E. Dodd, and Henry Steele Commager. *Our Nation's Development.* New York: Row, Peterson, 1934.

Barker, Eugene C., Walter Prescott Webb, and William E. Dodd. *The Growth of a Nation: The United States of America.* Evanston, Ill.: Row, Peterson, 1928.

Barnes, Alfred S. *A Brief History of the United States: For Schools.* 1871; reprint, New York: A. S. Barnes, 1872.

———. *A Popular History of the United States of America.* New York: A. S. Barnes, 1878.

Barnes, Mary Sheldon. *Studies in American History: Teacher's Manual.* Boston: D. C. Heath, 1893.

Bassett, John Spencer. *A Short History of the United States.* New York: Macmillan, 1913.

Beard, Charles A., and William C. Bagley. *The History of the American People.* New York: Macmillan, 1919.

Beard, Charles A., and Mary R. Beard. *History of the United States.* New York: Macmillan, 1921.

Beeby, Daniel, Joyce L. Hanna, and Clarence H. McClure. *Our Country.* Chicago: Laidlaw Bros., 1942.

Berard, Augusta Blanche. *School History of the United States.* Philadelphia: H. Cowperthwaite, 1855.

Bidna, David, Morris S. Greenberg, and Jerold H. Spitz. *We the People: A History of the United States of America.* Lexington, Mass.: D. C. Heath, 1971.

Blaisdell, Albert F. *The Story of American History for Elementary Schools.* Boston: Ginn, 1901.

Blum, John Morton, Bruce Catton, Edmund J. Morgan, Arthur M. Schlesinger, Jr., Kenneth M. Stampp, and C. Vann Woodward. *The National Experience: A History of the United States.* New York: Harcourt, Brace & World, 1963.

Bonner, John. *A Child's History of the United States.* 2 vols. New York: Harper & Bros., 1855.

Bourne, Henry Eldridge, and Elbert Jay Benton. *A History of the United States.* 1913; reprint, Boston: D. C. Heath, 1919.

Bragdon, Henry W., and Samuel P. McCutchen. *History of a Free People.* New York: Macmillan, 1958.

Brown, Gertrude Stephens. *Your Country and Mine: Our American Neighbors.* Boston: Ginn, 1963.

Brown, Gertrude Stephens, Ernest W. Tiegs, and Fay Adams. *Teachers' Manual, Including a Key, to Accompany "Your Country and Mine."* Boston: Ginn, 1958.

Brown, Richard C., William C. Lang, and Mary A. Wheeler. *The American Achievement.* Morristown, N.Y.: Silver Burdett, 1966.

Burnham, Smith. *The Making of Our Country: A History of the United States for Schools.* Chicago: John C. Winston, 1920.

Burton, Alma Holman. *The Story of Our Country: A Primary History of the United States.* Chicago: Werner School Book, 1896.

Butterworth, Hezekiah. *Young Folks' History of America.* Boston: Estes & Lauriat, 1882.

———. *A ZigZag Journey in the Sunny South.* Boston: Estes & Lauriat, 1886.

California State Text-Book Committee. *Introductory History of the United States.* Sacramento: State of California, 1905.

Canfield, Leon H., and Howard B. Wilder. *The Making of Modern America.* Boston: Houghton Mifflin, 1950.

Canfield, Leon H., Howard B. Wilder, Frederic L. Paxson, Ellis Merton Coulter, and Nelson P. Mead. *The United States in the Making*. Boston: Houghton Mifflin, 1937.

Carroll, Bartholomew R. *Catechism of United States History*. Charleston, S.C.: McCarter & Dawson, 1859.

Casner, Mabel B., and Ralph Henry Gabriel. *Exploring American History*. New York: Harcourt, Brace, 1931.

———. *The Rise of American Democracy*. New York: Harcourt, Brace, 1943.

Chadsey, Charles E., Louis Weinberg, and Chester F. Miller. *America in the Making*. 2 vols. Boston: D. C. Heath, 1927.

Chambers, Henry E. *A Higher History of the United States for Schools and Academies*. New York: University Publishing, 1889.

Chancellor, William Estabrook. *A Text Book of American History*. New York: Silver, Burdett, 1903.

Channing, Edward. *A Students' History of the United States*. New York: Macmillan, 1898.

Chapman, John A. *School History of South Carolina*. Newberry, S.C.: Newberry, 1893.

Coffin, Charles Carleton. *Building the Nation: Events in the History of the United States from the Revolution to the Beginning of the War Between the States*. New York: Harper & Bros., 1883.

———. *The Story of Liberty*. New York: Harper & Bros., 1878.

Coleman, Charles H., and Edgar B. Wesley. *America's Road to Now*. Boston: D. C. Heath, 1942.

Commager, Henry Steele. *The American Mind: An Interpretation of American Thought and Character Since the 1880s*. 1950; reprint, New Haven, Conn.: Yale University Press, 1965.

Commager, Henry Steele, and Raymond H. Muessig. *The Study and Teaching of History*. Columbus: Charles E. Merrill, 1980.

Cooke, John Esten. *Virginia: A History of the People*. Boston: Houghton Mifflin, 1884.

Cooper, Oscar H., Harry F. Estill, and Leonard Lemmon. *A History of Our Country: A Text-book for Schools*. Boston: Ginn, 1898.

Cousins, R. B., and J. A. Hill. *American History for Schools*. Boston: D. C. Heath, 1913.

Crabtree, Esther. *Understanding Your Country and Canada*. 1964; reprint, Boston: Ginn, 1968.

Cussons, John. *A Glance at Current American History, by an Ex-Confederate*. Glen Allen, Va.: Cussons, May, 1897.

———. *United States "History" as the Yankee Makes and Takes It, by a Confederate Soldier*. Glen Allen, Va.: Cussons, May, 1900.

Davidson, William M. *A History of the United States*. 1902; reprint, Chicago: Scott Foresman, 1906.

Dickson, Marguerite Stockman. *American History for Grammar Schools*. New York: Macmillan, 1921.

Dodd, William E. *Expansion and Conflict*. Boston: Houghton Mifflin, 1915.

Eggleston, Edward. *A History of the United States and Its People: For the Use of Schools*. New York: D. Appleton, 1888.

———. *A Household History of the United States and Its People for Young Americans*. 1889; reprint, New York: D. Appleton, 1896.

Eichel, Charles G., Harry Blickstein, and Sigmund Newman. *Pictorial History of America*. 2 vols. New York: Newman-Dupuy, 1931.

Eliot, Samuel. *History of the United States from 1492 to 1872*. Boston: Brewer & Tileston, 1874.

———. *Manual of United States History, from 1492 to 1850*. Boston: Brewer & Tileston, 1856.

Elson, Henry William. *School History of the United States*. New York: Macmillan, 1912.

Estill, Harry F. *The Beginner's History of Our Country*. Dallas: Southern, 1919.

Evans, Lawton B. *The Essential Facts of American History*. Boston: Benj. H. Sanborn, 1909.

Field, Lida A. *A Grammar School History of the United States*. New York: American Book, 1897.

Fish, Carl Russell. *The American Civil War: An Interpretation*. London: Longmans, Green, 1937.

———. *History of America*. New York: American Book, 1925.

Fiske, John. *A History of the United States for Schools*. Boston: Houghton Mifflin, 1895.

Fite, Emerson David. *History of the United States*. New York: Henry Holt, 1916.

Foner, Eric. *Give Me Liberty! An American History*, 5th ed. New York: W. W. Norton, 2017.

Forman, S. E. [Samuel Eagle]. *A History of the United States for Schools*. New York: Century, 1920.

Franciscan Sisters of the Perpetual Adoration. *The Cathedral History of the United States*. Chicago: Scott Foresman, 1923.

Gavian, Ruth Wood, and William A. Hamm. *United States History*. Boston: D. C. Heath, 1960.

Giles, Helen F. *How the United States Became a World Power*. New York: Charles E. Merrill, 1930.

Goodrich, Charles A. *A History of the United States of America: On a Plan Adapted to the Capacity of Youth, and Designed to Aid the Memory by Systematic Arrangement and Interesting Associations*. 1852; reprint, Boston: Hickling, Swan & Brewer, 1858.

Goodrich, Charles A., and William H. Seavey. *History of the United States of America, for the Use of Schools*. Boston: William Ware, 1867.

Goodrich, Samuel Griswold. *The First Book of History for Children and Youth*. Philadelphia: Desilver, Thomas, 1836.

————. *North America, or the United States and the Adjacent Countries. Parley's Primary Histories.* Louisville, Ky.: Morton & Griswold, 1847.

————. *Peter Parley's Geography for Beginners.* 1844; reprint, New York: Huntington & Savage, 1847.

————. *A Pictorial History of the United States . . . for Use of Schools and Families.* Philadelphia: E. H. Butler, 1866.

————. *The Tales of Peter Parley About Africa.* Philadelphia: Charles Desilver, 1860.

Gordy, Wilbur F. *A History of the United States for Schools.* New York: Charles Scribner's Sons, 1898.

Guerber, H. A. *The Story of the Great Republic.* New York: American Book, 1899.

Guernsey, Egbert. *History of the United States of America, Designed for Schools.* 1847; reprint, New York: Daniel Burgess, 1854.

Guitteau, William Backus. *The History of the United States: A Textbook for Secondary Schools.* Boston: Houghton Mifflin, 1919.

Hale, Salma. *History of the United States from Their First Settlement as Colonies, to the Close of the War with Great Britain in 1817.* 2 vols. 1827; reprint, New York: Harper & Bros., 1841.

Hall, Robert Green, Harriet Smither, and Clarence Ousley. *The Student's History of Our Country for Grammar Grades.* 1912; reprint, Dallas: Southern Publishing, 1914.

————. *A History of the United States for the Grammar Grades.* Dallas: Southern Publishing, 1920.

Halleck, Reuben Post. *History of Our Country for Higher Grades.* New York: American Book, 1923.

Hamer, O. Stuart, Dwight W. Follett, Ben F. Ahlschwede, and Herbert H. Gross. *Exploring the New World.* 1953; reprint, Chicago: Follett, 1962.

Hamm, William A., Henry Eldridge Bourne, and Elbert Jay Benton. *A Unit History of the United States.* Boston: D. C. Heath, 1932.

Harlow, Ralph Volney. *The Growth of the United States.* New York: Henry Holt, 1925.

————. *Story of America.* 1937; reprint, New York: Henry Holt, 1943.

Hart, Albert Bushnell. *Essentials in American History.* New York: American Book, 1905.

Hassard, John R. G. *History of the United States of America: For the Use of Schools,* 4th ed. 1878; reprint, New York: Catholic Publication Society, 1881.

Haworth, Paul L., and Alfred W. Garner. *Our Country's History.* 1921; reprint, Indianapolis: Bobbs-Merrill, 1926.

Hicks, John D. *A Short History of American Democracy.* Boston: Houghton Mifflin, 1943.

Higginson, Thomas Wentworth. *Young Folks' History of the United States.* Boston: Lee & Shepard, 1875.

Holmes, George Frederick. *New School History of the United States.* New York: University Publishing, 1886.

Horton, Rushmore G. *A Youth's History of the Great Civil War in the United States, from 1861 to 1865.* 1866; reprint, New York: Van Evrie, Horton, 1867.

Howitt, Mary. *A Popular History of the United States of America.* 2 vols. New York: Harper & Bros., 1860.

Hughes, R. O. *The Making of Our United States.* Boston: Allyn & Bacon, 1927.

Hulbert, Archer Butler. *United States History.* Garden City, N.Y.: Doubleday, Page, 1923.

Hunter, Thomas. *A Narrative History of the United States, for the Use of Schools.* New York: American Book, 1896.

James, James Alton, and Albert Hart Sanford. *American History.* New York: Charles Scribner's Sons, 1910.

Jarrell, Joseph. *United States History.* Greenville, S.C.: Bob Jones University Press, 2018.

Jernegan, Marcus Wilson, Harry Ellsworth Carlson, and A. Clayton Ross. *Growth of the American Republic.* New York: Longmans, Green, 1934.

Johnson, Edward Austin. *A School History of the Negro Race in America from 1619 to 1890.* Raleigh, N.C.: Capital, 1891.

Johnston, Alexander. *History of American Politics: Handbooks for Students and General Readers.* New York: Henry Holt, 1882.

Johnston, Alexander, and Winthrop More Daniels. *A History of the United States for Schools.* New York: Henry Holt, 1897.

Jones, John William. *School History of the United States.* Rev. ed. New York: University Publishing, 1901.

Keesee, Timothy, and Mark Sidwell. *United States History for Christian Schools.* Greenville, S.C.: Bob Jones University Press, 2001.

Kelty, Mary Gertrude. *The Story of the American People.* Boston: Ginn, 1931.

———. *Teaching American History in the Middle Grades of Elementary School.* Boston: Ginn, 1928.

Kennedy, William H. J., and Sister Mary Joseph. *America's Story: A History of the United States for the Lower Grades of Catholic Schools.* New York: Benziger Bros., 1926.

Lansing, Marion. *Makers of the Americas.* Boston: D. C. Heath, 1955.

Larned, Josephus Nelson. *A History of the United States for Secondary Schools.* Boston: Houghton Mifflin, 1903.

Latané, John Holladay. *A History of the United States.* Boston: Allyn & Bacon, 1918.

Lawler, Thomas Bonaventure. *Essentials of American History.* Boston: Ginn, 1902.

Lee, Susan Pendleton. *A Brief History of the United States with Questions and Summaries for Reviews and Essays Prepared for Use in Public and Private Schools.* Richmond, Va.: B. F. Johnson, 1896.

Leeds, Josiah W. *A History of the United States of America Including Some Important Facts Mostly Omitted in the Smaller Histories: Designed for General Readers and for Academies.* Philadelphia: J. B. Lippincott, 1877.

Lefferts, Walter. *American Leaders.* 2 vols. Philadelphia: J. B. Lippincott, 1919.

Loewen, James W., and Charles Sallis, eds. *Mississippi: Conflict and Change.* New York: Pantheon, 1974.

Long, William J. *America: A History of Our Country.* Boston: Ginn, 1923.

Lossing, Benson J. *A Pictorial History of the United States for Schools and Families.* New York: F. J. Huntington–Mason Bros., 1854.

Mace, William H. *A School History of the United States.* Chicago: Rand McNally, 1904.

Madgic, Robert F., Stanley S. Seaberg, Fred H. Stopsky, and Robin W. Winks. *The American Experience: A Study of Themes and Issues in American History.* Menlo Park, Calif.: Addison-Wesley, 1971.

Magill, Mary Tucker. *History of Virginia for the Use of Schools.* 1873; reprint, Lynchburg, Va.: J. P. Bell, 1914.

———. *Stories from Virginia History for the Young.* Lynchburg, Va.: J. P. Bell, 1897.

Manion, Clarence. *American History.* Boston: Allyn & Bacon, 1926.

Marshall, Thomas M. *American History.* New York: Macmillan, 1930.

Masoff, Joy. *The African American Story: The Events That Shaped Our Nation—and the People Who Changed Our Lives.* Waccabuc, N.Y.: Five Ponds Press, 2007.

———. *Our Virginia, Past and Present.* Weston, Conn.: Five Ponds Press, 2010.

McClure, Clarence H., and W. H. Yarbrough. *The United States of America.* 1937; reprint, Chicago: Laidlaw Bros., 1945.

McDonald, W. N., and J. S. Blackburn. *A Southern School History of the United States of America.* Baltimore: George Lycett, 1869.

McGuire, Edna. *The Story of American Freedom.* New York: Macmillan, 1957.

McLaughlin, Andrew C. *A History of the American Nation.* New York: D. Appleton, 1906.

McLaughlin, Andrew C., and Claude Halstead Van Tyne. *A History of the United States for Schools.* 2 vols. New York: D. Appleton, 1916.

McMaster, John Bach. *A School History of the United States.* New York: American Book, 1897.

Meany, Edmond S. *United States History for Schools.* New York: Macmillan, 1912.

Monroe, Walter Scott. *Objectives of United States History in Grades Seven and Eight.* Urbana, Ill.: Bureau of Educational Research, 1926.

Montgomery, David H. *The Beginner's American History.* Boston: Ginn, 1899.

———. *The Leading Facts of American History.* Boston: Ginn, 1895.

Monteith, James. *Youth's History of the United States: Designed for Intermediate Classes in Public and Private Schools.* 1858; reprint, New York: A. S. Barnes, 1882.

Morison, Samuel Eliot. *Oxford History of the United States, 1783–1917.* Oxford: Oxford University Press, 1927.

Morison, Samuel Eliot, and Henry Steele Commager. *The Growth of the American Republic.* New York: Oxford University Press, 1930.

———. *The Growth of the American Republic.* Rev. ed. 2 vols. New York: Oxford University Press, 1950.

Morris, Charles. *School History of the United States of America.* Philadelphia: J. B. Lippincott, 1916.

Mowry, William A., and Arthur May Mowry. *A History of the United States for Schools.* New York: Silver, Burdett, 1896.

Mumford, Thomas Howland. *The Child's First History of America.* New York: D. Appleton, 1856.

Muzzey, David Saville. *An American History.* Boston: Ginn, 1911.

———. *History of the American People.* Boston: Ginn, 1929.

———. *Our Country's History.* Boston: Ginn, 1961.

Nevins, Allan, and Henry Steele Commager. *America, the Story of a Free People.* Boston: Little, Brown, 1942.

Niles, Sanford. *School History of the United States.* St. Paul, Minn.: D. D. Merrill, 1890.

O'Hara, John P. *A History of the United States.* New York: Macmillan, 1919.

Peabody, Elizabeth Palmer. *First Steps to the Study of History, Being Part First of a Key to History.* Boston: Hilliard, Gray, 1832.

Perry, Arthur C., and Gertrude A. Price. *American History.* 2 vols. New York: American Book, 1914.

Pierson, Helen W. *History of the United States in Words of One Syllable.* New York: George Routledge & Sons, 1883.

Pollard, Edward A. *The Lost Cause: A New Southern History of the War of the Confederates.* Enlarged ed. New York: E. B. Treat, 1868.

Powell, Edward Payson. *Nullification and Secession in the United States.* New York: G. P. Putnam's Sons, 1897.

Quackenbos, G. P. *Illustrated School History of the United States and the Adjacent Parts of America.* New York: D. Appleton, 1859.

———. *Illustrated School History of the United States and the Adjacent Parts of America.* Expanded ed. New York: D. Appleton, 1871.

Redway, Jacques Wardlaw. *The Making of the American Nation: A History for Elementary Schools.* New York: Silver, Burdett, 1905.

Ridpath, John Clark. *History of the United States, Prepared Especially for Schools.* 1876; reprint, Cincinnati: Jones Bros., 1878.

Riggs, Eleanor E. *An American History.* New York: Macmillan, 1916.

Riley, Franklin L., J.A.C. Chandler, and J. G. de Roulhac Hamilton. *Our Republic: A History of the United States for Grammar Grades.* Richmond, Va.: Hunter, 1910.

Robbins, Charles L., and Elmer Green. *School History of the American People.* New York: World Book, 1925.

Robertson, William. *The History of the Discovery and Settlement of America.* New York: Harper & Bros., 1835.

Rugg, Harold. *America's March Toward Democracy: History of American Life: Political and Social.* Boston: Ginn, 1937.

———. *An Introduction to American Civilization. A Study of Economic Life in the*

United States. A Textbook in Geography and Civics with Historical Backgrounds. Boston: Ginn, 1929.

Rugg, Harold, and James E. Mendenhall. *Teacher's Guide for "An Introduction to American Civilization."* Boston: Ginn, 1934.

Schwartz, Melvin, and John R. O'Connor. *The New Exploring American History.* New York: Globe Book Co., 1981.

Scoppa, J. R. *A Century of Growth and Progress.* Chicago: Laidlaw Bros., 1943.

Scott, David B. *A School History of the United States.* New York: Harper & Bros., 1870.

Scudder, Horace E. *A History of the United States of America, Preceded by a Narrative of the Discovery and Settlement of North America and of the Events Which Led to the Independence of the Thirteen English Colonies: For the Use of Schools and Academies.* Philadelphia: J. H. Butler, 1884.

Simkins, Francis Butler, Spotswood Hunnicutt, and Sidman P. Poole. *Virginia: History, Government, Geography.* New York: Charles Scribner's Sons, 1957.

Simms, William Gilmore. *History of South Carolina from Its First European Discovery to Its Erection into a Republic: With a Supplementary Chronicle of Events to the Present Time.* Rev. ed. New York: Redfield, 1859.

Simms, William Gilmore, and Mary C. Simms Oliphant, eds. *The History of South Carolina.* Rev. ed. Columbia, S.C.: State, 1927.

Smallidge, Olive E., and Frederic L. Paxson. *Builders of Our Nation.* Boston: Houghton Mifflin, 1934.

Southworth, Gertrude Van Duyn, and John Van Duyn Southworth. *The Story of Our America.* New York: Iroquois, 1951.

Steele, Joel Dorman, and Esther Baker Steele. *A Brief History of the United States.* Barnes Historical Series. New York: American Book, 1885.

Stephens, Alexander H. *A Compendium of the History of the United States from the Earliest Settlements to 1872.* Columbia, S.C.: W. J. Duffie, 1872.

Stephenson, Nathaniel Wright. *An American History.* Boston: Ginn, 1913.

Swinton, William. *First Lessons in Our Country's History Bringing Out Its Salient Points, and Aiming to Combine Simplicity with Sense.* New York: Ivison, Blakeman, Taylor, 1872.

Tappan, Eva March. *Our Country's Story: An Elementary History of the United States.* Boston: Houghton Mifflin, 1902.

Thalheimer, M. E. [Mary Elsie]. *Eclectic History of the United States.* Cincinnati: Van Antwerp, Bragg, 1881.

Thompson, Waddy. *A History of the United States.* Boston: D. C. Heath, 1919.

Thorpe, Francis Newton. *A School History of the United States.* New York: Hinds, Noble & Eldredge, 1900.

———. *A History of the American People.* Chicago: A. C. McClurg, 1901.

Thwaites, Reuben Gold, Calvin Noyes Kendell, and Frederick L. Paxson. *The History of the United States for Grammar Schools.* 1912; reprint, Boston: Houghton Mifflin, 1924.

Todd, Lewis Paul, and Merle Curti. *Rise of the American Nation.* 1950; reprint, New York: Harcourt, Brace & World, 1961.

Tryon, Rolla M., and Charles R. Lingley. *The American People and Nation.* Boston: Ginn, 1927.

Turpin, Edna Henry Lee. *A Short History of the American People.* New York: Macmillan, 1911.

Vannest, Charles Garrett, and Henry Lester Smith. *Socialized History of the United States.* New York: Charles Scribner's Sons, 1931.

Wainger, Bertrand M. *The American Adventure.* New York: McGraw-Hill, 1957.

Wayland, John W. *How to Teach American History: A Handbook for Teachers and Students.* New York: Macmillan, 1914.

Webster, Noah. *History of the United States.* Louisville, Ky.: Wilcox, Dickerman & Co., 1832.

Wells, Louis Ray. *Industrial History of the United States.* New York: Macmillan, 1922.

Wertenbaker, Thomas Jefferson, and Donald E. Smith. *The United States of America: A History.* New York: Charles Scribner's Sons, 1931.

West, Willis Mason. *History of the American People.* Boston: Allyn & Bacon, 1918.

White, Henry Alexander. *The Making of South Carolina.* New York: Silver, Burdett, 1906.

Wilder, Howard B., Robert P. Ludlum, and Harriet McCune Brown. *This Is America's Story.* Boston: Houghton Mifflin, 1956.

Willard, Emma. *Abridged History of the United States; or, Republic of America.* New York: A. S. Barnes, 1846.

———. *History of the United States; or, Republic of America.* 1851; reprint, New York: A. S. Barnes, 1852.

Willson, Marcius. *History of the United States, for the Use of Schools.* New York: Mark H. Newman, 1845.

Wilson, Lucy Langdon Williams. *History Reader for Elementary Schools.* 1898; reprint, New York: Macmillan, 1929.

———. *United States History in Elementary Schools.* New York: Macmillan, 1899.

Wirth, Fremont P. *The Development of America.* New York: American Book, 1937.

Woodburn, James Albert, Thomas Francis Moran, and Howard Copeland Hill. *Our United States: A History of the Nation.* 1930; reprint, New York: Longmans, Green, 1935.

Woodson, Carter G. *The Negro in Our History.* Washington, D.C.: Associated Publishers, 1922.

Index

Page numbers in *italics* refer to illustrations.

Illustration Credits

100 Frontispiece to Benson Lossing's *A Primary History of the United States for Schools and Families,* 1863.

108 Emma Willard. From Ezra Brainard, *Mrs. Emma Willard's Life and Work in Middlebury,* 1918.

113 Mary Botham Howitt. Steel engraving on off-white wove paper, 11½ x 8¼ in., undated, after a painting by Margaret Gillies. Photograph by Barbara Katus. Courtesy of the Pennsylvania Academy of Fine Arts, Philadelphia.

122 Frederick Douglass. Photograph by Charles Milton Bell, 1881. Prints and Photographs Division, Library of Congress.

124 Charles Sumner. Framed lithograph by Leopold Grozelier, after a portrait by William Wetmore Story, 1854. Prints and Photographs Division, Library of Congress and National Portrait Gallery.

131 Elisha Mulford. Oil on canvas, 44 × 30¼ in., by James Harvey Young (1830–1918), 1890. Yale University Art Gallery, gift of classmates of the sitter.

136 Thomas Wentworth Higginson. Cabinet card by William Notman, Boston, 1905–11. Prints and Photographs Division, Library of Congress.

137 "The Last Moments of John Brown." Engraving by Frederick Juengling (1846–1889), after a painting by Thomas Hovenden (1840–1895), 1884, in the Metropolitan Museum of Art. Prints and Photographs Division, Library of Congress.

143 Edward Austin Johnson. From *How to Solve the Race Problem: The Proceedings of the Washington Conference on the Race Problem in the United States* (Washington, D.C.: National Sociological Society, 1904), p. 188.

151 "Slaves Escaping to Union Troops." From Hezekiah Butterworth, *Young Folks' History of America,* 1882, p. 433.

153 Charles Carleton Coffin. Engraving by Frederick T. Stuart, 1880–1896. Prints and Photographs Division, Library of Congress.

155 "Fit Only to be a Slave." From Charles Carleton Coffin, *Building the Nation,* 1883, p. 307.

158 "The Rising Power." From Charles Carleton Coffin, *Building the Nation,* 1883, p. 284.

159 "The Comfortless Cabin." From Charles Carleton Coffin, *Building the Nation,* 1883, p. 389.

160 "Death Rather Than Slavery." Wood engraving of Margaret Garner in *Harper's Weekly,* May 18, 1867, p. 308, after a painting by Thomas Noble. Reprinted in Charles Carleton Coffin, *Building the Nation,* 1883, p. 403.

168 "Colored Rule in a Reconstructed State (The members call each other thieves, liars, rascals, and cowards)." Wood engraving by Thomas Nast, *Harper's Weekly,* March 14, 1874. Prints and Photographs Division, Library of Congress.

171 "Savage Indians." From John Fiske, *A History of the United States for Schools,* 1895, after an illustration by Frederick Remington in Henry Wadsworth Longfellow's *Hiawatha.*

177 "Slaves in Field of Sugar Cane." From Helen W. Pierson, *History of the United States in Words of One Syllable,* 1889, p. 101.

184 Albert Bushnell Hart. George Grantham Bain Collection, Prints and Photographs Division, Library of Congress.

199 From Hezekiah Butterworth, *A ZigZag Journey in the Sunny South,* 1886, p. 239.

201 "They enjoyed getting together for a rollicking time." From Arthur C. Perry and Gertrude A. Price, *American History,* 2 vols. (New York: American Book Company, 1914), 2:135.

211 Laura Martin Rose, *The Ku Klux Klan; or, Invisible Empire,* 1914, pp. 77, 82.

218 "Ruins after the race riots," Tulsa, Oklahoma, June 1921. Prints and Photographs Division, Library of Congress.

220 Ku Klux Klan parade on Pennsylvania Ave., N.W., in Washington, D.C., September 13, 1926. Prints and Photographs Division, Library of Congress.

222 John Jay Chapman. Oil on canvas by Alfred Quinton Collins, c. 1895. National Portrait Gallery, Smithsonian Institution, gift of Chanler A. Chapman.

242 "Slaves at home, after the day's work was over. Negroes always have been fond of singing and dancing; and the banjo has been a favorite musical instrument with them." Drawing by Hanson Booth, from Fremont P. Wirth, *The Development of America,* 1937, p. 352.

250 David Saville Muzzey. Photograph, 1912. University Archives, Rare Book & Manuscript Library, Columbia University Libraries.

266 "Riders of the Ku Klux Klan. They worked at night." Image from D. W. Griffith's 1915 silent film *The Birth of a Nation,* in Southworth and Southworth, *The Story of Our America,* 1951, p. 351.

269 Mildred Lewis Rutherford. Frontispiece to Rutherford, *Four Addresses* (Birmingham, Ala.: Mildred Rutherford Historical Circle, 1916).

279 Sign displayed during riot at the Sojourner Truth U.S. federal housing project, Detroit, Michigan, February 1942. Photograph by Arthur S. Siegel. Farm Security Administration, Office of War Information, Prints and Photographs Division, Library of Congress.

285 Carter G. Woodson. Photograph, ca. 1915. Scurlock Studio Records, Archives Center, National Museum of American History, Smithsonian Institution.

289 William Edward Burghardt Du Bois. Photograph by Cornelius Marion Battey, 1918. Prints and Photographs Division, Library of Congress.

A Note on the Type

This book was set in Adobe Garamond. Designed for the Adobe Corporation by Robert Slimbach, the fonts are based on types first cut by Claude Garamond (ca. 1480–1561).

Typeset by North Market Street Graphics,
Lancaster, Pennsylvania

Printed and bound by Berryville Graphics,
Berryville, Virginia

Designed by Michael Collica